INSIDE THE KINGDOM

ALSO BY ROBERT LACEY

Robert, Earl of Essex

Henry VIII

The Queens of the North Atlantic

Sir Walter Ralegh

Majesty

The Kingdom

Princess

Aristocrats

Ford

God Bless Her!

Little Man

Grace

Sotheby's

The Year 1000

The Queen Mother's Century

Monarch: The Life and Reign of Queen Elizabeth II

Great Tales from English History: Cheddar Man to the Peasants' Revolt

Great Tales from English History: Chaucer to the Glorious Revolution

Great Tales from English History: The Battle of the Boyne to DNA

INSIDE THE KINGDOM

Kings, Clerics, Modernists, Terrorists, and the Struggle for Saudi Arabia

ROBERT LACEY

VIKING
CANADA

VIKING CANADA

Published by the Penguin Group

Penguin Group (Canada), 90 Eglinton Avenue East, Suite 700, Toronto, Ontario, Canada M4P 2Y3
(a division of Pearson Canada Inc.)

Penguin Group (USA) Inc., 375 Hudson Street, New York, New York 10014, U.S.A.
Penguin Books Ltd, 80 Strand, London WC2R 0RL, England
Penguin Ireland, 25 St Stephen's Green, Dublin 2, Ireland (a division of Penguin Books Ltd)
Penguin Group (Australia), 250 Camberwell Road, Camberwell, Victoria 3124, Australia
(a division of Pearson Australia Group Pty Ltd)
Penguin Books India Pvt Ltd, 11 Community Centre, Panchsheel Park, New Delhi – 110 017, India
Penguin Group (NZ), 67 Apollo Drive, Rosedale, North Shore 0745, Auckland, New Zealand
(a division of Pearson New Zealand Ltd)
Penguin Books (South Africa) (Pty) Ltd, 24 Sturdee Avenue, Rosebank, Johannesburg 2196, South Africa

Penguin Books Ltd, Registered Offices: 80 Strand, London WC2R 0RL, England

Published in Canada by Penguin Group (Canada), a division of Pearson Canada Inc., 2009.
Simultaneously published in the United States by Viking Penguin, a member of Penguin Group (USA) Inc.

1 2 3 4 5 6 7 8 9 10 (RRD)

Photo credits appear on page 403.

Manufactured in the U.S.A.

Maps and family tree by Jeffrey L. Ward
Family tree illustrations by Laura Maestro
Designed by Carla Bolte • Set in Granjon

ISBN 978-0-670-06402-1

Library and Archives Canada Cataloguing in Publication data available upon request to the publisher.
American Library of Congress Cataloging in Publication data available.

To Faiza, Fawzia, Ghada, Hala, Hatoon, Maha, Najat,
and all the mothers of Saudi Arabia

. . .

And to the memory of my own mother,
Vida Lacey (1913–2008)

CONTENTS

PART TWO

KINGDOM AT WAR

PART THREE

AL-QAEDA COMES HOME

SAUDI ARABIA
and Its Neighbors
Turkey
Caspian Sea
Tehran
Cyprus
Syria
Beirut
Lebanon
Damascus
Baghdad
Mediterranean Sea
Israel
Tigris
Karbala
Isfahan
Jerusalem
Amman
Iraq
Euphrates
Ar' Ar
Basra
Cairo
Jordan
Al-Jawf
Safwan
Kuwait
Kuwait City
Hafr Al-Batin
Tabuk
Al-Khafji
Persian Gulf
Hail
Al-Qaseem
Area of detail
Jubail
Nile
Buraydah
Sibillah
Bahrain
Dhahran
Unayzah
Egypt
Qata
Nejd
Sajir
Dariyah
Doha
Red Sea
Medina
Yanbu
Riyadh
Al-Kharj
Hejaz
Saudi Arabia
Al-Hauta
Rabigh
Rub Al-Khali (Empty Quarter)
Jeddah
Mecca
N
Taif
Asir
Abha
Najran
Sudan
Jizan
Hadramaut
Khartoum
Sanaa
Eritrea
Yemen
0 Miles 500
0 Kilometers 500
Aden
Gulf of Aden
Ethiopia
Djibouti
Somalia
©2009 Jeffrey L. Ward

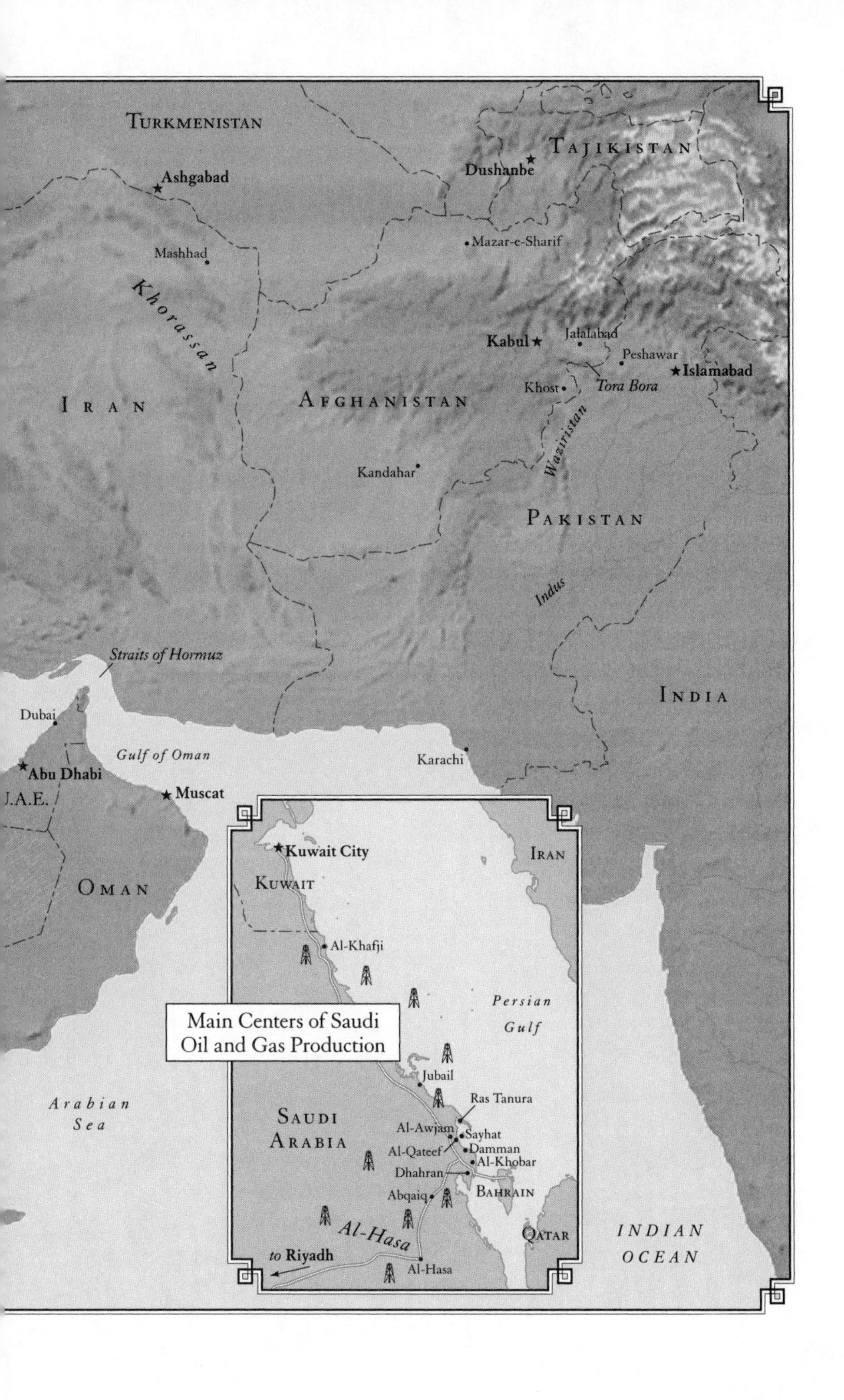
TURKMENISTAN
Ashgabad
TAJIKISTAN
Dushanbe
Mazar-e-Sharif
Mashhad
Khorassan
Kabul
Jalalabad
Peshawar
Islamabad
Khost
Tora Bora
IRAN
AFGHANISTAN
Waziristan
Kandahar
PAKISTAN
Indus
Straits of Hormuz
INDIA
Dubai
Gulf of Oman
Karachi
Abu Dhabi
U.A.E.
Muscat
OMAN
Kuwait City
IRAN
KUWAIT
Al-Khafji
Persian
Gulf
Main Centers of Saudi
Oil and Gas Production
Jubail
Ras Tanura
Arabian
Sea
SAUDI
ARABIA
Al-Awjam
Sayhat
Al-Qateef
Damman
Al-Khobar
Dhahran
Abqaiq
BAHRAIN
Al-Hasa
QATAR
INDIAN
OCEAN
to Riyadh
Al-Hasa

PREFACE

Welcome to the Kingdom

In theory Saudi Arabia should not exist—its survival defies the laws of logic and history. Look at its princely rulers, dressed in funny clothes, trusting in God rather than man, and running their oil-rich country on principles that most of the world has abandoned with relief. Shops are closed for prayer five times a day, executions take place in the street—and let us not even get started on the status of women. Saudi Arabia is one of the planet's enduring—and, for some, quite offensive—enigmas: which is why, three decades ago, I went to live there for a bit.

It was 1979. I had just published *Majesty,* my biography of Elizabeth II, which recounted the paradoxical flourishing of an ancient monarchy in an increasingly populist world. Now I was in search of more paradox, and it was not hard to find in Riyadh. After many a morning sipping glasses of sweet tea in the office of the chief of protocol, I finally secured an audience with King Khaled, the shy and fragile old monarch who had become the Kingdom's stopgap ruler following the assassination of his half brother Faisal in 1975. (The five Saudi monarchs who have ruled the Kingdom since 1953 have all been half brothers, with more than a dozen brothers and half brothers, not to mention their sons, still waiting in the wings—see the family tree on page XXIV.)

In the weeks of tea sipping I had given much thought to the important question of what I might *give* the king. What could I offer to the man who had—or could have—just about anything? I had decided on photographs. Before coming to the Kingdom, I had read the papers of the earliest British travelers to Arabia, intrepid servants of His Majesty's imperial government who had trekked across the desert sands in the early decades of the twentieth century in their solar helmets and khaki puttees. A surprising number had loaded their camels with the heavy wood-and-brass cameras of the time, complete with fragile glass plates and portable darkrooms so they could develop and print their negatives in their tents.

I made up an album of these images, which were then comparatively unknown, wrote out long captions and had them translated into classical Arabic, and bore my gift into the royal presence. It was *majlis* day—*majlis* meaning "the place of sitting"—and the bedouin had come out of the desert to sit with their king. Inside the manicured palace grounds were dusty Toyota pickup trucks parked higgledy-piggledy on the marble among the burnished Rolls-Royces and BMWs of princes and ministers. The trucks did not have sheep or goats in the back at that moment, but from their smell it was clear they had recently contained some woolly passengers.

I was already prepared for the theater that followed. The nose rubbing and hand kissing as the king met his people was a tableau unrolled for every visiting film crew and journalist—"our desert democracy," the minders from the Ministry of Information would proudly explain. Till that date I had managed to avoid a ministry minder (thirty years later I still proudly roam free), and I was developing my own rather cynical view of desert "democracy." It seemed to me to involve little more than the passing thrill of royal contact, the handing out of money, and the dispensing of favors that bypassed and undermined the fragile processes of proper government. So I was 50 percent skeptical as I entered the majlis—then 100 percent bowled over as I found myself treated to some direct royal contact of my own.

In front of the king was standing an old bedu, his bare toes scratching nervously at the rich silken carpet as he declaimed singsong lines of poetry, which he seemed to be making up as he went along:

Oh love of the people,
Oh Khaled, our king,
Oh lion of the desert,
Your promises we sing . . .

Listening to poetry is one of the occupational hazards of being king of Saudi Arabia. Elizabeth II shakes hands with a lot of district nurses. Saudi kings must nod appreciatively through the repetitive and often lengthy odes composed in their honor. In the meantime, there was a flurry of robed and shuffling hospitality, as thimblefuls of thin coffee got poured and trays of clear, sweet tea were circulated. The Riyadh equivalent of Buckingham Palace flunkeys were stern-looking, cross-belted retainers, wearing revolver holsters and swords.

Suddenly it was my turn to entertain the king, and I found myself ushered with my gift to the green brocade overstuffed sofa beside him—"Louis Farouk" is the decorative style favored in most Saudi palaces, a mixed allusion to the excesses of Versailles and the last, gaudy king of Egypt.

It was sticky to start with. How many times had this shy, long-suffering man had to accept the homage of stumbling foreigners? But as he turned the pages of the album, King Khaled started to "get it." He recognized uncles and cousins and places from long ago, and, above all, the pictures of his extraordinary, charismatic father, Abdul Aziz, "Slave of the Mighty"—the mighty one being God, whom Abdul Aziz served devotedly through the creed that outsiders call Wahhabism, central Arabia's harsh and fiercely puritannical interpretation of the Islamic faith.* Usually known in the west as Ibn Saud, or "Son of Saud," this warrior king had subdued and pulled together the tribes of Arabia between 1901 and 1925, then proudly (some said arrogantly) slapped his family name on the whole bundled-up conglomerate: Al-Mamlaka Al-Arabiyya Al-Saudiyya, the Saudi Arab Kingdom—Arabia as belonging to the House of Saud.

The great man's son Khaled was now turning the pages of my album with real interest, calling over cronies to look at such and such a face or to question whether such and such a caption was correct about the date or place—until he came to a photo dated 1918. It showed Abdul Aziz standing smiling and self-assured in a headdress and winter cloak, almost a head taller than a line of rather less confident relatives and companions, while a group of ragged little children in the front row squinted quizzically at the first European that most of them had ever seen. (See photo insert facing page 100.)

It was the children that attracted King Khaled's attention.

"One of those is me!" he exclaimed excitedly, recounting through a

*Many Saudis reject being described as "Wahhabis," since they see themselves as followers of true Islam, not members of a particular sect (see chapter 1, page 10, "The First 'Wahhabi'").

translator how he could remember this *khawajah* (Western gentleman) coming to meet his father, then taking them all outside to line up in the courtyard. The stranger had vanished under his blanket to peer at them through his curious machine, and the children had been told very strictly not to move. But little Khaled had not then understood why, nor had ever been shown the result. Six decades later, here it was—*"Wallah!"* ("By God," the most common and benevolent oath in Saudi Arabia).

The king happily slapped the album shut and ordered a servant to take it back to show the family that night. Meanwhile I was dismissed with a fatherly beam and was walked back to my place to sit through another hour of wafting incense and poetry, reflecting on the nature of this curious land. I had found my paradox—if not two. Blessed by geology with infinite riches, Saudi Arabia was ruled by a man who had started his life as a barefoot urchin in the sand. And while King Khaled was an absolute ruler of theoretically infinite power and wealth, he had lined up with his guests that morning after the last poem had been declaimed and, with no special precedence, had prostrated himself with them all in prayer.

. . .

So that became the theme of my book *The Kingdom,* published in 1981—the dazzling rocketing to modernity of a society that still insisted on tradition, and the delicate balancing act of the ruling family, whose fierce ambition had assembled the entire, scarcely credible creation.

"How did they do it?"

The Kingdom answered that question in 631 pages including index and notes. But life is short, and the book is out of print. So here, in just one paragraph, is why the House of Saud matters. Think of central Arabia as being in three parts—the oil fields in the east, the holy cities of Mecca and Medina in the west, and the largely barren desert in the middle. At the beginning of the twentieth century, and for most of the previous centuries of Arabian history, those three geographical units were separate countries and, to some degree, cultures. It was the modern achievement of the House of Saud, through skilled and ruthless warfare, a highly refined gift for conciliation, and, most particularly, the potent glue of their Wahhabi mission, to pull those three areas together so that, by the end of the twentieth century, the world's largest oil reserves were joined, sea to sea, to the largest center of annual religious pilgrimage in the world—and to their capital in the Wahhabi heartland of Riyadh.

That is the historical significance of the Saudi tribesmen. If it were not for Ibn Saud and his sons, the oil fields now called Saudi would probably be another overly affluent, futuristic emirate like Kuwait or Dubai along the Persian Gulf coast, all lagoon estates and Russian hookers. The oil fields, along with their incredible wealth and international influence, would be totally separate from the holy places of Mecca and Medina—and both those hypothetical countries would, almost certainly, be following a softer, more tolerant branch of Islam than the strict Wahhabism emanating from Riyadh.

"What if?" is a dubious game to play with the past. But, on the basis of the evidence, it seems reasonable to suggest that without the historic achievement of the House of Saud, the horrors of 9/11 would never have been inflicted on the United States, since Osama Bin Laden's poisonous hostility toward the West was a brew that only Saudi Arabia could have concocted. His attack on the twin towers was a maneuver in an essentially Saudi quarrel—played out with American victims.

• • •

That is the theme of the pages that follow: the story of the conflicts that made Saudi Arabia's paradoxes lethal for nearly three thousand people in New York's World Trade Center, at the Pentagon in Washington, D.C., and in a field in Pennsylvania on the morning of September 11, 2001—how an ancient religion came to define a modern state, fueling violence that spiraled far beyond the boundaries of Saudi Arabia. Think of the new words that we have had to learn in the past thirty years: *wahhabi, jihadi,* Arab-Afghan, Desert Storm, *fatwa,* Al-Qaeda. What do they all have in common? Which nation supplied fifteen of the nineteen hijackers on 9/11? One of the largest groups of foreign fighters captured in Afghanistan? The second largest contingent at the Guantánamo Bay detention camp? Plus several hundred terrorists and suicide bombers in Iraq?

Saudi problems have transformed the modern world. Saudi conflicts and growing pains got the twenty-first century off to a start that no one had anticipated, and we are still trying to work out what it means. I certainly did not begin to guess, when I brought my family to live in Jeddah three decades ago, at the world-shaking climax to which the contradictions and hypocrisies around me would lead. That is why I have written this book: to go back to 1979 and try to work out how it happened. It is a sequel to *The Kingdom,* but a sequel that must upend and reexamine everything that went before.

In 1982, a year after its publication in the United Kingdom and the United States, *The Kingdom* was banned by the Saudi government. The censorship office of the Ministry of Information listed ninety-seven objections to the text, and I was willing to accommodate only twenty-four of them. These all related to Islam, where I was happy to concede that a committee of Muslims knew more than I did about their religion. But I firmly declined to alter several long historical passages, particularly my accounts of the disputes between Abdul Aziz's sons Saud and Faisal, which resulted in the dethroning of King Saud in 1964. As a result, the book was banned from distribution or sale inside Saudi Arabia (its Internet translation remains blocked by Saudi servers)—and sales soared gratifyingly, especially in the Middle East. I had other books to write, and I did not go back to Saudi Arabia for a quarter of a century.

Then in 2006, the same Saudi friend who had secured me a visa in 1979 and weathered the minitempest of *The Kingdom*'s banning, suggested I return in the changed climate that followed the events of 9/11. I am grateful for his trust, as I am grateful to the many Saudis who have opened their hearts to recount their moving and sometimes painful personal experiences—this is their story. Several characters whom you meet at the beginning will pop up again in the narrative to carry their personal tales through to the end.

Like *The Kingdom,* this book is based on a stay in Saudi Arabia of some three years, as I have sought to experience the texture of life as much as a foreigner can, without losing the perspective that makes me a foreigner. Every word in the main narrative is as true as I can make it, checked and double-checked, wherever possible, against its original source. Then, set throughout the text, are some of the jokes and folktales that Saudis recount when they try to explain how things have come to be the strange way they are. It is a device I adopted in *The Kingdom* to reflect the rhythm and complexity of local narratives, recruiting fable to help explain the facts.

. . .

I am writing these words in a plane flying from the Saudi coastal oil fields to Riyadh. Comfortably ensconced by a window with my laptop, I am looking down on the arid, orange expanse of desert below me, and I cannot help thinking of the British adventurers who plodded across this same territory less than a century ago, taking more than a week to make the same journey. I am doing some time traveling of my own. The modern Saudi experience may seem remote, but it was not so long ago in the West—certainly in our parents' and grandparents' memory—that most people were devout and rather intolerant believers, scared and suspicious of other races and faiths: the "weaker sex" did not vote; capital punishment was considered a necessity; books and plays were censored (our movies still are); father knew best, and "nice" girls kept themselves pure until marriage. For centuries Western life was lived within the comfort of those structures and strictures, and it is only recently that we have started to look for new values—which we sometimes seek to define by criticizing those who are reluctant to abandon the proven security of the old ones.

As I look down on the desert, I can sense the trajectory of the plane make a shift. We will be landing in Riyadh shortly, after less than an hour in the air. So here we are, all of us, rushing into the future—with the Saudis, these days, starting to step out just a little faster than they did before. Their progress in the past three decades has been uplifting in some respects, but really quite shocking and destructive in others. It is a dramatic and important story, and as I set out to tell it, I cannot help wondering: Will they ban this book like the last one?

Robert Lacey
Riyadh, 2009

ABDUL AZIZ "IBN SAUD"
(1876–1953)

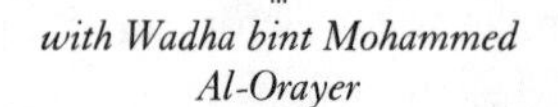

with Wadha bint Mohammed Al-Orayer

SAUD
(1902–1969)
Reigned 1953–1964

with Tarfa bint Abdullah Al-Asheikh

FAISAL
(1904–1975)
Reigned 1964–1975

with Jauhara bint Musaed Bin Jiluwi

MOHAMMED
(1910–1988)
Renounced his succession rights in 1964/1965

KHALED
(1912–1982)
Reigned 1975–1982

This family tree is based upon a list of the surviving sons of Abdul Aziz in undated order of precedence kindly supplied by Dr. Fahd Al-Semari of the Darat Al-Malik Abdul Aziz (the King Abdul Aziz Study Center) in Riyadh. Dates of birth have been estimated from this and from the family trees compiled by Michael Field and by Brian Lees, author of *A Handbook of the Al-Saud Ruling Family of Saudi Arabia* (Royal Genealogies, London, 1980). See Lees and also *The Kingdom* for details of all thirty-seven or so of Abdul Aziz's sons. The old king fathered a similar number of daughters, but the precise number of his children has never been publicly quantified.
Drawings by Laura Maestro.

RULERS OF THE KINGDOM

Abdul Aziz and His Sons—A Simplified Family Tree

with Hissa bint Ahmad Al-Sudayri

FAHD
(1922–2005)
Reigned 1982–2005

SULTAN (b. 1924)
Crown Prince 2005–

ABDUL RAHMAN (b. 1928)

TURKI (b. 1932)

NAYEF (b. 1933)

SALMAN (b. 1936)

AHMAD (b. 1941)

with Fahda bint Asi Al-Shuraim

ABDULLAH
(b. 1923)
Reigned 2005–

with nine other wives

Other living sons:

BANDAR (b. 1923)

MUSAED (b. 1923)

MISHAAL (b. 1926)

MITEB (b. 1928)

TALAL (b. 1931)

BADR (b. 1932)

NAWWAF (b. 1932)

MAMDUH (b. 1938)

ABDUL ELAH (b. 1939)

SATTAM (b. 1941)

MASHHUR (b. 1942)

HADHLUL (b. 1942)

MIGREN (b. 1943)

NOTE ON THE ISLAMIC CALENDAR

Muslim months begin and end with the phases of the moon. People scan the sky in every corner of Saudi Arabia, and only when the *hilal*—the new crescent moon—has actually been seen and attested is the month certified in court to have officially begun.

Twelve lunar months add up to some 354 days—eleven or so days short of the Western, Gregorian year. So a Muslim centenarian is not yet ninety-seven in terms of 365-day Gregorian years, and the shorter Muslim year is constantly creeping forward in relation to its Western equivalent. Celebrations like the end of hajj (the pilgrimage) and Ramadan (the holy month of fasting) arrive eleven days or so earlier in Western terms every year.

The calendar also has its own start date—the *hijrah,* or migration—the turning point in the birth of Islam, when the Prophet Mohammed forsook the hostility of unreformed Mecca (in the Christian year A.D. 622) and migrated to the community that would become known as Medina (see page 7). Islamic years are accordingly known as migration, or hijrah, years and will be denoted as A.H. (*anno hegirae*) in the pages that follow.

INSIDE THE KINGDOM

PART ONE

KINGDOM OF GOD

A.D 1979-1990 (A.H. 1400-1411)

Nothing is easier than to denounce the evildoer. Nothing is more difficult than to understand him.

—Fyodor Dostoevsky, *The Possessed*

CHAPTER 1

Angry Face

Juhayman means "Angry Face," deriving from *jahama,* the past tense of *yatajaham,* meaning to set your features grimly. Arabia's bedouin have a tradition of bestowing ugly, tough-guy names on their children. They believe it keeps trouble at bay in a troublesome world—though in the case of Juhayman Al-Otaybi, "Angry Face" of the Otayba tribe, the name came to stand for incredible trouble. With his wild beard and wild eyes, Juhayman had the look of Che Guevara about him, perhaps even Charles Manson. In November and December 1979, Angry Face horrified the entire Muslim world when he led hundreds of young men to their deaths in Mecca. It was a gesture of demented religious fanaticism, and the House of Saud did its best to disown him. This mingling of violence with religion was an un-Saudi aberration, explained government apologists—Juhayman was not typical in the slightest. Which was what they would say again, twenty years later, about Osama Bin Laden.

. . .

It went back to 1973, when King Faisal of Saudi Arabia announced a boycott on his kingdom's oil sales to the United States. Enraged by President Richard Nixon's military support for Israel in the October War against Egypt and Syria, the Saudi king had hoped to compel some dramatic change in U.S. policy. Yet as the Arab oil boycott caused the price of oil on the world market to multiply nearly five times, it was back home, inside the Kingdom, that the truly dramatic changes would occur.

"For about eighteen months nothing seemed to happen," remembers Dr. Horst Ertl, who was teaching chemical engineering at the College of Petroleum and Minerals in Dhahran. "Then, around the spring of 1975, just before the death of King Faisal, I drove across via Riyadh to the Red Sea coast. Suddenly everyone seemed to have money in their pockets. It was incredible. One moment just a few of the richer students had cars. Next moment, the university parking lot was filling."

After centuries of hibernation and a few recent decades of only gradual change, Saudi Arabia was suddenly turned on its head. Foreign money brought foreign ways—the good, the bad, and, in the eyes of many Saudis, the very definitely ugly. Women started appearing on TV and, even more offensively for many traditionalists, half-undressed beside hotel swimming pools. The Kingdom's cities became chaotic building sites, where blank-faced laborers in hard hats toiled in the dust like ants. The construction crane, it was said, was the new national symbol of the Kingdom, throwing up schools, universities, palaces, hospitals, mosques, office blocks, highways, more hotels—and shops, shops, shops.

"You'd go away for the summer," remembers Prince Amr Mohammed Al-Faisal, a grandson of the late king, "and come back to discover yourself surrounded by whole new neighborhoods. You got lost in your own town."

Petrodollars were the death of Jeddah's charming old Souq Al-Nada (the "Dew" marketplace), which derived its poetic name from the morning scent of moisture that wafted up from the beaten earth. In short order the soft earthen floor was cemented over with garish, trattoria-style ceramic tiles, and the scent of dew was replaced by petrol from the traders' noisy generators.

Faisal's successor, his half brother Khaled, who became king in 1975, looked on these changes with kindly bemusement. "Can you tell me, my sons," he would inquire of his nephews, bright young princes back from California with their degrees in business and engineering and political science, "what I should do with this fish that is opening its mouth, swallowing my money, and giving me back iron and cement? Are these riches a blessing to the Muslims, or a curse?"

The pious had no doubt. A society that had been safely closed for centuries was now ripped open to danger. Their pure world was under threat. Cocky children knew better than their parents. The English language counted for more than Arabic, God's own language in which He had revealed the Koran. Traditionalists could not glory in this jackpot moment, which was sullying their beautiful past. They felt scared and unprotected. They were outraged by these helter-skelter changes they were helpless to prevent, and they had a word for them—*bidaa,* innovations.

"Every *bidah* is a going-astray, and every going-astray leads to Hell-fire," went a saying attributed to the Prophet—though his condemnation, in the eyes of most modern Islamic scholars, referred to changes in the field of religious practice and ritual, not to technical innovations like the motorcar and television.

"Life before the oil boom had a sweetness and a closeness that we can now see was very precious—and very fragile," remembers Dr. Khaled Bahaziq, who was twenty-three years old in 1973 and studying in America. "When I was a child, we lived in one another's houses. We cooked food and shared it when we broke the fast at Ramadan. If the neighbors saw me misbehaving, they would tell me off, and my parents would say thank you. We were all family and friends, so we didn't need rules about the girls wearing veils. We were a community. Then the money came. Everybody bought cars, drove out of town and built themselves villas behind high walls—you were reckoned a failure if you didn't. And suddenly we found we were separate. We felt somehow empty inside. If we had a wedding to celebrate, we didn't get together like we used to, stringing out the lights round the neighbors' houses and yards. We'd hire a ballroom in some modern hotel."

Studying in America, Bahaziq filled the emptiness by seeking to become a better Muslim, forswearing the American temptations of alcohol and women. Back home in Jeddah for a vacation in 1975, he asked his family to find him a devout Saudi wife, in part to "innoculate" him against life in the States.

"My family made the choice. I had the right to meet her before the wedding—to 'inspect' her, if you like. But I felt that that was insulting to her. I trusted my family. I trusted her. I was happy *not* to be doing things in the modern and materialistic Western way. So the first time we saw each other was on our wedding day. Allah has blessed us ever since."

Bahaziq took his wife back to America, where he threw himself into Muslim activities, helping to organize the Islamic center at his university. As oil wealth increased in the late 1970s, Western newspapers gleefully reported the excesses of nouveau rich Arabs flaunting their fortunes in

Europe. But these Muslims who adopted Western delinquencies were not, it turned out, the Muslims who really mattered. The oil boom had produced a religion boom, and behind the headlines, the future was being seized by driven, pious men like Khaled Bahaziq, who would later wield a Kalashnikov in Afghanistan—and, even more dramatically, by a man called "Angry Face."

• • •

Juhayman Al-Otaybi overflowed with nervous energy.

"I never saw him sleeping," remembers Nasser Al-Huzaymi, who lived and traveled with Juhayman for four years in the mid-1970s. "He was like a father or brother to everyone, always ready to take care of you. When we went to sleep, he would make sure our blankets were pulled over us. People loved him. When he drove us in his GMC [truck] to recruit people in the villages, he would chant *'Allahu akbar!'* [God is great!] all the way. He was a leader. To use a Western word, he had 'charisma.'"

To a Western eye, Juhayman also had the air of an Old Testament prophet. In his short *thobe* and bared ankles, the straggle-haired fanatic seemed to be living in a different century from the "Gucci bedouin" of Jeddah, kitted out in their loafers and Porsches—and, in a sense, he was. Juhayman was repelled by bidaa, the innovations of the twentieth century. As the Westernizing affluence of the oil boom spread across the Kingdom, he sought refuge in the past, finding himself drawn backward in history, as is often the case with those who seek a fresh future in religion, to an earlier, simpler world, when the faith was fresh and new—so new, in fact, it was in the process of being created.

WHAT GOD REVEALED TO MOHAMMED

"Iqra!" "Recite!"

God started speaking to Mohammed when the Prophet was in his late thirties—forty years old in lunar years. "Recite in the name of your Lord who created humanity!" were the first words that came to the confused and earnest young merchant as he was meditating in a cave in one of the craggy hills surrounding Mecca. He felt, he later said, as if an angel had wrapped around him physically and was squeezing him tight.

God's fundamental instruction to his Messenger was to make the world a better place: the rich should provide money for the poor; women should be entitled to a portion of their parents' legacy; polygamy should be limited to four wives; retribution should be restricted to just one eye for an eye.

But this vision of moderated inequality—a model, for its time, of social reform—was not well received by the wealthy merchants of Mecca, whose fortunes were swelled by the pilgrims who came to worship the 360 gods of the city. Mohammed's insistence that there was only *one* God, in the tradition proclaimed by Abraham (Ibrahim in Arabic), seemed a mortal threat to the Meccans' income stream, and they did all they could to stifle the new movement, torturing the Prophet's followers and even devising a plot to murder him in his bed.

So Mohammed eventually gave his followers orders to leave this city where men were refusing to live as God intended. He told them to head north to the oases of Yathrib—a five-day camel ride away—and when the last of them was safely out of Mecca, he followed with his dear friend and ally Abu Bakr.

The two men's safe arrival in Yathrib provoked a riotous welcome. The followers had been waiting anxiously for days, scanning the southern horizon from the edge of the palm groves, and when they spotted the two distant figures late one evening, coming out of the sunset, they broke into cheers and celebration. "The Messenger is here! The Messenger has come!"

The hijrah (migration) of the Prophet from Mecca marks the beginning of Islamic history, since the members of the little community that now formed around Mohammed in Yathrib were able to live for the first time freely and openly as proper Muslims. In the weeks that followed, they built the first mosque, a low, brick-walled building around a courtyard, partially shaded with palm fronds; they listened to the first call to prayer (sung out proudly by Bilal, Abu Bakr's freed slave); and, following the Prophet's instructions, they instituted the first Islamic fast, the first Islamic laws, and a multitude of the practical traditions and regulations that came to define what it means to be a Muslim. Mohammed's social reform movement had become a real religion, built around the 6,236 verses of his recited revelation (the Arabic for recitation is *qur'an,* Koran).*

*Mohammed's recitations of the revelations he received over twenty-two years and five months were memorized by professional remembrancers (*huffaz*). They were written down by his secretary Zaid ibn Thabit and were finally compiled into one volume around A.D. 644, about a dozen years after the Prophet's death.

Yathrib was renamed. It became *Al-Medina,* "the City" of the Prophet, and since then every detail of the Prophet's life in Medina has been studied by Muslims with fierce intensity, for Mohammed did not preach a theoretical utopia somewhere in the future. Under the palm trees of Yathrib, he created life precisely as God wanted it. So at moments when Muslims have sensed that their world was going wrong, and that their lives might be taking on the wayward character of unreformed Mecca, many have tried to measure themselves—and to remold themselves—against the shape of the original template. Back to Medina!

• • •

In the mid 1970s Juhayman Al-Otaybi was already living in Medina, glorying in the chance to model his life on how Mohammed had lived in that very corner of the planet fourteen centuries previously. He had a home about half an hour's walk from the Prophet's Mosque, in Al-Harra Al-Sharqiyya, "the Eastern Terrain," a dry and infertile landscape of black volcanic rocks where he lived in a makeshift compound with his family. The devotees that he was starting to gather lived five minutes away in an even more makeshift hostel—Bayt Al-Ikhwan, the "House of the Brothers."

"We all slept on a mud floor," remembers Nasser Al-Huzaymi, who had dropped out of school and come to Medina seeking purpose in his life through religious devotion. "We had no telephone, and no plaster on the walls. We wanted to live as simply as possible, just like the Prophet's Companions. But we needed to read and study the Koran, so after some discussion, we considered that a single electric lightbulb was acceptable."

There were many such discussions.

"Did the Prophet eat chicken?" asked someone in the middle of a meal. "A good question," said Juhayman.

So the eating stopped, and the brothers pored over their copies of the Koran and the Hadith (the traditions and sayings of the Prophet). Juhayman kept his books in a huge, locked tin box that was welded into the back of his pickup truck, and at moments like this he undid the padlock to share the contents of his traveling library. It did not take much time to track down the authority for chicken consumption: one verse from the Koran envisioned the Companions relaxing in heaven, consuming "fruits, any that they may select, and the flesh of fowls, any that they may desire."

Chicken was OK, then—the meal could resume. Here was fundamentalism of the most basic sort. In a time of confusion, few things are more comforting than dogma. "The people of my own generation are the best," said the Prophet, according to one popular hadith, "then those who come after them, and then those of the next generation." This seemed a clear instruction to look backward. On this basis, every detail of life needed some sort of precedent from these three first and "best" generations.

It was a process that was going on all over the Arab world in the 1970s as Muslims worked out their different responses to the material and spiritual inroads of the West. Those who opted for back-to-basics called themselves *Salafi,* because they sought to behave as *salaf,* literally the pious ancestors of one of those three early generations that were mentioned with such approval by the Prophet. A group calling itself Al-Jamaa Al-Salafiya Al-Muhtasiba, "the Salafi Group That Commands Right and Forbids Wrong," had been active in Medina for some time, and Juhayman joined it when he came to town, plugging himself into some of the Kingdom's strongest and most ancient traditions of piety.

• • •

Medina's Salafi Group had been created around 1965 following a series of local disturbances known as "the breaking of the pictures" (*taksir al-suwar*) when zealous young vigilantes had taken it upon themselves to destroy pictures and photographs in public places, including portraits of the king.

"Hanging a picture on a wall may lead to exalting or worshipping it," ruled Sheikh Abdul Aziz Bin Baz, the austere president of Medina's Islamic University, "particularly if the picture is that of a King." After serving short terms in prison, the demonstrators decided to organize as a Salafi missionary group, and turned for approval to Bin Baz.

Blind from around the age of eight, Abdul Aziz Bin Baz was famous throughout the Kingdom as a holy man. With his eyes permanently closed, he seemed to be constantly in listening mode, his beard and strong-featured face cocked upward toward heaven, as if straining to catch God's least whisper. As his decree on royal pictures showed, Bin Baz was no respecter of earthly authority. According to U.S. documents, he was bold enough to confront Abdul Aziz himself in 1944 when he went to Riyadh to complain about the activities of American agricultural engineers in Al-Kharj, a town in the central region of Nejd. Thirty-two years old and *qadi* (judge) in the town, Bin Baz protested that the king was surrendering

Muslim land to infidels in contradiction of his duties as a Muslim ruler. The young qadi was particularly incensed that the engineers' wives had been mixing with local women and infecting them with liberated, Western ideas.

In the confrontation that followed, Abdul Aziz flew into a rage, imprisoning the young scholar and threatening to have him executed if he did not repent. But Bin Baz stood his ground. He had registered the unhappiness that many were coming to feel at the changes wrought by modernization, and as the years went by he came to be seen in Saudi Arabia as the modern repository of what the West called Wahhabism.

THE FIRST "WAHHABI"

Born in the Islamic, or Hijrah, year of 1115 (1703–4 in the Western, Gregorian calendar), Mohammed Ibn Abdul Wahhab learned the Koran at an early age. Traveling to the holy cities of Mecca and Medina as a teenager, he went on to Basra, in Iraq, to continue his religious studies. By the time he came to the dry and austere area of Qaseem, north of Riyadh, in A.H. 1153 (A.D. 1740), the thirty-seven-year-old preacher had come to feel that the Muslims of his time had gone grievously astray. People gave superstitious reverence to domes and tombs, even to rocks, caves, and trees that were associated with holy men; they dressed luxuriously, smoked tobacco, and indulged in singing and dancing that did not accord with his own austere reading of the Koran.

Ibn Abdul Wahhab ("Son of the Worshipper of the Giver") condemned these practices as *shirk* (polytheism). Calling on true Muslims to return to the central message of Islam, "There is no god but God," he led campaigns to stop music and to smash domes and gravestones in the name of God's Oneness. He and his followers liked to call themselves *muwahhidoon,* monotheists. They did not consider themselves a separate school of Islamic thought—they felt they were simply going back to the basics. But their critics derisively called them Wahhabis, and many of Nejd's settlements rejected the preacher's puritannical attacks on their pleasures.

Then the first Wahhabi encountered Mohammed Ibn Saud, the ambitious ruler of Dariyah, a small oasis town near the even smaller oasis of Riyadh. History was made. In A.H. 1157 (A.D. 1733) the two Mohammeds concluded a pact. Ibn Saud would protect and propagate the stern doctrines of the Wahhabi mission, which made the Koran the basis of government. In return, Abdul Wahhab would support the ruler, supplying him with "glory and power." Whoever championed his message, he promised, "will, by means of it, rule lands and men."

So it proved. In the following year the preacher proclaimed *jihad,* holy war, to purify Arabia, and after a series of bloodthirsty military campaigns, the Wahhabi armies swept into Mecca in April 1803 (A.H. 1218), extending Saudi authority from the Persian Gulf to the Red Sea. For a moment the House of Saud controlled more territory than the fledgling United States.

The empire did not last. Egyptian and Turkish troops marched into Nejd in the name of the Ottoman emperor to punish the Wahhabis for their presumption. In A.H. 1233 (A.D. 1818) the invaders brought cannons to Dariyah and bombarded its mud walls into rubble. But the Saudi-Wahhabi alliance proved strong enough to survive both this humiliation and the nineteenth-century family infighting that followed, to make its modern comeback under Abdul Aziz Ibn Saud (the great-great-great-grandson of Mohammed Ibn Saud). In his new Saudi Arabia the Koran ruled as it had ruled in Dariyah, and the tenets of Wahhabism remained the same—to revere God alone; to shun idols and man-made God substitutes; to pursue the original Muslim way of life with simplicity; and to command the good while forbidding evil.

• • •

These last two commandments, known together as *hisbah,* were the only elements that Abdul Aziz Bin Baz considered lacking in the proposal that Medina's Salafi Group brought to him in 1965 after the breaking of the pictures. He suggested they should add *hisbah* (adjectival form, *muhtasiba*) to their name, and so was born Al-Jamaa Al-Salafiya Al-Muhtasiba, the Salafi Group That Commands Right and Forbids Wrong. The blind sheikh became their *murshid* (spiritual mentor), and the group set off eagerly to spread the good word around the Kingdom.

Ali Saad Al-Mosa, an academic and columnist from the southern province of Asir, was sixteen when the missionaries of the Salafi Group arrived in the south in the mid-1970s. They were touring Ali's green and mountainous neighborhood on the border with Yemen.

"They seemed like ancient disciples," he remembers, "wandering all over the countryside. They camped together in our mosque for a week or so, and lived quite simply on whatever we could provide. I remember the gathering of beards."

Luxuriant beards were (and are) the most famous badge of Salafi conviction, based on a traditional belief, which some scholars dispute, that the Prophet never trimmed his beard.* Ali was especially impressed with the wild black beard of Juhayman, who had by then become one of the leaders of the group and was a powerfully effective preacher. As a lecturer in linguistics, Dr. Al-Mosa can today analyze the components of Juhayman's technique: "He started with some easy enemies," he remembers, "America, the West, and the wicked ways of the non-Muslim world. Then he made people feel guilty and scared, playing on their insecurities. 'You are a corrupt society,' he said. 'You must turn back to God.' He knew how to frighten simple folk. It was all about fear. He also criticized the media—too secular, with women's pictures in the papers; and the education syllabus—not enough religion. He was careful not to say anything directly about the royal family, but his whole attitude had an antigovernment drift."

Everywhere Juhayman looked he could detect bidaa—dangerous and regrettable innovations. The Salafi Group That Commands Right and Forbids Wrong was originally intended to focus on moral improvement, not on political grievances or reform. But religion is politics and vice versa in a society that chooses to regulate itself by the Koran.

"He disagreed with the government making it easier for women to work," remembers Juhayman's follower Nasser Al-Huzaymi, "and he thought it was immoral of the government to permit soccer matches, because of the very short shorts that the players wore in those days. He would use only coins, not banknotes, because of the pictures of the kings that were printed on the money. He thought that the coming of the rulers' pictures onto the banknotes was really bad bidaa. It was like television, a dreadful sin that had entered every home."

Juhayman's rejectionist thinking was shared by many occupants of the Bayt Al-Ikhwan hostel, particularly the newer recruits. Some opposed passports and identity cards on the grounds they showed loyalty to an entity that was not God. Others studied the scriptures to develop their own variations on traditional rituals—devising new rules, for example, on the

*The other "badge" is a shortened thobe, because the Prophet did not let his clothes brush the ground.

theology of whether or not to take off your sandals while praying. As news of these unorthodoxies filtered upward, the group's mentors became alarmed, and in the absence of Bin Baz, who had left for Riyadh in 1975 to take up grander religious responsibilities, a group of local sheikhs traveled out to the unwelcoming black lunar landscape of eastern Medina to try to reason Juhayman and his young zealots back onto the correct path.

"It was late in the summer of 1977," remembers Nasser Al-Huzaymi. "It was a hot night, so we all went up on the roof."

Built of rough cinder blocks, the House of the Brothers had never been fully finished, so there were bare pipes sticking up from the roof. In this raw setting beneath the stars, Juhayman took the lead aggressively on behalf of the radicals, arguing for "purity" and accusing the sheikhs of selling out to the government. They were not true Salafis, he said—they had not studied their holy books. Later he would even accuse his opponents of being police informers.

It was a bitter, personalized argument, and the rooftop meeting ended with a split. While the sheikhs departed with a minority that included certain founding members of the group, the younger, more hotheaded majority stayed at the hostel, taking their lead from Juhayman. From this moment onward, they started referring to themselves simply as the Brothers, Al-Ikhwan—a word that stirred up dangerous memories in Saudi society.

CHAPTER 2

The Brothers

In most Arab countries in the 1970s, the word *ikhwan* denoted the Muslim Brotherhood, the powerful network of Islamic activists, usually working underground, whose ideas influenced the young Osama Bin Laden. The Muslim Brotherhood was founded in Egypt, and from its steely roots came the extremists who would murder Egypt's president, Anwar Sadat, in 1981. But if you said "ikhwan" to most Saudis in the 1970s, especially to those of an older generation, their eyes would light up at the memory of another, earlier brotherhood that was particularly Saudi.

ABDUL AZIZ AND THE BROTHERS

The warriors from the bedouin tribes who supported Abdul Aziz, "Ibn Saud," in the early decades of the twentieth century called themselves Al-Ikhwan, the Brothers, and their ferociousness in battle was the key to his military success. Their imams had told them, in the historic tradition of Mohammed Ibn Abdul Wahhab, that to support the Saudi cause was to engage in jihad (holy war), so they burned with the conviction that those who opposed them were *kuffar* (infidels), and thus deserving of death. They also believed that any *mujahid* (holy warrior) who died in battle would go straight to heaven. This imbued the Ikhwan with such a lethal indifference to death that most towns would surrender at their approach, rather than risk being put to the sword.

In the course of the early 1920s the warriors of the Ikhwan helped extend Saudi power to the Red Sea coast. Abdul Aziz raised levies of *hadhar* (townsmen), but the Ikhwan were his ferocious vanguard, taking the fight to Mecca and Medina, and finally to the rich port city of Jeddah, which surrendered to the Al-Saud in 1925. The empire building was done, and Abdul Aziz packed his holy warriors back to their rural settlements with as much gold as he could muster. There were no more enemies left to fight, he told them. The time had come for his fierce, bearded warriors to go home to enjoy their wives and family making, and to practice the arts of peace.

But the Ikhwan were disinclined to settle. They were bedouin, after all. Their very lifeblood was to raid, and there were more battles left to fight, in their opinion notably against the impious Muslims of Transjordan and Iraq, their new neighbor nations to the northwest and northeast. Britain had created these pseudocolonies in the post–World War I carve-up of the defeated Ottoman Empire, and for the Brothers, an age-old principle was at stake: to mark their new boundaries, the *ingleez* (English) had set up frontier posts in the desert, seeking to limit freedom of movement where the bedu had traditionally wandered as they wished.

So in the late 1920s the more militant brethren, especially some members of the Mutayr and Otayba tribes, continued to go out riding and raiding as they had always done. They suspected their former leader had struck a deal to live in peace with the British, and, more seriously, that he had forgotten how to fight. Abdul Aziz had no real army, sneered the Ikhwan leader Faisal Al-Dawish to his counterpart, the Otayba chieftain, Sultan ibn Bijad. The Saudis were nothing but flabby cooks and soft men who slept on mattresses—"as much use as camel bags without handles."

The Ikhwan were correct about the British. Abdul Aziz had decided he had no choice but to live in harmony with the region's great colonial power. International frontiers had to be respected, particularly when it came to the British-protected states that now fringed his northern boundaries. That was why he instructed the Ikhwan to stand down from their raids and declared them rebels when they ignored his commands.

But the Brothers were quite wrong about the great man going soft. Abdul Aziz spent more than a year trying to conciliate with Al-Dawish before the showdown came. Early in March 1929 the Saudi king drove north from Riyadh with a convoy of open motorcars that had been mounted with machine guns and confronted the camel-riding mutineers on the windswept, open plain of Sibillah. He offered them one last chance to surrender, and when they ignored him and attacked, he gave the order to start firing. Hundreds of the Brethren and their camels were slaughtered.

The Al-Saud have always argued that Sibillah was a fair fight—that the balance of the battle and indeed the fate of the entire Saudi project hung in the balance. Their critics regard Sibillah as a cold-blooded massacre—and worse: In the context of the previous fifteen years it was a coldhearted desertion of the warriors whose fanaticism the Al-Saud had been happy to exploit when it suited their game.

"Saudi Arabia had virtually assumed its final shape as the result of constant war upon the infidel," wrote Harry St. John Philby, the first English chronicler of the country. "Henceforth the infidel would be a valued ally in the common cause of progress." The fanatics of the Ikhwan, on the other hand, must be discarded—they "could now serve no further useful purpose."

• • •

Among the Brothers who survived the machine guns of Sibillah was Mohammed bin Sayf Al-Otaybi, who had ridden to the battle with his leader, Sultan ibn Bijad, a renowned warrior and stubborn critic of Abdul Aziz. The Otaybi leader would end his days in a Riyadh jail—according to legend his final words were "Never give up." His follower Mohammed Al-Otaybi, meanwhile, went home to his Ikhwan settlement of Sajir, a spare collection of mud houses on the gravelly flatlands that mark the border of Qaseem, where, sometime in the early 1930s, he fathered the son to whom he gave the forbidding name of Juhayman.

Growing up in Sajir, Juhayman Al-Otaybi was immersed from the start in the ambivalent legacy of the Ikhwan. He loved to recount tales of their bravery, fighting for the Al-Saud and also against them. Around the age of twenty he joined the National Guard, the tribal territorial army that the Saudi state had formed from the Brothers who had stayed loyal to Abdul Aziz (the vast majority). The National Guard was known as the "White Army," since its members wore no uniform and reported for duty, rather haphazardly in those days, in their white thobes. Juhayman had left primary school unable to write with any fluency. But somewhere he had developed a prodigious appetite for religious reading and he began to collect the books that would fill his padlocked steel trunk.

The National Guard encouraged its members to pursue religious activities. All the units had imams and sheikhs who were dedicated to the

Wahhabi mission—though as agents now of the modern Saudi government, they no longer talked of jihad. Perhaps this was why Juhayman left the National Guard in the early 1970s to participate in the more stimulating activities of Medina's Salafi Group, supporting himself, according to Nasser Al-Huzaymi, through the shrewd buying, repairing, and reselling of vehicles in the car auctions of Jeddah. So long as the group was smiled upon by Bin Baz and the religious establishment, they received donations from pious local benefactors and from charitable funds.

"At one stage," remembers Al-Huzaymi, "Bin Baz was providing most of the money for Bayt al-Ikhwan."

But all this changed in 1977, following the fateful disagreement that occured amid the unfinished pipework on the roof. Until then Juhayman's subversive thoughts about banknotes and soccer players had been protected.

"When someone official got upset with us," recalls Al-Huzaymi, "Bin Baz would pick up the phone or go to see them. He would explain that we were only spreading the true faith, trying to make the country more pious. Quite a large group of the Brothers were arrested in Riyadh on one occasion, and the sheikh called up the Interior Ministry. He got them all released."

After the rooftop confrontation, however, and faced with the hostility of the sheikhs whom Juhayman had so brusquely rejected, the Brothers soon found themselves under pressure. Late in 1977 Juhayman got a tip-off from a friend in the local security forces, warning that he was due to be picked up for questioning.

"We packed up and drove away that very night," remembers Nasser Al-Huzaymi, who accompanied Juhayman. "We were escaping from the back door even as the police were arriving at the front."

From that moment forward, Juhayman was on the run. Thirty of the Brothers were soon taken in for more interrogation, detained for periods that ranged from a week to several months, and the whole dynamic of the movement shifted. Juhayman's own adventures set the tone, as he skulked in the northern deserts, experiencing the escapades of a Robin Hood. He had one narrow escape when he went to see his mother in Sajir, only to discover at the last minute that the police had the family home staked out. Suffering from a toothache on another occasion, he had to be smuggled to a friendly dentist who would not betray his identity. Being on the run created an atmosphere of paranoia and confrontation, and marked a new stage in the latter-day Ikhwan's campaign of reform—from alternative to radicalized, and now, increasingly, dedicated to subversive activities that were aggressive and underground. Terrorist, in fact.

. . .

No longer able to meet and talk easily with his followers, Juhayman turned to the written and spoken word. None of the cassettes that he recorded during his months in the wilderness has survived, but we do have his printed words, twelve angry diatribes that have become legendary among Islamic extremists over the years—"The Letters of Juhayman."

Their message was encapsulated in "The State, Allegiance and Obedience," the most political of these tracts. The Al-Saud, Juhayman complained, had exploited religion as "a means to guarantee their worldly interests, putting an end to jihad, paying allegiance to the Christians [America], and bringing evil and corruption upon the Muslims." That neatly summed up the fundamentalist case against the Saudi royal family, then and ever since—in a word, betrayal. It was the grievance of those earlier Brothers who did battle at Sibillah, and the essence of the message that Osama Bin Laden would deliver via his attacks on America on 9/11. The House of Saud were hypocrites; they exploited Islam to entice good Muslims to fight and die on their behalf, but when they had accomplished their worldly ends, they effectively machine-gunned the men who had put their lives on the line for them.

After his opening manifesto, Juhayman rather spoiled his case. He dived into the thickets of Islamic genealogy to demonstrate how the Al-Saud were not blood descendants of Mohammed—a pointless exercise, since they had never made any such claim. Juhayman had never been a disciplined thinker, and now he was caught up in the grandeur of his self-appointed mission. As ideas came into his head he dictated them to obediently scribbling associates. "He recited his thoughts out loud," remembers Nasser Al-Huzaymi, "just as the Prophet recited his revelations," so each of his Letters took on the rambling, declarative character of a Friday sermon.

"They all seemed a bit kooky to me," remembers Nabil Al-Khuwaiter, who, as a student at the University of Petroleum and Minerals in Dhahran, came across a selection of the pamphlets in October 1979. Crudely printed in green, yellow, and blue, the Letters of Juhayman, secretly published and smuggled across the border from Kuwait, had been scattered among the

Korans at the back of the little dormitory mosque where Nabil and his fellow students—the future oil technocrats of Saudi Arabia—went to pray five times a day.

"They were challenging the Islamic legitimacy of the Al-Saud to rule," Al-Khuwaiter recalls, "which was very shocking in those days. If criticism of the government ever appeared in the local press, it was never more than a mild complaint to a nonroyal minister about some aspect of his ministry's services. I didn't dare show the pamphlets to any but my closest friends and relatives—in fact, one relative even warned me that it could be some sort of *Mabahith* [secret police] trick to bait and snare potential dissidents.

"'Whoever heard of a name like Juhayman?' my relative said. 'If he is a real man, let him come out and give his real name, instead of trying to deceive impressionable young college students and get them to do his dirty work.'

"As I remember it, Juhayman argued that the use of ID photos proved that the government was *kafir* [infidel]. I couldn't really cotton on to his argument, but the Letters definitely caught the current of the times. On the one hand was the new wealth—the oil money flooding in with its invitation to go the Western way. On the other hand was the sense of loss as the old ways of doing things got swept away. There was this uncomfortable feeling that things were awry, so it was refreshing to see some alternative options set down on paper, however strange. I supported the idea that we needed more godly people in authority. That was how many young people were thinking at that time. It seemed so obvious—'Put the pious people in power.'"

• • •

The final stage in Juhayman Al-Otaybi's progression from earnest missionary to violent revolutionary occurred somewhere out in the northern deserts late in 1978, as the fugitive lay beneath his blanket looking up at the stars. Juhayman started to have dreams. For many years he had been contemplating the prophecies relating to the Islamic Messiah—the Mahdi, or "Right-Guided One"—who would come down to earth to correct the problems of mankind. The notion had carried some currency among the pious, and now, Juhayman dreamed, there was a need for someone who could correct the ills afflicting Arabia.

"When kings enter a village," ran a sura in the Koran that is not much repeated in the modern monarchies of the Middle East, "they corrupt it and demean the honor of its people."

Surely this applied to modern Saudi Arabia. In the very first of his Letters, Juhayman set out the traditions that connected the coming of the Mahdi, in his eyes, to current events in the Arabian Peninsula. "Great discord will occur," ran one prophecy, "and the Muslims will be drifting away from the religion." That was certainly coming true as the Al-Saud imported more and more Westerners to the country—and another tradition promised that the Mahdi would appear at the dawn of a new century. Well, it was now 1399 in the Islamic calendar.

This was where Juhayman's dreams came in, for they revealed to him the identity of the Mahdi—one of his own followers, Mohammed Abdullah Al-Qahtani, a good-looking and pious young man who had dropped out of university and made a small reputation as a poet. He was one of the members of the Salafi Group who had been locked up, then released, in Riyadh.

"The Mahdi will be of my [Qurayshi] stock," ran a hadith narrated by Abu Saiid Al-Khudri—"he will have a broad forehead and a prominent nose."

That physically matched the features of the handsome Al-Qahtani, whose first name and father's name corresponded to those of the Prophet, and whose non-Qurayshi name was explained away by a complicated story of adoption in an earlier generation.

Nasser Al-Huzaymi thought the whole thing was ridiculous.

"Al-Qahtani was a man," he says, "not a Messiah."

Al-Huzaymi was not convinced by the far-fetched tale of adoption and of Al-Qahtani's blood descent from the Prophet, and he grew alarmed by Juhayman's aggressive interpretations of other hadiths. These involved an army coming down from the north that would find itself swallowed up by the earth. Juhayman told the Brethren to get weapons before the end of the year, and to acquire small portable radios so they could listen for reports of the angels who would fly down from heaven to defeat the northern army. He traveled around the major cities gathering loyal survivors of the original '60s-era Salafi Group to brief them on the signs of the coming Mahdi. The recent arrests of pious Brothers had shown how the government was blocking the true path. Juhayman encouraged his followers to go out into the desert for target practice.

This all sounded like trouble to Al-Huzaymi, a mild and inoffensive character who was no lover of firearms. Like a number of others, he quietly made his excuses and slipped away from a movement that seemed to be losing touch with reality.

But Juhayman was a believer, and dreams are taken very seriously by Muslims—the angel Gabriel often spoke to the Prophet in his dreams.

"The fact that we dream," said one of the Brethren to Al-Huzaymi before he quit the group, "proves that we are more religious."

As Juhayman reported his visions of the Mahdi, his loyal followers responded with more and more dreams of their own, among them Al-Qahtani's own sister, who dreamed that she saw her brother standing inside the Grand Mosque in Mecca receiving the acclamations of the worshipers beside the Kaaba (the huge cube covered with black and gold embroidered fabric at the center of the Mosque's courtyard). Juhayman rapidly divorced his wife and married the woman, so that the Mahdi was his brother-in-law.

With the approach of A.H. 1400, a sense of purposeful hysteria began to permeate the Brotherhood. Coming and going in Mecca as religious insiders, Juhayman and his followers had their eyes on the *khalawi,* the warren of cellars and study rooms that lay beneath the floor of the Grand Mosque. Privileged worshippers were allowed to descend to the khalawi, where long corridors of simply furnished rest areas and cubicles were set aside for private prayer and meditation. These underground rooms would become their headquarters, they decided—an easily defensible bolt-hole where they could hole up and wait for their prophecies to be fulfilled.

Though by now openly critical of the royal family, the rebels do not appear to have had a coherent plan to subvert the Saudi government. They evidently believed that if they put themselves in the right place at the right time, God's cataclysm would do the rest—and they would have front-row seats. Bribing an official of the Bin Laden company, the building and maintenance contractors in charge of the site, they were able to drive their pickup trucks straight into the basement. As A.H. 1399 drew to a close they came and went openly through the streets of Mecca as they stocked the khalawi with supplies—dates, water, and dried yogurt, but also ammunition and weapons.

They tried to keep their plans secret, but there were several hundred rebels, some of whom were euphoric at the approaching fulfillment of one of Islam's most famous and fantastic prophecies, so it was not surprising that hints of their scheme leaked. Early in November, Ali Saad Al-Mosa, the bright young student who had heard Juhayman speak a few years earlier, was at a family funeral down in Asir.

"It was a very cold night," he remembers, "and someone from the village started talking loudly, saying that Al-Khidr ["the Green One," a shadowy Islamic righter-of-wrongs sometimes confused with the Mahdi] would be arriving with the new century, and that there would be changes. Everyone listened very seriously and nodded their heads. A lot of people, it seemed to me, believed him."

. . .

Saudi coffins are not wooden boxes: they are more like stretchers—open litters on which the dead are transported to their resting place beneath a shroud. One of the perks of being a Meccan is that your relatives can shuttle your corpse into the holy of holies for a farewell prayer at the very heart of Islam. So twenty or so such "coffins" provided the ideal cover for Juhayman and his followers to smuggle their final consignments of weapons into Mecca's Grand Mosque in the small hours of November 20, 1979—the first day of Muharram, the first Islamic month of the year 1400. Beneath the shrouds were dozens of firearms: pistols, rifles, Kalashnikovs, and magazines of ammunition.

Fajr, the predawn prayer, would be called that day at 5:18 A.M.—it is timed to the moment before sunrise when the first glimmer of brightness shows along the horizon—and the "mourners" aroused no special interest as they filed through the ghostly light. The shrouded cargoes were coming and going all the time, and on this particular morning the light was more ghostly than usual. As Juhayman and his followers fanned out quietly with their weapons around the coolness of the Grand Mosque's massive tiled courtyard, the *hilal,* the thinnest of crescent moons, could be discerned in the sky above them: new moon, new month, new year, new century—though, as Riyadh's governor, the sardonic Prince Salman, would later point out, the old century would not be truly complete until the *end* of 1400, with the new, fifteenth century beginning on the first day of 1401.

As the first prayer call of A.H. 1400 sounded, the slight, barefoot figure of Juhayman went scampering up the steps to the public address system to jostle aside the imam and commandeer his microphone. Celebratory shots rang out. Men were firing rifles into the air while the Brothers were clustering around Mohammed Al-Qahtani, the Dreamed-of One, shaking his hand and offering him homage.

"Behold the Mahdi!" they were shouting. "Behold the Right-Guided One!"

Now was the time for Juhayman's prepared proclamation to be read out by one of his followers.

"The Mahdi will bring justice to the earth!" rattled the message from the loudspeakers, providing the small number of confused and sleepy policemen around the Mosque with the first explanation of what was amiss. "Juhayman is the Mahdi's brother! He calls on you to recognize his brother! Recognize the Mahdi who will cleanse this world of its corruptions!"

From beneath their robes several dozen more men produced rifles, joined in the shouts and fanned out purposefully toward the Mosque's twenty-five double gateways. At this cue a couple of hundred men leaped up from among the worshippers. Policemen and a young assistant imam who tried to resist were shot dead. The gunmen reached the gates. The doors were shut, and the shrine revered by Muslims as the holiest place on earth was sealed off. The House of God had been hijacked.

CHAPTER 3

Siege

The extraordinary news that the Grand Mosque had been kidnapped was received in Riyadh with consternation and something approaching panic.

"I wish they had done that to my palace, not to the Mosque," exclaimed the pious old King Khaled with horror.

The sixty-seven-year-old Khaled had come to the throne four years earlier in the aftermath of a family compromise. In terms of seniority, the brother in line after Faisal was Khaled's forceful elder brother Mohammed. But age has never been the sole criterion for authority in Arabia. The tribe searches for the candidate who can best bring consensus, and the inner councils of the Al-Saud had long been wary of Mohammed as *too* forceful. Known as Abu Sharrain, "the Father of Twin Evils," the elderly prince had a vile temper that would be revealed to the outside world in 1977 when he ordered the deaths of his granddaughter and her lover, who had tried to elope. This tragic scandal was later depicted in the British TV film *Death of a Princess,** and might have caused the Al-Saud even more embarrassment had Mohammed not agreed to step aside from the succession in the 1960s. Sidelined from public office, paid off with land grants and endless deference, his prickly pride was salved by the knowledge that the prince who replaced him was his full blood brother.

*The screening of *Death of a Princess* on British television provoked the expulsion of the British ambassador from Jeddah in 1980. See *The Kingdom*, chapter 48. The romantic legend has subsequently developed that the ill-starred couple were not murdered—reports of their deaths were confused—and that they were smuggled out of the country to start a new life elsewhere. This seems far-fetched.

Khaled's mild and conciliatory style made him an altogether better guardian of the clan's equilibrium. He was generally assumed to be a cypher whose function was to rubber-stamp the executive decisions of his westernized younger half brother Fahd, the crown prince. But Khaled had bedouin shrewdness and two very relevant strengths—his links with the tribes, who embraced him as they never embraced Fahd, and his similarly warm relationship with the council of the *ulema* ("those who possess learning"—the religious sheikhs). These traditional connections were exactly what the crisis of the Grand Mosque called for, and on the first day of the new century Fahd happened, in any case, to be far from Riyadh—the crown prince was representing the Kingdom at an Arab League summit in Tunis.

"We were awoken by phone calls very early that morning," remembers Prince Turki Al-Faisal, the young director of Saudi foreign intelligence who was also attending the conference. "The crown prince told me to go back at once. There were important issues in Tunis, so he was going to stay at the summit."

The soft-spoken Turki was one of the rising stars of the family. Educated at the Lawrenceville prep school in New Jersey, Georgetown, Princeton, *and* Cambridge, he had the gravitas of his father, Faisal, and the insouciance to spend four months in his twenties driving a new Lamborghini home from London to Arabia. When he got back to Mecca on the night of Tuesday, November 20, 1979, he rapidly discovered the nature of the foe the Al-Saud was up against. As he reached out for the handle of the door at the Shoubra Hotel, where his uncles had set up their headquarters, a bullet shattered the glass in front of him. Juhayman had stationed snipers in the soaring minarets of the Grand Mosque, and they had already claimed victims.

* * *

The task of recapturing the Mosque had been assigned to Fahd's full brothers, Sultan, the defense minister, and Nayef, the interior minister, assisted by Nayef's deputy and younger brother, Ahmad. With Salman, the governor of Riyadh, they made up the core of the so-called Sudayri Seven, Abdul Aziz's seven sons by his cleverest wife, Hissa Al-Sudayri.* The Sudayris were the powerhouse at the heart of the Al-Saud, owing

*See family tree, page xxiv.

their influence partly to their numbers (no other grouping of blood brothers numbered more than three), but mainly to their mutual loyalty, ambition, and extraordinary appetite for work—qualities instilled in them by their mother. To her dying day, the formidable Hissa insisted that all seven of her boys, no matter how grand they had become, should gather in her home once a week for lunch.

Sultan and Nayef had reached Mecca by nine that morning and started deploying their forces—some local army regiments and a couple of companies of the Special Security Force, a unit of Nayef's Interior Ministry. The Mecca regiments of the National Guard also moved into the town. Their commander, Abdullah, would shortly fly back from a holiday in Morocco.

A respectable military grouping had been put in place within hours. But its princely commanders had no authority to assault the Grand Mosque—that permission would have to come from the grand council of the ulema, who were being hastily assembled in Riyadh. Nor at this stage did the princes know much about who or what they were supposed to be fighting: rumors ran the gamut from Iranians to the CIA or Israeli agents. It turned out that the grand ulema could help with that as well.

• • •

The religious sheikhs held a regular meeting with their monarch every Tuesday. It was broadcast on the TV news, with Bin Baz, blind-eyed and head cocked heavenward, seated in the place of honor beside the king. In theory, the ulema disapproved of television. But since it existed, they judged themselves a better subject for the screen than more trivial fare such as cartoons. Now, as they shuffled hurriedly over the plush carpeting of the Maazar palace in Riyadh, they had more unpleasant realities to confront.

They already knew exactly who had taken the Grand Mosque. The cleric whom Juhayman had jostled aside that morning to seize the microphone had been the respected Sheikh Mohammed ibn Subayl, principal imam of the Mosque and one of the teachers at whose feet Juhayman and his followers once sat in earlier, more submissive days. Ibn Subayl had recognized his former pupils with dismay, and knew all about the Salafi cause they had served. He had taken refuge in his office to telephone the news to his colleagues. Later, jettisoning his gold-trimmed cloak and wrapping his headdress around his shoulders in the fashion of foreigners, he had managed to escape from the Mosque in a group of Indonesian pilgrims.

Juhayman was keeping Arabs inside the Mosque as conscripts for the Mahdi's army, but he had given orders to release non-Arabic speakers, who would not understand what he or the Mahdi were saying.

King Khaled wanted guidance from the sheikhs. What should his soldiers be doing? Every Muslim knew the rules against violence in God's house—that was what made the action of these violators so shocking. So was it permissible for Saudi troops to attack the kidnappers with guns and bombs inside the *haram* (holy place), with all that implied for damage to the Mosque?

The religious sheikhs, who included Bin Baz, played for time. Neither then, nor ever since, has any Saudi cleric admitted the slightest responsibility for the monster that, Frankenstein-like, they had nurtured in Juhayman. But their long delay in condemning him and his latter-day Ikhwan suggested deep embarrassment. The ulema granted the king an emergency fatwa (judgment) to take "all necessary measures" to "protect the lives of Muslims inside the mosque." Then they sat down for three full days to ponder the detailed measures to be taken against the pious young men they had once blessed as their missionaries.

• • •

Mahdi Zawawi saw two women sauntering in the deserted Mosque courtyard with rifles. He could not believe his eyes. He was one of the helicopter pilots flying patrols over the haram, peering down on the rebels from a thousand feet. The women were dressed in black and totally veiled—with bandoliers crisscrossed over their robes, and automatic weapons in their hands.

"They were very tall," he remembers. "And they were carrying themselves proudly. It was quite a sight—two women, scarcely anyone else, walking slowly round the Kaaba, talking to each other and wearing pistols in their belts! Those bedouin wives . . ."

Zawawi was flying at too great an altitude to see any more—or to hear the *tak-tak-tak* coming from the snipers in the minarets. When he got back to his base in Taif, in the mountains above Mecca, he discovered that a bullet had pierced his fuselage. The hole it made was less than half an inch from the fuel tank.

• • •

Down on the ground, meanwhile, a lull had descended. Events were proceeding in a curiously haphazard fashion.

"I went over as a spectator," remembers Khaled Al-Maeena, then working as a sales director for Saudi Airlines in Jeddah. "I could see the snipers up in the minarets taking potshots. Beside me were some Yemenis who'd arrived wearing their white pilgrim towels. They knew nothing about the trouble. The government had blanked out the news for the first twenty-four hours. So these guys had turned up to do their *umrah* [small pilgrimage]."

Girls on a school roof were playing ball—unconcerned to be in sight, and also in range of the minarets. Arriving home in a nearby street after a long business trip, Maatooq Jannah knew nothing of the trouble until he knocked on his mother's door to be greeted not by a welcome but by a horrified scream—"Trim down that beard at once!" she cried. "You'll get us all killed!" In just a few hours the rebellious connotations of wearing a bushy Salafi beard had already spread around Mecca.

As the twilight darkened, the reporter Ali Shobokshi noticed how difficult it was becoming to see clearly in the open plaza around the Mosque, and he sensed a business opportunity. Like many a Saudi, the journalist had his own freelance enterprise on the side, a floodlight-rental business—so he hurried off to the Saudi command headquarters in the Shoubra Hotel to propose a deal. The princes had their fatwa in hand, and they were planning to attack and recapture the building that very night.

• • •

The bombardment started at 3:30 A.M. Bright flashes and deafening explosions blasted through the darkness as artillery on the hills around the town lobbed nonpercussive shells, intended to minimize physical damage, into the Mosque. Under cover of the shelling, groups of commandos raced for the haram gates, aiming particularly for the Bab Al-Salaam, the Peace Gate, in the middle of the 490-yard-long Safa-Marwah gallery, which ran along the eastern side of the Mosque. This was where, in normal times, pilgrims would move to and fro, replicating the Koranic story of Abraham's wife Hagar as she ran desperately looking for water.

Juhayman and his marksmen were waiting. They fired down on the attackers, only opening the Peace Gate momentarily to pour out a stream of bullets into the ranks of the hapless commandos. The attack was a fiasco. Dozens of Saudi troops were killed. It was deeply disheartening. When a battalion of paratroopers from the northern city of Tabuk arrived soon after dawn, the princes insisted that they should go immediately into action.

Their commander, Colonel Nasser Al-Homaid, was not so sure. He suggested it might be better to wait until that evening, after darkness, when floodlights could be used to blind the defenders. But he was countermanded by his royal superiors.

"You are not a man!" shouted one of the senior princes, dismissing the colonel's strategic thinking as cowardice. Loss of life did not matter anyway in this mission, as the royal commander saw it, since any soldier killed would be considered a martyr and would go straight to Paradise.

It is not known who this senior prince was. Turki Al-Faisal, then a junior prince, denies that any such conversation took place. But on Thursday, November 22, 1979, someone in royal authority certainly commissioned a daylight attack on the Mosque that was virtually identical to the attack that had just failed so miserably under cover of darkness.

These were days of high tension, and there are many reliable tales of angry princes snapping out contemptuous orders—starting with Prince Fahd shouting imperiously into the phone, first from Tunis and then from Jeddah when he got back on Friday. It is, regrettably, the Saudi way, and it is not an exclusively royal failing. Many Saudi teachers and even some university lecturers adopt the same dismissive, autocratic style with their students. Promotion? Positive reinforcement? These are, literally, foreign concepts when it comes to the exercise of authority in Saudi Arabia.

So later that day in broad daylight the brave Colonel Al-Homaid dutifully led his paratroopers into the Safa-Marwah gallery, where, as it happened, the supposed Mahdi, Mohammed Abdullah himself, was waiting in ambush with several dozen marksmen. A junior paratroop officer, Lieutenant Abdul Aziz Qudheibi, later described in the newspaper *Al-Riyadh* the courageous way in which his commanding officer met his death, along with many of his comrades. Since the paratroopers had flown south from Tabuk, there was a macabre sense in which an army from the north had been swallowed up—though not by angels.

The young Qudheibi himself was wounded and captured. The Ikhwan bathed his wounded forearm with water from the haram's holy spring of Zamzam, which, they assured him, was more healing than any man-made disinfectant. Eager to convert the young officer, they shared the exciting news about the coming of the Mahdi. Henceforward, they explained, television, radio, khaki uniforms, and salaries paid by the Ministry of Defense would all be forbidden. These things were offensive to the Almighty.

. . .

Next day the ulema finally reported. Impatience at their tardiness had been expressed all around the Muslim world. From Cairo the grand sheikh of Al-Azhar had sent a telegram urging "quick decisive action"—by which he meant a meeting of the world's leading Islamic scholars that would "save the Holy House of God." This proposal to remove the issue from Saudi hands was an ill-concealed rebuke of the stewardship of Bin Baz and his colleagues, who had allowed this tragedy to happen.

The defenders of the three-day delay pointed out the difficulty of discovering what the religious sources had to say about violence in the haram. Their critics pointed to a verse in the Koran itself, the most reliable authority, that seemed to make the issue crystal clear: "Do not fight with them in the Sacred Mosque until they fight with you in it. But if they do fight you, then slay them; such is the recompense of the unbelievers."

This proved to be the verse on which the ulema ultimately based the verdict they issued late on Friday, November 23, 1979. But since they knew very well that the young men inside the Mosque were *not* unbelievers, they also issued an explanatory statement that set out the problem with which they had had to wrestle: "Although this verse has been revealed in connection with the infidels, its connotations include . . . those who acted like them." They were not prepared, in other words, to deny the Muslim faith of the rebels.

Their language was curiously restrained. The sheikhs had a rich vocabulary of condemnation that they regularly deployed against those who incurred their wrath, from *kuffar* (infidels) to *al-faseqoon* (those who are immoral and who do not follow God). But the worst they could conjure up for Juhayman and his followers was *al-jamaah al-musallaha* (the armed group). They also insisted that the young men must be given another chance to repent. Before attacking them, said the ulema, the authorities must offer the option "to surrender and lay down their arms."

By now those at the very top of the government had discovered the truth about the compromising relations between the religious sheikhs and Juhayman.

"They [the religious sheikhs] knew them all well," says Prince Turki. "The so-called 'Mahdi' had been a pupil."

Prince Nayef was anxious to make clear that his Mabahith (secret police) had identified Mohammed Al-Qahtani and a number of the Ikhwan as troublemakers. They had got them all safely locked up months before—only to release them at the request of Sheikh Bin Baz. As Fahd put it ruefully in an interview in January 1980: "We had earlier taken action against them, but some people intervened for their release out of good intentions. . . . Those who intervened believed that perhaps they were something useful for the propagation of Islam."

These words are, so far as is known, the closest the Al-Saud ever got to issuing a rebuke to Bin Baz or to any member of the ulema for their enabling role in the Grand Mosque debacle. Princes are pragmatists. The fatwa of Friday, November 23, was a wishy-washy document, but its conclusion gave the government the authority they needed: "The ulema, therefore, unanimously agree that fighting inside the Sacred Mosque has become permissible. . . . All measures can be taken."

As darkness fell that evening the floodlights were switched on in Mecca and a military jeep with loudspeakers drove slowly around the outside of the massive compound. "To all those who are underground and inside the Mosque," crackled out the message that had been requested by the ulema. "We warn you so that you can save your souls. Surrender or we shall force you. . . . You have to surrender."

No one moved. The jeep went on driving and broadcasting. Around and around the walls of the Grand Mosque it drove—for one hour, two hours, three hours, calling out the same surrender message, only to be greeted with silence. For some reason the snipers in their gun nests gave no response.

They might have done so if they had known what would happen next. Suddenly the truce was ended as, one by one, the Mosque's towering minarets were struck by TOWs—tube-launched, optically tracked, wire-command-link guided missiles—that exploded with a deafening bang. As they struck the marble balconies, a cluster storm of shrapnel and orange flames carbonized every sniper in the gun nests. Now the minarets really were silent, as plumes of thick smoke drifted over the parapets.

The TOW missiles were part of the Kingdom's enormous arms sales program with America, as were the M113 armored personel carriers that had started lining up around the Mosque, waiting to crash their way in. A small tracked armored vehicle that looked like an undersized tank with an automatic weapon on top, the M113 was a rare U.S. success story in the Vietnam War. It could hold up to eleven soldiers. As a succession of these motorized battering rams smashed into the gates, Saudi soldiers jumped out to pursue the rebels who retreated into the pillared arcades.

It was a bitter battle. None of these young assault troops had ever seen action like this, stalking deadly enemies a few miles from their homes. Creeping through the pillars, Lieutenant Mohammed Sudayri, only a year out of Sandhurst (Britain's West Point), heard the sound of a magazine being loaded a few yards away.

"I knew it was not one of my men. I had checked every magazine before we started. They had all loaded up correctly. So I went round the pillar with my rifle ready."

There the young officer—a distant cousin to Hissa, mother of the Sudayri Seven—saw a rebel standing, a few yards away, with his back to him, loading his magazine.

"My first thought was to arrest him. But I remembered how others of them had pretended to surrender, then produced hidden guns, daggers, grenades even, and killed us. They had no scruples. When one of their comrades died, they poured petrol on his face and burnt it so we could not find out who he was. They gave the job to their women. And whenever those women found one of our men, they cut off his private parts."

Like all the troops, the lieutenant had heard the fatwa read out: "If they do fight you, then slay them." This was a contest to the death. He raised his rifle, took point-blank aim at the rebel's head, and pulled the trigger.

• • •

On the Brethren's side, Mohammed Abdullah Al-Qahtani was enjoying his immortality as Mahdi. He had fought recklessly in the Safa-Marwah corridor. Now, as the Saudi soldiers advanced through the forest of pillars throwing hand grenades, he would run forward whenever he heard a grenade hit the marble. He would pick it up and fling it back in the brief second before it detonated, scoring hit after hit—until his luck ran out. As he bent down to pick up another grenade, it exploded. When the government eventually located the bloodstained proof of his mortality, they lost no time photographing his corpse, his face still curiously handsome, and published it in the newspapers.

Rumors had been swirling since the beginning of the siege, and according to one, King Khaled had sent for Al-Qahtani's mother. The perplexed old king wanted to investigate the truth about her son, which she found easier to grasp than he did.

"If my son is the Mahdi, he will kill you," she said bluntly. "If he is not, you will kill him."

It is a good story, but the Al-Saud say it did not happen.

• • •

By Sunday morning Saudi forces controlled the Mosque from ground level upward, and Turki Al-Faisal went inside through the shattered gates to survey the damage with his brother Saud, the foreign minister. What struck him, he later told the author Yaroslav Trofimov, was the eerie silence in the shrine, which he had always experienced as so crowded—and the lingering aura of the evil that he knew had occurred there.

It was by no means over. As the government troops moved through the pillars, Juhayman had ordered his long-planned change of tactics, a strategic retreat down into the khalawi below the Mosque's pavement. The insurgents had already stashed boxes of food, water, and spare ammunition in the honeycombed maze of prayer rooms and were planning to hold out for weeks. They refused all appeals to surrender. They could not expect to live very long or very pleasantly if they did turn themselves in. So they blackened their faces and holed up in the grubby little catacombs with mattresses, their womenfolk, some unfortunate children who had been brought along, plus what was left of their dates and water.

Saudi assault troops flooded the cellars and flung live electrical cables into the water. They had more success when, after some delay, they smashed holes in the Mosque pavement and dropped down canisters of paralyzing CS gas that had been flown in from Paris by French commandos. Technically known as *o*-chlorobenzylidene malononitrile, CS was similar to the lethal chemical used by Russian troops to liberate the Moscow theater seized by Chechen rebels in 2002. An irritant that blocks breathing, CS gas "knocks out" those who inhale it and can cause death in sufficient concentrations. The compound used in Moscow killed more than 170 people.

One of the French commandos later claimed that he had briefly sneaked into the Grand Mosque before the attack, but this was denied by his commanding officer and by his two companions who had helped him train the Saudi gas handlers. By all reliable accounts, the three French agents did not fight in Mecca. They recall waiting up in Taif during the final attack with their telephones cut off, feeling rather helpless in their luxurious hotel rooms as they gave a Saudi medic advice on how to deal with the sinister effects of CS gas.

The hard work was done by Saudi assault troopers wearing gas masks, plodding day after day through the now filthy darkness of the khalawi catacombs, flinging out gas canisters, then stumbling forward through the toxic fumes.

"The defenders," remarks Prince Turki, "definitely had the advantage."

Not a single rebel surrendered voluntarily; they sprang ambushes and fought viciously to the bitter end. Finally, on Tuesday, December 4, 1979, two weeks to the day from the beginning of the siege, the attackers burst through a metal door to find a huddled group of men, their faces blackened with soot, their ragged clothes soiled with blood and vomit. The gas had had its effect. Some were shivering uncontrollably. But one, hidden among crates of weapons and piles of colored pamphlets, retained the wild, and now surprisingly frightened, eyes of a cornered beast of prey.

"What is your name?" asked the Saudi captain, pointing his gun.

"Juhayman," came the oddly subdued reply.

. . .

The capture of Juhayman did not end the rumors—indeed, they swirled more fiercely than ever. One described Abdullah bin Abdul Aziz, commander of the National Guard and number three in the royal heirarchy behind Khaled and Fahd, going to see the blasphemous culprit as soon as he was captured. Juhayman was lying on the ground, and when the black-bearded commander-prince caught sight of his former National Guardsman, he started growling with rage. Handicapped with an embarrassing stutter, Abdullah was notorious for being a man of few words, and, according to the story, he wasted none on Juhayman. He simply walked across the cell and, without more ado, stood firmly on the rebel's head. The story was not true, but it contained a truth—the House of Saud did not build a country the size of a small continent by being soft with their enemies.

Prince Turki Al-Faisal went to get his own firsthand look at the insurgent leader in the hospital, where he was lying shackled to his bed.

"Forgive me," cried Juhayman beseechingly, his bravado suddenly gone. "Forgive me, *tal omrak* [May God prolong your life]. Please ask *ammi* Khaled [my uncle Khaled] to forgive me!"

In saying "*ammi* Khaled" Juhayman was using the term of endearment traditionally employed by slaves and retainers in princely Saudi households, and the young intelligence chief ignored his plea, furious at the familiarity and also at the loss of life that had stemmed from this man's delusion that he knew the truth of Islam. The government had lost 127 soldiers dead and 461 injured, along with 117 rebels and a dozen or so of the worshippers who were killed in the first morning's gunfire. The prince pointed derisively at the captive's matted beard and electrified, wispy hair.

"So that's Islamic?" he sneered.

• • •

The soldiers led them out just before dawn—a shuffling group of men shackled hand and foot, shivering a little in the cold. There were soldiers on the square and up on the roofs around the old bedouin marketplace in central Riyadh, with a huddle of robed princes and ministers in the darkness, waiting on a balcony to see justice done. Sixty-three men were due to be executed that morning in eight towns around the country,* starting with Juhayman in Mecca. Here in Riyadh the tall, square-framed governor, Prince Salman—the brother whose looks, say the family, most resemble those of his father, Abdul Aziz—was reading intently down a list.

"He was checking the tribal names of the soldiers," recalls an eyewitness, "to make sure that the killing was done by and in front of their own. They are masters, that family, at doing things the tribal way."

One of the prisoners was screaming and writhing. He was an Afghan, one of the twenty or so foreigners whom Juhayman had swept up in the preceding months and on the day itself. The official roll call listed Yemenis, Pakistanis, Sudanese, and Egyptians.

"I am innocent!" cried the Afghan as they led him in front of the executioner. He was wriggling so much that the blade missed its mark, slicing into his shoulder. His screams got shriller as the uniformed soldiers

*Mecca, Medina, Dammam, Buraydah, Hail, Abha, Tabuk, and Riyadh—to cover every corner of the Kingdom.

struggled to keep their hold. An officer stepped forward to finish him off with a revolver shot to the head.

But it was the first of the victims whose death would set the sinister tone of that chilly morning. No one who saw him would ever forget. He was one of the Mahdi's friends who had helped organize the Riyadh Ikhwan, and he carried himself as a leader, defiantly raising his shackled arms in prayer.

"*Bismillah, Al-Rahman, Al-Raheem*—In the name of God, the Compassionate, the Merciful!" he called out in a strong and confident voice, quite unafraid. "You know what they have done," he cried—and here he raised his blindfolded eyes toward heaven. "You have witnessed their sins and their corruption. May their end be most horrible!"

With a proud stiffening of his back and shoulders, he invited the executioner to do his work. He flexed his body and seemed almost to rise into the sword as it descended. The blind, utter belief of the man was breathtaking. He was God's warrior, and having done God's work, he had no doubt at all that he was now going to heaven.

CHAPTER 4

No Sunni, No Shia

If there was one member of the House of Saud who most powerfully embodied everything against which Juhayman and his Brethren had protested, it was the complex figure of Crown Prince Fahd bin Abdul Aziz. He was Mr. Modernity, playing the dynamic CEO of Saudi Enterprises Unlimited to King Khaled's genial chairman of the board. Fahd had been appointed the Kingdom's very first minister of education by his brother Saud, then served under Faisal as minister of the interior. In both positions he had gained a reputation for shifting Saudi life in a Westerly direction. Now with the oil boom he was taking things further.

The shocking assassination of King Faisal in 1975 had had one upside in the eyes of progressive Saudis—his death had loosened the national purse strings. The old king had been cautious with his own money, and he was still more cautious with that of the country. A tale that his sons admitted was probably apocryphal, but which they liked to relate just the same, described an angry Henry Kissinger threatening Faisal during the 1973 oil embargo with the possibility that America might choose to stop consuming Saudi oil.

"In that case," replied the hawk-faced monarch, "we shall go back to our tents and live on camels' milk. But what will *you* do, Mr. Kissinger, without any gas for your cars?"

Faisal's parsimonious policy was to save oil profits for the Saudi equivalent of a rainy day, but his Westernized younger half brother was not afraid of spending. Fahd believed with a passion that the national revenues should be invested as soon as possible inside the Kingdom to create more wealth: Within months of Faisal's death, the crown prince was forming committees and drawing up spending plans in which words like *infrastructure* and *take-off* figured prominently. Hospitals, schools, highways, airports; two new industrial cities, one on each coast; more planes for Saudia, the national airline; more weapons for the armed forces; and a set of huge "military cities" to defend each vulnerable corner of the country.

"He was a visionary," recalls one of the technocrats in Fahd's inner circle. "Nobody was wild about his project for the two industrial cities. But he dug out the money and he fought them through. He was a man with real guts. Now Yanbu and Jubail are two of Saudi Arabia's great success stories."

It was Fahd's ambition to bring Saudi Arabia the best from the West, and his private life tended in the same direction. In his youth the prince had been the classic example of the Monte Carlo Arab, prowling the baccarat tables in his open-neck black shirt. King Faisal had rebuked his younger brother more than once for his disappearances to Europe on extravagant gambling binges. Fahd's name meant "desert leopard," but as the years went by—he was fifty-six in 1979—the crown prince's generous appetites were making him look less and less leopardlike.

Fahd also served himself generously when it came to business. As he doled out the petrodollars to sweep away sleepy old Saudi Arabia, the crown prince saw no reason to conceal the financial favors that he lavished on his family and his friends. *"Nahhab, wahhab,"* said his critics. "He steals, then he gives." It was an accusation that could have been leveled at many members of the royal family. They had built the Kingdom. It carried their name. It was hardly surprising if a large number of princes found it difficult to distinguish between what was theirs and what belonged to the still-growing state.

The crown prince's power base lay among his dynamic group of hardworking Sudayri brothers, but most of the family backed his manifesto to supervise an outward-looking program of national development. Fahd's confidence in a succession of "five-year plans" was accepted with a reverence that a Soviet commissar might have envied—and he was never afraid to think big. He liked to joke with European friends that he would one day commission the construction of a grand national opera house in Riyadh, in which *Aida* would be performed with not one, but ten elephants.

It was not a joke that he shared with Sheikh Abdul Aziz Bin Baz. The religious sheikhs had long viewed Fahd with a skeptical eye. So that made it all the more tricky in November 1979, when, as the crown prince wrestled with one bitter religious revolt at Mecca in the west of his kingdom, he found himself confronted by another in the east.

• • •

In the village of Al-Awjam, Ali Al-Marzouq watched his fellow villagers as they beat themselves with chains—a long, snaking line of men dressed in black, their jaws set grimly, swaying from side to side and bringing their metal flails down in unison with a hearty *whack!* across their shoulders. The village lay in eastern Saudi Arabia, home to the world's very richest concentration of oil fields. Billions of dollars' worth of "black gold" lay below the earth on which these young devotees were stomping. All of them, like Ali, were Muslims of the Shia persuasion (*Shia* means "followers," "faction," or "members of a party"), and they were marking their doleful anniversary of Ashura.

Ashura is Arabic for "tenth" and refers to the date of the Shias' defining annual ritual, the tenth of Muharram—which fell on November 30 in 1979. The villagers of Al-Awjam, along with the other five hundred thousand or so Shia Muslims then living in the Eastern Province, were marking the emotional climax of their religious year, even as Juhayman and his followers were battling it out with the Saudi security forces in the Grand Mosque on the other side of the peninsula.

Ali decided to go into town to watch the ceremonies in Al-Qateef, the Shia headquarters of the area. This sprawling, dusty settlement ringed with date palms was home to more than two hundred thousand inhabitants, the vast majority of them Shia. The town's crumbling Turkish mud fort recalled the days before the Saudis came, when the date groves and trading enterprises of the hardworking population made Al-Hasa (the nineteenth-century name of the whole province) a valuable corner of the Ottoman Empire. Now the area was still more valuable, thanks to its efficient and productive oil fields, whose smooth working owed much to the reliability and industriousness of the local labor force, 60 percent of them Shia, virtually the only native-born Saudis then willing to carry out modern, industrial-style manual work. The growth of Aramco, the Arabian American Oil Company, was built on American expertise and the stringent Shia work ethic—when meeting for business appointments, the Shia are among the few Saudis who will ring to warn you they are running ten minutes late.

The whole of Al-Qateef was quivering with Ashura fever as Ali Al-Marzouq, then a slightly-built schoolboy of sixteen, made his way toward the Al-Fateh ("Victory") Mosque on Abdul Aziz Street, not far from the marketplace and the stalls of the fish auction. Hundreds of young men had gathered to listen to a religious lecture over the mosque's loudspeakers, spilling out onto the street to fill an overflow corral of wooden barriers. Their emotions were roused by the traditionally tearful nature of Ashura lectures, but also by recent events outside Saudi Arabia. The ayatollahs' revolution in Iran had been a dazzling assertion of Shia power and identity, and it gave extra meaning to this first Ashura of the new Islamic century. "No Sunni! No Shia! All Muslims together!" chanted the crowds outside the mosque, beating their chests and sobbing as the lecture came to an end. Someone had brought along some posters of the Ayatollah Khomeini and had hoisted them high.

"It felt safe and comforting," remembers Ali Al-Marzouq, "to be with my brothers, shoulder to shoulder."

But the bedouin soldiers of the National Guard, standing shoulder to shoulder on the other side of the barriers, felt anything but safe. They were not Shia. Quite the contrary. They were proud to be Sunni, like the majority of Saudis—and, indeed, like the large majority of Muslims throughout the world—meaning that they took their directions from the sunna, the words, actions, and example of the Prophet. To them the Shia were a heretical and miserably misguided sect whose loyalties lay with "the Persians"—the Shia in Iran. Unlettered Sunnis (as well as a good few who were educated) spread stories of how the Shia had forked tails hidden beneath their thobes and enjoyed unnatural sexual practices, notably at this time of year, when they would gather in their *husayniyas* (meeting rooms) to switch off the lights, strip off their clothes, and engage in writhing mounds of group sex. The resulting babies, many Sunnis believed, were then venerated by the Shia community and grew up to become their mullahs.

Wahhabi sheikhs regularly denounced the Shia as deviants in another, more theological fashion. They described the Shia as *rafada,* or "rejectionists" of the correct Islamic succession, since they had complicated God's simple truth, introducing the first and most harmful innovation of all.

WHY THE SHIA ARE DIFFERENT

One of the very first people to become a Muslim was the Prophet's bright young cousin Ali, who lived in the Prophet's household and heard God's teachings from an early age. Mohammed called him "brother." When the clans of Mecca prepared their devilish plot to kill Mohammed, sending one assassin from each clan with a dagger, it was Ali who bravely rolled up in the Prophet's blanket as a decoy, risking his own life to save Mohammed's. When, eventually, the Muslims returned to Mecca in triumph, it was Ali who helped Mohammed open the door to the Kaaba to bring out the idols and smash them to smithereens.

Since the Prophet could neither read nor write, Ali wrote his letters for him. Mohammed gave Ali his favorite daughter, Fatima, in marriage, and at least one hadith suggests that the Prophet may have viewed his popular son-in-law as his successor. "Whoever recognizes me as his master," Mohammed was heard to declare as he rested on his way back from his final pilgrimage, "will recognize Ali as his master." When the Prophet died shortly afterward, in A.H. 10 (A.D. 632), Ali was entrusted with the job of washing his body and preparing it for burial.

But even as he was carrying out this sacred family duty, Ali was being marginalized by a hurriedly summoned conclave of Companions, who decided that Abu Bakr should become the first successor, or caliph, of the Prophet. Venerable and pious, Abu Bakr had been greatly loved by Mohammed, and he came from outside the Prophet's family. Many of the Companions felt strongly that leadership of the faith should not become the property of one clan.

So young Ali lost out—he was still only in his early thirties—and he accepted the decision. One of this remarkable man's remarkable qualities was acceptance. If anyone embodied submission, which is the literal meaning of the word *Islam,* it was Ali. He served Abu Bakr with loyalty, as he served the next two caliphs, Omar and Othman, even though his supporters maintained that he had been repeatedly excluded from the succession by sharp practice. For the Shiat Ali, the party or followers of Ali, it became a defining idea that the tradition of the Prophet could only be passed down adequately through the bloodline of Mohammed.

When Ali was eventually chosen as the fourth caliph, early in A.H. 36 (A.D. 656), he certainly manifested some of the Prophet's charisma. He proved an inspiring leader of the *umma,* the Islamic community of believers, while also exhibiting bravery on the battlefield as he wielded his legendary fork-tongued sword, Zulfiqar.

"There is no hero but Ali," became a Shia cry, "and no sword but his Zulfiqar!"

But this hero worship proved fatal. The multiple strands of the early Muslim world had already produced the earliest movement of Islamic dissent, the khawarij, literally "those who come out and depart." It was less than thirty years since the Prophet had died, but already the Kharijites were complaining that the *umma* had departed from his ways. True Muslims, they believed, were confined to those who adhered strictly to the example of Mohammed, and they introduced a deadly new idea to Islam—*takfeer* (condemnation or excommunication): those who did not follow God's word precisely were kuffar, infidels deserving of death. When Ali was killed by a Kharijite wielding a poisoned sword during Ramadan in A.H. 40 (A.D. 661), he became one of the earliest victims of Islamic terrorism.

"There is no authority except God, oh Ali," cried his assassin, "not you!"

• • •

So, in the fortieth year after the Hijrah, Ali became the first martyr of the Shia, starting them down their emotion-laden path of sorrow and faith. This was infused with the sense of life being stacked against them—of having, somehow, been robbed—and it would reach its fulfillment twenty years later at the battle of Karbala in Iraq, to the south of Baghdad. Fought on Ashura, the tenth of Muharram, in A.H. 61 (A.D. 680), Karbala would be commemorated ever afterward at the Shias' annual religious ritual of "the Tenth," their tear-stained Good Friday with no Easter Resurrection to follow.

From their earliest years, young Shias imbibe every detail of Karbala, as surely as Christian children know the story of the three crosses on the hilltop. How Husayn bin Ali, Ali's son by his marriage to Mohammed's daughter Fatima, and hence the Prophet's grandson, stood with just a few brave companions against the massive army of the caliph Yazid; how the enemy cut off their water; how Husayn implored their mercy, carrying out his infant son, dying of thirst, to be greeted by a hail of arrows that killed the boy; and how, finally, Husayn himself, sorely wounded and by now the sole survivor, mounted his horse, taking a Koran in one hand and a sword in the other, to ride into the merciless barricade of death, striking down dozens before he himself was eventually subdued.

The story of Karbala epitomized bravery, martyrdom, hopelessness, injustice—all the causes to which the Shia would relate their own bitter experience over the years. They were a persecuted religious minority, and in few corners of the Muslim world had they been persecuted as systematically as by the followers of Mohammed Ibn Abdul Wahhab, who reserved special condemnation for the Shia. For Ibn Abdul Wahhab, the Shia adoration of Ali and Husayn, which went along with the veneration of tombs and shrines, represented the ultimate in *shirk* (polytheism) and called for takfeer—the sentence of death. Inspired by his teachings, the first Saudi army raided Al-Hasa in A.H. 1216 (A.D. 1802) to purge it of idols and shrines, then headed north to the ultimate Shia shrine, built on the battlefield of Karbala. They were responding to an Iraqi attack, and when they got to Karbala they made sure that they destroyed the tomb of Husayn.

• • •

As Ali Al-Marzouq and his chest-thumping Shia comrades faced off against the Saudi National Guard in Qateef a century and a half later, there was some potent history between them. While paying lip service to plurality, the modern Saudi state had treated the members of its Shia community as second-class citizens. Out on the oil rigs, Shia made up the drilling gangs, but usually worked to the orders of a Sunni foreman. There were at that time no Shia diplomats in the Saudi foreign service, no Shia pilots in the national airline—and certainly none in the air force. They could not become head teachers or even deputy heads in local schools, where, if they did teach, they were expected to follow a syllabus that scornfully denigrated Shia history and beliefs. Local zoning rules even banned them from building dens or basement areas beneath their homes, for fear that they might use them as secret husayniyas for subversive worship and for their alleged sexual congresses.

It seemed appropriate, when long-distance telephone dialing was introduced to the Kingdom, that Riyadh should be allotted the code 01 and Jeddah and Mecca 02, while the east, the source of the country's wealth, had to make do with 03. A cartoon of the time showed a cow straddling the map of Saudi Arabia: it was grazing in the east and being milked in the west by a merchant who handed the bowl to a princely individual doing nothing at all in the middle.

For many years the Saudi Shia had endured this situation with passivity. Like Judaism and other persecuted faiths, Shia Islam had developed a tradition of quietism as a survival mechanism, along with *taqiya*—literally, discretion or "cautionary dissimulation." Shia were authorized to pretend, in self-defense, that they were not Shia—which gave Sunnis another reason to denounce them as deceptive and unreliable.

Then, in the mid-1970s, an eloquent young Shia preacher, Sheikh Hassan Al-Saffar, started raising consciousness in Qateef. He was a quiet, modest character with downcast eyes, very much the cleric with his neat beard and round white turban, but with a subtle determination. Drawing inspiration from Karbala, Al-Saffar (pronounced As-Saffar) praised the bravery of Husayn's determined resistance to discrimination and the unfair distribution of wealth. Where, he asked pointedly, might one see such injustices today? While in the pulpit, he was careful not to mention the Saudi regime directly—he kept his specifics firmly in the days of Husayn. But his listeners got the point.

Behind the scenes, Al-Saffar talked more frankly to the young Shia activists that he had organized into a secret discussion group, the Islamic Revolution Organization (IRO), whose pamphlets listed their complaints aggressively: "When the people look at the squandering of the national wealth, while every area in which they live is deprived, miserable and suffering, is it not natural for them to behave in a revolutionary way, and for them to practice violence, and to persist in fighting for their rights and the protection of their wealth from the betrayal of the criminal Al-Saud?"

The gloves were off—and that was just fine by the several thousand hurriedly deployed Wahhabi National Guardsmen on the streets of Qateef. They happily adopted the solution of their Ikhwan forebears to the raucous challenge posed by Ali Al-Marzouq and his overexcited Shia friends. The rhythmic chest-thumping and the cries of "Islamic Republic!" were all tokens of deviancy. The posters of Khomeini were evidence of loyalty to a foreign power. Suddenly the guardsmen were over the barrier, laying into the crowd with sticks, thrashing about them wildly.

"You could see the blood everywhere," remembers Ali.

He tried to shield himself, but the guardsmen had them surrounded, and Ali cowered with his companions as the blows rained down. "They shouted out that we were kuffar and broke open the head of the man beside me. The blood went all over my back. When I finally got home that night there was so much blood, my parents thought I had been shot."

• • •

Ali was lucky. A few days later Dr. Jon Parssinen, an American professor in social sciences at the "Oil College," as the University of Petroleum and Minerals was known, noticed two empty seats in his classroom on the hill beside the Aramco headquarters in Dhahran. The class shifted uneasily when he asked where the students were.

"After the class," recalls Parssinen, "one of their friends took me aside and quietly told me they had been shot in Qateef. Nobody, but nobody, discussed what had happened. Their places remained empty for the rest of the semester, two bright young men who had been heading for important careers in petroleum engineering. It was very sad, but in those days you just did not talk about it."

According to official estimates, seventeen people were killed in the riots that consumed the Qateef area for the next five days, with more than a hundred injured. More than two hundred were arrested. Buses were overturned. The offices of Saudia, the national airline, were burned, and the local branch office of the Saudi British Bank was ransacked.

"Qateef was cut off for several days," recalls Clive Morgan, the bank's area manager for the Eastern Province, who went to assess the damage. "We had to talk our way through various military checkpoints until we reached the National Guard Headquarters Command Post—which was very reminiscent, to my mind, of television scenes of the Vietnam War."

Saudi National Guardsmen were attacked and suffered casualties, and several Shia communities barricaded themselves off, defying the authorities for days. From the other side of the Gulf, Radio Tehran incited its fellow Shias with the ayatollahs' take on the Saudi royal clan: "The ruling regime in Saudi Arabia wears Muslim clothing, but inwardly it represents the U.S. body, mind, and terrorism."

"Oh Khaled, release your hands from power!" shouted the inhabitants of Sayhat, a Shia community to the southeast of Qateef. "The people do not want you!" It was a humiliating loss of face for a ruling family that prided itself on being habitually in control.

CHAPTER 5

Vox Populi, Vox Dei

Since the early 1960s the House of Saud had been on the lookout for trouble—investigating and arresting Communists, socialists, and "godless" radicals of all sorts. Serious opposition, everyone anticipated, would be coming from the left.

But the attacks of 1979 had come from the very opposite direction—from those on the right and from directly behind the royal family. "Godless" was the reproach that was now being thrown at the king and princes of the House of Saud. It might have been expected that the long-suppressed Shia of the Eastern Province would one day rebel, but Juhayman and his radical ilk had been nurtured in the traditional territory of Wahhabi mosques and religious scholars that the Al-Saud considered their heartland. Conservatives, it seemed, could also cause turmoil.

Publicly, Crown Prince Fahd professed himself undismayed. "The reaction of the country was like a national opinion survey," he declared. "Everyone came to fight against Juhayman."

But in private the crown prince was less confident. The Shia intifada, or uprising, in the Eastern Province worried him particularly.

"He kept talking about Iran," remembers his friend Adnan Khashoggi. "He could not get over what had happened to the Shah."

Revolutions are disruptive by definition, but the Iranian upheaval had had an extra, unanticipated ingredient. In 1776 the American Revolution showed that colonialism could not last forever; thirteen years later the French Revolution marked the end of the road for absolute monarchy; and Russia's 1917 Revolution came as confirmation of this—the old institutions were on their way out.

But Iran did not fit into this satisfying slide toward secular modernity—quite the contrary. An apparently impregnable, Westernizing autocrat, smiled on by America, with a huge army, an efficient secret police, and burgeoning oil revenues, had been brought down without a serious shot being fired—all the Shah's modernization had proved helpless against the supposedly outmoded power of religion.

Fahd was not well read, nor had he been conventionally educated. His upbringing in the isolated mud city of Riyadh in the 1920s and '30s was dominated by Koranic instruction and what were officially described as "traditional desert pursuits"—riding, shooting, hunting, and sitting for long hours in his father's majlis. But he had learned much through watching how carefully his father handled the religious sheikhs. The Shah had got on the wrong side of the mosque, reckoned Fahd—and that was the side on which the former playboy already feared himself to be. So the crown prince did not argue when his elder brother Khaled came up with a fundamentally religious answer to Juhayman's unexpected challenge.

• • •

The traditional old monarch got the idea from his regular meetings with the ulema. The sheikhs had no doubt as to a solution—photographs of Saudi women, they said, should no longer appear in the newspapers. They had always said this was un-Islamic—Bin Baz had issued many a fatwa on the subject—and the desecration of the Grand Mosque was the proof. In the months following the siege, the blackened and bullet-scarred carcass of the Mosque, with the gaping holes smashed through its marble flooring, made a sight on which many pondered.

"Those old men actually believed that the Mosque disaster was God's punishment to us because we were publishing women's photographs in the newspapers," says a princess, one of Khaled's nieces. "The worrying thing is that the king probably believed that as well."

In fact, of course, the proliferation of pictures and photographs *had* been a major element in the grievances of Juhayman and his followers. When King Khaled passed on the sheikhs' verdict to his advisers he did not go into details about the complaints of the rebels, but his firmness suggested he believed that God had intervened personally in Mecca at the beginning of Muharram in A.H. 1400. Everybody knew, he argued, that photographs of unveiled women were un-Islamic. So why had the government been allowing them?

The younger members of the government were dismayed. The "Ph.D. set" of technocratic ministers recruited by Fahd to turn the oil revenues into modern infrastructure were appalled at the irrelevance of the gesture as much as at its check on the progress of women. But when it came to religion, the old king was operating in one of those areas he considered his own—and he did not even take the matter to the Council of Ministers. Khaled had come to agree with the sheikhs. Foreign influences and bidaa were the problem. The solution to the religious upheaval was simple—more religion.

Crown Prince Fahd had, in fact, already announced a more progressive, secular, and essentially Westernizing strategy. For nearly twenty years the House of Saud had been promising constitutional reform—the establishment of a Majlis Al-Shura, or "Consultative Council" of nominated worthies who would scrutinize legislation. In the long term, it was hinted, the Shura Council might even develop into some sort of elected, representative parliament. King Faisal had first proposed this in 1964, as part of a package of reforms to be known as the "Basic Law" (*constitution* was a taboo word, since the Kingdom already claimed to possess a perfect constitution in the form of the Koran). On succeeding Faisal in 1975, Khaled had renewed his own commitment to the Majlis Al-Shura and the Basic Law, and after the siege of the Mosque, Fahd announced that the reform plan was still on track.

"We shall soon have a Consultative Council," declared the crown prince in one of a flurry of post-Juyhayman interviews that he gave in the closing days of 1979, showing his seriousness by promising fifty, sixty, or maybe as many as seventy members. "Initially its members will be appointed. We must move gradually."

How fast was "gradually"? he was asked.

"Within a period," he promised, "which, I believe, will not exceed two months."

But when the two months was up, the crown prince did not announce the new Majlis and Basic Law. Instead he resorted to a standard Saudi delaying tatic, the creation of a committee to reexamine the practicalities of the proposal—in this case, a panel of religious and government worthies to be headed by his cautious brother Nayef.

"Once we embark on this path," warned Fahd meaningfully in his private briefing to the committee, "there will be no coming back. In the end we will have to face direct elections—nobody says that we have to do that now."

This was hardly the way to stir action in any committee, let alone in a quorum of the cautious Saudi establishment. So no more was heard about a Consultative Council—let alone a national opera house or a multi-elephant *Aida*.

• • •

In January 1980, Samar Fatany had just returned from studying in Cairo to join the English language service of Radio Jeddah. She came from an old Mecca family—her uncle was an Islamic judge who had taught in the Grand Mosque.

"So many young graduates were coming back from abroad with plans and ideas to make our country a better place," she remembers of the early 1980s. "They were exciting days, with lots of challenges. There were bazaars and plays and fashion shows—international events, with the women from different countries wearing their national costumes. There were at least four cinemas in Jeddah. I got a job on the local radio, reading the news."

But after Juhayman came the clampdown. The Saudi security services did not intend to be caught napping again.

"You had to get permits for everything—from the governor, from the ministry—and things could be canceled at the last minute. They made things so difficult that, after a time, you gave up."

This jumpy, repressive atmosphere was given another jolt by the changes made to appease the ulema. Jeddah's movie houses were shut down. Older folk compared it to the 1920s, when the Wahhabis conquered the Red Sea kingdom of the Hijaz. The grandmother of Sami Nawar, modern Jeddah's director of historic conservation, recalled stuffing muslin down the horn of the family's windup gramophone to avoid trouble with the combative Ikhwan.

"It's that climate up in Nejd," she would explain, "with such extremes of hot and cold. That's where their extreme ideas come from, poor dears."

"Christmas used to be such fun in the compounds," remembers Dr. Enaam Ghazi, an Egyptian physiotherapist. "People put lights in the trees. The lights didn't show from the street, but you could ride round on your bicycle and enjoy them. That stopped after Juhayman. No more Halloween. No more Valentine's."

King Khaled's ban on female photos in the newspapers was followed by the complete package of changes demanded by the ulema—particularly in education.

"Modern science, geology, the history of civilization, the history of Europe—I remember studying all that in my Saudi school in the 1970s," says Mahdi Al-Asfour, an Aramco planning consultant. "That vanished. Now it became just the history of Islam and the Al-Saud, with hours of extra religious studies—and even science and math had to include some Islamic content. When my child went to school, he came home crying one day because one of the teachers told him that he would be going to hell. Why? Because he listened to music and because his thobe was not cut short enough."

Over in the east at the University of Petroleum and Minerals, the American lecturer Jon Parssinen noted how international relations was dropped from the Oil College's social science program—"too Western, too secular"—while the course entitled Social Change in Developing Countries was handed to a safe pair of Muslim hands. Psychology survived only as long as the tenure of the dean who was its protector. Then it vanished with him, judged inappropriate in an Islamic institution. Parssinen found himself spending more time than ever with the dean, ripping contentious pages from the course textbooks.

"We'd sit down together and spot a bare-breasted African lady in a cultural-geography book, or a chapter on homosexuality in the sociology primer—'Tear it out!' We'd lay the books on our knee and rip out whole sections. It was serial murder. If students ever asked me about the missing pages, I'd quietly arrange to give them copies after class."

One enterprising instructor had been teaching English by getting his pupils to chant ABBA songs—"Thank you for the music, the songs you're singing." That vanished very early.

Islam was the watchword. Headed by a descendant of Mohammed Ibn Abdul Wahhab, the Ministry of Higher Education Islamized the curriculas of the colleges and energetically set about expanding the religious faculties. Saudi universities had started out almost totally religious in the 1950s, and now they went back to that. By 1986 no fewer than sixteen thousand of the Kingdom's one hundred thousand university students would be pursuing religious studies whose foundation involved long hours devoted to learning the Koran by heart.

Instructors in nonreligious courses found themselves under extra pressure.

"One September two of our best professors, ladies from Canada and the United States, arrived back at Jeddah for the start of the new year," remembers a bright young Saudi woman who was studying English literature at King Abdul Aziz University in Jeddah in 1983. "They were sent home. They had been teaching the origins of the English novel—*Tom Jones, Moll Flanders* and all that bawdy stuff. Someone had reported them. There were a group of 'veilers' in our class—'the fanatics with eyes.' They considered themselves the guardians of our virtue."

The fundamentalists in the class did appreciate one piece of Christian literature, however.

"We were reading John Milton," remembers the student, "*Paradise Lost* and *Paradise Regained,* in which Eve was depicted as a seducer, the source of all human sin and wickedness. Trouble arrives with the very first woman—the veilers just loved that. Eve is treated quite kindly in the Koran: we don't talk badly about her in our religion; for Muslims she is the mother of mankind. But for Milton she was the temptress, the reason for man's descent from heaven to hell. 'There you are,' these religious women would say. 'We women are sinful. We are misleaders of men. That is why we should all stay at home and be veiled.' "

. . .

Heaven and hell—most people in modern Saudi Arabia believe in them quite literally. Good Muslims will go one way, bad Muslims the other, with the all-powerful, all-watching Deity keeping score. Every action that you take in your life—every decision that you make—helps decide whether you will spend your eternity with comely virgins or whether you will fry.

"We like you so much," say Muslims sadly to their Western friends. "We hate to think of you in the fire."

Hell and heaven are not, for most Saudis, symbolic concepts, as many liberal Westerners today find it comforting to believe. For a Saudi—as for most devout Muslims—your eternal destiny will depend literally and inescapably on (a) being a Muslim and (b) following the demands that Allah makes of you. The life that matters is the afterlife—which makes for an earthly existence disciplined by fear and punishment.

It therefore follows that the fundamental duty of the state is to make sure that its citizens end up in the right place. As laid down by the Saudi

Basic Law, the objective of the Saudi state is nothing so transitory as personal earthly freedom. It is to make people good Muslims—the *hisbah* that Sheikh Bin Baz had proposed as a mission to his Salafi protégés: command the good, forbid the bad. Schools start the job with children, and mosques continue the shaping into adulthood—with practical assistance from the local Committees for the Promotion of Virtue and the Prevention of Vice, the groups of state-subsidized vigilantes known to Westerners as the "religious police." In 1980 these bearded zealots were the government's obvious allies in the post-Juhayman campaign of godliness—as well as potential sources of disaffection that needed to be bought off.

People noticed that imams and religious folk seemed to have more money to spend from the early 1980s onward. The petrodollar went pious. Saudi clerics were shoeless no longer, with the religious police benefiting most obviously from government injections of cash. They started to appear in imposing new GMC vans, with their once humble local committees of *mutawwa* (volunteers or enforcers) taking on the grander, "Big Brother" aura of their original, collective name—Al-Hayah, "the Commission." They developed attitude to match.

"In the old days," recalls the scholar and media businesman, Abdullah Masry, "you'd see the shopkeepers kneeling outside their shops at prayer time. People were free to follow their own spiritual practices as ordained by their faith. Now the religious police told everyone that they had to lock up and go to the mosque."

In Jeddah, the recently constructed French hotel, the Sofitel on Palestine Road, had opened a pair of segregated gyms. They had separate entrances for men and women, but within months of the opening, the busy women's gym was closed down. "Single women going alone into a hotel building?" remembers one of the female members sardonically. "*Haram!* The ultimate sin!"

The segregation was extended to the humblest coffee shop, with separate entrances and screens creating an area known as the "Family Section": men were allowed to enter only if they were accompanied by a related female—their sister, mother, wife, or adult daughter—which, ironically, gave a certain power to the women. This separation had always been the rule in Nejd. Now it was extended with strictness all over the country. Music shops were closed down, and Jeddah's ancient tradition of the downtown street vendors and sweets makers singing songs to celebrate Ramadan was suppressed.

It was difficult not to cause offense. Western women had always worn modest versions of Western dress. Long-sleeved, high-neckline Laura Ashley muslins suited the bill perfectly. This gave expatriate gatherings the character of a *Little House on the Prairie* costume drama, with a preponderance of pastel greens and pinks. But now foreign women started to cover their costumes with the black *abaya,* Saudi-style. Westerners were clearly starting to feel uncomfortable, and Samar Fatany noticed the difference in her foreign colleagues.

"They couldn't mix and mingle with Saudis—it became Them and Us. I had some great friends at the radio station, two Australian women. But they decided to leave. It wasn't fun anymore. In fact, it became distinctly edgy. Then I was stopped from reading the news."

One year Saudi TV had broadcast footage of the immensely popular Lebanese singer Fairuz with a strange black lozenge on the screen masking her chest, to conceal her crucifix. Now she, and all other women, vanished completely. The religious police became more and more evident, harassing people on the street.

"You couldn't walk around with your husband without your ID cards," remembers Samar. "They would accuse you of infidelity."

Sometimes even ID cards were not enough. Muslim women do not surrender their names on marriage—they keep their own family names throughout their life. So when Samar Fatany and her husband, Khaled Al-Maeena, turned up in Riyadh for a conference in the early 1980s, they encountered trouble at the check-in desk of the Radisson.

"They were very polite," remembers Al-Maeena, "but they said they needed proof we were married. It so happened I'd just written an article for *Al-Muslimoon* ["The Muslims"]. That was the holy of holies when it came to religious things. But it wasn't good enough. I had to go to the police station with a male friend so he could swear that my wife was my wife."

The House of Saud had executed Juhayman. Now they were making his program government policy.

CHAPTER 6

Salafi Soccer

The faculty blocks of King Abdul Aziz University rise from the eastern outskirts of Jeddah like so many huge white shoe boxes—plain, workaday structures that are thoroughly in keeping with the noncontroversial teachings that the students are expected to absorb. You go to a Saudi university to imbibe the canon of received knowledge without question, not to learn how to think, critically or otherwise, and certainly not how to reorder the world. But in the late 1970s and early '80s the university's lecture rooms were buzzing with some of the most radical and potentially subversive ideas to be heard in the Middle East.

For nearly twenty years, starting in the days of pro-Soviet President Gamal Abdul Nasser of Egypt, the Saudi government had been giving refuge to the God-fearing opponents of the Arab world's secular regimes—and particularly to members of the Muslim Brotherhood, the underground soldiers of Allah who were at risk of torture and death in Nasser's political prisons. It was a matter of policy, part of King Faisal's strategy of combating godlessness at home and abroad. Sober, purposeful, and above all devout, the exiled members of the Muslim Brotherhood provided the Kingdom with a disciplined cadre of teachers, doctors, and administrators at this formative moment in the country's development. Thousands arrived to stiffen and staff the expanding Saudi infrastructure, particularly the ministries, universities, and schools, where they inculcated children with the need to be virtuous young Muslims. Female members of the Brotherhood, many of them from Syria, were particularly successful at persuading their teenage pupils to shun degenerate Western culture and to wear the full veil, the *niqab*.

The founder of the Muslim Brotherhood was himself a schoolteacher, Hassan Al-Banna, an Egyptian who blamed the weakness of the Arabs on their failure to follow the "straight path" as commanded by God at the beginning of the Koran. The key to gaining strength, Al-Banna believed, was not to become more Western. Muslims should do quite the opposite, searching for their answer in the pure and original message that God delivered to the Prophet—though that did not stop Al-Banna from adopting some of the West's political techniques. As he studied the success of the Communist and Fascist parties in 1930s Europe, he built the Brotherhood around a structure of self-contained cells (he called them *usar*—"families"), while using sport and physical fitness, Hitler Youth–style, to attract young recruits. He developed his own, Islamic form of the Boy Scouts, and he made sure, like Hamas and Hezbollah today, that those who supported the Brotherhood were supported in turn by a grassroots network of social facilities, particularly schools and health clinics. These were often more accessible and efficient than anything provided by the state.

Al-Banna founded the Brotherhood in 1928. The movement's eloquent modern campaigner was Sayyid Qutub, also from the Egyptian school system, in this case a schools inspector who had been sent on a training course to America in the late 1940s and had returned home horrified at the moral laxity of the West. Qutub was particularly appalled by the sexually explicit style of Western women, which he noted in compulsive detail: "expressive eyes and thirsty lips . . . round breasts, full buttocks . . . shapely thighs, sleek legs." His views were further soured by some unpleasant encounters in New York and Colorado when his Arab looks became the object of racial prejudice.

Hassan Al-Banna was assassinated in 1949, allegedly by King Farouq's secret police, after building up his welfare network and a pious membership that came to number millions. Sayyid Qutub was imprisoned and eventually hanged by Nasser in 1966. But his brother Mohammed escaped to Jeddah, to be welcomed at Mecca's university of *Umm Al-Qura* ("Mother of Villages"—one of the names bestowed on Mecca by the Prophet), where he gave lectures that propagated Sayyid's call to reject the West:

> Look at this capitalism with its monopolies, its usury and so many other injustices. . . . Look at this "individual freedom," devoid of human sympathy and responsibility for relatives except under force of law.

The Western habit of dispatching parents to retirement "homes" struck Sayyid Qutub as typical of what one Iranian critic would later describe as "Westoxification."

> [Look] at this materialistic attitude which deadens the spirit; at this behavior like animals, which you call "free mixing of the sexes"; at this vulgarity which you call "emancipation of women" . . . at this evil and fanatic racial discrimination.

To counter Westoxification, Sayyid Qutub looked to religion. "Islam," he proclaimed, "is the answer." And having been brutalized in Nasser's prisons, he was no pacifist. Those who would deny jihad's active and aggressive character, he wrote, "diminish the greatness of the Islamic way of life."

The ambitions of the Muslim Brotherhood were similar to those of the Salafis and also of the *dawah wahhabiya* (Wahhabi mission)—to reestablish the order of Allah and to bring about the perfect Islamic state. But the rhetoric of the Brotherhood dealt in change-promoting concepts like social justice, anticolonialism, and the equal distribution of wealth. Politically they were prepared to challenge the establishment in a style that was unthinkable to mainstream Wahhabis, who were reflexively deferential to their rulers and enablers, the House of Saud.

It was heady stuff for the young students of Jeddah, taking the Wahhabi values they had absorbed in childhood and giving them a radical, but still apparently safe, religious twist. They had learned of jihad at school as a distantly romantic concept—part of history. Now they were hearing of its practical possibility today, and they could even make personal contact with jihad in the barrel-chested shape of Abdullah Azzam, who gave lectures in both Jeddah and Mecca in the early 1980s. A Palestinian, Azzam had taken up arms against the Israeli occupation of his family home in Jenin, on the West Bank, after the Six-Day War of 1967, the humiliating defeat ruefully known throughout the Arab world as "Al-Nakba," the "Disaster." But this eloquent warrior sheikh, whose long beard spilled over his chest like a rippling gray waterfall, had no time for Yasser Arafat or his PLO henchmen, whom he considered insufficiently religious.

The Saudi government had welcomed ideologues like Azzam and

Mohammed, the surviving Qutub,* to the Kingdom as pious reinforcement against the atheistic, Marxist-tinged thinking of their Middle Eastern neighborhood. But in the process they were exposing young Saudi hearts and minds to a still more potent virus—hands-on, radical Islam. As the 1980s progressed, hundreds of young men, many of them from outside the university, gathered on Fridays to pray and listen to the booming, inspirational sermons of Abdullah Azzam.

"I went to hear him several times," remembers Jamal Khashoggi, the young second cousin of Adnan, the business tycoon. Jamal had been studying in America and was just getting his start in journalism. "It was a huge gathering. There were so many listeners that the mosque was full. People had to sit and pray outside in the street."

Among the throngs who gathered to absorb the ideas of Azzam and Mohammed Qutub in the shade of the dusty neem trees on the Jeddah campus was a tall and thin, rather thoughtful young student with a smooth olive complexion, high cheekbones, and a hawklike nose. As a sign of his Islamic consciousness, the young man had for some time been trying to cultivate a long and wispy beard.

• • •

Osama Bin Laden was a demon center forward.

"We used to make up teams and go out to the desert by the Pepsi factory," recalls Khaled Batarfi, a football enthusiast who was three years' Osama's junior. The advantage of having Osama on your team, Batarfi remembers, was his height. Already approaching his adult stature of six feet four, the lanky beanpole would soar effortlessly above his opponents to head the ball into the goal. He was the Peter Crouch of Jeddah pickup games.

Today the Pepsi factory area of Jeddah is occupied by the glittering shops and malls of Tahliah Street. In the late 1970s the *tahliah* (desalination plant) lay beyond the northern limits of the city. Batarfi and Bin Laden would bump out across the scrubby wasteland as the heat of the day wore off, their cars full of chattering friends.

"We'd play a game, then kneel together and pray the *maghreb* (sunset prayer)."

*Azzam would later travel to Afghanistan. Mohammed Qutub lives in Mecca to this day.

The boys sat side by side in the warm darkness, munching sandwiches and drinking cans of juice and fizzy drinks from the cooler.

"Osama was very quiet and shy," remembers Batarfi. "He was always soft-spoken. But he had this strange authority about him. He loved football, but he didn't approve of the very short shorts that players wore in those days. He wore long shorts to the knees, then tracksuit slacks, and we all copied him. He divided us into four groups—Abu Bakr, Omar, Othman, and Ali, named after the Companions of the Prophet who were the first four caliphs. Then he'd ask us questions: 'When was the Battle of Uhud?' 'Three years after the Hijrah,' someone would say. 'Right,' he'd say, 'that's five points to Abu Bakr.' It was like a TV quiz show, but without the clapping—that, he explained, is not Islamic. When someone got the right answer we'd all sing out *'Allahu akbar!'* "

Osama's religiosity—and his love of soccer—would have given great pleasure to his late father, Mohammed, once one of the most respected and powerful businessmen in Saudi Arabia.

THE BUILDER

King Abdul Aziz and his friend Mohammed Bin Laden had just two working eyeballs between them—one each. Their handicapped sight was one of the personal bonds that linked the two men. Another connection was that, through multiple marriages, they had both derived great pleasure from the fathering of several dozen children each. Abdul Aziz had lost his eye to trachoma, and legend had it that the Yemeni-born Bin Laden had won royal favor by offering one of his own eyes to the king in an unsuccessful eye transplant.

This myth was respectfully whispered in the ranks of the Bin Laden construction company, but the truth was more prosaic. A fanatical footballer when young, Mohammed Bin Laden had lost his eye in a wild game of pickup soccer when he was a building laborer in the Sudan, a decade before he set foot in the Kingdom, where he built up his own business in the 1940s and '50s as a construction tycoon.

The one-eyed center forward made his fortune through hard work and by avoiding shortcuts. Mohammed Bin Laden paid his fellow Yemenis fairly and he did not overcharge his clients. His fortune derived less from his customers' pockets than from his own shrewd investment in bargain-price land around his developments—and when it came to royal projects, he asked for no payment until the palace was finally completed to the prince's total satisfaction. He served Abdul Aziz as director of public works and played the same role unofficially, after 1953, with his son King Saud.

Mohammed Bin Laden never scuttled from a job on which he was losing money. He was "the Builder"—he always delivered. He was admired across the Kingdom for the solidity of his work, and he was known to be a pious man. He had been the obvious choice for contractor in the 1950s when the House of Saud decided they wished to expand the grand mosques of Mecca and Medina, recasting the old prayer halls with soaring, Alhambra-style arcades, and enlarging the covered area no less than sixfold.

The new buildings featured colorful Maghreb tiles that were plastered over miles of steel-reinforced concrete of extraordinary strength—as the Saudi National Guard and army discovered in Mecca in 1979 when they tried to blast holes in it.

"We should give the Bin Ladens a medal for their workmanship," said the jaunty young Prince Bandar bin Sultan at the time. "Then behead them."

It was a common shortcut for Saudi contractors to skimp on materials, so the siege of the Grand Mosque provided an unexpected endorsement to the thoroughness of Mohammed the Builder, who died in a plane crash in 1967.

. . .

Mohammed's son Osama disapproved of Juhayman—he thought the man had been crazy. "How can you seize the holiest place in Islam," he'd say, "then bring in weapons and kill people?"

But at this stage of life his own path to piety was that of the Salafi. The evidence was in the lengthening of his beard. As Osama and his friends studied the Koran, they started to shorten the length of their trousers and thobes, and to wear wrinkled shirts that had not been ironed—they had found no evidence that the Prophet or his wives had ever used irons.

"Osama would fast on Mondays and Thursdays," remembers Khaled

Batarfi. "He was consciously following the Prophet's example. But he wasn't overbearing in his religion, and he certainly wasn't violent—not at that time in any way. He'd invite us to his home sometimes to record Islamic chants—just chants, of course: music for him was already strictly *haram* [forbidden]."

Osama's half brothers and half sisters were, on the whole, a more worldly crew. With the boom of the 1970s the original Bin Laden construction company had diversified, like many a Saudi family business, moving into equipment supply, water storage and desalination, motor vehicle distribution (Audi, Porsche, and Volkswagen), import-export trading, telecommunications, and also franchise ventures in food and catering: the Holy Mosque contractors were also the Saudi distributors of Snapple. But while Osama benefited, like all his siblings, from the considerable family wealth, he had been brought up separately by his mother. His parents divorced soon after his birth. The boy had no full blood brothers or sisters in the family, and he seemed to cultivate his separateness.

This isolation may explain his receptiveness to the approaches of a member of the Muslim Brotherhood while he was at school. A Syrian phys ed teacher recruited Osama and four other young pupils for after-hours soccer training, which soon developed into candlelit sessions of Islamic storytelling.

"The Syrian was mesmerizing," recalls one of Osama's fellow students. "He was a born storyteller. But his stories got darker and darker. Osama seemed to like them, but it was too much for me—it caused me to leave the group. The teacher told us a story about a boy of our age who had come to God, but who had found his father standing in his way. This father was not a true believer—he would pull the prayer rug out from beneath his son, for example, when the boy tried to pray. As the teacher told us this tale, he built up the suspense: how this 'brave and righteous' boy determined that he would *fight* for the right to pray; how he got hold of his father's gun; how he found the bullets; how he learned how to load the gun, how he made a plan. The story must have gone on for a full twenty minutes, with the candlelight flickering in the darkened room, and all of us sitting round with our mouths open. Then the climax came—the boy shot his father dead.

"It was a deeply shocking story, because we are taught in Islam to love and respect our father in every situation, even if he is a nonbeliever. But the Syrian turned that teaching on its head. *'Wallahi!'* he exclaimed, 'the Lord be praised—with that shot, Islam was finally liberated in that home!' "

CHAPTER 7

Jihad in Afghanistan

Ahmed Badeeb was a genial and roly-poly science teacher at Jeddah's select Al-Thagr (the Harbor or Haven) school on Mecca Road; one of his pupils was Osama Bin Laden. But Ahmed, who held a master's degree in secondary education from Indiana State University, moved on from teaching to join Saudi Arabia's CIA, the General Intelligence Department (GID), or Istikhbarat, and one morning in the spring of 1980, he was called in by his boss, Prince Turki Al-Faisal. A high-ranking Pakistani general was arriving the next day to meet the king and the crown prince, explained Turki, and he wanted Ahmed to make all the arrangements.

Ahmed did not attend the meeting with the crown prince, but he did join his boss afterward for dinner with the visiting general, Akhtar Abdur Rahman, who turned out to be head of Pakistan's powerful military intelligence organization, the ISI (Inter-Services Intelligence). The conversation was all about Pakistan's beleaguered northwestern neighbor, Afghanistan, invaded a few months earlier by the Soviets. Muslim freedom fighters, the mujahideen, local Afghan warriors, were mounting fierce resistance, and Pakistan was supporting them.

Three days later Ahmed received further instructions.

"You have a task to accomplish," said Prince Turki, handing him an envelope. "His Royal Highness [the crown prince] has agreed to help our Afghan brothers. We are going to buy them their first shipment of weapons, and you must take the money for them to Pakistan—in cash."

"In cash?" queried Ahmed.

"In cash," repeated the prince, handing him the crown prince's letter, where Ahmed read the words "No trace."

"At the beginning," explains Prince Turki today, "it was most important that the Russians should not be able to link the mujahideen to any national entity, neither to ourselves nor to Pakistan. We needed deniability. The plan was to use the money to buy Kalashnikovs and RPGs [rocket-propelled grenade launchers] for the Afghans, along with other old Russian weapons that the freedom fighters could have picked up from anywhere."

Ahmed Badeeb went to the bank and quoted an account number. He declines to say how many fresh $100 bills he requested, but he confirms that the sum was in the millions, and that he was able to lift and carry the money in one large carryall. Experienced couriers report that $2 million is the most that a reasonably fit individual can hang from one arm without staggering too obviously under the weight of the bills (nearly forty-one pounds).

"What sort of job do you do, sir?" asked the teller curiously as he checked the account balance.

"I'm a businessman," replied Ahmed.

Two days later he went back to receive the notes, each million packed in its own custom-made wooden box. Ahmed took the money out of the boxes, wrapped the bundles in metal foil from his kitchen, and enveloped the whole package in a black plastic garbage bag, which he carried as far as Karachi.

"That bag's too big to carry on the plane," he was told at the domestic check-in for Islamabad.

"Not at all," he insisted, cavalierly jiggling the bag up and down, trying to give the impression that it was filled with party balloons.

When the bag went through the X-ray machine, the kitchen foil bounced back a plain image, and when the security guard asked to open the bag, Ahmed told him there was sensitive film beneath the black plastic. Producing his diplomatic passport, he decided that the time had come to ring General Akhtar.

"Your people are giving me a hard time with the documents," he said.

"You have arrived so quickly!" said the general in surprise—scarcely a week had passed since the dinner.

Badeeb's destination was the home of Pakistan's president, Mohammed Zia-ul-Haq.

"It was a very humble, very simple place," Ahmed remembers. "A small villa with only three or four rooms. The president was just getting ready for the *maghreb* [sunset] prayer, and we prayed it together."

Badeeb had met Zia-ul-Haq the previous year when he carried a message from Saudi Arabia requesting that Pakistan should not hang the deposed prime minister Zulfikar Ali Bhutto, sentenced to death on corruption charges. That request was not granted, but his current mission met with more success. The Saudi sat with the president late into the night discussing the problems of Afghanistan and Pakistan, while Zia's small son zoomed around the room on a little bicycle.

"I have brought the amount you requested of His Majesty," said Badeeb.

"Give my thanks to His Highness," replied Zia. "Please tell him I will come for *umrah* [small pilgrimage] very soon."

Meanwhile, in an adjoining room, five generals of the ISI had opened Badeeb's bag and were toiling away, counting every one of the crisp $100 bills.

• • •

Osama Bin Laden could not wait to get to Afghanistan. Within two weeks of the Soviet invasion the twenty-two-year-old was visiting Peshawar, the atmospheric town on the Pakistani side of the border where the bearded mujahideen loped down the streets with their Kalashnikovs slung over their shoulders. Returning to Jeddah inspired, Osama lobbied wealthy friends and relatives to raise what one associate described as a "huge" sum of money to support the mujahideen.

There were not many devout young Muslims who could afford to drop their studies to fly to Pakistan on an impulse, and some historians have doubted whether Bin Laden traveled to Peshawar at such an early date. But there is no evidence to contradict his story. Osama certainly had the funds to take him just about anywhere in the world, and if his personal wealth was exceptional, his impulse was not. The plight of the invaded Afghans woke an immediate and powerful response in a society where outrage was habitually rationed. Here was an injustice where protest could be permitted—encouraged even—by the Saudi government, which had had no diplomatic relations with the atheistic Soviets since 1938.* Better that anger should be directed into jihad abroad than into Iran-style revolution at home.

With the government's blessing, the Friday pulpits took up the cause. Newspapers reported Communist atrocities against innocent Muslims—while their columnists ignored the "red lines" that restrained their aggression on other issues. Charities were created. Collection boxes appeared in supermarkets and mosques, and Saudi schoolchildren were encouraged to raise money for the poor Afghans.

"People became very generous with their money," remembers a government minister of the time. "It was an inspiring and romantic idea that people wanted to help—those few brave men in the mountains resisting the mighty Soviet Union."

Religion was the catalyst. Early in the 1980s Rafiq Hariri, then CEO of the construction company Saudi Oger, astonished the *Washington Post* reporter David Ottaway by smuggling him into the Muslim-only area of Medina, where he proudly showed off the massive Koran printing plant he had been commissioned to build for the government. It was by far the world's largest. Hundreds of machines stood ready to churn out tens of millions of Korans in multiple languages with commentaries approved by Bin Baz and the Saudi ulema. It was part of the Kingdom's worldwide missionary effort to combat the Shia teachings of Khomeini's Iran, and particularly in Afghanistan, where it would ensure that young Afghans were fortified against Marxism with "the true Islam." Korans and textbooks would be distributed free to the madrasas (schools) inside Afghanistan and along the Pakistani border.

Less than six months after the Soviet invasion, the Saudi foreign minister, Saud Al-Faisal, the elder brother of Turki, announced that fund-raising among ordinary Saudi citizens had accumulated no less than 81.3 million Saudi riyals ($22.1 million). In May 1980, Saud handed a check for that amount to the secretary general of the Islamic Conference in Islamabad. The money was destined for Afghan refugee relief. But by that date his

*The USSR was the first major nation to recognize Ibn Saud, establishing diplomatic relations on February 16, 1926, ahead of the British on March 1, 1926—and the United States in 1931. But the Soviet representative was recalled from Jeddah during Stalin's purges in 1938 and was never replaced.

brother Turki's General Intelligence Department had already secretly disbursed a great deal more than that—on weapons.

• • •

Since taking charge of Saudi foreign intelligence in 1977, Prince Turki had doled out large sums of money for the fighting of covert wars. In the mid-1970s, Saudi Arabia had become a founding member of the Safari Club, the brainchild of Count Alexandre de Marenches, the debonair and mustachioed chief of France's CIA, the SDECE (Service de Documentation Extérieure et de Contre-Espionnage), suppliers of the CS gas that finally ended the Mecca siege. Worried by Soviet and Cuban advances in postcolonial Africa, and by America's post-Watergate paralysis in the field of undercover activity, the swashbuckling Marenches had come to Turki's father, King Faisal, with a proposition.

"His idea was," recalls the prince, "that since our American friends were off the playing field, as it were, and could not launch undercover operations at this critical time, we should get together a group of like-minded countries to try and keep the Communists out of Africa with money, arms, soldiers—any sort of skullduggery. Calling it the 'Safari Club' was a sort of joke by Marenches, but the aim was deadly serious."

The French spymaster had it all worked out. His SDECE would supply the technical equipment and expertise; Morocco and Egypt would supply arms and soldiers; Saudi Arabia would supply the money. Marenches also invited the Shah to join—which led to the premature revelation of the club's activities when the Iranian leader fled from Tehran in 1979 without destroying his papers. By then, however, the Safari Club already had an impressive list of achievements to its credit. In March 1977 Moroccan troops (paid and armed by the Saudis) had fought off a Cuban-Angolan attack intended to oust Mobutu Sese Seko from Zaire; Somali president Mohammed Siad Barre had been bribed out of the Soviet embrace by $75 million worth of Egyptian arms (paid for again by Saudi Arabia); and Saudi money had enabled both Chad and Sudan to keep Libya's Muammar Al-Qadhafi at bay.

"We did it for America," remembers Prince Turki, "but we also did it, obviously, for ourselves. From the earliest days Saudi Arabia had always looked on Marxism as anathema to human well-being, and also to religion. We saw it as our job to fight against Soviet atheism wherever it might threaten."

Now Marxist ideology and Russian arms were threatening Afghanistan—and the whole Gulf region. Zia-ul-Haq had a dramatic-looking red triangle that he would place on the map of Afghanistan to show how the Soviets were seeking to drive a wedge through the region to push south and achieve the historic Russian goal of a warm-water port. The Pakistani president got out his triangle for the benefit of William Casey, Ronald Reagan's newly appointed head of the CIA, when he arrived in Islamabad in 1981, but Casey had no need of the lesson. Jimmy Carter, the outgoing president, had laid down U.S. policy a year earlier in his State of the Union address, a few weeks after Russian tanks had rolled into Afghanistan: "Let our position be absolutely clear. An attempt by any outside force to gain control of the Persian Gulf region will be regarded as an assault on the vital interests of the United States of America, and such an assault will be repelled by any means necessary, including military force."

Early in February 1980 Carter agreed to a covert program that would put his doctrine into practice—a secret agreement that Saudi Arabia and the United States would match each other, dollar for dollar, to fund an undercover guerrilla campaign in Afghanistan that would hand the Soviets "their own Vietnam." The two countries would eventually spend more than $3 billion each, according to Rachel Bronson, an authority on U.S.-Saudi relations, in a collaboration that would turn out to be world-changing. It was a partnership that could hardly have been imagined half a century earlier, when America and Saudi Arabia, so remote and so dramatically different from each other, had first drifted into contact.

CHAPTER 8

Special Relationship

It was no coincidence that American geologists started arriving in Saudi Arabia in the depths of the Great Depression. Abdul Aziz needed the money. By 1931 the worldwide recession had cut the annual flow of pilgrims, his chief source of income, from 130,000 to fewer than 40,000. Previously the Saudi king had sniffed at the Gulf sheikhs of Bahrain and Qatar who sold off the mineral rights in their territories. Given the choice, he would have preferred not to have infidel foreigners snooping around his lands. But with no money to pay the tribes, he swallowed his pride. Tribal loyalty was the basis of his power. Things had become so bad, he confided to one British diplomat, that he could no longer entertain the chiefs as custom required. He had had to restrict their visits to the time of the Eids (the two Muslim feast days following Ramadan and the Hajj).

In the spring of 1933 Abdul Aziz welcomed representatives of Standard Oil of California (Socal, later Chevron) to Jeddah. After spending a week or so playing them off against Britain's Iraq Petroleum Company (IPC), whose surveyors doubted there was much oil in Arabia, he signed an exploration contract with the Americans for £35,000. It was a measure of the deal's novelty that the already mighty U.S. dollar still carried little weight in the primitive barter-and-bullion economy of Arabia. Abdul Aziz wanted to be paid in gold sovereigns, which were duly shipped to Jeddah in a wooden chest that was placed for safekeeping, according to cherished Saudi legend, under the bed of his finance minister, Abdullah Al-Suleiman. Later that year Socal's geologists started work in the east, and the king sent word that these non-Muslims should be greeted in his name and protected as honored guests.

But not everyone welcomed the Christians.

ABDUL AZIZ AND THE SON OF THE TIGER

One Sabbath in 1933 Abdul Aziz was sitting in the baked-mud mosque a few steps away from his baked-mud palace in the heart of Riyadh. It was around noon on Friday, the moment when the male inhabitants of the town shuffled into the mosque for the principal prayer gathering of the week. The floor was strewn with thick and richly colored carpets, and the Saudi king's sons sat around him as they listened to the sermon of Sheikh Ibn Nimr ("Son of the Tiger"), one of the great Wahhabi preachers of the day.

The sheikh had taken as his theme some verses from sura 11 of the Koran—"Incline not to those who do wrong, or the fire will seize you. You have no protectors other than Allah, nor shall you be helped." The sheikh was indignant at the recent appearance of non-Muslims in the Kingdom—he promised damnation to those who dealt with the infidels—and as the preacher developed his theme, Ibn Saud's annoyance became more and more obvious.

Suddenly the king interrupted the sermon. He told the Son of the Tiger to step down, and then rose to his feet to offer another set of verses, which he recited perfectly from memory: "Say to those that reject [your] faith," he declaimed, citing the more tolerant words of the Koran's sura 109, "I worship not that which you worship, nor will you worship that which I worship. . . . You have your religion and I have mine."

"Live and let live" was Abdul Aziz's sermon for the day.

• • •

The U.S.-Saudi relationship may have been founded on money, but for Ibn Saud it always had a personal and even sentimental dimension. The first Americans he met were Christian medical missionaries based on the island of Bahrain. These doctors and nurses from the Reformed Church in America treated his soldiers on several occasions after 1911, and came across from the island quite regularly—their painstaking archives record the treatment of nearly three hundred thousand mainland patients in the course of Abdul Aziz's reign. Thirty-five hundred of these patients required surgery, including the king himself, who summoned Dr. Louis Dame urgently to Riyadh in 1923 to operate on an alarming and painful "cellulitis of the face" that had caused one of his eyes to swell to the size of a baseball.

Dr. Dame, who, like all the mission doctors, spoke Arabic, lanced the inflammation and solicitously attended the king and other members of the royal family for nearly a week. He was particularly caring toward the king's aging father, Abdul-Rahman. Grateful and much impressed, Abdul Aziz insisted that the Reformed Church's medical facilities should be matched and expanded by Socal when the oil company started work in the Eastern Province, and in 1936 Dr. Dame was recruited to help set up the service.

Having pieced together his own independent kingdom largely on his own terms, Abdul Aziz now invited the United States to play, in some respects, the role of his colonial power. He felt no threat from idealistic Americans like Louis Dame, Christian missionary though he was, nor from the proliferating legion of Socal oil prospectors—booted and bearded pioneers who were pursuing their own mission of gushers and derricks. When it came to the political machinations that might be hatched by the government of these good-hearted men, the Saudi king took comfort from the fact that, as he candidly put it to one American visitor, "you are very far away!" His translator, Mohammed Al-Mana, later recalled the pleasure at court in 1933 as it became clear that Socal was outbidding Britain's IPC for the oil concession, "for we all felt that the British were still tainted by colonialism. If they came for our oil, we could never be sure to what extent they would come to influence our government as well. The Americans on the other hand would simply be after the money, a motive which the Arabs, as born traders, could readily appreciate and approve."

This optimistic Saudi view of the United States as a generous and detached power that was somehow more moral than the rest of the world neatly chimed, of course, with America's own exceptionalist image of itself. The loss of innocence over subsequent years would provide both sides with a succession of painful and poignant moments. The first came in February 1945 when Abdul Aziz traveled up the Red Sea for his first-ever encounter with a Western head of state, President Franklin Delano Roosevelt, who had come to Egypt following the Yalta conference. It had been a hopeful and novel jaunt up from Jeddah for the Saudi party on board the USS *Murphy,* the king's cooks and coffee servers slaughtering sheep on the deck of the destroyer, while his sons enjoyed the titillating sight of Miss

Lucille Ball cavorting in various states of undress, courtesy of the movie projector in the crew's quarters.

But then FDR sprang his bombshell—he invited the Saudi king to help him secure a home in Palestine for the Jewish people. The Jews of central Europe had suffered most terribly at Hitler's hands, the president explained, and he felt a personal responsibility to help them—he had committed himself indeed to finding a solution to their problems. Did the king of Arabia have any suggestions to make?

The king certainly did, and he based his proposal on simple bedouin principles.

"Give them [the Jews] and their descendants," he said, "the choicest lands and homes of the Germans who oppressed them." There was no reason why the Arab inhabitants of Palestine should suffer for something the Germans had done. "Make the enemy and the oppressor pay," he said. "That is how we Arabs wage war."

Jewish immigration into Palestine had been a major and universal Arab grievance since the 1920s, with Britain attracting most of the blame, since London administered the Palestine mandate and had been the architect of the Balfour Declaration, which first expressed "favor" toward the prospect of a "national homeland" for Jews in the Middle East. Now, it appeared, the United States was also an endorser of the Zionist project, though as he said good-bye to Abdul Aziz, Roosevelt promised the Saudi king that "he would do nothing to assist the Jews against the Arabs, and would make no move hostile to the Arab people."

FDR's successor, Harry Truman, broke this pledge in Saudi eyes when America supported Israeli statehood at the United Nations in 1948. Dwight Eisenhower was judged more evenhanded. Following the attempt of Britain, France, and Israel to seize the Suez Canal in 1956, Eisenhower sternly compelled the three conspirators to withdraw their forces. But this humiliating illustration of where postwar power lay prompted some creative thinking in Jerusalem. Nine years later, the purposeful marshaling in Washington of what would become known as the Jewish lobby helped ensure U.S. acquiescence and effective support for Israel's 1967 conquest of Jerusalem, the West Bank, and Gaza in the Six-Day War. When Egypt sought revenge six years later, taking Israeli troops by surprise as they marked the ceremonies of Yom Kippur 1973, Richard Nixon threw the weight of U.S. armaments behind the defense of Israel. In the twenty-eight years since FDR and Ibn Saud met, America had moved from tentative patron to firm guarantor of the Zionist project. As the Saudis saw it, Israel had become America's fifty-first state.

Publicly King Faisal bin Abdul Aziz reacted in fury, launching the Arab oil boycott of 1973. But in private it was a different matter. U.S.-Saudi relations were embedded in many fields—Aramco was America's largest single private overseas investment anywhere in the world. Throughout the oil boycott and Faisal's vehement protests at U.S. support for Israel, two U.S. military missions remained stationed in the Kingdom, training the Saudi Army, Air Force, and National Guard, while the king and his agents deployed the country's profits from the anti-U.S. oil embargo to finance the Safari Club's pro-U.S. activities in Africa. When it came to sheer, bottom-line survival, where else could the House of Saud turn but to America?

"After Allah," Faisal had told President Kennedy in 1962, "we trust the United States."

This neatly encapsulated the Saudi balancing act—but staying upright on the tightrope depended on keeping quiet about the friendship to those who might find it offensive at home. Successive Saudi kings chose to downplay the alliance to the average Saudi man-in-the-mosque, whose Fridays were regularly inflamed by pulpit warnings against the Western *shaytan* (Satan), laced with unashamed doses of anti-Semitism. To his dying day King Faisal believed implicitly in the anti-Jewish forgeries *The Protocols of the Elders of Zion,* and funded modern republications of its fabrications. In Washington, meanwhile, U.S. administrations who were courting the Jewish vote tended to restrict White House appearances by bearded Arabs in headdresses, particularly near election time.

"There goes New York State," remarked President Kennedy in January 1962 after photographers had caught him visiting the ailing King Saud in Palm Beach.

The more intimate and intertwined the U.S.-Saudi relationship grew, the more it became, for both sides, a friendship that could not afford to own its name.

• • •

The summer of 1981 saw the arrival in Washington of Prince Bandar bin Sultan, a self-assured young Saudi Air Force squadron commander, sent to ease the passage through Congress of a massive Saudi arms deal. U.S.-Saudi collaboration had been proceeding smoothly both in Afghanistan and with the undercover campaigns of the Safari Club, but the Kingdom's security had been compromised closer to home. Iraq's emerging dictator, Saddam Hussein, had thrown the first of his aggressive foreign policy surprises when he attacked Iran the previous September. If his gamble failed, the ayatollahs might extend their power westward, and Riyadh needed to know what was going on over the Iraqi horizon. The answer lay in AWACS—America's recently developed airborne warning and control system.

Deriving its intelligence from a huge radar dish tacked on top of a Boeing 707, the AWACS system was capable of tracking 240 hostile aircraft simultaneously and directing fighters to intercept them. Patrolling thirty-five thousand feet above the oil fields, the "flying mushroom" could give the Saudi Air Force a twenty minute advantage over intruding enemy aircraft—time for an F-15 to make at least one extra pass. Lacking AWACS patrols, Riyadh had been humiliated even as Bandar arrived in Washington that June when Israeli fighter-bombers flew hundreds of miles to and fro through Saudi airspace to destroy Saddam Hussein's nuclear reactor at Osirak, near Baghdad. Osirak made the Kingdom even more determined to acquire AWACS—while, as Israel saw it, the intelligence planes would give a dangerous combat edge to a potential enemy. On Capitol Hill the Israel lobby vowed to fight the purchase every step of the way.

Bandar bin Sultan already had some experience of the ways of Washington. Three years earlier he had been seconded from his flying duties at the suggestion of his brother-in-law Turki Al-Faisal to serve as a military attaché to the Saudi embassy, lobbying for the purchase of the F-15 fighter.

"My vote will cost you $10 million," he was told at the time by Senator Russell B. Long of Louisiana, who unashamedly explained the system perfected by his father, Huey "King Fish" Long, the legendary governor of Louisiana: "I want you to assure me that your government will deposit $10 million in a bank in my town, and before you do that, let me know so that I can tell the bank president. . . . He will pay for my reelection. You can then draw your money back anytime, once I have been reelected."

It was no problem at all for the Saudi Ministry of Finance to shift $10 million from New York to Louisiana—and Saudi Arabia had a great deal more than that on deposit in the Chase Manhattan Bank. Keen to help a wealthy customer, the bank's chairman, David Rockefeller, had promised to use his influence to pull in the votes of several senators. But as the weeks went by, Bandar got the impression that Rockefeller was treading water.

"What do you suggest?" asked his uncle the crown prince on the phone.

"You can order the finance minister to move $200 million from Chase Manhattan to J. P. Morgan," replied Bandar.

"Next day," recalls Bandar, "David Rockefeller called me at eight in the morning. I was asleep. He called me at nine; I was busy. He called me at ten; I was out. At four o'clock in the afternoon, the hotel reception phoned me to say that a Mr. Rockefeller was in the lobby."

It was once said that becoming president of the United States would have represented a demotion for David Rockefeller. Now the arch-networker had apparently traveled from New York to Washington to court a thirty-two-year-old fighter pilot. Bandar recalls keeping the banker waiting till six, then telling him he was too busy for a meeting—he was on his way to the Hill to work on the votes he had been promised.

"I'm going to stay here in Washington," promised Rockefeller, as Bandar remembers it, "until I get you all the votes you want."

"Every night for three days," according to Bandar, "he would call me and tell me 'I've got Senator so-and-so.' About three days later when he'd got all the senators he'd promised—and two more—I told our Finance Ministry to move the $200 million back to Chase Manhattan."

Today David Rockefeller says there are "a rather large number of factual inaccuracies" in Prince Bandar's recollection. He calls the tale "preposterous," and questions the mechanisms by which the Saudi Arabian Monetary Authority could, hypothetically, have switched funds in the casual way that the prince suggests. But he agrees that he met with Bandar, and also with Turki Al-Faisal and the Saudi ambassador at the time, Ali Alireza, in the Saudi embassy in March 1978, two months before the sale of the F-15s was approved in Congress.

Smiles, gifts, and smoothly conveyed threats—it was the classic strategy that the Al-Saud had deployed for generations. It had worked with the bedouin. Now it may have worked just as well with American politicians. In European terms, the young pilot's relentless pursuit of his goals was pure Machiavelli—and that added an extra dimension to the nickname that Bandar soon acquired in DC's corridors of power: "the Prince."

. . .

Little did Washington realize how precarious that princeliness was. Bandar was born as the result of a brief encounter between Prince Fahd's full Sudayri brother Sultan bin Abdul Aziz, the swaggering Saudi defense minister, and a servingwoman, a black slave. The boy was kept at arm's length by his father for much of his childhood.

"I was conceived out of wedlock, and my mother was a concubine," Bandar would say frankly in later years, explaining how, by custom, if a slave "gets pregnant and you acknowledge it before she has the baby, then it is automatic freedom from slavery. But you still have to deal with the cultural realities; you'll always be the kid who's a different color, whose parents never got married."

Young Bandar had an African appearance, with darker skin and black, frizzy hair. In this, his looks were little different from those of many Arabians—Arabs and Africans have been crisscrossing the Red Sea since time immemorial. But this has not eliminated racial prejudice in Saudi Arabia. On the contrary—some Saudis practice the most unashamed (and un-Islamic) ethnic snobberies, discriminating on the basis of skin darkness and facial features, right down to the flatness of a man's nose. Bandar's nose was definitely flat, so when it came to choosing falcons on a hunting expedition, he remembers getting the last pick—a scruffy bird with mottled black and brown feathers at which everyone laughed.

But the boy's scruffy champion outperformed the nobler specimens—and that proved a metaphor for his own scrappy and defiant attitude to life. Hearing that King Faisal's beautiful daughter Haifa was unhappy with her father's choice of husband for her, a much older prince, Bandar put in his own bid, and he won her hand. Determined to be a fighter pilot despite the indifference of his father, who, as defense minister, could have fixed the deal with a flick of his pen, Bandar made his own arrangements, faking his date of birth to secure early admission to the Royal Air Force College at Cranwell.

The fact that Bandar's mother was not of royal or tribal lineage theoretically relegated her son to second-rank royal status. Bandar's own generation, the more pedigreed grandsons of Abdul Aziz, referred to him behind his back as "the son of the slave." But the slur seems to have inspired him to overcome the disadvantage of his birth. Hugely energetic, overflowing with charm, and rubber-ball irrepressible, Bandar had been brought up in the household of his powerful aunt Lulua bint Abdul Aziz, Sultan's full sister, then in the home of Hissa Al-Sudayri herself. Through these forceful women, Bandar got the chance to know, and to impress, his uncle Crown Prince Fahd.

Fahd took a shine to his able young nephew, making him ambassador to Washington in 1983 and giving him primary responsibility for fostering the U.S.-Saudi relationship. In many ways Fahd fathered Bandar better than Sultan—and Bandar returned the compliment, growing closer to Fahd than some of the crown prince's own sons. Walter Cutler, the two-time U.S. ambassador to Riyadh who met Bandar regularly through the '80s, cannot recall a single meeting that was not interrupted at some stage by a call from the crown prince—after 1982, the king.

Bandar deployed his charm similarly in the Reagan White House, where he ingratiated himself with Nancy Reagan and, with a shrewd eye on the future, became the occasional racquetball partner of a rising young soldier with political ambitions, Colin Powell. Reagan's muscular and robustly anti-Communist foreign policy matched precisely with the Saudi view of the world—and made the Kingdom a valued ally when Congress explicitly blocked such ventures as U.S. funding for the anti-Marxist Nicaraguan contras. Following a personal request by Ronald Reagan to Fahd over breakfast in the White House in 1985, Bandar set up the channels to get funds wired to the contras to the tune of $1 million and later $2 million a month, using bank account numbers supplied to him by Reagan's national security adviser, Robert "Bud" McFarlane. The account itself had been set up in Switzerland by the deputy director of political-military affairs in the National Security Council, Oliver North.

When the Iran-contra scandal broke, the Walsh Report revealed that Saudi Arabia had secretly channeled a total of $32 million to the contras on Reagan's behalf. But that was small beer compared with the sums the Kingdom was dispensing in other areas. In Angola, Ethiopia, the Sudan, and Chad, the Safari Club kept up its anti-Marxist activities—with more vigor, if anything, in the absence of the Shah. And then there was Afghanistan.

"You are not alone, Freedom Fighters!" proclaimed Ronald Reagan grandly in his 1986 State of the Union address, promising that America would provide "moral and material assistance" to those who fought against Communism in Afghanistan, Angola, and Nicaragua.

America certainly did its part. But doing the sums, it is now clear that through the eight years of Ronald Reagan's presidency, 1981–89, Saudi Arabia actually provided more material assistance to the world's varied assortment of anti-Communist "freedom fighters" than did the United States, thus hastening the end of the Cold War and helping accomplish the downfall of the "Evil Empire." For America it was a very good return on thirty-five thousand gold sovereigns.

CHAPTER 9

Dawn Visitors

In the early 1980s, Fawzia Al-Bakr became one of the first Saudi women to write in the newspapers under her own name.

"Women used to hide behind bylines like *Bint al-Badia* ['Daughter of the Desert']," she remembers. "I thought that was stupid. I had nothing to hide."

Twenty-one years old and a teaching assistant at the University of Riyadh, the forthright Ms. Al-Bakr delivered her views through a weekly full-page column in the relatively conservative newspaper *Al-Jazeera*.*

"I wrote about women and freedom and things like the wrongness of modern men having more than one wife. I argued the need for civil organizations in Saudi Arabia to advance human rights."

Al-Bakr never went into the *Al-Jazeera* office—there were no facilities for women to work there—and she never met the male editor of her page. She was planning to do so, but one morning in June 1982 when she was organizing exams at the university, she was summoned to the principal's office. Two men in thobes were waiting for her, with a woman, who asked politely if they could escort her to her home. It was her first contact with the fabled Mabahith, literally "the detectives," Saudi Arabia's secret police.

The Mabahith are a department of the Saudi Ministry of the Interior, so vast and pervasive in their watchfulness that *secret* is scarcely the word for them. They have woven themselves into the very fabric of Saudi life.

*Popular shorthand for the Arabian Peninsula—*Al-Jazeera Al-Arabiya* means the "Island of the Arabs." Based in Riyadh, *Al-Jazeera* newspaper is not connected with the Qatar-based TV news network of the same name.

There is a Mabahith informant praying in every significant Saudi mosque, ready to make a phone call should the imam's sermon get too fiery, nor would any university faculty be complete without its careful listener by the coffee machine. The proudly worn badge of the Interior Ministry's security forces actually depicts a huge, staring eye—though in 1979 they had been caught out by both the eastern intifada and by the seizing of the Grand Mosque. It was not entirely their fault—they had captured the "Mahdi" himself before the seizure, after all, only to be told to let him go—but it had spurred them to redouble their intelligence gathering, with mixed results. While the intensified border patrols of the ministry had not picked up many militants, they had gathered a rich harvest of alcohol smugglers. The price of black-market whisky in Jeddah had exploded from one hundred dollars to as much as four hundred dollars per bottle.

As Fawzia Al-Bakr reached her family home in the company of her polite but unsmiling escorts, she tried to warn her teenage brother.

"Wasalu zuwwar al-fajr!" she whispered—"The dawn visitors have arrived!" Her brother's eyes opened wide with horror.

The plainclothes officers escorted her up to her bedroom, where they searched through her desk and cupboards.

"They took all my notebooks and files," she recalls. "I told my mother it was something to do with missing exam papers."

It was not until Al-Bakr found herself at an office of the Interior Ministry that she realized the full danger of her situation.

"There was a crowd of other women who had been brought in, with a lot of policemen milling round, and I thought I must be dreaming. Then they started reading out the names—'the prisoner Fawzia Al-Bakr.' I nearly fainted. One of the women had to hold me upright."

The new prisoner was issued a blanket and a dirty gown, then locked alone in a cell inside the ministry building.

"The food was atrocious. It was prepared by bedouin women who looked after us. They were very nice ladies, but also very simple. They could not read or write. I think they were the wives of soldiers or National Guardsmen."

In the small hours of every morning, at around 2 A.M., the police summoned Al-Bakr for questioning. One of the bedouin women escorted her to the interrogation room.

"They were very civil. There was no suggestion of torture or intimidation, but they kept on asking the same things. The interrogators changed, but the questions they asked were the same: 'Have you seen these leaflets?' 'What do you think of the government?' 'Do you belong to Al-Haraka Al-Wataniya [the National Movement]?'"

Al-Haraka Al-Wataniya was a group of liberals who were campaigning for reform in the late 1970s and early '80s. They were particularly opposed to the conservative trend of social policy since Juhayman, and because political gatherings were forbidden in Saudi Arabia, they were, by definition, an "underground" organization. Academic and intellectual, with a high proportion of members who had completed their educations in the West, they included freethinkers and atheists who liked to label themselves "Communist," risking the fierce shariah law penalties on those who renounce their faith. But their agenda did not extend far beyond talk.

"I'd turned down invitations to join various organizations—there was one called Al-Islahiyoon [the Reformists]. I just wasn't interested in joining things. I only wanted to write my columns. But I was obviously campaigning for the same sorts of changes as the Reformists, the National Movement, and all the others. Who wouldn't, the way things were going?"

After a week the women were moved from the ministry cells to villas in the Riyadh suburb of Suleymaniya.

"I think they'd pulled in so many people they couldn't cope. There was a great panic in those years after Juhayman and the Shia riots. The government was overwhelmed. They must have rented these villas—compounds built for expatriates. They were quite comfortable, we each had our own room. But the windows were blocked, and we could not meet with each other. We spoke to each other through the lavatory pipes. I got to know one woman, Zahrah, a Shia, an artist—she could not stand being on her own. She was screaming all the time. And every night they'd take me for the same questioning for two hours or more."

The worst thing for Al-Bakr was having no contact with her family.

"They had no idea where I was, if I was dead or alive—whether I would ever come back. My father went every day to Prince Salman's office. Nothing—they wouldn't tell him anything. It was terrible for them."

Making the family feel the pain was part of the Mabahith technique.

"It's good to get the family involved," explains a currently serving Mabahith officer. "It means that they'll probably put pressure on the troublemaker when he (or she) comes out of detention. We have also found that while many detainees might be willing personally to go back inside again, they moderate their behavior for the sake of sparing their family—particularly their mother."

The assistant professor kept up her own spirits by trying to memorize the Koran, the only book she was allowed.

"It was good for my Arabic language. You can use any experience that does not break you to build yourself up. One lady tried to commit suicide, so they took all our mirrors away. That was surprisingly difficult, not being able to see yourself. After a time you begin to wonder if you are still there."

One day, with no warning, after nearly three months of detention, one of the female guards came to tell her to pack up her things.

"'*Khalas!*' she said—'It's finished'—I could go home. Some official phoned my family to say I was coming out that night, and they were all there to greet me, my cousins and my aunts—it was a wonderful party."

Great was the rejoicing at the university.

"My boss, the dean, Dr. Mansour Al-Hasmy, gave me a special award—Honorary Employee of the Year. He made a big deal of it. He wanted to make a public point on the campus about freedom. And he worked really hard to get me a scholarship the next year to go to the University of Oregon. The newspaper, *Al-Jazeera*, had also been supportive—they had kept sending me my paychecks all the time I was inside."

But her mother found it hard to celebrate.

"My mother is a loyal Saudi citizen, but to this day she is mad at Prince Nayef."

From the traditional, family point of view, Fawzia's three months behind bars had been a social catastrophe.

"What angered my mother most was that it had ruined my marriage prospects. What family would allow their son to marry a girl who had been to prison?"

IN SEARCH OF THE ORYX

The gazellelike oryx is Arabia's most graceful form of wildlife, and, according to an old Saudi joke, the survival of the oryx became a matter of concern to the Ministry of the Interior. So they called in the world's top security forces, America's FBI and Britain's SAS, to see if they could track down a specimen—while also inviting their own secret police, the Mabahith, to show what they could do.

After a day, the FBI reported in. "We've located an animal a few miles from our camp. We've got it in our sights. Give us the word and we'll pull the trigger."

A day later, the SAS called. "We've got one surrounded, but she appears to be pregnant. We recommend approaching with extreme caution."

But from the Mabahith came no word—not that day nor the next. After a week of waiting, a search party was sent out, which eventually located the elite corps of Saudi detectives, miles from the oryx grounds, all huddled around in a circle, menacing a frightened rabbit. One of them was holding the rabbit up by the scruff of the neck, while another was indulging in the Mabahith's then nationally notorious form of torture—beating the prisoner hard with a stick on the soles of its feet. This tactic is said to derive from a saying of the Prophet that punishment should leave no mark on the body, so as they walloped away at their victim's leathery soles, Saudi interrogators could comfort themselves with the reflection that their torture was truly "Islamic."

"Come on, come on! Stop wasting our time!" the interrogator was shouting at the captive rabbit. "We know the truth! Admit that you're an oryx!"

• • •

The work of the Mabahith was scarcely more subtle in real life. Working as Riyadh editor for the English language newspaper *Saudi Gazette,* the young American journalist Peter Theroux noticed how his office telephone would go dead at crucial moments.

"It was as if certain phrases triggered a cutoff," he remembers. "An American woman once rang me offering a story about strange things that her husband was discovering at a military facility. The moment she mentioned the name of the base, the phone line went dead. She rang back, and the connection cut out again the moment she mentioned the name."

It was not the sort of story that Theroux would have touched with a barge pole, in any case. He had soon learned the so-called red lines (*khutoot hamra*) within which the Saudi media had to operate. There were a set of undefined but generally understood conventions—the Palestinians could do no wrong, the Israelis could do no right, there should be not a whisper of dissent about the king or the religious establishment, and there should be no "bad news" stories that might make readers discontented. It sometimes seemed that too many paragraphs about the Kingdom's appallingly high rate of traffic accidents could be judged seditious.

To avoid any doubt, the editors in chief of all the newspapers were summoned to a monthly meeting at the Ministry of Information to discover the red lines of the moment—some papers actually published photographs of their editor with the minister "discussing the topics of the day." Peter Theroux remembers the outcome of one such discussion in the spring of 1982 following the horrific, Guernica-style destruction of the flourishing town of Hama by the Syrian government that February. Intent on eliminating the Muslim Brotherhood, the Assad regime had organized the brutal murder of ten thousand or so opponents, and as many more innocent bystanders. Hama remains a backwater to this day.

"How could you ignore something as ghastly and inhuman as that?" recalls Theroux. "It was beyond dispute that the massacre had happened, and there was no doubt that our readers would be looking for some comment in the editorials. It was not as if Syria was any special friend to the Saudis. But the word came down from the ministry not to criticize: 'Syria is an Arab sister. Bash Begin [Menachem Begin, the Israeli prime minister] instead.'"

Theroux found humor the best recipe for survival, surprising visiting journalists by offering to guess the number of the room in which they were staying at the Intercontinental Hotel. He would always get it right—room 103. He had been allocated the same room himself when he first arrived in Riyadh. It was the room with the hidden microphones.

• • •

Control became the watchword of the 1980s in Saudi Arabia—particularly for women. Freshly elected to the committee of a women's charity in Jeddah, Maha Fitaihi decided to organize a forum on women's issues and obstacles to development—until news reached the Ministry of Social Affairs, which supervised all charitable activities. They told her to change the subject or cancel the event. Saudi women did not suffer from any obstacles to their development, she was confidently informed by one of the all-male staff of the ministry, and whatever problems they might encounter could be solved by their religion. A lecture on women's health issues, drugs, and AIDS provoked a similar response. "A few isolated cases don't make an 'issue,'" she was told, and an official letter soon arrived, sternly instructing her not to organize any further educational or awareness gatherings, unless they were focused on "Islamic" affairs.

Up in Riyadh, Hatoon Al-Fassi encountered even more drastic difficulties when she tried to organize a graduation ceremony for her class at King Saud University. It was an all-female occasion—every mother had been allocated two tickets—held in the gymnasium hall on the male side of the campus. Through the year, Hatoon and her sporting colleagues had been visiting the gym every Thursday to train at gymnastics, volleyball, and handball, and the plan was for these sports to feature in the end of year celebrations.

But Wahhabi religious orthodoxy was opposed to women's sports. Reflecting this, there had never been organized sport or games for girls at Saudi state schools, whose control was handed to the religious establishment by King Faisal in the early 1960s. Energetic physical activity was considered harmful, in some unspecified way, to feminine bodily functions, and also involved the wearing of immodestly revealing athletic costume. For their sports activities, Hatoon and her athletic friends—graduates, for the most part, of the Kingdom's private academies—dressed in tracksuits with long trousers and long sleeves. It made their volleyball hot, but respectable.

The entertainment for the graduation evening involved the finals of the sporting tournaments, interspersed with folkloric music and dance from different corners of the peninsula, with a spectacular roller-skating exhibition whose participants (also in long sleeves and trousers) had been rehearsing for months.

But as the program got under way, there came heavy knocking at the doors of the building. It was the religious police calling for the music to be stopped. The mutawwa did not actually enter the hall, but they kept patrolling noisily outside, their angry male presence intimidating the women trapped inside the gym. Hatoon and her friends tried to keep up the spirit of the ceremony with loud applause for the trophy presentations, but they found themselves whistling in the dark—literally. At 10 P.M. some malevolent male hand outside threw the power switch, and all the lights in the hall were extinguished.

There was no female sports program at King Saud University the next year, and no music or dancing when the women's degrees were conferred.

There were also new attendance regulations. Women had to be on campus by eight in the morning, after which the gates would be closed until noon. No female undergraduate could leave the university between those hours, unless she was a wife or mother and could show a paper as proof—and the paper, of course, had to be signed by her male guardian.

• • •

In just a few years, it seemed, the triumph of the religious was complete—and it was marked by the increasing number of beards. In the immediate aftermath of the Grand Mosque siege, Saudi men had tended to trim their beards. They did not want to be associated with the hairy excesses of the rebels. But as the 1980s passed, facial hair made a comeback. Religious conservatives gloried in their long and luxuriant Islamic beards. Sprouting defiantly from every facial follicle, the Salafi beard became the badge of piety, superiority, and the capacity to inspire fear. You could easily identify the religious police as they advanced toward you in the street. They looked like a posse of menacing Juhaymans.

Every face of authority seemed to be conspiring to shut down Saudi society in the early 1980s. In fact, the Mabahith and the mutawwa answered to different masters. While the Mabahith were government officials taking their orders from the Ministry of the Interior, the mutawwa were comparatively unregulated: their network of local committees for the "promotion of virtue and the prevention of vice" gave them the character of freelance vigilantes, taking their cue from the local pulpit. A strong king or local princely governor could have called them sharply to heel. But following the capture of the Grand Mosque, there was not a member of the royal family inclined to do so.

CHAPTER 10

Stars in the Heavens

In June 1982 (coincidentally the month that Fawzia Al-Bakr went to prison) old King Khaled died. His personal 747, a huge white and green Boeing jumbo jet, contained an operating theater equipped with the latest heart-monitoring and resuscitation devices with links to his surgeons in the Cleveland Clinic. Yet the precautions failed to save him. Venerable, bluff, and widely loved, Khaled had been the Ronald Reagan of Saudi kings.

Now it was time for a touch of Nixon. Saudis appreciated the competence of Fahd the Leopard, but few felt great fondness for him, and the new king made a bid for sympathy in his first broadcast to his people. He was now responsible, he said, for ruling "in accordance with God's revelation," and he had to confess that he found these divine requirements a heavy duty—his heart was "trembling," he said, "for fear of failure and retribution." Fahd warned of the problems ahead, and of the threats from the great powers hatching plots "to divide and fragment" the Arabs. "What is most to be feared," he cautioned, "is that they will attack us from within by the sowing of dissension and driving our citizens to extremism." He did not suggest that the impetus to extremism might be coming from *inside* the Kingdom. The enemies were all outside. Saudi youth, in particular, "must not imitate the lost youth of the West and be carried away by corrupt pleasures."

The fearful and almost apologetic address was an opening gesture by the liberal-minded king to appease the religious conservatives.

"If an election were held here tomorrow," Fahd once confided to a colleague, "Bin Baz would beat us without even leaving his house."

This basic awareness was drilled into every young member of the House of Saud.

"Without exception," says a minister who has worked with the family for many years, "they are brought up to have respect and to show respect toward the religious scholars."

This respect was in singular contrast to the ill-disguised contempt that the Shah had shown toward Iran's mullahs.

"I have no doubt that Fahd has gone to heaven," said one of his admirers after his death. "It is only fair. His life on earth was such hell being perpetually polite to those religious fanatics."

One aspect of Fahd's purgatory was that the new king felt obliged to rein in some of his pleasures. In the early 1980s he had accepted the gift of a rakish twin-funneled luxury motor yacht from his friend John Latsis, a Greek shipping tycoon whose Saudi oil-refining and construction business, Petrola, owed much to the favor of Fahd. Complete with its own helipad and disco dance floor, the *Abdul Aziz,* later the *Prince Abdul Aziz*, was the longest yacht in the world, and Fahd liked to moor the 482-footer off Marbella, on the southern coast of Spain, where Latsis helped him raise a huge white-pillared palace that was a bizarrely accurate replica of the White House in Washington. Helicopters hovered overhead, and private jets flew in to nearby Málaga every day with exotic flower displays and a never-ending supply of wealthy visitors. When the Saudis came to town, calculated one local publication, their combined spending contributed $10 million per day to the resort's hedonistic economy. It was small wonder that the mayor of Marbella announced that he was proposing to name a street in the Saudi monarch's honor.

Once he became king, however, Fahd felt able to make only one trip to Marbella—his family had to go and have the fun without him. The king confined himself to the palace that Latsis built him on a man-made island off Jeddah, and when in Riyadh he was an austere Wahhabi, receiving the ulema every Tuesday as his predecessor had done, with Sheikh Bin Baz sitting beside him in pride of place.

Bin Baz, for his part, was seeking to enter the twentieth century. The blind sheikh had become notorious among liberals for a fatwa he had issued a dozen years earlier when American astronauts were landing on the moon—"On the Possibility of Going into Orbit." His judgment had cast such doubt on the American achievement and on the proven facts of the moon landing that people accused Bin Baz of doubting the roundness of the earth. This was not totally fair. There are Western websites to this day that assert that the U.S. moon landings were staged in a TV studio, and the sheikh's main point in his fatwa was to be skeptical: "We cannot believe anyone who comes and says 'I was on the moon' without offering solid scientific evidence." In fact, wrote Bin Baz, "we see nothing in the Koran against the possibility that men may reach the moon. . . . We know there are spaces between earth and sky. There is nothing to say that the rockets cannot fly in them."

The sheikh's ruling—in response, he said, to numerous queries he had received from "the Muslims"—was a detailed and touchingly open-minded attempt to square the dry facts of modern science with the mystic teachings of the Koran and its talk of genies flying between the planets. But Bin Baz's suspicions of the Americans weighed heavy: "We must make careful checks whenever the *kuffar* [infidels] or *faseqoon* [immoral folk] tell us something: we cannot believe or disbelieve them until we get sufficient proof on which the Muslims can depend."

At a superficial reading it was possible to assume that Bin Baz had gone beyond questioning the moon landing to denying it, and soon afterward the sheikh gave an interview in which he mused on how we operate day to day on the basis that the ground beneath us is flat, even though science asserts, against our physical experience, that the world is spherical.

"As I remember from when I could see," he said, "it seemed to be flat."

It was an honest expression of paradox, particularly moving from a man who had been blind most of his life, and it led him to the belief that he was not afraid to voice and for which he became notorious—Bin Baz believed that the earth was flat.*

At least one senior member of the ulema reproved Bin Baz for his embarrassing assertion, which radicals had seized on to satirize the Wahhabi establishment as "members of the Flat Earth Society." But the sheikh was unrepentant. If Muslims chose to believe the world was round, that was their business, he said, and he would not quarrel with them religiously.

*It is often said that Bin Baz issued a fatwa asserting that the earth was flat. After extensive research I have only been able to discover his fatwa "On the Possibility of Going into Orbit," in which he does not state this in so many words and in which he appears, to this author at least, to weigh the available scientific evidence contradicting his beliefs with more open-mindedness than many a modern "creationist" in the West.

But he was inclined to trust what he felt beneath his feet rather than the statements of scientists he did not know: he would go on believing the earth to be flat until he was presented with convincing evidence to the contrary.

In 1985 the evidence presented itself. Prince Sultan bin Salman, the thirty-eight-year-old son of the governor of Riyadh, was selected by NASA to serve as payload engineer on one of its *Discovery* space shuttle flights, and the prince went to Bin Baz for advice. Much of the training, and the first few days of the flight, would fall in Ramadan, so what should he do about fasting?

"You can apply the Prophet's rules about traveling," replied the scholar without hesitation. These rules made clear that Mohammed permitted the traveler, if he wished, to postpone his fast until his journey's end: then he could make up the lost days in his own time.

Prince Sultan, however, was not so keen. He had tried making up fasting days in the past, and he had not enjoyed doing his penance when everyone else had gone back to eating normally. He preferred to fast as he went along—and NASA was, in fact, delighted at the chance to monitor the impact of daytime food and drink deprivation on the young Muslim. It proved minimal.

The prince called Bin Baz from the Kennedy Space Center every day or so.

" 'Look,' " Sultan remembers telling him, " 'we're going to be traveling at eighteen thousand miles per hour. I'm going to see sixteen sunrises and sunsets every twenty-four hours. So does that mean I'll get Ramadan finished in two days?' The sheikh loved that one—he laughed out loud."

After some discussion, the two men agreed that everything should be reckoned in normal, earth time, from the time and place of launch in Cape Canaveral. This would also apply to the five daily prayer times, which, because of weightlessness, would have to be carried out in an upright position, with the prince strapped into his seat and wearing his space boots.

"It would be no good trying to face Mecca," remembers the prince. "By the time I'd lined up on it, it would be behind me."

Sultan bin Salman would be the first Muslim ever to fly in space and Bin Baz was eager for his firsthand observations.

"Keep your eyes open," were his parting words on the day before blast-off. "I want to hear about everything you see."

"I shall never forget it," says Prince Sultan today, "the sight of the earth, so small and round and bright in the blackness. Everything was very clear and sharp. We have a saying in the Koran, 'Verily, we have mansions of stars in the heavens.' That summed it up for me. Twenty years later it remains woven into everything that I believe."

Back in Taif, the young prince received a hero's welcome. His uncle Fahd was there to greet him on the tarmac, along with his proud father, Salman, and a multitude of admiring brothers and cousins. Later that evening the young prince escaped to the home of Bin Baz, where the sheikh had gathered a reception committee of the Kingdom's most learned religious figures. They wanted to hear the firsthand facts about what was revolving around what in the universe.

"The sheikh was so excited," remembers the prince. "He met me by the front door and embraced me and led me in to meet all the sheikhs, keeping hold of my hand the whole way. *'Allahu akbar!'* he kept repeating. He kept asking me questions. How was it that we didn't fall out of the sky? How could the shuttle fly that fast without using its engines?

" 'Let this not be the last time!' he said. 'Who's going to go next?' "

In the light of the prince's clear testimony that he had looked down on a spherical globe, Sheikh Bin Baz ceased his assertions that the earth was flat. It was important for the Muslims, he always said, to be open-minded and to accept the clear evidence that God put before them. But the blind sheikh knew what he knew, and he never formally recanted what he had said. Many doubted whether, in his heart, Abdul Aziz Bin Baz, who would rise to be the most senior religious figure in Saudi Arabia, ever truly abandoned his belief in the evidence of what he felt beneath his feet and had gazed on before his sight was taken from him.

. . .

By 1985 the Kingdom's greatest asset was becoming its major problem—oil had plummeted from spectacular boom to disastrous slump. Around forty dollars per barrel when the decade opened, the price started to slip in 1981, with production dropping by a third in Fahd's first year as king. The world economy was being flooded with new supplies from Canada, Alaska, and the multiplying North Sea oil platforms, while demand was decreasing as a result of economic recession, more fuel-efficient cars, and the conservation measures prompted by the high prices of the boom years. Virtually all of America's power-generating industry switched back in these years from oil to coal. "Oceans of Oil," bemoaned *Texas Monthly* magazine in a 1984 special issue devoted to the world glut of energy.

In 1981 Saudi oil income had stood at a healthy SR 328 billion per year. Over the next four years it would decline steadily to a quarter of that. The fall had a disastrous impact on Fahd's government spending plans, and he took out his frustrations on his world-famous oil minister, the handsome, dark-eyed Sheikh Ahmad Zaki Yamani.

"Why haven't you been round to see me recently?" he would complain over the phone.

The king resented the minister's high profile abroad and the fact that the articulate Yamani—who, unlike Fahd, could speak fluent English—delivered his opinions to the world not just on questions of oil, but on Israel-Palestine and U.S.-Saudi relations as well. Scarcely a month went by in the early 1980s without Sheikh Yamani giving an interview or a prestigious lecture to an admiring—usually Western—gathering. He was on the cover of every news and business magazine.

Many in the royal family shared Fahd's unhappiness that a commoner should be treated as the voice and face of Saudi Arabia. Yamani had been Faisal's protégé in the 1960s, and his successors came to feel that Zaki had grown too big for his boots. The Al-Saud particularly disliked the way that the outside world referred to him as "Sheikh."

"Yamani was plain *ustaz*—Mister Yamani," says an adviser to the royal court. "*Sheikh* is an honorific reserved for tribal chieftains and for religious scholars."

For his part, the oil minister resented being roused at two in the morning to attend the impromptu cabinet meetings called by Fahd, and for being blamed for events that, in his opinion, were the nature of the market. Many of the new fields coming on line around the world had been made economically feasible by OPEC's price rises, and the West had "got religion" on energy conservation under the same pressure of price. There had never been great affection between Fahd and Yamani, and over the years their relationship grew openly hostile. In October 1986 Fahd sent Yamani a cable at an OPEC meeting instructing him to push for a price of eighteen dollars a barrel. The king had agreed to this strategy after long discussions with the rulers of Kuwait and other Gulf states, and was furious to hear afterward, as they told it, that Yamani had treated the agreed policy with ill-concealed disdain.

"I don't know how I can work with this guy any longer," Yamani had declared impatiently to a ministerial colleague who telephoned him during the meeting on Fahd's behalf to confirm the king's instructions. Later, he had a direct and acrimonious confrontation with Fahd on the phone.

The oil minister had gone several steps too far, and he seemed to know it. On his return from the OPEC meeting Yamani flew briefly to Jeddah, then headed for Riyadh, where he waited, as if expecting the end—which came within a matter of days. A brief official statement made no pretence of "resignation," but stated baldly that the oil minister had been dismissed. Yamani was playing cards with his family when the news was announced on television. He was a fan of *baloot,* Saudi Arabia's most popular card game, a version of the French game *belote.* "Turn up the volume," he said without looking up from the table—and went on playing cards.

In later years a myth developed that King Fahd deliberately kept the price of Saudi oil low through the 1980s in a devious scheme devised with Ronald Reagan to diminish Russia's income from its own oil and gas sales and eventually bankrupt the USSR, thus securing Cold War victory.

"That was simply impossible," says the oil economist Dr. Ibrahim Al-Muhanna of the Saudi Ministry of Petroleum. "No single producer could then or now 'control' the price of oil. In 1986 Ronald Reagan actually sent [Vice President George H. W.] Bush to Riyadh begging us to push the price *up,* and we would certainly have pushed the price up if we had had the power to do so. The national budget was in desperate need of the revenues. No one liked or wanted the low oil prices of the mid-late 1980s. Everyone suffered, Saudi Arabia most of all. It was a very bad time."

. . .

Between 1981 and 1986 Saudi oil production would fall from nearly ten million barrels per day to less than four, with a catastrophic impact on government revenues. To start with, the Finance Ministry could draw on its investment reserves, put aside for just such a day as this. For a dozen years the Saudi government had been cautiously piling its surpluses into foreign bonds and currencies, mainly the dollar. But in 1985 the budget tipped from surplus into deficit and the government started to borrow and to draw down still more heavily on the surpluses accumulated in the boom years.

"The money just dried up," recalls one of Fahd's associates. "Things got so tough that ministries had to struggle to pay the salaries at the end of the month."

The once mighty Kingdom was on its way to being a debtor state, and in a government-dominated economy, that meant widespread unemployment and hardship.

The young suffered most. High birthrates and the excellence of the expensive new medical system were producing tens of thousands of young male Saudis with little prospect of suitable or steady work. Thanks to the post-Juhayman "reforms" to the education syllabus, Islamist teaching did less than ever to prepare young minds for the realities of the modern world—and the products of the rote-learning religious colleges were particularly lacking in the practical skills that their society needed. Young Saudis were being taught to scorn what the West was giving them, while also being encouraged to blame the West for their ills.

It was a prescription for trouble. Frustrated in their search for the support and self-respect of a decent living—which would also have enabled them to pay the high Saudi bride price to get married—these young men became easy targets for radicalization, sublimating sexual frustration into religious extremes. As part of the program to make the country more pious, thousands of Koranic study groups had been set up in the early 1980s in mosques and, during the holidays, inside government schools. Koranic recitation competitions featured regularly in the newspapers. Boys who memorized some or all of the Koran were rewarded by the Ministry of Education with awards of one thousand to two thousand riyals ($250 to $500)—money prizes that were especially attractive to children from poor backgrounds. Religious extremists had a field day in these apparently innocent Koranic classes and quizzes, the Saudi equivalent of American spelling bees. They were fertile recruiting grounds for the fundamentalist campaign that was coming to be known as the *sahwah*—"the awakening."

Discontent was not eased by a widespread understanding of how much of the oil boom's revenues had gone into the pockets of those around the king. People could live with royal extravagance in the good times—any self-respecting Saudi family was expected to enrich itself, starting with the family at the top. But with less gravy to go around, resentments were more deeply felt, particularly as Fahd made little apparent effort to check his personal spending. Rumors started to circulate about the favor the king lavished on his latest, prettiest young wife, Al-Johara ("the Jewel") and her son Abdul Aziz, on whom Fahd doted. The boy became known in common gossip as "Azouz" or "Azouzi." A soothsayer was said to have warned the king that he risked being assassinated like his brother Faisal if he did not keep Azouzi beside him wherever he went—which resulted in the eleven-year-old turning up at the White House for the state dinner in honor of his father's visit to Washington in February 1985. The bemused Reagans gave the teenager a model of the U.S. Space Shuttle and sat him beside Sigourney Weaver.

Soothsayers are not uncommon in Saudi Arabia. Newspapers regularly report the arrest of witches and fortune-tellers. As the slump continued and people looked back nostalgically to the boom years of King Khaled, the superstitious started to award Fahd that most damning of titles—an unlucky king.

MODERN SAUDI HISTORY IN FIVE EASY LESSONS

If you did not go hungry in the reign of King Abdul Aziz, you would never go hungry.

If you did not have fun in the reign of King Saud, you would never have fun.

If you did not go to prison in the reign of King Faisal, you would never go to prison.

If you did not make money in the reign of King Khaled, you would never make money.

If you did not go bankrupt in the reign of King Fahd . . .

• • •

What could be done? Some of the younger princes dared to suggest that the time had come to enact the long-promised Basic Law with its Majlis Al-Shura (Consultative Council). This would be one step at least, they argued, toward change and reform. But Fahd would only smile at them.

"I used to say that very same thing to my brother Faisal," he would recall. "I would urge him to sign the Basic Law and enact the Shura Council. But now that I'm in the same position that he was, with the document in front of me, I feel the same doubts. What did my brother know, I wonder, that made him hold back?"

Fahd had, in fact, set in train the construction of a grandly domed building that could house the Consultative Council at some time in the future. Actually to fill the building with argumentative councillors, however, was a step too far. The reluctant reformer decided instead to curry more favor with the religious establishment. In 1984 the presses of Medina's massive $130 million King Fahd Holy Koran Printing Complex rolled into action. That year, and every year thereafter, a free Koran was presented to each of the two million or so pilgrims who came to Mecca to perform their hajj, evidence of Wahhabi generosity that was borne back to every corner of the Muslim community. The Kingdom's seventy or so embassies around the world already featured cultural, educational, and military attachés, along with consular officers who organized visas for the hajj. Now they were joined by religious attachés, whose job was to get new mosques built in their countries and to persuade existing mosques to propagate the dawah wahhabiya.

"No limit," announced a royal directive, "should be put on expenditures for the propagation of Islam." The government allocated more than $27 billion over the years to this missionary fund, while Fahd devoted millions more from his personal fortune to improve the structures of the two holy sites in Mecca and Medina. Vast white marble halls and decorative arches were raised by the Bin Laden company at the king's personal expense to provide covered worshipping space for several hundred thousand more pilgrims.

To set the seal on this campaign, Fahd decided to award himself a new title. King Faisal had liked to be known informally by the ancient style of *khadem,* or servant, of the two holy places—Al-Haramain Al-Sharifain, the mosques of Mecca and Medina. The much-venerated title went back to the time of the caliphs, and in 1986, while opening the new television station in Medina, Fahd announced that he no longer wished to be known as king, but wanted people to address him in future by "this title that is closest to my heart."

His surprise announcement provoked disrespectful ribaldry. "His Majesty says 'Don't Call Me Your Majesty,'" ran the imagined headline of an imaginary Saudi newspaper, while foreign humor concentrated on the

Ministry of Information's decision to upgrade the translation of *khadem* from humble "servant" to the more pompous "custodian." To American ears the result was quite the opposite, since "custodian" conjured up the image of a downtrodden man with a mop and a bucket. A cheeky young U.S. diplomat seized on these janitorial connotations to draw a cartoon that depicted a forlorn-looking king kneeling on the floor in a sleeveless vest and ragged pants, scrubbing away while a long-bearded cleric supervised him sternly.

"Be careful, Fahd," the imam was saying. "Mind that you clean the place properly!"

The point of the cartoon, which hung in a private office in the U.S. consulate in Jeddah for many years, was to wonder who was pulling the strings in Saudi Arabia. The more complex challenge, which involved the essence of Saudi survival, then and now, was to work out how religion could "ground" a fast-changing society with the heavy anchor it needed in a world of flyaway secular tendencies. The ancient and modern contradictions in King Fahd's character were easy to laugh at, but they were the contradictions that lay at the very core of the Saudi soul.

CHAPTER 11

Into Exile

King Fahd liked to start his meetings with a lengthy soliloquy. He would launch into a cascade of thoughts and meditations that could go on for as long as forty minutes, spitting out ideas and volubly soaring with riffs and jinks that displayed the nimbleness of his mind. The royal speeches struck one British ambassador as resembling the diatribes delivered by the soapbox orators at Speaker's Corner in London's Hyde Park—except, of course, that no one in Saudi Arabia was allowed to stand up and deliver speeches in the street. King Fahd was the only soapbox orator in his Kingdom.

The king had another, more practical, speech that he liked to deliver to his provincial governors, less a diatribe than a briefing. Since the days of Abdul Aziz the Kingdom had been administered by local emirs who operated as regional mini-kings, sitting in majlises, hearing grievances, settling disputes, and passing on the regulations that arrived from Riyadh. In the early days these viceroys had often been trusted chieftains and magnates from local tribes, but as the Al-Saud multiplied, increasing numbers of the family were dispatched from Riyadh to the provinces—and were treated, on the whole, to a warm reception. People liked the idea of taking their problems to a prince who could pick up the phone and get straight through to the king or one of his senior brothers.

On this principle, Fahd dispatched his son Mohammed to govern the Eastern Province in 1984. Several years previously, immediately following the riots and bloodshed of 1979, he had tasked his American-educated younger brother Ahmad, the deputy interior minister, to come up with an emergency program of reform.

"We noticed the difference in a year or so," recalls Clive Morgan of the Saudi British Bank. "Money was clearly being spent. The Shia areas of Qateef and Sayhat had always seemed to me the poor relations of the Eastern Province. Now they started getting modern infrastructure—new roads, hospitals, and schools."

Fahd appointed the most successful and dynamic of his sons to take over where Ahmad left off. Deploying his own close family was a generally understood sign of the priority that the king attached to the job. One of the advantages of Fahd's not having Wahhabism in his bloodstream was that he had no particular prejudice against the Shias.

"If you see a poor man come into your majlis, try to speak to him before you speak to the other people," the king told his son. "Never make a decision on the spot. Say you will give your decision later. Never sign a paper sending someone to prison unless you are 100 percent convinced. And once you've signed, don't change your mind. Be solid. You will find that people try to test you."

Fahd was delivering his basic course in local leadership—Saudi Governance 101.

"If you don't know anything about a subject, be quiet until you do. Recruit some older people who can give you advice. And if a citizen comes with a case against the government, take the citizen's side to start with and give the officials a hard time—the government will have no shortage of people to speak for them."

Fahd advised his son to get tribal disputes settled rapidly.

"Try to solve the problem in your private presence, not in front of other people. Take the two men to your office and sit them down quietly. Embrace them warmly—and don't let them leave until they have embraced each other."

For decades the Al-Saud had delegated their authority in the east to a tough old bedouin branch of the family, the Bin Jaluwi, notorious for their tendency to solve local difficulties with hearty lashings and the executioner's sword. Mohammed bin Fahd—whose mother was a Bin Jaluwi*—

*Mohammed bin Fahd's Bin Jaluwi heritage is another example of the Al-Saud's "tribal way." A number of regional governors are related to local magnates and dynasties through their mothers. Prince Saud bin Abdul Muhsin, governor for many years of the northern province of Hail, is descended, via his mother, from the Rasheeds, who ruled Hail before being ousted by the Al-Saud.

would set a very different style. American-educated and smoothly charming, he was at that time the royal family's most successful businessman. His rivals in the Saudi brotherhood of merchants alleged that Mohammed had taken unfair advantage of his royal *wasta* (influence or connections), but they were not averse to using a little wasta of their own. Many a Saudi fortune, royal and nonroyal, derived from the commission charged to foreign businesses in these hectic years of infrastructure building. It was perfectly legal to charge commission—it was compulsory, in fact. Any foreigner who wished to operate in the Kingdom had to share a proportion of his business with a Saudi partner—which effectively put local wasta up for sale.

Now the king told Mohammed to hand the running of his business empire to his brother and sons and to devote his considerable energies to the cajoling of more government money into the east. Following the recommendations of his uncle Ahmad, Shia districts would benefit particularly. When the thirty-four-year-old prince arrived in Dhahran, he also brought an introductory sweetener from his father—a general amnesty for all Shia activists who had been detained since the 1979 riots. Hundreds of prisoners were released.

• • •

Ali Al-Marzouq was one of them. He had been politicized by his experience in the riots and had wasted no time in joining Sheikh Hassan Al-Saffar's IRO, the Islamic Revolution Organization—though he found, once he joined it, that the revolution of the title was intended to be spiritual.

"The Sheikh always told us," remembers Ali, "that our aim must be to seek peace, and that we must learn to handle confrontation, both with other groups and with individuals, in a nonviolent way. We must learn to be calm."

Ali became a dedicated disciple of his leader's seemingly infinite pacifism. Some Westerners compared the tranquil and impassive Al-Saffar to Gandhi, whose philosophy he had studied. The sheikh looked rather like a Buddha as he sat straight-backed and cross-legged on the square cushions of his husayniya, wearing his turban and quietly teaching his followers. But Al-Saffar's approach stemmed more fundamentally from the Shia tradition of quietism exemplified by Husayn at Karbala—the almost masochistic acceptance of whatever disaster life might throw one's way.

"We always tried to follow the example of Husayn," says Ali. "Abu Hadi ["father of Hadi," the pseudonym of Hassan Al-Saffar] told us that acceptance was the way. But we also wanted freedom—freedom to discuss and publish our new ideas about Islam. After the intifada [uprising of 1979] we talked a lot about freedom, and I decided that I wanted to seek freedom for myself, the true, personal, inside freedom that Islam can give to the mind and the spirit. I would become a religious guy."

Ali dropped out of high school and ran away to Kuwait, where there were seminaries that trained young Shia imams.

"My father brought me back [Ali was one of nineteen brothers and sisters—all by the same wife]. He said he wanted me at home and, like a lot of parents at that time, he felt afraid for me and for my questioning ideas. That was a very nervous time. One day my father took all the books and magazines he could find out of the house and buried them in the sand."

In 1982 the nineteen-year-old Ali had gone "up the hill" to take a job at Aramco, whose main offices clustered on the Dammam dome around the oil well that had got the company started nearly half a century earlier. He worked in the transport department for a few months. But that Ramadan he took a holiday, traveling with a group of Islamic Revolutionary friends to the holy city of Mashhad, in northeastern Iran. Every evening they listened to lectures from Al-Saffar, who had fled the Kingdom soon after the intifada, along with the other leaders of the resistance movement. They made up a large and happy group of Shia Saudis, talking about home, fasting, and praying together through the rituals of Ramadan.

"We didn't plot or organize anything," recalls Ali. "But the Mabahith obviously didn't like Shia leaving the country to go and talk with Abu Hadi. They presumed we had signed on as agents for Iran. As I got off the plane in Bahrain coming home, I was arrested."

Saudi intelligence had a strong presence on the minuscule, theoretically independent offshore island that was in the process of being connected to the Saudi mainland by a six-lane causeway. The Mabahith were on the lookout for young Saudis who had taken Iranian money and might be willing to abet the ayatollahs' openly hostile attitude to the Kingdom.

"I had long hair, and the Bahrainis cut it off and stuffed it down my underpants. They also hit me round the head. But that was nothing to what the Saudis did when they got hold of me. The Mabahith kept beat-

The Saudi army on the march in eastern Arabia in 1911 (photographed by Captain William Shakespear, Britain's political agent to Kuwait). Their flag displays the words of the *Shahada*, the Muslim declaration of faith: "There is no god but God, and Mohammed is his Prophet"—the design and wording of the Saudi flag to this day.

Abdul Aziz, "Ibn Saud" (in light robe, third from left), photographed with his family in Riyadh in 1918 by the British explorer and colonial official Harry St. John Philby. In 1979 King Khaled bin Abdul Aziz (born in 1912) recalled posing for this photograph with his father. Khaled is seen here immediately in front of Abdul Aziz, with his elder brother Mohammed to his left.

Oil well number 15 on the hills overlooking Dhahran in eastern Saudi Arabia. Shortly after the discovery of oil in commercial quantities in 1938, King Abdul Aziz ordered that the first oil revenues should be spent on a place of worship for the oil workers, hence the mud domes being built in the foreground—decorative and insulating features of the mosque roof. The white-painted mosque with its multidomed roof stands on the hill to this day. The oil well has since been capped.

King Abdul Aziz "Ibn Saud" meets U.S. president Franklin Delano Roosevelt on board the USS *Quincy* anchored in Egypt's Great Bitter Lake on February 14, 1945—the start of the U.S.-Saudi "special relationship."

An Aramco (Arabian American Oil Company) classroom at Dhahran in the late 1940s. At the typewriter is Ali Al-Naimi (b. 1935), today Saudi Arabia's minister for petroleum and mineral resources.

Ahmad Zaki Yamani, Saudi Oil Minister 1962–86, the "voice of OPEC" in the eyes of the oil-consuming world—charmed by his manner and infuriated by his policies.

Time magazine's view of OPEC (the Organization of Petroleum Exporting Countries) in March 1979, drawn by Don Wright of the *Palm Beach Post*. The price of oil had risen from $2 per barrel on the open market in 1973 to $37 in early 1979.

King Faisal in 1967, the year in which Saudi Arabia joined a short-lived Arab oil boycott of the United States and Britain in protest of their support for Israel in the Six-Day War. In 1973 Faisal would organize his oil boycott of the West more effectively.

King Faisal (second from left) leads the *ardha*, the Al-Saud's traditional sword dance, with his half-brothers and future kings Khaled (left), Fahd (second from right), and Abdullah (far right).

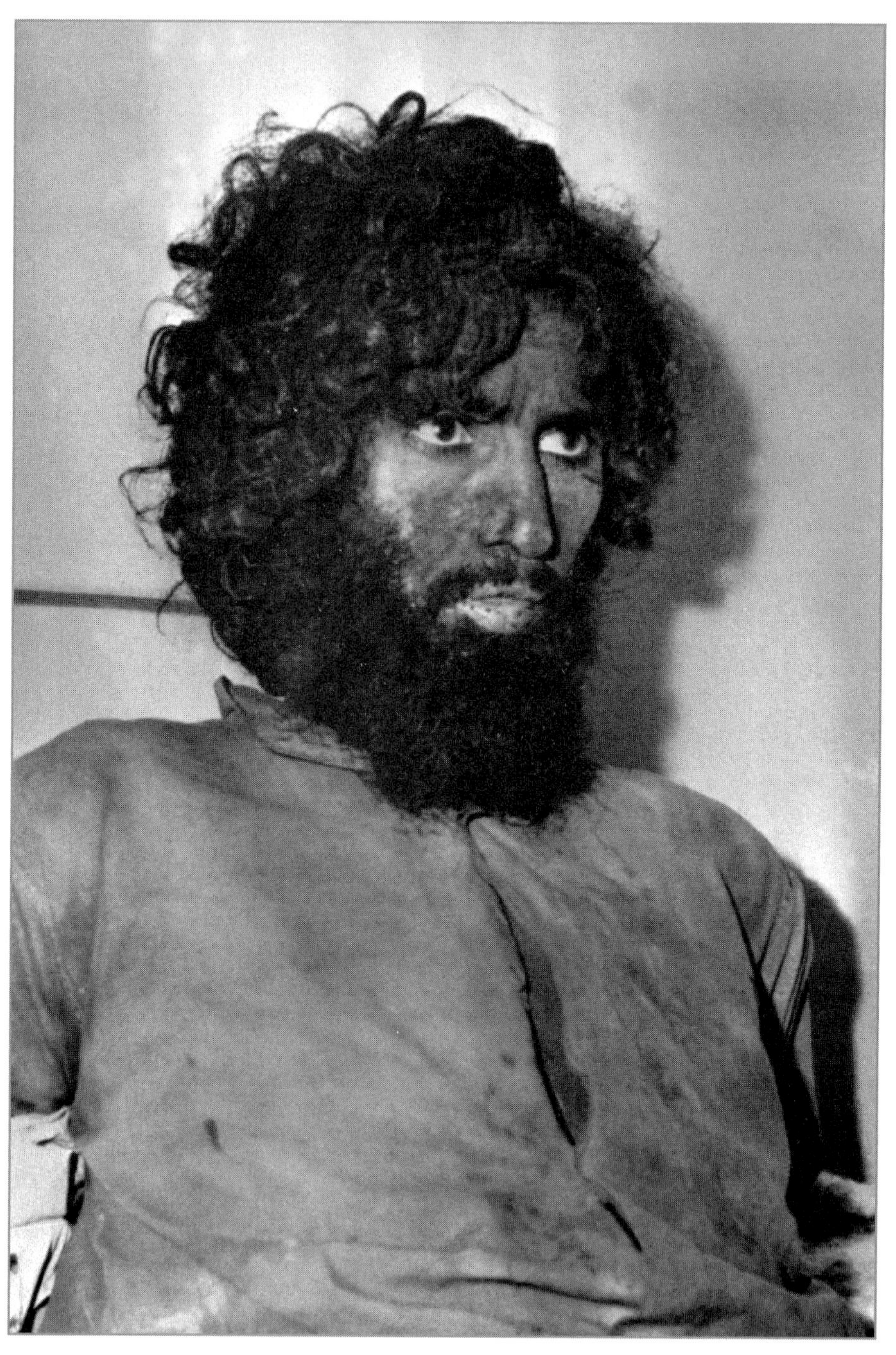

"Angry Face" Juhayman Al-Otaybi photographed after his capture at the end of the Grand Mosque siege in December 1979.

Juhayman's early mentor, the blind Sheikh Abdul Aziz Bin Baz, later grand mufti (principal religious leader) of Saudi Arabia, notorious for having asserted that as he experienced it, the earth was flat.

Juhayman's followers under arrest following the recapture of the Grand Mosque. Sixty-seven were executed with Juhayman on January 9, 1980.

Sheikh Hassan Al-Saffar, spiritual leader of the Shia Muslims living in Qateef and other towns in eastern Saudi Arabia.

Early November 1979—three weeks before the Shia uprising in Qateef. Ali Al-Marzouq, aged 15, delivers a reading in his village mosque in celebration of the Eid Al-Ghadeer, the anniversary of Mohammed's final sermon, in which, Shia believe, the Prophet named his son-in-law Ali as his successor. Sunni Muslims do not accept that Mohammed named Ali as his successor, and do not celebrate the Eid Al-Ghadeer.

ing and beating me on the soles of my feet. I couldn't walk for a week. When they broke one stick, they brought a new one, and when the beating was over, they kept me standing up and awake day after day, night after night. They would not let me sleep. After ten days I gave in and signed what they asked for—a confession that I belonged to the IRO. Straightaway the beatings stopped and they let me go to sleep. That was the end of it. All they'd wanted was that piece of paper. I should have confessed on the first day."

In the course of two years in jail, Ali made many new Shia friends.

"A lot of them had done nothing wrong. None of us had made any plans for bombings or shootings. We were not training or planning for violence. It was crazy to lock us up. At night in my cell I remember hearing men screaming for hours from the beatings. My cousin, the son of my father's sister, lost his mind completely. They let him out early, but he has never been the same again. It was horrible. Shia are usually pretty quiet, conservative guys. But when we came out, it was hard to feel great kindness toward King Fahd and his son."

• • •

Mohammed bin Fahd faced an uphill task as he took up his Eastern Province duties in 1984, for the general bitterness that lingered from the intifada of '79 had been assiduously stoked by pamphlets and broadcasts from Ayatollah Khomeini and the Iranian government. The ayatollah made no secret of his wish to discomfit Saudi authority, and he viewed the Shia worshippers in the Qateef area—around a third of the local population*—as potential allies to his cause. In these years Radio Tehran broadcast regular appeals to Saudi Shias to rise in revolt against their princely "oppressors."

Khomeini particularly resented Saudi claims to the guardianship of the holy places. Since 1980, Iran's now revolutionary pilgrims had been using their annual hajj to promote their cause in Mecca, smuggling in posters of the ayatollah and brandishing them outside the Grand Mosque while shouting derisive slogans. "Fahd, the Israeli Shah" was a favorite. These essentially political demonstrations offended Saudi sensitivities, and,

*In 2007, estimates based on the latest census figures showed a total population in the Eastern Province of 3,400,157, made up of: native Sunni, 1,541,379; native Shia, 914,765; and foreign, 944,013. In Al-Hasa, Shia composed some 40 to 45 percent of the 908,366 inhabitants, and some 87 percent of the 474,573 registered inhabitants of Qateef.

indeed, the feelings of many other Muslims, who felt that the pilgrimage was not the place for advancing the Khomeini cult of personality.

Then in 1986 a consignment of luggage from Tehran was found to include suitcases whose false bottoms had been packed with plastic explosives, and Mohammed bin Fahd was not inclined to take chances. How could he tell which of the local Shia were sleeping with the enemy? IRO followers inside the Kingdom started to feel the heat again, especially since their leaders, Sheikh Hassan and his lieutenants, were all living in Iran with the blessing and support of the Iranian government.

"I heard that my friends were getting taken in for questioning," remembers Ali Al-Marzouq, "and I was not ready for two more wasted years—so much time erased from my life. When I had been in jail before, I was not allowed to read. There were no books. I'd just sat there day after day with my mind going round. Never again—and in 1986 I had just gotten married. So I talked about it with my wife and we decided we would leave. We got fake passports, and drove up to Kuwait. From there we flew to Syria. We both knew it would be a long time. We cried from the bottom of our hearts as we were leaving, but once we had crossed the border I said, 'OK. This is a new life.'"

That did not prove the end of Ali Al-Marzouq's travels. In August 1987 the Iranian demonstrations on the pilgrimage escalated one further and fatal step. Excited Iranians paraded through Mecca proclaiming "God is great! Khomeini is leader!" violating Islamic tradition by carrying knives and sticks beneath their pilgrim towels, according to Egyptian pilgrims who managed to escape the massacre that followed. A total of 275 Iranians, 85 Saudis, and 42 pilgrims of other nationalities were killed, most of them trampled to death in the pileup that resulted from the attempts by the Ministry of the Interior Special Forces to check the demonstration, which had been called by Mehdi Karrubi, Ayatollah Khomeini's personal representative in Mecca. The Saudi government refused to condemn their soldiers' actions. Preserving the peace at Islam's greatest annual gathering was a responsibility they took very seriously. They had no doubt that the Iranian Shia were responsible for the tragedy—and Khomeini responded with fury. He denounced the House of Saud as murderers and called on all loyal Shia in the Kingdom to rise up and overthrow them.

Hassan Al-Saffar and the IRO had had no involvement in the Mecca tragedy, nor had any Shia from the east. But Khomeini's incitement to revolt put them in an impossible position—they were forced to take sides.

"We were not willing to be the tool of a foreign government," remembers Sheikh Hassan today. "There were a number of people in authority in Iran who wanted to recruit us against the Saudi government. They came to us—they made quite a few approaches to us. But we told them that we wished to remain independent."

His aide Jaffar Shayeb did the political talking on the sheikh's behalf.

"We listened to what they said," says Shayeb of the Iranians. "But we were never willing to be part of their games."

From the moment of his arrival in Iran, Al-Saffar had made clear his disagreement with the most radical of the Ayatollah Khomeini's ideas—the doctrine that the ulema (religious scholars) are qualified not simply to advise the ruler, but to exercise government in their own right. This is the revolutionary concept—Khomeini's own—that justifies Iran's "government of the godly." The executive power held by Iran's clerics sets Iran apart from any Muslim government in history, and the doctrine was perceived as deeply subversive by the House of Saud. Sheikh Hassan Al-Saffar agreed with Riyadh.

"This is not in the Koran, nor in the Prophet's teachings in the Hadith," he says. "The scholars give advice to the ruler. They do not rule."

Al-Saffar gave the order for his followers to leave Iran, and the Saudi Shia were once again on their travels. They could not stay in Iran, but they could not return home either. Late in 1987 the entire community of exiles started packing their bags and dispersed to Syria, Cyprus, London, and Washington.

Ali Al-Marzouq was sent to Cyprus to coordinate the IRO's press activities, where he and his wife survived on a meager stipend from the organization, plus whatever help their families could send them.

"Sometimes the money arrived," Ali remembers. "Sometimes it didn't. If we were lucky, we could afford one chicken per month. My wife became very good at cooking biryani—with lots of rice."

Back in the Kingdom, meanwhile, Prince Mohammed bin Fahd continued with his program of Eastern Province reform and infrastructure building—though in the absence of senior Shia figures he could hardly accomplish the high-level talking and conciliation for which his father wished. Saudi Arabia was not operating in a vacuum. It was living in a dangerous neighborhood where people and events outside its borders could have unforeseen consequences back home.

CHAPTER 12

The Dove and the East Wind

When Prince Khaled bin Sultan was studying air-defense tactics in the early 1980s at the Air War College in Maxwell, Alabama, he regularly took part in war games. A few years later he found himself on the edge of the real thing. On June 6, 1984, the prince was flying in a helicopter over the port of Jubail in eastern Saudi Arabia when his radio picked up the voice of an Iranian fighter pilot who was talking excitedly to his base. The Iranian had just flown his F-4 fighter onto the wrong side of the "Fahd line," the air frontier that the Saudis had defined down the center of the Gulf as the Iran-Iraq War heated up.

The purpose of the Fahd line was to provide Saudi air defenses with more reaction time. Unauthorized planes that crossed the line would be shot down, Riyadh had warned, and this pilot had already been given two warnings. Alerted by their AWACS patrols, manned at that time by U.S. Air Force personnel, the Saudi Air Force had already put two of their own F-15 fighters in the air. When the Iranian ignored their requests and kept his plane plowing onward toward the Saudi coast—and the Saudi oil fields—the reaction was uncompromising. One of the F-15s shot the intruder down. The Iranian's radio cut off as his fighter spiraled down into the sea.

It was a crisp and effective Saudi victory, but it raised worrying issues. The dogfight was part of what became known as the "Tanker War," in which Iranian planes menaced ships that were carrying oil not only from Iraq but from Iraq's two major allies and bankers, Kuwait and Saudi Arabia. This was a threat to the entire world economy—any trouble in the Straits of Hormuz could disrupt oil supplies for weeks—and King

Fahd sent an urgent appeal to the White House. The Reagan administration responded promptly, shipping four hundred short-range ground-to-air Stinger missiles to Riyadh, along with an air force aerial tanker that could extend the patrolling and fighting distance of the Saudi fighter planes.

But the president had sold these weapons to Saudi Arabia without consulting Congress, and the lawmakers were furious. The Stingers were particularly effective missiles. What if the Saudis passed on a few to their Palestinian friends? When the Kingdom presented a formal application later that summer to purchase a range of weaponry that included advanced F-15 fighter jets and Lance surface-to-surface missiles, the reaction was hostile. Israel made clear that it did not want to see such powerful weaponry in Saudi hands. The Kingdom had been obstructive of the Camp David process, and there was a widespread perception that, sooner or later, the Al-Saud would go the way of the Shah.

The pro-Israeli grouping that Bandar bin Sultan had so narrowly outmaneuvered to secure the AWACS sale four years earlier regrouped with renewed determination. This time the Saudi sale would not pass. In 1985 the chances of Ronald Reagan actually accomplishing the downfall of the "Evil Empire" still seemed less than plausible, even to those who agreed with his ambitions, and the Saudi contribution to America's secret wars remained hidden by necessity. The president could not, for example, reveal that the pro-Palestinian Kingdom of Saudi Arabia had, with his blessing, already purchased Stinger missiles by the hundreds and then passed them on to the freedom fighters of Angola and Afghanistan.

The Saudi arms package stalled in Congress, and in February 1985 Reagan reluctantly admitted defeat. To procure their planes, Bandar and his father, Prince Sultan, the defense minister, turned to Mrs. Thatcher's Britain, where, within months, they negotiated a multibillion-pound package—the Al-Yamamah deal—to acquire Tornado fighter-bombers and other weaponry, and also to build some military bases.

"That woman," Bandar liked to say of the British prime minister, "was a hell of a man."

At the time, the Al-Yamamah contract was said to be worth some $5 billion. By the year 2000 it had escalated to tens of billions as air base construction and service contracts were written in—more than the Kingdom had by that date expended on every U.S. military purchase in its history.

"My friends, let me tell you, we are not masochists," said Bandar, explaining to a group of McDonnell Douglas executives why the Saudis had so dramatically diverted their petrodollars away from the U.S. defense industry. "We don't like to spend billions of dollars and get insulted in the process."

• • •

The Al-Yamamah deal has become notorious. Perhaps, with hindsight, it was asking for trouble to name history's largest ever bilateral weapons deal after the bird of peace (*al-yamamah* in Arabic means "the dove"). It was certainly foolish of British Aerospace (which later became BAe Systems), the manufacturer of the Tornado fighter, to allow the setting up of a fun-and-games fund for prominent Saudis when they came to London, and for their travel agent to list every detail of how they spent it in meticulous ledgers that would later find their way to the newspapers. Thus in July 2004, the readers of the *Sunday Times* were able to read how, over a thirteen-year period, Peter Gardiner, a St. Albans travel consultant, spent £60 million supplying Saudi royals and dignitaries with chartered yachts in Cannes, whole floors of the world's top hotels, including the Plaza in New York and the George V in Paris, and luxury cars, including the gift of a £170,000 Rolls-Royce to one lucky princess.

Joining in the fun, the glamorous Miss Anouska Bolton-Lee told the readers of the *Mail on Sunday* how her charming Saudi prince, Turki bin Nasser, deputy commander of the Saudi Air Force and brother-in-law of Prince Bandar, had set her up in a Holland Park apartment for which the not unreasonable rent of £13,000 a year was paid—and had also helped with her education. Life on the Al-Yamamah payroll was not all Cristal champagne and Dolce & Gabbana sheepskin coats at £12,000 a pop, she explained: the arms company had generously put her through drama school, financing a two-year course at the prestigious Lee Strasberg Institute, whose speciality was Method acting.

It was Bandar bin Sultan's freewheeling lifestyle that carried the highest price tag: £75 million for a top-of-the-range wide-bodied Airbus jet, capable of seating some two hundred passengers—or one Saudi prince and his friends. Legally the jet was not Bandar's property: it was registered to the Saudi Air Force. But Bandar used it for personal and family trips as he wished, and he had the aircraft painted blue and silver, the livery of his favorite football team, the Dallas Cowboys.

"Yes. So what?" was Bandar's unapologetic reply to an interviewer who asked him if there was corruption in Saudi Arabia—and his lawyers hastily added that the prince did not consider the Al-Yamamah deal to be corrupt. All the gifts and side payments transferred through the contract—said to total £1 billion paid in batches of £30 million per quarter for more than a decade to Riggs Bank, Washington—had been approved by the Saudi Ministry of Defense (headed by his father, Prince Sultan). Bandar had personal charge of the Riggs account, but it was not "a corrupt personal benefit." It was "Saudi government money from start to finish," he explained, and he embarked on a robust defense of what he received and spent in an authorized biography by William Simpson, an old friend from his RAF fighter pilot days.

Far from being corrupt, Al-Yamamah was "a utopian arrangement," according to Simpson, citing "sources close to Bandar" to explain the "ingenious diversity of Al-Yamamah." The side payments from the contract provided some of the untraceable cash Saudi Arabia needed to fund its secret battles with Communism from Chad to Afghanistan. Using bartered oil and offshore bank accounts, Al-Yamamah was designed to produce large sums of money of which there was no government record. The prince might fly his Airbus to St. Lucia, Honolulu, and his luxurious home in Aspen, but he also used it for the official shuttle diplomacy that took him to London, Paris, and Moscow on the Kingdom's behalf. One trip of which Bandar was particularly proud was his secret 1983 journey to Rome, on which, he claimed, he had handed over a suitcase containing $10 million to a priest in the Vatican Bank. This was before Al-Yamamah increased the prince's cash flow, but it demonstrated, in his eyes, the usefulness of money that was off the books. In this case, according to Bandar, the Saudi $10 million went to the Christian Democrats' election campaign that helped keep the powerful Italian Communist Party at bay—though his claim is impossible to verify, and the Vatican has always denied it.

Bandar was saying, though Simpson did not put it this clearly, that the Saudi government knowingly paid BAe vastly more than their actual weaponry was worth, then requested BAe to give the overpayment back to them to use for purposes ranging from the subversion of Communist governments to fun and games in Holland Park. According to Bandar, his government was quite happy with this.

"The Defense Ministry audited and approved every penny," says one of his aides.

By this account, the Saudis were, in effect, bribing themselves. But they were also cheating themselves, since money that was spent on mistresses or family plane journeys rather than on, say, notional anti-Communist activities, was being embezzled from the Saudi state.

As Bandar saw it, Al-Yamamah had nothing to do with anybody but Saudi Arabia, and he could not see what the British press was complaining about when the story broke in 2004. It had not cost Britain a penny. Presents and favors were part of the traditional method of doing business at all levels in the Middle East. Why should Britain complain if the Kingdom chose to overpay for British armaments and to breathe some life into the moribund UK defense industry? It would have died without Al-Yamamah. For more than twenty years the contract had kept thousands of doughty Lancashire workers in the money producing Tornado fighter planes and Hawk trainers at the BAe factory in Warton, on the edge of Preston—a rust-belt town whose fortunes would be very different without the billions pumped into the local economy by Saudi Arabia.

Arguing his corner, Bandar liked to finish up with the aircraft themselves. If the Kingdom had succeeded in its original bid to push the purchase of F-15s through Congress, he would explain, all the planes would have had to carry armament restrictions to placate the Israelis. For the same reason they could have been configured only as defensive, fighter-interceptors. But under the terms of Al-Yamamah, forty-eight of the seventy-two Tornados purchased by the Saudis were advanced-strike fighters without deployment restrictions, and all the Hawks had attack capacity. In the context of defending his country, the prince considered his duty more than done. He saw no need to apologize for a blue and silver Airbus—nor even for the Method acting lessons of Miss Anouska Bolton-Lee.

• • •

The Iran-Iraq War of 1980–88 was a beastly and bloody business. Hundreds of thousands of ill-trained young men went to their deaths in its World War I–style trenches and "human wave" bayonet charges—a tragedy in which, after 1983, Saudi Arabia and the United States were both complicit. When Iran launched a successful counterassault in that year against Saddam Hussein's unprovoked invasion of September 1980, the

Saudis financed the Iraqi leader as a Sunni Arab "brother." Saddam was the best available barrier to the scary prospect of the ayatollahs taking power in Baghdad, while the United States backed the Iraqi tyrant as part of Washington's enduring attempt to gain some redress for the humiliation of the Iranian hostage crisis of 1979–81.

In 1985 the conflict went literally ballistic, when the two protagonists started launching Soviet Scud missiles at each other's capitals. This so-called War of the Cities gave added urgency to Saudi Arabia's wish to boost its air defenses, since the Kingdom had no missiles with which to defend itself or to serve as a deterrent. Al-Yamamah had supplied fighter planes and conventional weaponry, but where could the Kingdom locate the equivalent of the Lance missiles whose sale Congress had blocked? The ever-resourceful Prince Bandar found an answer—in Communist China. Saudi Arabia was already financing Chinese weapons sales to Iraq and was allowing the shipments to travel overland through Saudi territory. Why not increase the shipments to include some Chinese CSS-2 Dongfong ("East Wind") missiles, Bandar suggested to his uncle Fahd. The missiles could be discreetly off-loaded into Saudi care before they reached the Iraqi border. As the prince later explained with glee: "I came and asked my friends, the Americans, for missiles—a ground-to-ground missile with an eighty-mile range called the Lance. But we were told no, because it's a threat to somebody [Israel]. So we went and got a sixteen-hundred-mile-range missile."

This was not, in fact, as clever as it sounded. Sixteen hundred miles meant that, fired from Riyadh, China's East Wind missiles could hit not only Baghdad and Tehran, but Egypt, Libya, Turkey, Pakistan, western India, much of east and central Africa, and, most crucially, any city or settlement in Israel—the equivalent, by the mid 1980s, of threatening American soil. Saudi acquisition of these lumbering super-Scuds would represent a colossal change in the Middle East balance of power, particularly since the CSS-2s were configured to carry nuclear warheads—which made Bandar's next move particularly cheeky. Having heard that Iran was seeking to buy Chinese weapons, he claims that he secured a meeting with U.S. secretary of state George Shultz. Shultz says he has no recollection of this meeting.

"Would it be OK," Bandar says he asked Shultz, "if we go to China and make them an offer they can't refuse—that we will buy all the weapons they were going to sell to Iran and then give them to Iraq?"

In discussing the details of how to acquire China's missiles, Fahd had given his nephew strict instructions: he must not tell any direct lies to the Americans, and Bandar felt that his proposition met that test. Shultz would appear to have felt otherwise, however, when he discovered what Bandar actually did. Having obtained some sort of American blessing, the prince flew to Beijing, where he did the small-arms deal as proposed—but also laid the groundwork for the purchase of some twenty-five nuclear-capable, sixteen-hundred-mile-range East Wind missiles, complete with launchers and trainers, for an estimated $3 billion.

• • •

The job of completing the deal and installing the missiles secretly was handed to Bandar's half brother Khaled, the chief of Saudi air defense who had listened on his helicopter radio to the downing of the Iranian pilot at the opening of the Tanker War. A tough and meaty figure, Khaled had survived the humbling rigors of Sandhurst to come home and specialize in air defense. Having studied in U.S. missile schools, he was the ideal person to execute the East Wind project, and he took particular pleasure in the secrecy involved—on one visit to Hong Kong his Chinese counterparts, fearing hidden cameras, arrived with aluminum-foil-lined umbrellas, which they opened and held over their documents while trying to negotiate in whispers.

In Saudi Arabia, the arrival and the installation of the missiles had to be arranged when there was no U.S. surveillance overhead.

"We knew the timings of the satellite," remembers the prince. "We knew when it was coming over."

The Saudi troops who were assigned to the East Wind project vanished so effectively, their families assumed they must have been sent on a secret mission to help the Afghani mujahideen, a rumor that Khaled encouraged. Some enterprising wives got hold of his private number.

"By our religion, you must inform us if our men are dead," they told him.

"By our religion," he replied, "I swear that they are alive. I will divorce my wife if they are dead—and I am telling you that with her sitting beside me."

As air-defense commander, the prince had proposed that the installation of the missiles should be revealed once they were operational with their crews fully trained, sometime around the middle of 1989—the whole point of a deterrent was that enemies should be aware of its existence and power. But the news broke fifteen months earlier. According to one account, American alarm bells started ringing when a satellite analyst studying pictures of a high-security missile base in China spotted a delegation of men in beards.*

"Nuclear weapons, for fuck's sake!" exploded Richard Murphy, assistant secretary of state for the Middle East, when he confronted Bandar bin Sultan with the satellite pictures. George Shultz cut off all links with the prince—he had never spent much time with Bandar in any case. If the Saudi ambassador had anything to say, he could talk to a desk officer. Given the scale of the deception, the secretary of state saw no reason to believe Saudi assurances that they had paid extra money to have the missiles adapted for non-nuclear warheads. Washington was furious from the White House to Congress.

"Congratulations," sniffed Richard Armitage, the assistant secretary of defense, to Bandar. "You've just put yourselves squarely at the top of the Israelis' targeting package. If the balloon goes up anywhere in the Middle East, you're going to get hit first."

In American eyes, Riyadh's sneaking of the East Wind missiles into range of Israeli territory was a smaller version of the Cuban missile crisis of 1962—except that the smuggling had been done by a nation that claimed to be a loyal friend. Even the urbane Colin Powell lost his cool.

"You guys have done something really stupid," he has recalled yelling to Bandar. "You'd better hope the Israelis don't bomb it—but I don't think they will, because it's not a very good system you've bought."

The East Wind missile system was, indeed, slow to load with liquid fuel and notoriously inaccurate, which is why it was a serious threat only when carrying nuclear warheads. Lucky to land within a mile of its target, the CSS-2 was scarcely worth firing with conventional warheads, and Israel showed its scorn by sending strike aircraft to "buzz" Saudi airfields. Flying low over the ground, the Israelis released empty fuel tanks (inscribed

*A U.S. official based in the Kingdom offers a more prosaic explanation. He says that the base was stumbled on by accident when a young U.S. diplomat took his girlfriend camping in the desert south of Riyadh.

with Hebrew characters) to prove they could drop real bombs there anytime they chose.

King Fahd sent Ronald Reagan his personal assurance that the missiles did not carry nuclear warheads and that they would not be used for a first strike on Israel, adopting a considerably humbler tone than he was employing in public. But the State Department was not mollified. When Philip Habib, Reagan's Middle East envoy, went to meet Fahd in April 1988 to discuss Israel, Palestine, and Lebanon, he was accompanied by Hume Horan, the recently arrived U.S. ambassador, who insisted on raising the missile question the moment that Habib had finished his business. Horan was a master Arabist, and he was just launching eloquently into his official protest when the king exploded in fury. The ambassador was back in Washington within a week.

The curious story was put about that Horan was sent home because King Fahd "did not like his Arabic," and that was true in a way. Yet like everything to do with the East Wind affair, this was only part of the story. In the long-running U.S.-Saudi marriage of convenience, Riyadh's acquiring of Chinese weaponry had to be rated a serious and deliberately pursued infidelity—though, once the ritual pots and pans had been flung, the dysfunctional marriage jogged along very much as before. The couple clearly met each other's basic needs more than either of them cared to admit.

So far as is known, Saudi Arabia's East Wind missiles remain in service, and on standby, to this day. The Saudi government continues to deny that the missiles' warheads are nuclear.

CHAPTER 13

Vacationing Jihadi

Khaled Bahaziq and his wife first went to Peshawar, near the Afghan border, for a working holiday in the mid-1980s. "We wanted to work with the refugees for a week or so," remembers Khaled. "We experienced the Russian invasion as something personal. It was an attack upon our brother Muslims, and we wanted to help. Our own government was making it so easy. They were giving big discounts on air tickets. You just needed a letter from one of the relief organizations. Quite a number of our friends were there."

Among those friends was Osama Bin Laden, who had recently opened a guesthouse in Peshawar, Bayt Al-Ansar, the "House of the Helpers." In Islamic history the *ansar* were the helpers who welcomed Mohammed to Yathrib and gave him shelter when he left Mecca. Osama welcomed Arab volunteers who had come to Pakistan to do relief work among the Afghanis. At this stage there were only a few Arabs who had actually come to fight.

"When Osama talked about jihad in those days," remembers Bahaziq, "it was more about building than fighting. He was gentle and rather quiet, with this deep, slow voice that came up from his chest. You could not see him going to the battlefield. I thought he was very soft and unwarlike. At this stage he was just starting to bring in his company's construction equipment, sending machines over the border to build roads for the mujahideen. It was good to see him again after Jeddah. We had long conversations about the jihad and the importance of implementing Islamic values. I found it very, very comforting to feel part of the jihad, and he felt the same.

"Don't forget that in those days Osama was not a villain, and he was not in any way anti-Saudi. Quite the opposite. He was a hero of the community, using his wealth to help a noble cause that was supported by the Saudi government—and by the American government as well. The Muslims saw the fight as strengthening Islam. The West saw it as a battle to bring down Communism. In those days everyone was fixated on kicking out the Russians. I don't remember anyone who looked ahead and saw a clash.

"Osama and I would pray together. We were friends and more than friends—our families both came up from Yemen in the early days. When we were kids we would go horseback riding together, doing jumps on a spare piece of land that we owned. Osama was always very athletic. He was the first person I remember—Muslim or non-Muslim—who insisted on eating and drinking things that were pure and natural. After our riding I would offer him fruit juice from the fridge at my house and he'd refuse. 'This has got preservative,' he'd say."

In Peshawar Bin Laden had teamed up with Abdullah Azzam, the inspirational Palestinian *jihadi* from the Jeddah and Mecca university campuses. Azzam had set up his own Afghan relief network, the Maktab Al-Khadamat (Office of Services), to welcome Saudi volunteers and money. He would accommodate volunteers in the frontier town, then channel them off to the training camps in Afghanistan and the Khyber Pass, which opened just nine miles to the west.

"Azzam was another man of principle," remembers Bahaziq. "He was very handsome, with his bushy, gray beard. I really loved the moments I had with him. He was always smiling—very calm, not stern. I'd met him when he came lecturing in America in the 1970s. Now he was putting his ideas into practice. He was helping jihad on the ground."

Azzam's Office of Services produced pamphlets and newspaper articles, drumming up international support for the Afghan war effort, and Khaled Bahaziq was one of those who responded. In the course of the 1980s he made no less than ten trips from Jeddah to Peshawar—like many Saudis, a vacationing jihadi.

"I'd buy my weapon when I got to the border. There was a huge weapons souk outside Peshawar—the guns were hanging there in rows, hundreds of them. You could buy any weapon you fancied, and go on your way. I would always get a Kalashnikov. It cost a thousand riyals [about three hundred dollars]. I would use it while I was there, then, when I left, I'd give it as a present to one of the Afghan brothers. Across the border there were lots of stalls selling hashish and opium flowers—very beautiful looking. But that was not for true jihadis, not in any way. I'd rent a car, or sometimes I'd buy one that I'd sell when I went home. If I was going up to the northeast where the roads were not paved, I would get a four-wheel drive, a Toyota or a jeep."

Bahaziq had a job as a university lecturer in Jeddah, as well as a share in a medical supplies business with his brother-in-law. His brother was a full-time mujahid, one of the small group of "Arab Afghans" who were fighting their own battle against the Russians.

"When I went to the front, it was a very good feeling. I had a sensation of calmness and peace. Jihad was doing God's work, and I felt very close to God. I always felt—and my brother used to say this—that we were defenders. We were not there to kill, but to defend. There was great fellowship, we were all brothers, with a lot of joking. I used to make this life-size human dummy: it had a headdress that made it look like an Afghan, so I would stick it up over the trench and the Russians would fire at it. We laughed and teased each other—we felt very easy with the bullets flying around. If one of them caught us, we knew it would take us to heaven. I remember one expedition in the mountains where we had no jeeps. We had our weapons on donkeys, and it got dark and cold. One of the young guys decided to give his donkey a name—Nadia. 'Please, Nadia,' he said, 'come into the cave with me, just for warmness. I'm not married, and I want the feeling that I have a woman to keep me warm.'"

Bahaziq brought his wife to vacation with him on several occasions, taking her into the firing zone.

"So my wife, you could say, is also a terrorist. One day I was teaching her how to throw hand grenades. I had one in my hand with the pin out, holding it tight so it would not explode. 'Am I your king?' I asked her. 'Am I your master on the earth? If I release this, what happens after three seconds will be horrible—worse than death.' 'Please, Khaled,' she said, pleading with me, 'please, yes indeed, you are my master.' So I threw the grenade far away and it exploded. 'Right,' she said, taking a grenade for herself and pulling out the pin. 'Now let *me* tell you who *you* are.'"

Coming and going, often during his Ramadan holidays, and sometimes bringing his children, whom he would leave in one of the Peshawar guesthouses, the vacationing jihadi had no illusions as to who were the serious warriors in the battle against the Russians.

"The Afghans were like their goats, scaling the mountains so nimbly. Somehow they always got themselves up above the Russians, firing down on them in their tanks. They had such toughness. They did not show pain. I remember one had had his finger cut off, and I was dressing that wounded hand with a bandage. Meanwhile, he had his walkie-talkie in the other hand and was giving out orders. Another time I was with an Arab and an Afghan when both of them got shot. At once the Arab started rolling on the ground screaming. The Afghan just looked at him."

• • •

For several years Osama Bin Laden was an armchair warrior, traveling to Peshawar to bring money and supplies, helping the mujahideen with his road-making work, but not actually joining the Afghans on the field of battle. Later he confessed his shame that he had not been braver—"I asked forgiveness from God Almighty," he wrote in one account that he prepared for Abdullah Azzam, "feeling that I had sinned."

But in 1986 he started work building a military base, a camp to house several dozen Arab fighters, near the Afghan village of Jaji, about ten miles from the Pakistani border. It was a turning point in his career—it brought him into contact with real fighting. The following summer Soviet jets made a series of attacks on the camp, diving down on Jaji, their engines screaming. The lanky young Saudi, now thirty years old, dived for cover as the shells rained down.

"The mountains were shaking from the bombardment," as he later described it. "The missiles that landed outside the camp were making a huge noise that covered the sound of the mujahideen cannon as if they did not exist. Bear in mind that if you heard those sounds alone, you might say there could not be anything louder! As to the missiles that landed inside the camp, thanks to God, they did not explode. They landed as iron lumps. I felt closer to God than ever."

By Bin Laden's melodramatic account, the mujahideen cannon managed to bring down four Soviet planes.

"I saw with my own eyes the remains of [one of] the pilots—three fingers, a part of a nerve, the skin of one cheek, an ear, the neck, and the skin of the back. Some Afghan brothers came and took a photograph of him as if he were a slaughtered sheep! We cheered."

Osama described the battles of Jaji to the young journalist Jamal Khashoggi, who had come out to write about the Arab Afghans for *Al-Majallah* magazine.

"He was very proud," remembers Khashoggi. "He showed me how he'd figured out that he could defend the whole valley from a certain vantage point. The Afghans, he said, did not think tactically like that."

Like Khaled Bahaziq, Bin Laden was full of admiration for the bravery of the Afghan fighters. Unlike the Arabs—and Bin Laden himself—they had not dived for the trenches. They had stood their ground, firing up at the infidels, serene in their faith, accepting life or death as it was dealt to them.

"Reliance upon God is the main source of our strength," Bin Laden told Khashoggi. "These trenches and tunnels are merely the military facilities God asked us to make. We depend completely on God in all matters."

Osama was coming to feel that his life—and death—was totally in God's hands.

"I became more convinced of the fact," he later wrote, "that no one could be injured except by God's will."

When a Russian mortar shell fell at his feet shortly after this, he waited fatalistically for it to explode and kill him.

"I felt *sakina* [serenity]," he later told the British journalist Robert Fisk—*sakina* being the Islamic concept that removes you mentally from the material aspects of the world. Linked with God in another existence, you feel elevated, exhilarated—quite indifferent to whether you live or die. It is the nirvana to which suicide bombers aspire.

"It was quite clear talking to him," said Fisk, "that this was a very important moment in his life—he had conquered fear and the fear of death. And once you do that, you start discovering that perhaps you love death . . ."

. . .

The Soviet attacks on Jaji were Osama's baptism of fire, launching his career as a holy warrior. The Saudi press took up the story, glorifying "Abu Abdullah" ("Father of Abdullah," Osama's jihadi name) and also the role of the young Saudis who fought beside him—as many as ten thousand according to an Interior Ministry survey of exit-stamp destinations in the 1980s. This scarcely compared to the 175,000 to 250,000 native Afghans estimated to have been fighting the Soviets, but the Saudis had given lavishly (with America) to support the war, and some of the payment was in blood. The bodies of the Arab dead were dispatched home in cold storage, embalmed in sweet-smelling fluid whose scent consoled grieving parents, convincing them that their sons had died martyrs.

It was a new and very pleasant sensation for Arabs to feel they had played their part in a military victory. "Progressive" Arab leaders like Nasser and Sadat had flung well-armed Arab armies against Israel, and had delivered humiliation. They had not included religion in their strategy. But now victory was going to those who grounded themselves in Islam. Small and simple groups of holy warriors were humbling one of the world's two superpowers. God was smiling on the faithful in the mountains—as He was also smiling on the domestic jihad that was restoring godliness to Saudi society.

• • •

The Sahwah—the Awakening—was coming good. As the 1980s progressed, the tone of Saudi preachers grew sharper in the Friday pulpits, and their sermons circulated through a jazzy new medium—compact recording cassettes. Once condemned as vehicles for decadent Western music, cassette tapes were now welcomed as a way of spreading the word of God. Popular sermons sold in the thousands through stalls in the souk, along with stories of the Prophet and early Islam. Young devotees collected and swapped these cassettes the way their Western contemporaries collected Michael Jackson tapes. There was an exciting sense of momentum—and some of these preachers were extremely young men.

• • •

Mansour Al-Nogaidan, aged eighteen, was an eloquent young preacher from the town of Buraydah in Qaseem, the Wahhabi heartland two hundred miles north of Riyadh. To this day the sheikhs of Qaseem consider themselves the true keepers of the Wahhabi flame, proudly showing visitors the small, conical mosque, an oversize beehive made of mud where, they say, Abdul Wahhab stayed at least once when he came to Qaseem to carry out his mission. In all the Arabian Peninsula, they believe, they remain the most faithful to the monotheistic, reforming truth of the Wahhabi mission.

Not surprisingly, in 1979 Qaseem had contributed a generous number of supporters to the cause of Juhayman. Mansour Al-Nogaidan can remember his classmates bunking off school in the early days of 1980 to watch their execution. Age eleven at the time, he was too nervous to join them.

"The beheading platform was only four hundred yards from our school," he recalls "But my knees would not allow me to go."

Juhayman's movement had been explained to Mansour and his friends in terms of black magic.

"His hands were tied behind his back, according to our teachers, because if he were let loose he could fly. He was the bogeyman. Mothers told their children that Juhayman would come and get them if they did not behave and go to bed."

From his early teens, Mansour was proud to consider himself a Salafi, memorizing the Koran, attending extra lectures at the mosque, and drifting into the orbit of the local fundamentalist preachers who called for the destruction of television as the machine of the Devil. Inspired, the boy would secretly pour water through the holes in the back of the family television set. The antihierarchical nature of Salafism made the movement deeply appealing to the teenage rebel in search of a cause.

Salafism also played on the fears of a scared inner child. At the religious summer camps that Mansour attended, adult teachers deliberately cultivated their charges' fantasies about heaven and hell.

"After listening to the teachings, my mind would dwell on the scorpions and spiders in hell, and the two blue angels who would be coming to my grave to take me to the fire. I would go to bed crying and scared."

Abdullah Thabit, a young Salafi recruited in Asir in these years, remembers actually being taken to his grave.

"I had this mentor—each new recruit had one. After dark he would drive me to the cemetery and instruct me to lie down in one of the freshly dug graves. I would shiver there in the darkness looking up at the stars, while he terrified me with tales of hellfire and the tortures that awaited me if I did not find the way to God."

The mentor also, however, offered his young charge a personalized, fatherly protection against these ultimate fears—a crucial element in Islamist recruitment tactics. While ostensibly anti-Western, the recruiters deployed Western parenting techniques, extending to vulnerable youngsters a one-on-one warmth, interest, and support that contrasted sharply with the authoritarian style of traditional Saudi fathers, who doled out whatever personal affection they had to offer among numerous wives and a large brood of children. Mansour Al-Nogaidan found his own way to God revealed when he was coming down the steps of the mosque and felt his shoulders being held warmly by a venerable and kindly old sheikh.

"He had a 'white face,'" Mansour remembers. "That's an expression we use for someone whose faith is shining out of their features."

This man, Sheikh Mohammed Al-Saqaabi, was famous in Buraydah for following the ways of the Prophet in the most literal possible fashion, living in a mud hut without electricity and shunning the motorcar to travel by horse and buggy.

"'Look, my son,' he said to me. 'I'm sure you're attending the public education [the local state school], and I am here to tell you that is the worst thing that can happen to you. You must leave, and attend more of these lectures at the mosque. Your family will get angry with you, but you are here on this earth to satisfy God.'"

Mansour's family was, indeed, as angry as the sheikh predicted. His mother wept, and his brothers threatened to beat him and drag him back from the madmen into whose hands he had fallen. Many ordinary Saudis did not sign on to the extremism of the Sahwah. But the "awakening" was smiled upon by the religious establishment, and—like the jihad in Afghanistan—its agencies received easy support from the rich and vicariously pious: there was no shortage of funds to print pamphlets and circulate cassettes. The government gave no sign that it discouraged the development of this mystical and rather wild strand in national life. On the contrary, King Fahd had denounced the "lost" youth of the West: he could only approve, surely, of young Saudi men becoming *more* religious—while for the young men themselves, the confident certainties of fundamentalism offered comforting solutions and a clear way ahead through the confusions that afflict any teenager.

"It now seems to me," says Mansour, "that I struck a sort of deal with God—that He would take away my personal fears and worries if I gave up everything to devote myself to Him, following the Salafi way. That was the bargain: if I lived like the Prophet, I would find peace of mind. And in due course, after several years, I myself could become a 'sheikh.'"

Mansour left home to go and live with the local Salafis, the "Brothers of Buraydah," a community of fundamentalists who occupied their own particular corner of town—three hundred families or so, with their own school and mosques. In front of the family his father had sternly warned Mansour that he would be on his own if he left. But he clearly sympathized with his son's religious direction: he secretly bought the boy books and helped him out financially for a year, until he died. For SR 1,500 ($400) a year Mansour was able to rent a semiderelict old house among the Brothers. "It was a mud hut," he remembers. He grew his beard long and cut his thobe short. As he studied at the feet of the local Salafis, his mentors encouraged him to start teaching and preaching in his own right—and, after a year or so, even to start issuing fatwas.

Mansour's first fatwa, published when he was eighteen, was that there should be no ceremonies of congratulation for boys who had completed their Koranic memorization or for men who were starting on the religious life. There was no record in the Koran or the Hadith, he argued, of Mohammed conducting such rituals.

Appalled at his youthful presumption, the local "government" sheikhs reported Mansour to the royal court in Riyadh. Within days the teenage preacher was arrested by the Mabahith and taken to their notorious Al-Haier prison south of Riyadh.

"I sobbed—I was just terrified," he recalls. "I thought I was going to get hanged."

But when the eighteen-year-old found himself released after little more than two weeks, he continued his crusade against what he saw as the hypocrisy of the Wahhabi establishment. A year later, in 1989, he issued a fatwa condemning the World Youth Soccer Cup, which was being held in Saudi Arabia. Soccer was haram (forbidden), in his view, like many sports, and there should be no infidels competing in the holy land. Back Mansour went behind bars, this time to Riyadh's Alaysha prison. After fifty-five days he signed the Mabahith's standard "get out of jail" card, a promise that he would, in future, be a good Saudi citizen and do nothing to annoy the *wali al-amr*—the country's authorized leadership. When he got back to Buraydah, he discovered that his congregation was larger than ever.

• • •

As the 1980s drew to a close, the Saudi Sahwah (Islamic Awakening) was going from strength to strength. It caught a widespread mood of dissatisfaction, while providing activity and a sense of purpose for the Kingdom's many unemployed young men. It was also boosted by the spectacular triumph of its fighting arm in Afghanistan. In 1988 the Russians started withdrawing, and on February 15, 1989, the Soviet Union announced that the last of its soldiers had left the country.

It was an extraordinary defeat—Russia's own humiliating Vietnam, as the U.S.-Saudi alliance had hoped. But the victors interpreted its roots and reasons in different ways. Within months the West was celebrating the scarcely believable collapse of the entire Soviet monolith. Europeans danced on the Berlin Wall, and the exact details of how and by whom the Afghan victory had been accomplished were swallowed up in a generalized tale of Cold War triumph—free enterprise, capitalism, deterrence.

But Saudis remembered their prayers at school assemblies. They had shaken their collecting boxes, and had sent off the bearded young heroes to jihad. The photos and film footage of the bandolier-slung fighters in the mountains was compelling. Afghanistan had been *their* triumph—and it certainly owed much to the massive injections of Saudi government funds via Pakistan, along with private, charitable cash.

Khaled Batarfi remembers the celebratory gatherings in Jeddah's grandest homes, with groaning buffets, trays of fruit juice, and the guest of honor, Osama Bin Laden, doing the rounds to be embraced and kissed. Thirty-two years old in March 1989, the young man was as quiet and soft-spoken as ever, but he was clearly gathering a sense of destiny. After the meal the room fell silent as the victorious mujahid rose to tell tales of caves and of the mountains, of battles won and of brave companions who had not returned, but who were now, of course, all sitting beside God as martyrs in heaven—*"Al-hamdu lillah,"* "God be praised," murmured the room in unison.

Invited to look into the future, the warrior came up with an unusual prediction that he derived from the war between Iraq and Iran, which had just petered out. Both sides had fought themselves to a standstill. But now, warned Osama, Saddam had a huge army on his hands—hundreds of thousands of young men for whom he had no peacetime jobs. The Iraqi dictator was feeling humiliated, and, with the continuing oil glut, he was desperately short of cash. Far from being grateful to the countries that had helped him out, he was angry and full of blame. Having been brushed off by Iran, he would be casting around for another target.

PART TWO

KINGDOM AT WAR

A.D. 1990–2001 (A.H. 1411–1422)

So intimate is the connection between the throne and the altar that the banner of the church has very seldom been seen on the side of the people.

—Edward Gibbon, *The History of the Decline and Fall of the Roman Empire*

CHAPTER 14

Desert Storm

"It was a Wednesday night, going into Thursday morning," remembers Ahmed Badeeb, who received a call in the small hours from the director of the Saudi intelligence bureau in Kuwait. "He told me he was up on top of the office with his binoculars—the Iraqis had driven over the border, and he was watching them. They were heading into the city with armored cars and tanks."

Helicopters were landing special forces troops in the city, guided down by men on the ground waving flashlights—a group of Iraqi air-traffic controllers, it was later discovered, that had come to Kuwait pretending to be a football team.

Badeeb put in a call to King Fahd, who was cruising in the Red Sea on his yacht.

"Nonsense, Ahmed" scoffed the king. "You're making it up. I was on the phone just five minutes ago with the emir of Kuwait."

But Fahd called the Saudi ambassador just the same, and Badeeb listened on the line as the ambassador climbed the stairs to report from his own roof.

"There's nothing at all, *tal omrak* [may your life be long]. I can't see anything. Wait a minute—*wallahi* [by God], I am mistaken! I can hear bullets!"

"Escape at once!" Badeeb heard the king shouting. "Line up the cars! Get yourself out of there now!"

. . .

"Sons of the Arabian Gulf!" ran a plaintive and unsourced statement issued on a Kuwait radio frequency that was picked up by the BBC that morning. "Men of the desert shield . . . an Arabian Gulf country is asking for your help. How could an Arab occupy the land of his Arab brother? . . . Kuwait of Arabism, which has never abandoned its pan-Arab duty, today appeals to Arab consciences everywhere. God is above the aggressor . . ."

And with that pious expression of hope, the BBC's monitors could pick up no more.

. . .

A few hours later Prince Mohammed bin Fahd was awoken in Al-Khobar by a call from the captain of the Al-Khafji frontier post on the Saudi-Kuwait border—the emir of Kuwait had just driven in and wanted to speak to him.

In fact, the emir wanted to speak to Mohammed's father, the king, but no one knew his number in Jeddah. For two hours Fahd and his son tried to persuade Emir Jaber, a timid and depressive man, to stop waiting at the border and drive down the coast to Dhahran. In the end, Fahd told his son to drive up and get him.

Mohammed bin Fahd and his guards jumped into a 4x4 and headed northward up the coast road, past a long stream of Kuwaitis heading south.

"The emir did not want to leave the border," he recalls. "He kept looking across at his country and phoning to Kuwait City to try and find out what was going on."

Fahd was phoning his son every half hour.

" 'You've got to bring him south,' he told me. 'It's not safe! You've got to move! Now!' "

Eventually Mohammed bin Fahd persuaded Jaber to leave the border. The prince drove the now stateless ruler south and delivered him to Dammam late that afternoon.

. . .

If Saddam's invasion surprised the Saudis, they were still more shocked by the reaction of countries they had considered their friends—especially that of the biggest client on their payroll, Yasser Arafat, who came out for Iraq. By one estimate, the Saudi government had paid $1 billion or more to the Palestine Liberation Organization in the course of the 1980s. Then, as now, Saudi Arabia was by far the largest financial supporter of the Palestinians.

"We watched the Palestinians chanting against us on television," remembers Princess Latifa bint Musaed. "I couldn't believe what they were shouting: 'With chemicals you must kill them, Saddam!' I was so angry. Ever since I could remember I had been sending riyals to help support the poor oppressed Palestinians every month. So did my friends. Helping the Palestinians was a thing that good Saudis did."

King Hussein of Jordan also came out in support of the Iraqi invasion, telling CNN that Saddam could be forgiven for assimilating Kuwait—the little emirate, he said dismissively, was "a British colonial fiction." This was rich coming from a man for whose family the British had invented the Kingdom of Transjordan only two generations previously, but Hussein seemed to have forgotten that particular episode in Hashemite history.

"Even if I were not a king, I would still be the *'shareef'* [descendant of the Prophet]," he told a gathering of Jordan's tribal and parliamentary leaders, referring back to the title his ancestors had borne for the seven pre-Saudi centuries during which they had ruled in Mecca. "Indeed, now you may call me shareef."

To emphasize his claim to rule on Saudi soil, the king chose this moment to grow a beard that made him look remarkably like the last but one shareef, his great-grandfather Hussein, who had packed up his gold and fled from Jeddah in 1924 as the Saudi armies approached. Sixty-six years later, it seemed, the great-grandson was ready to return.

Yemeni television redrew its television weather map to relocate its borders hundreds of miles northward, painting vast swaths of Saudi territory in Yemeni colors. The electronic land grab crossed the peninsula just south of Riyadh. When the Saudi government revoked the favored-neighbor privileges extended to Yemeni workers in the Kingdom, the Yemenis walked off jauntily.

"We'll be back," chortled one group to their Saudi employers, "and when we come back, *we*'ll be occupying *your* houses."

It was the revolt of the have-nots who had long resented the Saudi blend of windfall wealth and self-righteousness. Now they showed their true feelings. Libya, Tunisia, Sudan, Algeria, Mauritania—even the Afghan government recently installed in Kabul with Saudi money—all distanced themselves from Saudi Arabia. A leaked recording from the Cairo summit summoned to discuss the crisis exposed Arab leaders shouting insults at one another across the table.* Saddam had not disclosed the direction he would be heading after he had swallowed Kuwait, but it did not sound as if his freshly declared friends would object too much if he staked his claim to the oil fields of the Kingdom.

• • •

Fahd said nothing—in public. Behind closed doors the Saudi king was on the phone constantly to his allies, particularly President Mubarak of Egypt, who, like Fahd, had accepted Saddam's personal assurance that he would not invade Kuwait. Like Fahd, the Egyptian felt bitterly betrayed. But the king kept his counsel. As the days went by, it seemed possible to some observers that Saudi Arabia might be planning to accept the Iraqi occupation in some messy compromise that would be covered up with assurances of Arab brotherly love. The Desert Leopard, they insinuated, was in a funk.

"Not at all," recalls a member of his kitchen cabinet. "He did not want to show his hand too early. It was a tactic he took from poker. Fahd never took any decision without running it right through the consensus—all his brothers, the main ministers, the military, the tribes, and the religious sheikhs."

The sheikhs most of all. Faced with an armed threat on his border, Fahd obviously spoke to his military, but his most important calls were to the religious establishment, and to Abdul Aziz Bin Baz in particular. Would the ulema support him, asked the king, if he had to turn to America for military assistance?

The answer was a prompt and unanimous no. The Wahhabi tradition—upheld in the past by the "Son of the Tiger" and by Bin Baz himself when he was qadi of Al-Kharj—was to seek separation from nonbelievers: "Let there not be two religions in Arabia." This well-known hadith was one of several authorities that fundamentalists liked to cite as prohibiting the presence of infidels in the Kingdom. There remained many a true believer in the towns of Unayzah and Buraydah who would walk the other way if he saw a foreigner in the street. Such cautious and fearful folk constituted

* At the emergency Arab League summit convened in Cairo on August 9, 1990, the motion condemning Saddam and approving the dispatch of Arab troops to free Kuwait was opposed by Iraq, Libya, and the PLO; Algeria and Yemen abstained; Jordan, Sudan, and Mauritania expressed reservations, while Tunisia failed to attend. The twelve members approving the resolution were Bahrain, Djibouti, Egypt, Kuwait, Lebanon, Morocco, Oman, Qatar, Saudi Arabia, Somalia, Syria, and the United Arab Emirates.

the deep roots of the Kingdom's believing community, and it was for them that the sheikhs now had to speak.

Fahd kept on trying, recruiting his brothers Salman and Nayef, who had more pious reputations. All the senior princes maintained close ties with the ulema, and with Bin Baz in particular, some of them visiting him in his home and seeking spiritual guidance. The keener princes rather enjoyed sitting in Bin Baz's majlis to watch the blind sheikh conduct his teachings, when his students would read out sections of the Koran or Islamic writings, then earnestly scribble down the wisdom that the great man delivered at the end of every paragraph.

The scholar's home was a little cluster of modern two-story buildings where he lived with his wives and children in the Shumaysi neighborhood of Riyadh. This was royal territory. Talal bin Abdul Aziz and other princes had palaces nearby. In fact, the compound had been a gift to Bin Baz from the royal family. This did not make it a bribe. All senior Saudi clerics lived in homes that were gifts from rich benefactors and foundations. Still, it was a reminder of the underlying reality of the royal-Wahhabi alliance. The Al-Saud needed the Wahhabi clerics for their legitimacy, but the clerics, for their part, depended equally upon the Al-Saud. In no other Muslim Arab country did senior religious figures enjoy such prestige and closeness to the government centers of power. There would be no more cars and plush houses for the sheikhs if Saddam Hussein marched into Riyadh.

It took a few days of arguing, but once the discussion had started, Fahd reckoned that the initial No would not stand.

"'Praise be to God, the Cherisher and Sustainer of the worlds," came the announcement, eventually, on August 13, 1990. "The board of senior ulema has been aware of the great massing of troops on the Kingdom's border and of the aggression of Iraq on a neighboring country. . . . This has prompted the rulers of the Kingdom . . . to ask Arab and non-Arab countries to deter the expected danger." It was the duty of the good Muslim ruler, continued the statement, "to take every means to deter aggression and the incursion of evil. . . . So the board thus supports all measures taken by the ruler."

It was hardly a ringing endorsement, but it would do. In the meantime, the Saudi king had been talking to Washington. On Saturday, August 4, General Norman Schwarzkopf received a phone call from his boss, Colin Powell, chairman of the Joint Chiefs of Staff.

"King Fahd is asking for someone to brief him on the threat to his kingdom," said Powell. "When you get there, you'll have to play it by ear."

"Is the U.S. government saying we're prepared to commit forces?" asked Schwarzkopf.

"Yes," replied Powell. "If King Fahd gives his permission."

. . .

The bulky figure of the Saudi king was waiting for the Americans in the far left-hand corner of the majlis in his Jeddah palace beside the Red Sea. Down one side of the plush green and gold room were lined the princes—Abdullah; Saud Al-Faisal, the foreign minister; Bandar bin Sultan, just in himself from Washington; Abdul Rahman, Sultan's Sudayri brother and vice defense minister—all in robes, headdresses, dark mustaches and beards. Down the other wall, dressed in shirts, ties, and Western business suits and every one of them clean-shaven, were seated the American officials—Defense Secretary Dick Cheney, Pentagon strategist Paul Wolfowitz, Deputy National Security Adviser Robert Gates (later defense secretary to both George W. Bush and to Barack Obama), and Ambassador Chas Freeman, along with their bemedaled and uniformed military delegation.

Schwarzkopf strode forward with his array of charts and aerial photographs, and, since there was no seat available, he went down on one knee in front of the king to begin his presentation.

Embarrassed, Fahd called for a servant to bring a chair, so the husky four-star general found himself seated with his display materials in his lap, while the Saudi king looked over one shoulder and Crown Prince Abdullah peered over the other.

"I had imagined," Schwarzkopf recalls, "that they would listen to my briefing politely, then go away to discuss it among themselves."

In fact, he found himself in the middle of an animated discussion in Arabic, only snippets of which were translated into English by Bandar. The U.S. photographs, taken a few days earlier by surveillance planes and satellites, showed Iraqi armored vehicles and troops massed in the desert along the Saudi border, with a handful of tanks—no more than five—clearly inside Saudi territory. Schwarzkopf was inclined to think that this was unintentional. The Saudi-Kuwaiti border was not delineated on the ground at that point. But Fahd took it very seriously.

"I don't care if it's only one tank!" said the king indignantly. "They've trespassed on Saudi sovereignty."

Schwarzkopf said bluntly that America had no inside intelligence of Iraqi intentions, and he now laughs at the often-canvassed Arab conspiracy theory that the United States had doctored the aerial photographs to make the threat seem worse than it was.

"They were regular reconnaissance photographs, sharp and clear, taken on some very bright days, but they did not show a definite picture. If we had doctored them we could have done a much better job. I explained that we could only make an educated deduction from the facts on the ground: these were identifiably some of the Iraqi Army's very best units; they were clearly pausing to rearm, refuel, and reequip as taught by their Soviet instructors. We had observed them regroup that way during the Iran-Iraq War. They might or might not be preparing to attack. But it could hardly be said that their posture looked defensive. The tanks were facing south."

Schwarzkopf concluded with a presentation of the substantial forces that the United States could provide to protect the Kingdom, then he yielded the floor to Cheney for a final statement. President Bush was willing to make this military commitment immediately, said the defense secretary: "If you ask us, we will come. When you ask us to go home, we will leave. We will seek no permanent bases."

This was the point at which Schwarzkopf had expected the Saudis to retire to conduct their deliberations privately. But the princes continued their discussion briskly and briefly in front of their visitors—with the turning point coming in a sharp exchange between Fahd and Abdullah.

"We must be careful not to rush into a decision," said the crown prince.

"Like the Kuwaitis!" retorted Fahd caustically. "They did not rush into a decision, and now there is no Kuwait."

"There is still a Kuwait," persisted Abdullah.

"And its territory," replied Fahd, "consists of hotel rooms in London, Cairo, and elsewhere."

Abdullah conceded the argument, and as the other princes in the room agreed, the king turned to Cheney and spoke his first and only word of English—"OK," he said.

• • •

Within days U.S. planes and troops were flooding into Saudi Arabia's airports and bases in every corner of the country. Schwarzkopf's rule of thumb was simple. He wanted five U.S. soldiers on the ground for every Iraqi, and by the end of September thousands of young Americans in combat gear were driving their jeeps around the streets and highways of the east. The trouble was that quite a number of these Americans were women—attractive young female GIs who swung their vehicles around as if they were back in North Carolina. This set alarm bells ringing in the Saudi Ministry of Defense, and, after talks with General Schwarzkopf, the U.S. lady drivers were confined to U.S. camps, the Aramco compound, and out in the desert (where bedouin women also drove).

But the ban did not apply to the several thousand Kuwaiti women who had recently arrived in the Kingdom. They went on driving their cars to the shops—they could be seen every day in Al-Khobar and the sprawling cities of the oil fields, loading their cars with groceries and ferrying their children to and from the beach. There was no law that explicitly banned women from driving in Saudi Arabia. There is none today—the Kingdom's notorious female driving ban is a matter of social convention, fortified by some ferocious religious pressures. So some Saudi women started looking thoughtfully at their Kuwaiti sisters.

• • •

Dr. Aisha Al-Mana came from a religious family on her mother's side—"all imams and bearded ones," she recalls. Her father was Mohammed Al-Mana, Abdul Aziz's literate companion and translator whose charming memoir, *Arabia Unified*, vividly captures the leisurely atmosphere of Riyadh before the oil wealth came.

"My father," she remembers, "always warned me against joining parties and factions, either left or right. 'Be yourself,' he used to say."

Aisha took his words to heart. As a politically active student in America she had fought a losing battle against the Islamist takeover of the Arab student organizations in the 1970s.

"In those days the U.S. government encouraged the religious hardliners as a counterweight to the Arab nationalists," says Aisha. "I remember how the State Department used to give money to the fundamentalist students—the Arabs and also the Iranians. They gave them air tickets for their conferences and helped them organize. I saw it myself. They thought they were fighting Communism, and they ended up with Khomeini. All this Islamism—it's not religion: it's only politics, and it was America that helped create these extremists. They just ride on religion, these born-agains—in Iran, in Saudi Arabia, and in the southern states of America too: they're all after their own piece of the cake."

Expressing such views forthrightly after she returned to Saudi Arabia got Dr. Al-Mana into trouble with the Ministry of the Interior. Her work as a school principal, lecturer, and women's activist in Riyadh and the Eastern Province earned her invitations to foreign conferences, but the Mabahith had other ideas.

"They call you in and ask you to sign a *taahud,* a pledge, in which you promise not to repeat something you have said which they do not like. So you sign it. Then you say the same thing again, or write it in an article, and when you go to travel you get to the airport and discover there's something on the computer: they won't let you leave. You're there with your bags all packed, and you have to go home again. Then after a year or so you hear from a friend who was also banned, but has now been allowed to go. So you try again, and this time you find that you can walk through the barrier. They don't tell you officially. The ban just melts away—till the next time you annoy them."

A wife, mother, school principal, and activist, Aisha Al-Mana had been banned like this on four occasions, and she found the battle tiring.

"I've been active in women's rights since my personal awakening. I used to refuse to wear the abaya. I thought I could change the world single-handed."

The war rekindled her fire. It was Friday, October 19, 1990, and Aisha was traveling inland from Al-Khobar, heading down the highway to Riyadh, with heavy U.S. trucks and desert-camouflaged troop transporters rumbling on either side, towering over her car.

"I believe that wars are fought by rulers, not by the people—it's the people who suffer. So when I saw those huge American convoys traveling, I knew that they had not come here for me, for my people, or for my government. What a nonsense to say that they had come halfway round the world to protect me! They had come to protect their own interests—because they didn't want Saddam to control their oil. It made me feel bad. People were taking decisions about me somewhere else. Then I thought, Why shouldn't I have a say? There *is* something I can do."

Aisha Al-Mana told her driver to stop the car, get out, and go and sit in the backseat. Then she got into the front, took her place behind the wheel, and drove all the way to Riyadh—a distance of nearly two hundred miles. She had learned to drive as a student in America and, like many Saudi women, was accustomed to driving whenever she was abroad.

"I felt wonderful. I felt like I was flying. When I came to the checkpoints along the road, the guards asked, 'What's going on?' I told them, 'What's going on is what you can see is going on.' I laughed and showed them my ID, so they laughed. 'That's all we have to check for,' said one. They were bedouin. They were not shocked. They had seen women drive. Their wives could have been driving the family pickup somewhere over the hill at that very moment, for all we knew. I smiled at them and they smiled at me. They waved me through. We were all kind of happy."

. . .

When Aisha Al-Mana got to Riyadh, she shared the tale of her glorious journey with a group of women who had gathered to discuss what they could do to help the national emergency.

"They asked me to join them. We all wanted to help—to help with first aid, perhaps, if there were going to be bombs and missiles. We wanted to do something. But a lot of us were helpless. Many of our foreign drivers had been repatriated. How could we get to hospitals or schools, or wherever we might be volunteering? So here was a good reason to ask for permission to drive—it was religious. Islam is a very flexible religion. If you are traveling, you can delay or combine your prayers. If you have nothing to eat, you can eat pork. So we said, 'Let's start with this.' Let's get in touch with some officials and say we want to help with the defense of our country, and to do that we need to be able to drive ourselves—like the Kuwaiti women are already doing."

In the days that followed, Aisha spoke to some ministers she knew, while others of the group spoke to officials and princes who might be favorably inclined. A week later the women convened again.

"We had all received the same answer. 'Thank you very much. It's a kind offer and a great idea—but this is not the best moment.' That is what you are always told when you suggest change in Saudi Arabia—'I agree with you, of course, change has to come. But just wait a little. Be patient. Now is not the right time.' We had had enough of that. We decided that now *was* the right time."

The women agreed to meet the following Monday.

"I arrived late, and by the time I had got there, they had taken the decision to drive. They had fixed the location and the route. We decided to dress properly, with abayas and veils (head scarves, not full niqab), and to send a letter to Prince Salman [the governor of Riyadh] telling him what we intended to do, why we thought it was the right time. I delivered the letter to his office first thing next day."

The letter, if delivered, did not reach the prince, who would proceed through his working day in blithe ignorance of the planned demonstration—until he was woken from his afternoon nap with the news.

The women had chosen a circular route through some of the busiest and most modern shopping streets of Riyadh, along King Abdul Aziz Road, down Tahliah (Desalination) Street, through the Olaya district and back. There were forty-seven of them in fourteen cars.

"We could have had more. We could have had hundreds. But we'd decided just the evening before—in less than twenty-four hours. And we didn't want to make it too big. We wanted this to be symbolic.

"Look," explains Aisha Al-Mana. "I don't like driving. I never did. But it is a basic necessity for ladies who work and are supporting families. A foreign driver costs you seven hundred to a thousand riyals [$180 to $250] per month. Then there is his food and health care and his accommodation—which may be in bachelor accommodation with other drivers, which causes problems in its own right. There are more than a million male foreign drivers in Saudi Arabia, doing nothing else but driving the women around.

"So say a lady who works earns four thousand riyals [$1,000] a month. A third of that has to go on paying her driver—money that goes out of the country. Then think of the mother who stays at home and doesn't work—how is her husband to afford a driver for her if he is a teacher or a civil servant? He has to do all the driving himself, taking her to the shops, taking the children to and from school. Think how the productivity of those men would rise, if they were not taking time off work every day to act as chauffeur."

The economic arguments in favor of women driving seem irrefutable to a Western sensibility, as does the main religious one—that the effect of the driving ban is to place a respectable Saudi woman, usually alone and often for long periods of time, in a confined space with a single man who is not her husband or permitted male relative. One might have thought that this last argument would have some purchase with the members of the Commission for the Promotion of Virtue and the Prevention of Vice.

"This is what shows you that none of this is religious," says Aisha. "It's all social. These men need to keep control of their womenfolk. It's a matter of their pride. And as part of their pride, they cannot believe that a decent Saudi woman would choose to misbehave with a non-Saudi man."

. . .

The convoy of cars had made their planned progress nearly twice around the circuit, when a traffic patrolman spotted them. Reem Jarbou, then a teenager sitting excitedly beside her mother, Wafa Al-Munif, a businesswoman and charity worker in Riyadh, saw the policeman look casually across the road, then look back again in a horrified double-take at the procession of women sedately driving their cars down Tahliah Street.

"He had no idea what to do. I saw him reach for his radio, and his call must have been monitored by the religious police, because suddenly they were all over us—jumping out of a dozen or so of their huge trucks and swarming everywhere in their headdresses and thobes and long beards. Then the regular, uniformed police arrived, and there was a standoff. Here we were, a group of women, standing by our cars, a little shaken, wondering what would happen next and rather proud of what we had done, while the men were standing round in the street arguing. Whose jurisdiction was it? Which of them would have the honor of taking us into custody?

"Luckily all the police, religious and regular, answered to Prince Salman. He was not going to let us fall into the hands of the religious maniacs, and they were furious—beside themselves. One got into our car beside the policeman who drove us to the police station. He was just steaming, a great big angry lump of indignation in the front seat: he kept muttering curses and insults as we drove. He said he wanted to kill us, and I really think he meant it."

. . .

Among those arrested was a happily pregnant Fawzia Al-Bakr. Her time in prison eight years previously had not hampered her marriage prospects—on the contrary. Her notoriety had attracted the attention of Fahd Al-Yehya, a young medical student who would become one of the Kingdom's most eminent psychiatrists. The couple had got married in 1985—"I think he liked my writing," says Dr. Al-Bakr, who earned her Ph.D. in comparative education at the Institute of Education, University of London, in 1990.

Fawzia had borrowed her brother's car to take part in the demonstration, and as she stood beside it, she recognized one of the policemen who came toward her out of the melee.

" 'Dr. Fawzia,' he said, 'do you remember me?' It was one of the Mabahith who'd interviewed me all those years back when I was locked up in the villas. 'You never stop, do you?' he said, and he sort of smiled.

"Later on, when we got to the police station, he came across to me again and told me what to write on the report form as I was filling it in. 'No,' he said. 'Don't say your brother knew that you were borrowing his car. He'll only get in trouble. Say that you took the car without his consent.' "

Unlike the Mabahith, the religious police could not see the funny side. As darkness fell, husbands and brothers started arriving at the station to take their womenfolk home. They were showered with scorn by the bearded ones.

"Weaklings!" They hissed. "Don't you know how to control your women?"

The insult went to the heart of the matter, for control of womenfolk is the basis of every tribal society: let your women go off (and therefore, ultimately, procreate) with anyone they choose, and that is the end of male tribal authority—of the tribe itself, in fact. Whatever the military outcome of King Fahd's war, the women's driving demonstration made clear that the social consequences were going to be incalculable.

• • •

While Prince Salman was wrestling with the problems caused by one demonstration in Riyadh, his nephew Bandar in Washington was trying to encourage another. To help sway U.S. public opinion behind the war, the ambassador called a meeting of Saudi students in Washington. The embassy sent airline tickets to fly in the leaders of the Saudi student clubs from universities all over the country.

"This is a grave moment in your country's history," he told them as they gathered in the Radisson Renaissance hotel on Seminary Road in Alexandria, Virginia. "Now is the time for you to go out and demonstrate. Show the Americans how you feel. Be vocal! Make banners! Think up slogans! Go out into your campuses and in the streets and make your feelings felt!"

There was an awkward silence.

"Thank you, Your Royal Highness," said one of the students. "But how shall we do this? We have never been educated to do such things—we've always been told that it's un-Saudi to demonstrate. How do you expect us to do this now?"

. . .

Back in Riyadh, the demonstrators who *had* made their feelings plain were suffering the consequences. All the women lecturers at King Saud University were suspended and banned from the campus. Religious conservatives denounced them fiercely in the newspapers, and their criticisms seemed to meet with popular support. The loudspeakers of the Friday sermons positively quivered with fury. Abdul Aziz Bin Baz issued a fatwa against women driving.

"The situation of women," declared one of the milder cassettes that circulated, "is the reason for all these woes that are falling on the nation."

It was a reprise of the arguments that had followed the uprising of Juhayman ten years earlier—with a sinister edge. Leaflets were distributed that publicized the names of the women and their husbands. Good Saudis and Muslims were urged to take action against these "Communist whores." The cruelest cuts came from young traditionalists among the lecturers' own female students—they spat on their teachers.

"The king was truly shocked," remembers one of the royal family. "After the war he invited the women to his majlis to let them know that he felt for their suffering. 'You are our daughters,' he told them."

Dr. Aisha Al-Mana did not attend the meeting.

"So far as I know," she says, "that meeting was *not* the king's idea. It was requested by some of the women who wanted to say they were sorry—they were worried about their jobs. They felt they needed to apologize, and that is their right. But I am not sorry. In my opinion we did nothing for which we should apologize. To drive as Saudi women—*that* is our right."

CHAPTER 15

Battle for Al-Khafji

By the middle of January 1991 the little settlement of Al-Khafji on the Saudi-Kuwaiti border was a ghost town. Life in the northeastern corner of Saudi Arabia had grown ever more hectic as preparations accelerated for the U.S.-Saudi military campaign to recapture Kuwait. But Al-Khafji stood deserted—a peppering of empty, angular buildings and forlornly looping power lines on the salt flats of the Gulf coast. Saudi guards had abandoned the northern frontier post to which the emir of Kuwait had driven in such distress on the morning of August 2, 1990. The town was undefendable, decided the commander of the Arab armed forces of the U.S.-Saudi coalition, Khaled bin Sultan, who dug in his first line of fortifications some twenty-five miles to the south.

The serious business of the war was being conducted overhead. Taking off from an arc of bases and hastily constructed desert landing strips in the early hours of January 17, 1991, aircraft of the U.S.-Arab coalition roared into action with a blitzkrieg of precision-guided bombs and missiles that would rain down on Iraq for thirty-eight days and nights, their mission to demoralize and, where possible, destroy, the Iraqi armed forces.

As it turned out, the weeks of remorseless aerial bombardment, followed by the classic outflanking maneuver that Norman Schwarzkopf executed to recapture Kuwait, produced a remarkable victory for the U.S.-Saudi coalition and their allies. Saddam's army would surrender after less than one hundred hours of ground combat.

But such success seemed anything but guaranteed as January 1991 drew to a close. The Iraqi Army was huge and menacing, with a proven inventory of intimidating chemical weapons. On January 18, 1991, Saddam launched seven of his Scud missiles against Tel Aviv and Haifa, then directed twenty of the missiles at Riyadh and Dhahran in a succession of alarming nighttime attacks. There were disputes within the coalition—Schwarzkopf and Prince Khaled clashed regularly, a pair of oddly similar man-mountains with egos to match. How much firepower should be directed against Baghdad? Should not more be done to degrade Saddam's vaunted Republican Guard? The fear of everything that might go wrong was reflected by the coalition's provision of chemical suits and by some eighteen thousand hospital beds in the theater of operations. It was at this moment, on the night of January 29–30, 1991, that Iraqi tanks of the 5th Mechanized Division, one of Saddam's crack units, rumbled over the undefended Saudi border with troop carriers and occupied the town of Al-Khafji.

. . .

For the second time in less than six months, Saddam Hussein had successfully invaded another Arab country, and he lost no time in trumpeting his triumph. In Riyadh King Fahd was furious.

"I am lucky," Khaled bin Sultan later admitted, "he did not strip me of my command that night!"

The king called his nephew incessantly, insisting that he take instant action to oust the Iraqis and demanding to know what had gone wrong. The prince's strategy in abandoning Al-Khafji, which was at the mercy of artillery fire from Iraqi guns on the Kuwaiti border, had been based on the assumption that coalition airpower could deal with any Iraqi land incursions. But air cover of this no-man's-land was the responsibility of the U.S. Marines based around the "elbow" of the Saudi-Kuwaiti border, thirty miles to the west, and they had been busy throughout the night fending off an Iraqi attack on their own positions.

The Saudi commander felt let down by his allies, and he got on the phone to Ahmad Al-Sudayri, the Saudi director of air operations.

"Forget about the Joint Forces!" he recalls himself shouting. "If the U.S. Air Force or the Marines don't come at once, I want you to take our air assets out of the coalition and send them all to me! I need the Tornados, the F-5s, everything you've got!"

His ultimatum produced results. U.S. air command switched B-52s and AC-130 Spectre gunships to the coastal road, where they went into action on the afternoon of January 30, blocking Iraqi attempts to send down reinforcements. The thousand or so Iraqi troops who had occupied Al-Khafji were cut off.

But even as the prince was drafting his plans to recapture the town, he had an additional item of intelligence to digest. Two ANGLICO (Air Naval Gunfire Liaison Company) teams—one of five, the other of six U.S. Marines—had been operating secretly among Al-Khafji's deserted houses, using their advanced undercover position to guide and call down artillery and air attacks on the border. They had not had time to escape, and they now found themselves surrounded by Iraqi troops—though the Iraqis did not yet know that the Americans were there. Khaled realized immediately that this changed everything.

"Our first priority," he told Sultan Adi Al-Mutayri, his major general in charge of the assault, "is not to free Al-Khafji. It is to get the Marines out."

Four years later the prince was honest enough to admit his motives.

"I was extremely worried," he wrote in his memoirs, "that Schwarzkopf might use American troops, either U.S. Marines in an amphibious attack or a heli-borne U.S. Army unit, to free *my* town in *my* sector. The shame would have been difficult to bear."

Major General Al-Mutayri did not let him down. As dusk fell, a detachment of Saudi National Guard armored cars drove up the coast road, heading for the spot where the ANGLICOs were hiding. Iraqi snipers shot out the tires of the vehicles, immobilizing ten of them, but the fully armored tanks of the Saudi Land Forces were following up. By midnight the eleven Americans were liberated unharmed—if the Iraqis had known they were there, they might have fought harder. Now the Saudis faced the more formidable task, the full liberation of Al-Khafji.

"We were scared," admits Suleiman Al-Khalifa, then a young captain under the command of Sultan Al-Mutayri. "We had never fought in a real war before."

Al-Mutayri was an inspiring leader.

"He had been up twice to reconnoiter Al-Khafji itself," remembers Al-Khalifa, "driving round the outskirts and getting shot at by the Iraqis. Our generals don't usually do that."

Al-Mutayri knew he must keep his forces away from the salt flats of the coast, where several Iraqi and Saudi tanks had got stuck in the swampy terrain. Tanks would be the basis of his assault—his U.S.-made M60A3s had double the range of the Iraqis' Soviet weaponry. But the job would ultimately have to be done by his foot soldiers, advancing under cover of the tanks' gun barrels and fighting from house to house.

"It was a two-pronged attack," recalls Al-Khalifa, one of the foot soldiers who fought his way up Mecca Street between the salt marshes on one side and the greasy oil-change garages on the other. "Some of the Iraqis defended really fiercely. They kept on shooting to the end. There was one officer, I remember, in the beach hotel, who absolutely refused to surrender. He was a fanatic for Saddam. Then there were others who were loaded down with video recorders and women's clothing—they seemed more keen on looting than on fighting."

The attack started at 8 A.M. on the morning of Thursday, January 31, a combined maneuver by Saudi National Guardsmen, Royal Saudi Land Forces, and two mechanized Qatari companies that were part of the coalition. Eighteen Saudis were killed in the assault and thirty-two wounded, but by midday, Al-Mutayri's troops were in the middle of Al-Khafji, having killed some thirty-two Iraqis and taken more than four hundred prisoners. The major general radioed the happy news to his commanding officer, who relayed it immediately to the king. Fahd was ecstatic, ordering his nephew to get up to the town itself as soon as possible with a contingent of press to show the world that Saddam's men had been kicked out of Saudi Arabia.

It was sunset as Khaled bin Sultan reached Al-Khafji, where he was stopped at a Saudi Marine checkpoint. The officer in charge, Colonel Ammar Al-Qahtani, who had known the prince since childhood, pleaded with him not to go farther. There were snipers in the town, he explained, and the mopping-up operations were not complete. At that moment an incoming Iraqi shell exploded nearby.

"Court-martial me if you like," cried Al-Qahtani, suddenly getting hysterical, "but I will not let you through!"

He thrust himself in front of the prince's jeep, raising his arms in the air—then relented just as suddenly, reaching inside the jeep emotionally to kiss his commanding officer on the top of his head.

The truth of the colonel's warning was revealed the next day, when a group of twenty armed Iraqis surrendered only three hundred yards from the spot where Khaled had chosen to give his press conference. From their vantage point, they said, they had had the Saudi commander directly in their gun sights. They could easily have killed the prince as he stood brightly illuminated by the lights of the TV crews, but they were not Saddam fanatics, and they had wisely calculated that to open fire would have resulted in their own deaths. They asked to be treated as military refugees, not prisoners of war, as a reward for not pulling their triggers.

• • •

The triumph of Al-Khafji transformed morale across Saudi Arabia. It was the largest battle fought on Saudi soil in modern times. The destruction of Iraq's 5th Mechanized Division eliminated one of Saddam's finest armored units and had provided a genuine test of Saudi (and Qatari) fighting resolve. Saudis had risked their lives—and lost their lives—to recapture a corner of their country. The government lost no time proclaiming the eighteen men who died in the retaking of the town to be martyrs.

Al-Khafji was, in fact, the only pitched battle of the entire Gulf War. Everything else, as Khaled bin Sultan later put it, was "just movement." By the time the coalition's aerial bombardment was finished and the ground troops went into action on February 24, 1991, the Iraqi forces had either fled or surrendered—which suddenly raised a question to which surprisingly little thought had been given: How to define "victory"?

• • •

Just over a month earlier, on January 10, 1991, James Baker, the U.S. secretary of state, had been talking frankly in Riyadh with the U.S. ambassador Chas Freeman.

"What do you think," he suddenly asked, "our war aims ought to be?"

Hostilities were then only seven days away, and the ambassador's first reaction was to find the question "shocking." But on reflection he came to see that his boss's inquiry was not as naïve as it sounded. Baker had wrought miracles to pull together a coalition the likes of which the world had never seen—prickly Arabs, skeptical Europeans, the suddenly ex-Communist Russians working with the West for the first time, the silent support of Israel. But lining up these disparate elements had depended on being vague. The allies had only resolved on the need to expel Saddam from Kuwait. Beyond that, the great coalition had no agreed aims.

Razored by five weeks of merciless bombardment from the skies, the demoralized Iraqi Army surrendered in just four days. But as Norman Schwarzkopf and Khaled bin Sultan went to Safwan airfield on March 3, 1991, to negotiate the details of the cease-fire with their Iraqi opposite numbers, they were told to restrict themselves to technical matters—the line of control between the two sides, the handling of prisoners of war, and restrictions on overflight of southern Iraq by Iraqi planes. No mandate existed to enforce an Iraqi surrender, nor to define in any way the total and catastrophic nature of Saddam Hussein's defeat.

"The Iraqi generals," recalls Chas Freeman, "must have had great difficulty as they walked out of that tent in restraining a smile."

Lacking a definition of final victory, the coalition never compelled Saddam Hussein to admit that he had lost and they had won the Gulf War of 1991—the tyrant remained in his palace. As the years went by, that failure was to engender a train of painful consequences.

"In my personal view," says Khaled bin Sultan, "the manner in which the Gulf War was concluded did not match up to the way it was waged. . . . The view of our American and British allies was: 'Let's not take any more. Let's wrap up the loose ends and get out fast.' "

Received wisdom in the West would later argue that the coalition was wrong to have halted as it did on the outskirts of Kuwait, and that the victorious allies should have marched decisively onward to Baghdad. But that had never been the mandate of the coalition, and like every other Arab nation, Kuwait included, Saudi Arabia would have balked at such a plan. Apart from the wish to mend fences, King Fahd and his brothers were well aware that toppling Saddam would have handed Iraq over to its Shia majority, thus magnifying the mischief-making power of Iran.

Norman Schwarzkopf was opposed on military grounds. "Had we taken all of Iraq," he wrote in 1992, "we would have been like the dinosaur in the tarpit."

Later that year President Bush said essentially the same thing, writing with his national security adviser, Brent Scowcroft, in the journal *Middle East Report*. To have moved on from Kuwait to invade Iraq, the president argued, "would have incurred incalculable human and political costs. . . . We would have been forced to occupy Baghdad and, in effect, rule Iraq. . . . Had we gone the invasion route, the United States could conceivably still be an occupying power in a bitterly hostile land."

Perhaps the most cogent arguments against invasion were delivered by Bush's defense secretary, Dick Cheney.

"Do you think," he was asked in 1994, "that the U.S., or UN forces, should have moved into Baghdad?"

"No," he replied without hesitation in a CNN interview that has since been replayed by millions of viewers on YouTube. "If we had gone to Baghdad . . . there would have been a U.S. occupation of Iraq. . . . Once you got to Iraq and took it over, took down Saddam Hussein's government, then what are you going to put in its place? That's a very volatile part of the world, and if you take down the central government of Iraq, you could very easily end up seeing pieces of Iraq fly off . . .

"It's a quagmire if you go that far and try to take over Iraq. . . . The question for the president, in terms of whether or not we went on to Baghdad and took additional casualties in an effort to get Saddam Hussein, was how many additional dead Americans is Saddam worth? Our judgment was, 'Not very many' and I think we got it right."

Ten years later, as vice president to George W. Bush, Dick Cheney was to argue exactly the opposite. In that decade the former defense secretary had become a principal advocate of the argument that America should send troops to Baghdad to "take down" the government of Saddam Hussein and clean out the palace. This was partly because of events inside Iraq following the unsatisfactory conclusion of the Gulf War. But it was mainly the consequence of what happened next in Saudi Arabia.

CHAPTER 16

Awakening

When the news had come through of Saddam's invasion in August 1990, Osama Bin Laden knew exactly how he could help. He got in touch with the comrades who had fought with him in Afghanistan, both Arabs and Afghans, and came up with a plan—they would revive the old Saudi-Afghan alliance. He and his mujahideen companions had defeated the Soviets in the mountains. Now they would chase Saddam and his Iraqis through the streets of Kuwait and back to Baghdad. Muslims would flock from around the world, he was sure, to help push back this un-Islamic aggression.

The triumph of Afghanistan had inspired Osama to see jihad as a process that he could take anywhere, with himself as one of its leaders. Before leaving Afghanistan he had recast his organization, giving it a new name—Al-Qaeda.

"He rang me to explain," remembers Jamal Khashoggi, the young journalist who had first interviewed Bin Laden in Afghanistan in the 1980s. "He said that Al-Qaeda was an organization to record the names of the mujahideen and all their contact details: a database, which is one of the things that *qaeda* means in Arabic. So wherever jihad needed fighting, in the Philippines or central Asia or anywhere in the world, you could get in touch with the fighters quickly."

Osama's first plan, before the Iraqi invasion of Kuwait, had been to set up some Afghan-style training camps in the mountains of Yemen, where the craggy terrain provided ideal guerrilla territory. Islamists along the Saudi border were bidding for power against the Communists of the south, offering Osama the chance to advance the Salafi cause in the homeland of his father.

"He had developed this love for revolution and fighting," remembers Prince Turki Al-Faisal. "Battle was becoming his solution for everything. He saw his mujahideen fighting all over the world, winning victory after victory for Islam. He was not best pleased when I told him he should stay out of Yemen. The Saudi government was not interfering there, I told him. He should not even think of it. When the invasion of Kuwait happened that summer, I think he reckoned he'd give us one last shot."

Osama had worked out a step-by-step strategy to cross the Saudi border and infiltrate Kuwait, then wage an urban guerrilla campaign, fighting from house to house until the Iraqis were expelled. It was far from implausible, and he decided to present his proposal to a senior prince to whom he and his family felt particularly close, Ahmad bin Abdul Aziz, the vice minister of the interior.

Forty-eight years old in 1990, Ahmad was the youngest of the seven Sudayri brothers. He was one of the first sons of Abdul Aziz to be educated in America, where he studied political science at Redlands University, in California. Within the family he had a reputation for quiet seriousness. In 1980 his elder brother Fahd had chosen him to investigate the grievances of the Shia following the Qateef uprisings of the previous December, and it had been Ahmad's proposals that started the program of infrastructure building in the east that was later continued by Mohammed bin Fahd. For a dozen years Ahmad had labored as the loyal assistant to his brother Nayef at the Interior Ministry, concentrating on security issues. As deputy governor of Mecca before that, he had grown close to the Bin Laden family, so he seemed the ideal conduit for Osama's Kuwait liberation plan.

"Bin Laden was greatly concerned about security," recalls Prince Ahmad. "He said that King Fahd should move out of his palace in Jeddah because he thought that it was too close to the sea—it could easily be attacked. He had brought along his eldest brother, Bakr [head of the Bin Laden company] to show that he was serious and that he had the family backing. He was very keen to show that he was a good Saudi citizen, and he was very proud of this plan he had devised to raise volunteers for the safety of his country."

Ahmad was not convinced.

"His idea did not seem practical to me. It did not sound organized or professional. Nor did it begin to match the scale of the problem."

Like Turki Al-Faisal, Ahmad noted Bin Laden's eagerness for a fight—almost for its own sake.

"He several times used the word *jihad.* I knew that he had been speaking a lot in mosques. It was clear that he had got used to fighting and was finding it hard to give it up. But *jihad* means that you go to war, then stop."

The prince responded with courtesy.

"I thanked him very much. I told him that we were very grateful for the help he was offering of these volunteers, but that we had professionals who were preparing a strategy and that we hoped that the situation would not come to that. I told him that the Bin Laden family had always been loyal friends to our family, and that we looked forward to many more years of that friendship. We would get in touch with him if we thought it necessary."

Ahmad's rejection could not have been more polite, nor more summary. According to some sources, Osama attempted to present his proposals to other senior members of the family and met with the same response—Thanks, but no thanks. According to someone who was present at another meeting to which Osama brought a five-page document setting out his strategy, Bin Laden's face went "black" with anger when his proposal was dismissed.

• • •

When the House of Saud turned down Osama's mujahideen in favor of the godless Americans, they did not just offend his pride. They offended his religious beliefs—and those of many other pious Saudis. "Let there not be two religions in Arabia," ran the text thundered out in sermons across Arabia following the arrival of the American troops, in contemptuous defiance of the ulema's government-supportive fatwa.

"To defend ourselves we have invited the help of our real enemies," complained Dr. Safar Al-Hawali, a young middle-ranking cleric who was not afraid to take on the establishment. "The point is that we need internal change. The first war should be against the infidels *inside.* Then we will be strong enough to face our external enemy."

Al-Hawali was the dean of theology at Umm Al-Qura, the Islamic University of Mecca, where he had made his name with his thesis "Al-

Ilmaniya" ("Secularism"). This, he argued, was a Western concept insidiously designed to undermine Islam from within—and the arrival of the Americans was proof of it. The Gulf War had been coordinated, as Hawali saw it, first to control and eventually to destroy Islam, and would result in Western military bases being set up around the Gulf. It was a sin, in his opinion, to have allowed "crusader" troops—Christians, Jews, and women—into the land of the two holy mosques.

Abdul Aziz Bin Baz, who had played a leading role in coaxing the ulema to support the government, took issue with Al-Hawali and the other Sahwah (Awakening) preachers. The two holy mosques were on the opposite side of Arabia, he pointed out in press interviews—621 miles distant from the American troops stationed beside Kuwait and the Iraqi border.

"The Americans," he argued, "have come to protect, not to seize the *haramain* [holy places]. They have come to repel the aggression and to remove injustice."

He then embarked on a discussion of the Koran's Al-Maeda sura, in which God listed the foods forbidden to Muslims: "dead meat, blood, the flesh of swine, that which has been killed by strangling, or by a violent blow, or by a headlong fall, or being gored to death." The sura concludes by telling Muslims that while these foods are forbidden, they *can* be eaten by someone who is starving. So today, on the same basis, argued Bin Baz, "the state has had to use some infidel states to stop this brutal enemy."

It may have pleased some of the blind sheikh's listeners to hear America's troops compared to the flesh of swine, but the devotees of the Awakening were not impressed. Bin Baz, they said scornfully, had become "a government sheikh."

. . .

The fertile farming area of Qaseem, northwest of Riyadh, is famous for its dates, and famous also for its Wahhabism. When it comes to holiday jobs, the date farmers select only the most serious young Muslims as fruit pickers. So during the Gulf War harvests of 1990 and 1991, the date groves of Qaseem were centers of particular Islamic fervor, seething with indignation at the Al-Saud's embrace of the infidels. In Qaseem the Sahwah's eloquent mouthpiece was Sheikh Salman Al-Awdah, a black-bearded cleric who had been preaching the Awakening quietly in Buraydah before the war. Now he proclaimed it loudly, and his sermons circulated around the peninsula in best-selling tapes.

"This country is different," he proclaimed. "It is united under the banner of Islam, not because of this person or that person . . ."

". . . Or because of that family," was the additional message readily captured by his listeners. The sheikh was proposing a religiously based, non-Saudi identity for Saudi Arabia. In his best-selling tape "Why Do States Disintegrate?" Al-Awdah talked scornfully of the Egyptian pharaohs, who would hand out money to their subjects but were hated all the more for that. As the sheikh described how the pharaohs showed their contempt for their people's minds, interfering with their religion and restricting their intellectual freedoms, it was not difficult to work out who his real target was.

All Saudi mosques broadcast their Friday sermons loudly to the neighborhood via their minaret loudspeakers, so it became the weekend chore for junior diplomats in Riyadh to go and sit in their cars outside the capital's most radical pulpits and make recordings of what the imams were declaiming.

Inside the U.S. embassy, David Rundell spent hours listening to the Sahwah tapes.

"Ninety percent of it was 'Don't beat your wife and be a good neighbor,'" he recalls. "But the remaining 10 percent was pretty virulent. The only one with a sense of humor was Safar Al-Hawali. He'd paint these unattractive word pictures of an overweight American, with his shirt unbuttoned, a thick gold chain around his neck, walking his dog while holding hands with his wife. 'Be careful,' he'd say, 'or your daughter will end up working in a shoe store.'"

Dogs and shoes are unclean to all Muslims—hence the widespread Arab delight when an Iraqi protestor hurled both his shoes at George W. Bush in 2008—while Wahhabis take a dim view of wearing gold, holding hands in public, or unbuttoning your shirt to reveal chest hair.

• • •

For the radical young fatwa-issuing preacher Mansour Al-Nogaidan, America's military "occupation" of his country in August and September 1990 was the first step on his own personal path to rebellion. Less than two months later came the second—the women's driving demonstration in Riyadh. Al-Nogaidan had no doubt that the two events were connected.

"I got a phone call that day," he remembers, "from a friend in Riyadh.

'The women are driving!' he told me in a panic. 'Thank God the mutawwa have stopped them.' 'Thank God,' I echoed. But as we found out more, it seemed very clear that Prince Salman was supporting the women."

Al-Nogaidan was just twenty, opinionated beyond his years and well respected in his Salafi community. But he was beginning to fret at the passivity of his Buraydah brethren.

"We were always very pleased to hear the news from Afghanistan," he recalls. "We were obviously happy at the success of our Muslim brothers. But we kept ourselves to ourselves. We were not passionately committed to the jihad—nor, for that matter, to the progress of the Sahwah."

This reticence troubled him. Salman Al-Awdah was preaching a few mosques away from Mansour's neighborhood in Buraydah, but the Brothers warned Mansour to keep his distance. " 'Those Sahwah sheikhs are accusing the government of infidelity,' they said. 'Be very careful.' "

Ultimately, the Brothers were conventional, loyal-to-the-emir Wahhabis in the Bin Baz mold, and Mansour was coming to reject this blind obedience that lay at the heart of the traditional Wahhabi mission.

"When I listened to the tapes of Al-Awdah, I got the message immediately. It was embedded in every sentence, and it was so very cutting—his criticism of the Al-Saud."

Mansour was making new young mujahid friends who had fought in Afghanistan and who excited him with their proactive, vigilante-style approach.

"They laughed and were enthusiastic. They were so different from the passivity of the Brothers who were always saying, 'We must accept the punishment of God.' The mujahideen had trained themselves to make a difference. They had fought to change things in Afghanistan, and now they were mobilizing to change things at home."

Mansour started going down to Riyadh to stay with his radical new friends in the neighborhood of Hay Al-Rabwah, where young Salafis bunked together in communal guesthouses, Afghanistan-style. This was where Juhayman had camped when he was rounding up recruits in support of the Mahdi, and now, a dozen years later, the climate again seemed ready for his fevered style of revivalism. Some young jihadis owned copies of the rebel's famous Letters, which they read to one another and discussed. At night during the Gulf War they sat up on the roofs to watch

Saddam's Scud missiles fly overhead. Those who could afford a car would shuttle around picking up the others for Koran meetings or morning prayers.

"It was very Boy Scoutish and even cultlike," recalls a jihadi from those days. "We organized sentries and lookouts, the whole communal thing. You felt like it was you against the world. There was no one who mattered outside your own tight little group."

The neighborhood was so pious that there were no cigarettes in the shops.

"We watched a lot of videos of the jihad—the death and burial of Abdullah Azzam," recalls Mansour Al-Nogaidan. "I admired these men who had fought in Afghanistan, and I wanted to go there myself. But when I went to get my passport, I was told I was banned from traveling. Why? I asked. 'If you want to know,' they told me, 'you'll have to go to the Ministry of the Interior.' "

By now Mansour had served three spells in jail—sixteen days for criticizing religious graduation ceremonies in 1987, fifty-five days in 1989 for his Youth World Cup protest, and forty-seven days in 1990 for a lecture he had delivered in Buraydah in which he had attacked the irreligiousness of the Saudi education system, and had encouraged pupils to forsake school as he had done. He was building up his credentials as a champion of the Islamist cause, and in the middle of 1991, only months after the Kuwait war had ended, he received an invitation that seemed the crowning accolade. Sheikh Osama was looking for someone with good religious knowledge who could teach in Jeddah. A house and salary went with the job.

Mansour flew down to Jeddah as soon as he could, going to Bin Laden's famously austere house in Macarona Street. But by the time he got there, Osama was gone.

. . .

In a matter of months Osama Bin Laden had moved from being the applauded colleague and partner of the House of Saud to considering himself their dedicated foe. For many years his reflexive loyalty to his family's patrons had been a quiet joke among the faithful. When King Fahd paid a state visit to Britain in 1987, the Queen had invested the Saudi ruler with the Royal Victorian Chain, whose elaborate insignia contains a large white enameled Maltese Cross, prompting people in Peshawar, when they saw the photographs, to whisper that the Saudi king must have forsaken Islam.

"For God's sake," Osama scolded them, "don't discuss this subject. Concentrate on your mission. I don't permit anyone to discuss this issue here."

But eighteen months in the Kingdom had transformed Bin Laden's attitude—he did not appreciate the double rejection by the Saudi government of his offers of help. He had already ignored Prince Turki's prohibition and was starting to organize armed Al-Qaeda camps in Yemen.

"He introduced me one evening to some friends who were helping him fight the jihad in Yemen," recalls Jamal Khashoggi. "He was proud of it. I told him, 'You can't do that without the government's permission.' He just looked at me and smiled."

Soon barbed wire appeared along the top of the high wall surrounding Osama's Macarona Street house.

"He must have feared some sort of retaliation from Yemeni agents," says Jamal Khashoggi. "The government told him to take the wire down and to stop making speeches. His passport was confiscated."

The liberal reformer and lawyer Mohammed Saeed Tayeb met Bin Laden in these months.

"It was at a weekly gathering in Mecca," he recalls. "I saw this man, very tall and beautiful, sitting at the end of the majlis. He was wearing a pistol outside his thobe—which seemed normal in those months of the war with Iraq, though no one else was wearing a pistol. That was the only time in my life that I saw Bin Laden, and I was struck by how very quiet he was, and how polite. If anyone else started talking in the salon, he instantly stopped talking himself."

Saeed Tayeb was a veteran of constitutional jostlings with the Al-Saud. By 1991 he had already been in and out of jail on three occasions for a total, at that date, of seven years behind bars (he has since racked up more). So when Bin Laden had stopped speaking about the need to battle the corruption and false façade of Communism in Afghanistan, Saeed Tayeb tackled him on the need for a battle closer to home.

"Mr. Bin Laden," he asked. "Why have you been spending all your time and money fighting in a foreign land? The true corruption and the false façade is *here*—to our left and to our right. It is above our heads and below our feet."

As an old-fashioned Arab nationalist (he named his first son Abdul Nasser in honor of the famous Egyptian leader), Saeed Tayeb had always been against the Afghan enterprise—he felt that Bin Laden and his fellow Islamists had been gulled into an essentially American project to defeat the Soviets. But Bin Laden refused to be drawn.

"Afghanistan," he replied quietly, "has been a place for training our young men in how to fight and to use weapons."

Osama declined the chance that he was being offered to engage in criticism of the Al-Saud, and he gave no clue as to his feelings. He was under official warning, after all, and his immediate priority at this moment was to regain his confiscated passport.

Using family connections, he managed to retrieve the passport in the summer of 1991, and instantly left the country for Afghanistan. Sources differ on how long he spent there—possibly more than six months—then he flew with his followers and friends to Africa. Hassan Al-Turabi, the ideologue of the recent Islamist coup in the Sudan, had invited Bin Laden to transfer his headquarters to Khartoum, and Osama had decided to take up the invitation. Here was a wonderful chance to locate his fighting "base" in a country where he was supported by a genuine Islamic government. How very different from Saudi Arabia—where, as events turned out, he would never set foot again.

CHAPTER 17

Stopping the Sins

"If the government will not act against the sins, what can we do to stop them?"

By November 1991, a few months after his abortive trip to meet Osama Bin Laden in Jeddah, this question was at the top of Mansour Al-Nogaidan's agenda.

"Educating and counseling other people was no longer enough for me," he remembers. "The world had become so polluted, I was coming to feel that I wanted to change reality itself."

His new jihadi friends provided him with an answer as they sat and talked one evening in the Riyadh suburb of Al-Suwaydi.

"Tonight we have a mission," they told him. "We're going to burn down the Bel-Jone video shop, and we want you to join us."

The Bel-Jone was Riyadh's largest video store.

"I don't have the courage," Mansour told them bluntly. "And it is not correct."

His friends looked at one another, then looked back at him. They had been to the video store a few days earlier, they explained, and had tried to talk to the owner and "educate" him about the sinfulness of what he was doing. The man had not been receptive. So since their polite request to stop promoting evil had been refused, it was now their duty to promote the good. This could not be a sin. In advancing these arguments, they were observing the protocol of Islamic law on military attacks—the need for advance warning, discrimination in the selection of the target, and care to ensure that the planned punishment should match, and not exceed, the offense. They were inviting Mansour, in other words, to no casual act of violence, but to jihad—a carefully considered godly mission.

Mansour sat and thought. He prayed. He needed no reminding that videotapes were the degenerate channels by which secular, non-Islamic poisons were Westernizing the minds of young Saudis—the government sheikhs were always complaining about them, but doing nothing. His friends, on the other hand, were serious and committed Muslims who were prepared to put their principles into practice: they had already burned down video stores in Unayzah and Buraydah. In planning to stop the sins tonight, they had made sure that they would not be endangering human life; they had checked that there would be no one inside the Bel-Jone once it closed. It was a freestanding building, so no other property would be harmed.

The mixture of theology and human consideration convinced him.

"After two hours," he remembers, "I said OK. I would do it as an honor: it was a compliment to be invited by my friends."

The petrol had already been purchased at nine different gas stations, along with three natural-gas canisters that would be stationed to blow open the doors. Arriving at the video store in the darkness of the small hours, his friends worked with experienced speed. Having studied the store's layout, they poured gasoline over the roof, and through openings in the walls around the air conditioners. When they were sure the fuel was distributed to maximum effect, they laid the final trail—a narrow stream of gasoline across the front step that flowed under the doors and into the store. Mansour lit his match and tossed it. He started to run away even as the petrol exploded with a warm *whoosh*.

A few hours later, after the dawn prayer, the conspirators drove back past the scene of their crime. They could hardly contain their delight. The entire, sprawling Bel-Jone video store and its noxious contents had been burned to the ground. The sins had been stopped! *"Al-hamdu lillah!"* they cried out together. "Thanks be to God!"

. . .

Buraydah was the next target—a women's charity for widows and the poor, where, the group was convinced, the females of the community were being taught bad things.

"They felt sure," recalls Mansour, "that the charity was a front for liberalizing and Westernizing women—teaching them to take off their *hijab* [head covering] and to become very free. I was not so sure and asked them for proof. I said my *istikhara* [the Muslim prayer for guidance] for two hours before I decided to go, and even then I did not feel happy."

The charity was in a villa behind a high wall, which concealed Mansour and his friends as they broke in and started to search the rooms.

"There had been no fatwa against the charity," remembers Mansour. "So we had to search for the evidence of sin. We were expecting to find sex videos, but all we found was a hair salon. We found one room that was equipped with exercise machines for the handicapped, so we decided to leave that. Then we found a shelf of religious books—how could we burn those? We decided to take out all the Korans. On the director's desk I found a file with the names of three hundred poor families. I was astonished to see the names of three families that I knew. They were related to me and they were receiving aid. It made me unhappy, but then one of the friends found a controversial book lying around. It was by the fundamentalist scholar Mohammed Nasser Al-Deen Al-Albani arguing that it was OK for women to show their face.

" 'This is as we suspected,' said the friend in triumph. 'This book shows the sin that they are truly plotting to accomplish in this building.' Everyone else agreed. So we started stacking the rooms with petrol and with gas canisters."

The jobs in the group had been carefully apportioned. The person who poured the petrol did not light it, and this time the job of striking the crucial match had been handed to another newcomer. As with the video store, the results were devastating.

"The building was burnt out," Mansour recalls. "But this time I did not feel happy as I had the time before."

• • •

He did not have long to contemplate his remorse. In less than ten weeks—early in January 1992—Mansour and his friends were tracked down by the Mabahith and found themselves in the dock facing Sulayman Al-Muhanna, a venerable and sheikhly figure who was the senior judge of all the Riyadh courts.

"My son," the sheikh inquired with an apparent sympathy that Mansour had not expected, "are you feeling guilty or not guilty for what you have done?"

"I did not do anything wrong," replied Mansour defiantly. "And if I said I won't do it again, I would be a liar."

He then launched into a recitation of all the hadiths and authorities that justified his taking action in the stopping of sins—to be cut short by the judge.

"I am not here to argue with you," said Sheikh Al-Muhanna, who had suddenly become a great deal less sympathetic. "I am here to sentence you."

He dispatched Mansour and his fellow fire bombers to prison for sixteen years.

• • •

Mansour Al-Nogaidan and his fellow arsonists-in-the-name-of-God were the most spectacular protesters in an unprecedented fusillade of protests that marked the Kingdom's reaction to the Gulf War. After a decade of domestic docility, Fahd's welcoming of U.S. troops seemed to have broken some kind of spell. If the king could overturn the conventions, so could everyone else. Women claimed the right to drive, while forty-three liberal reformers from Jeddah, Riyadh, and the Eastern Province, the much imprisoned Mohammed Saeed Tayeb prominent among them, set out their ideas for comprehensive democratic reform in a petition they submitted to the king. The House of Saud brushed this off as elitist and Westernized—"Just what you'd expect from Jeddah," in the dismissive words of one Nejdi thinker. But then came a double onslaught from the Wahhabi heartland, Khitab Al-Matalib (the Letter of Demands) signed by fifty-two religious figures, many of them Sahwists, followed in May 1992 by a still stronger document, Mudhakkarat Al-Nasiha (the Memorandum of Advice). These petitions did not place the accent on Western-style democracy, which was not a priority for men who sought wisdom in the Koran rather than in the fickle and earthly will of the people. "Consultation" was the watchword, along with judicial and administrative reform—particularly of government corruption—more accountability, the restoration of Islamic values, and a reduction of the expatriate labor force.

The Memorandum was drafted and presented by Dr. Ahmad Al-Tuwayjri, a member of an intellectual clan who had made their name in government service. His father had run the royal office of telegrams for Abdul Aziz for a period and then for his eldest son Saud, tapping out the Morse code messages through which the Saudi monarch communicated with the outside world.

"On summer nights we slept up on the roof," remembers Al-Tuwayjri, who spent much of his childhood in Taif. "My father kept the radio beside him to listen to the BBC, and sometimes he'd switch the channel, so we could listen to [the singer] Umm Kalthum, or to other poems and Egyptian music."

As an undergraduate at Riyadh's King Saud University, Al-Tuwayjri had campaigned unsuccessfully for the formation of a student union, confirming his reputation as a troublemaker when he returned from America in the mid-'80s: he gave a lecture that not only deplored the rigidity and intolerance of the religious establishment, but called for a Majlis Al-Shura that would represent the collective wisdom of the community.

Such a Consultative Council was one of the key demands of the Memorandum on which Al-Tuwayjri, now the Dean of the College of Education at King Saud University, worked with other academics and religious figures in the months following the Gulf War. Many of his friends hosted weekly forums in their homes, where men sipped tea and coffee together and often shared a light supper while they debated the issues of the moment.

"Everyone agreed," remembers Al-Tuwayjri, "that things had gone wrong and that something had to be done."

As reform plans were discussed in the forums, Al-Tuwayjri looked for a balance between the conservative and moderate proposals. It was a sign of the prevailing sense of crisis that the Consultative Council, once mistrusted by some as a secular or even Western innovation, was now generally desired with certain safeguards. Every constituency saw the council as the means to advance its own particular cause with the government. Having invited ideas from forums outside Riyadh, and particularly from those in the Wahhabi heartlands of Unayzah and Buraydah, Al-Tuwayjri eventually produced a manifesto that covered three pages. University colleagues helped him boil it down to a single sheet of bullet points, and having secured the signatures of some distinguished religious sheikhs, he took it to his mentor, Abdul Aziz Bin Baz.

"Sheikh Bin Baz was one of the most open-minded people I have ever known," says Al-Tuwayjri, "the very opposite of the 'flat earth' reputation that was played upon by the newspapers. His name suffered from the pressures he was put under by the government, and also by the sheikhs, to issue some truly weird fatwas. Sometimes he tried to reconcile the impossible. But I can tell you that he was a great scholar—with a very kind heart. I remember the look of dismay and sadness on his face when I told him about two of the lady lecturers in my college who were sacked after the driving demonstration. His color changed. He was the person who intervened with the king and got them their jobs back."

Now Al-Tuwayjri went to Bin Baz's house in Al-Shumaysi with the final draft and read out its calls for reform.

"The sheikh listened very carefully, then he signed straightaway. The document contained criticism, but it was *loyal* criticism. It was working within the system to achieve change, so that was acceptable to his principles. He always wanted to be patriotic."

Delivering the Memorandum was more difficult.

"We decided on a small delegation: Sheikh Abdul Muhsin Al-Ubaiqan [a conservative religious scholar], Sheikh Saeed bin Zuair [another fundamentalist sheikh whose radical views had previously landed him in prison], and Muhsin Al-Awaji [a fundamentalist]. They all got in a car and went round to the palaces. At Fahd's and Sultan's they were told to leave the document. Nayef and Salman each invited the petitioners in and received the Memorandum personally."

Then there was silence.

"The Memorandum," says Al-Tuwayjri, "took them completely by surprise. They were stunned. The ideas had come from everywhere—from north, south, east, and west, and from people of real weight, men who were very devout and conservative. There were famous judges, academics, successful businessmen, and ulema, headed by Bin Baz of all people. It was a consensus of people who mattered. We had worked very quickly and quietly, so the Mabahith had not got wind of it—or perhaps they did not imagine that we would actually present it."

After two days, the delegation that had presented the document received calls from Prince Salman's office proposing a meeting two days hence. But in the meantime, details of the Memorandum had leaked. A wide circle of people had read its suggestions, and the meeting was abruptly canceled.

"It was the leaking of the details that got them really mad," recalls Al-Tuwayjri, "the fact that the contents of the document—and the names on it—got spread around. For them the fact that people *knew* about it was a betrayal. By the time a group of us got to the governor's office to see Prince Salman he was furious and a conflict started in minutes.

"Luckily both sides realized that they were there to solve a problem, not create another one. After all, nothing in the Memorandum was actually against the royal family. It was about helping them—about offering them expert consultation and advice. That's what we stressed. In the end the meeting went on for an hour, and it all ended quite reasonably."

As governor of Riyadh, Prince Salman had been chosen by the senior group of Al-Saud brothers to negotiate a compromise that saved some royal face. The petitioners were absolutely unwilling to retract a word, but they were prepared to apologize for the unintended way that the Memorandum had been leaked. For their part, the government agreed that a committee should be established to act as the vehicle for accepting well-intentioned suggestions and complaints, and to start the ball rolling, the king announced the establishment of the Consultative Council more or less at once. Fahd had had the plans on his desk, as part of the so-called Basic Law, for more than a dozen years—a sixty-seat, all-male, nominated chamber with limited powers of scrutiny, whose building had already been completed. In 1980 he had promised the Shura after the seizing of the Grand Mosque. Now "crusader" troops and some domestic agitation had brought to pass what Juhayman could not.

THE DONKEY FROM YEMEN

Soon after the end of the Gulf War, the government of Yemen sent a peace offering to King Fahd—a donkey carrying two heavy baskets, one on either side of its back. One basket contained a beautiful and shapely woman, the other was stacked full of gold nuggets.

"Wonderful!" cried the king. "I shall give the beautiful woman to my poor brother Sultan [the much married defense minister]. He doesn't have enough of them. And I shall send all that gold to my poor son Abdul Aziz. He's down to his last fifty billion riyals."

"What about the donkey?" asked his courtiers. "It's so loud and stupid."

"Excellent!" cried the king. "Send it to the new Shura Council. That's just what we need there!"

. . .

The arrests started a month after Prince Salman had brokered the peace.

"A group of officers from the Mabahith arrived at my house," remembers Al-Tuwayjri. "They were dressed in thobes. They were extremely polite and respectful. But in Saudi Arabia we have no rights. They said they had orders to search my house and take me to headquarters. So that is what happened. There were seven or eight of us arrested and they took us all to Al-Haier [the Mabahith prison in the south of Riyadh]."

Every night Al-Tuwayjri was cross-examined by three Mabahith officers.

"They wanted to know if there was a plot. That was the purpose of the whole thing. They had been caught out by the Memorandum. Now they wanted to be sure we had not been conspiring to overthrow the government.

" 'If I'd wanted to do some overthrowing,' I told them, 'I'd have worked in secret. I wouldn't have gone to the government and given it my advice.' "

The government justified the arrests on the grounds that Al-Tuwayjri and his friends had gone outside the protocols of *shura* (consultation). It was not the Saudi way to broadcast criticism in a way that might provoke agitation and dissent.

"I hope that efforts will be confined to giving advice for the sake of God," declared King Fahd. "If, however, someone has things to say, then he can always come to those in charge and speak to them in any region, in any place. As advice, this is wanted and desired."

"Trust your local prince," in other words. After a week Al-Tuwayjri was transferred to join his fellow petitioners in a collection of cells with their own communal area.

"I volunteered to do the cooking for everyone, and it made for quite a cozy atmosphere. After a time the officers would drop in for a chat and watch sports on the television with us. We were allowed to get books from the prison library, or send someone out to buy them. We had a sort of club going. It was almost sad when they sent us home after forty days. You hear terrible stories about the prisons in Egypt, Libya, Syria, and just about every other Arab country. On the basis of my own experience, I have to say that in Saudi Arabia we definitely have a better class of jail."

• • •

Al-Tuwayjri's forty days of confinement reflected Fahd's anger and frustration. The Saudi king had taken big risks and had acted with rare speed and decisiveness to save his country—only to be thanked with criticism from almost every quarter. His indignation was understandable. In addi-

Prince Fahd bin Abdul Aziz, 33, Saudi Arabia's first education minister, tests out the latest in British desk design with Miss M. G. Green, headmistress, in a class of female pupils at Kidbrooke Comprehensive School, London, in November 1954. There were at that date no girls' schools in Saudi Arabia, and many conservatives refused to countenance the notion. It would be another ten years before Fahd's half-brother Faisal introduced publicly funded girls' education—with armed platoons of soldiers deployed to protect the first female pupils and their parents from the possible wrath of religious extremists.

A carefree King Fahd greets the press at Nice on the French Rivera in April 1987, a few months after he assumed the title Custodian of the Two Holy Mosques.

From 1983 onward, Saudi Arabia spent, by some estimates, as much as $40 billion supporting the bitter and bloody war that Saddam Hussein's Iraq waged against Iran and the Ayatollah Khomeini. In this picture, taken sometime in the mid-1980s, the grateful Iraqi dictator shows off his weaponry to his Arab brother, the Saudi king.

Fahd's twin-funneled private yacht, the 482-foot-long *Prince Abdul Aziz,* the longest private yacht built in the twentieth century.

U.S. president Ronald Reagan and Saudi Crown Prince Fahd first met in 1981 at the North-South Economic summit in Mexico. As king, Fahd would next meet Reagan in Washington in 1985, when, over breakfast, Reagan asked Fahd to supply the secret funds—ultimately some $32 million—that led to the Nicaraguan Contra scandal.

Fahd's private palace in Marbella, southern Spain, which displays an uncanny resemblance to the White House.

Prince Turki Al-Faisal, director of the Saudi CIA (the Istikhbarat, or General Intelligence Department) from 1977 to 2001. He helped fund and supervise the expulsion of Soviet forces from Afghanistan in the 1980s, and presided over the 1990s era that saw the emergence of the Taliban and Osama Bin Laden's Al-Qaeda. After serving in London as ambassador from 2002 to 2005, he was named ambassador to the U.S., but resigned his Washington post only a little more than a year later, in circumstances that have never been fully explained.

Prince Bandar bin Sultan as a fighter pilot. He trained at Britain's Royal Air Force College at Cranwell and later serrved as Saudi ambassador from 1983 to 2005.

Prince Bandar helped lobby the U.S. Congress for the purchase of AWACS surveillance aircraft (left) by Saudi Arabia in 1981. President Reagan backed the sale, so when Israel's prime minister Menachem Begin spoke out against it, the Saudis came up with the slogan "Reagan or Begin?" The Senate finally approved the sale 52–48.

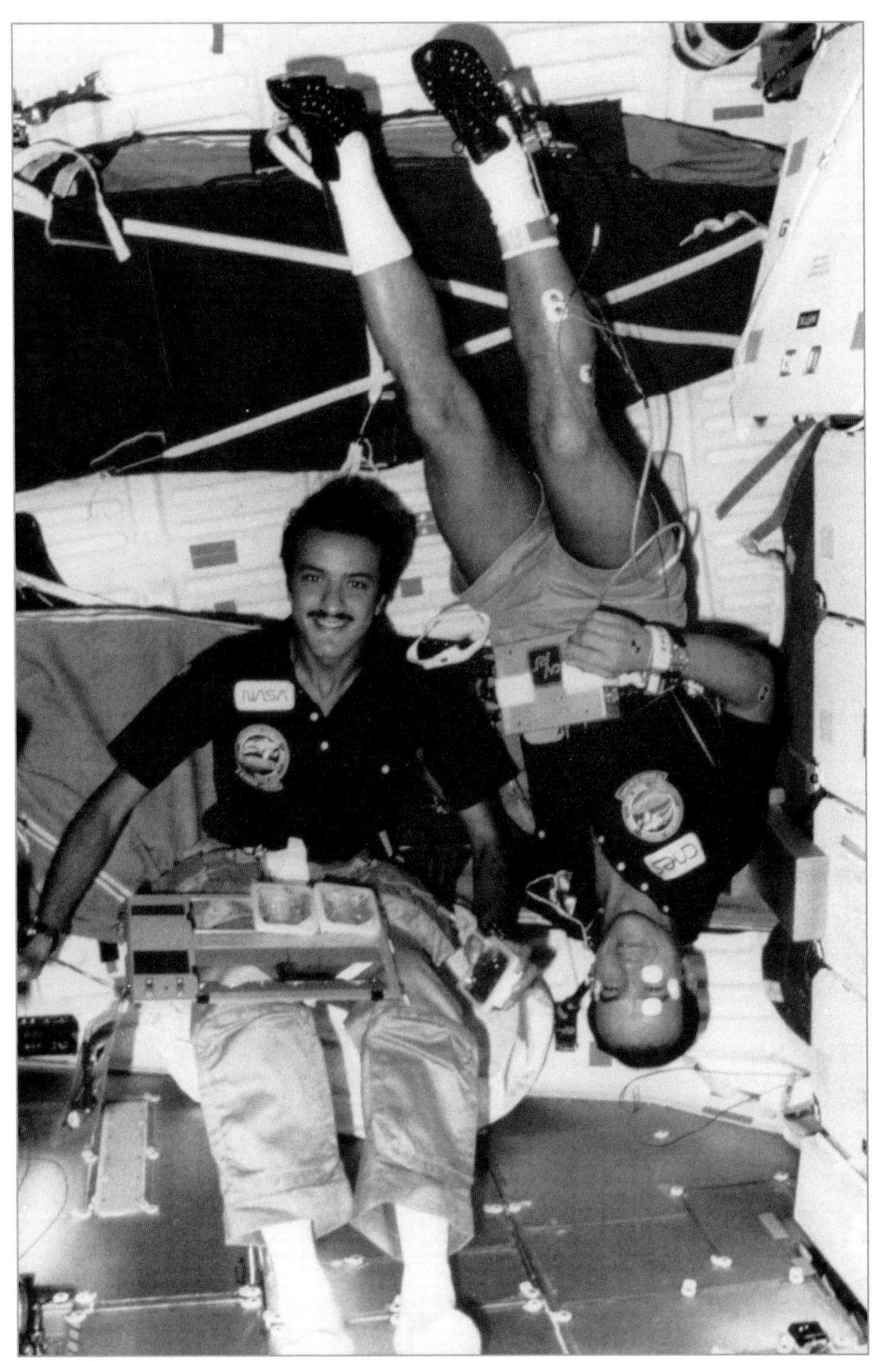

Prince Sultan bin Salman, 29, the first Arab in space, weightless on board the Space Shuttle *Discovery* in July 1985 with the French payload specialist Patrick Baudry (in shorts).

Prince Salman bin Abdul Aziz, center, in a plain dark *thobe,* joins the *ardha,* the traditional Saudi sword dance. The second-youngest of the powerful Sudayri Seven princes, Salman has been governor of Riyadh since 1962, presiding over the development of the capital from a sleepy desert town to a bustling and largely efficient capital city of more than four million inhabitants.

Since 1975, Prince Nayef bin Abdul Aziz has presented a firm face to the world as minister of the interior and director of the Kingdom's police, security, and secret police (the Mabahith). Shown here in front of his ministry's all-seeing-eye symbol, he presents arrangements for the 2006 *hajj* (pilgrimage), which the Kingdom regards as its foremost security task. In March 2009 Nayef was named the Kingdom's "Second Deputy Premier," making him the presumed successor to his elder brother Sultan as Crown Prince.

Crown Prince Sultan bin Abdul Aziz has been in charge of the Defense Ministry and its armaments contracts since 1962, deploying his massive fortune to the benefit of his exceptionally large family—more than thirty sons and daughters—and to lavish charitable enterprises.

In 1988 Osama Bin Laden, pictured here, aged 31, in his command HQ (a cave) was Saudi Arabia's hero of the hour. His Arab Afghan fighters had helped trounce the godless Soviets to create an inspiring new role model for Saudi youth—the modern holy warrior for Islam.

Desert Storm. January 6, 1991. King Fahd and General Norman Schwarzkopf review troops of the thirty-four nation alliance assembled to expel Saddam Hussein's Iraqi invasion forces from Kuwait. After more than a month of aerial bombardment, the coalition forces invaded Kuwait, directly and via Iraq, on February 24. After less than one hundred hours of ground fighting, Iraq's forces laid down their arms, signing cease-fire terms at Safwan airfield on March 3.

In the small hours of January 30, 1991, Iraqi tanks and troops crossed the Saudi-Kuwaiti border to occupy the deserted frontier town of Al-Khafji. The following day Saudi National Guardsmen and two Qatari mechanized units fought their way north to recapture Al-Khafji in the only seriously contested battle of the Gulf War—also liberating two groups of U.S. Marines who had been hiding in the town on aerial guidance missions. Eighteen Saudis were killed and thirty-two wounded.

tion to his domestic critics, a group of dissidents had started fomenting trouble in exile. Following the failure, as they saw it, of the Letter of Demands and the Memorandum of Advice, two radical academics from Riyadh's King Saud University—Saad Al-Faqih, a professor of surgery, and Mohammed Al-Massari, who was chairman of the physics department—had relocated to London, where they made skillful use of the BBC and other international media to launch scathing critiques of the Saudi regime, and of Fahd in particular. The king's well-documented taste for Western pleasures made him an easy target, eagerly taken up and spread by the early websites of the 1990s—and by a campaigning Palestinian journalist, Said K. Aburish, whose particular focus was the destructive influence of oil on the Arab character and culture. Fahd's double identity illustrated this precisely, in Aburish's opinion, and his book *The Rise, Corruption, and Coming Fall of the House of Saud* became a best-seller when it was published in London in 1994.

The king was no bookworm, but he did understand the power of television. Satellite TV dishes had started appearing on Saudi rooftops in the early 1990s and had provided Sahwah activists with another focus for their anger. The dishes were routes, declared the sheikhs, by which foreign decadence was being channeled directly into Saudi homes, corrupting the minds of the young—and of women, in particular—with frivolity and alternative, non-Islamic lifestyles. Particularly ardent zealots, including members of the religious police, had taken out their hunting rifles to aim potshots at these very visible symbols of Westernization, and the regular civil police had not shown much energy in pursuing them.

Sheikh Bin Baz came to see the king to explain the outrage that good, pious Muslims were feeling about the satellite dishes, and Fahd—whose every palace had at least one huge satellite dish—was all sympathy. Satellite television should be banned, he agreed. In 1994 an official decree made it illegal to manufacture, import, or install the dishes, and as the ban took effect a number of princes jumped into the now very profitable dish-importing business. For ordinary customers, buying a princely dish meant buying a certain immunity.

The biggest investment of all was in the production of television programming to be broadcast on the burgeoning satellite networks. The government controlled the Kingdom's terrestrial TV channels through the Ministry of Information—the main studios were inside the ministry's

Riyadh compound, where the tall, onionlike TV tower provided a proud symbol for the ministry on all its letterheads and leaflets. Satellite television would obviously bring reporting and ideas into the Kingdom that were beyond royal control—unless the royal family controlled the satellite stations. So in the early 1990s Fahd began to invest in the TV business through Abdul Aziz and Khaled Al-Ibrahim, brothers of the king's now favorite wife Al-Johara (and therefore uncles of young Abdul Aziz bin Fahd, the much indulged Azouzi).

"The king realized," says one of his kitchen cabinet, "that television, and these satellite channels in particular, were going to have a profound effect on how Saudis came to think. It was their window to the outside world. It would open their eyes to everything. There was no way to stop it in the long run—banning satellite dishes was just a gesture. So why not try to have some sort of control or influence?"

Thinking of control and influence, Fahd also turned his gaze eastward. He had an inner circle of contacts that he would call, often in the small hours of the morning, to test out ideas or to request instant policy papers. It was the king's telephone think tank, and in the months following the Gulf War Fahd started using his early-morning phone calls to solicit ideas on how to deal with the long-standing problem of his subjects who were Shia.

CHAPTER 18

In from the Cold

Soon after Saddam Hussein invaded Kuwait, in the summer of 1990, Iraqi agents started appearing at the ancient, blue-tiled shrine of Zaynab in Damascus. Shias had been visiting the shrine for centuries to honor Zaynab, spirited sister of the martyred Husayn (see the glossary, page 342). Since leaving Iran, Sheikh Hassan Al-Saffar, leader of the Saudi Shias in exile, had set up his headquarters here, and it was to the sheikh that the Iraqis now came with a message from their president.

Saddam had always had a special place in his heart for the interests of the Saudi Shias, explained his emissaries, and had decided to offer Sheikh Hassan a radio station of his own in Iraq. This would enable the sheikh to beam his spiritual messages directly to his oppressed followers inside the Kingdom, while also encouraging them to rise up against the tyranny of the House of Saud. Along with the radio station there would also be funds to help support the expenses of the sheikh and his movement—and, perhaps, even, the use of a plane. Sheikh Hassan and his group of Shia exiles were being recruited to join Saddam in his anti-Saudi war effort.

"It was not worth even the effort of responding"—says the sheikh today with a sniff—"the idea that Saddam Hussein genuinely cared about the rights and worship of the Shia people."

"We rejected the approach out of hand," says Tawfiq Al-Seif, who was then the sheikh's deputy. "We'd left Iran in order to prove our independence. Our loyalty was not to Iraq, but to a reformed Saudi Arabia."

By the summer of 1990, Sheikh Hassan was heading the most effective opposition the House of Saud had faced to that date, thanks to the movement's change of emphasis following their departure from Iran. Al-Saffar and his followers had abandoned the theme of Islamic revolution with its connotations of Khomeini. They were now presenting themselves in more universal terms, as the International Committee for Human Rights in the Gulf and the Arabian Peninsula—a hot button to press in these months that saw the collapse of the Soviet Union.

"Our 'Human Rights' label attracted the American media like a magnet," remembers Fouad Ibrahim, the historian of the dissident Shia movement. "Congressional researchers came asking for data. We received inquiries from the United Nations. We started working with activists like Amnesty International and Human Rights Watch—and we used our contacts inside the Kingdom to hand out news stories around the world on Saudi arrests and scandals."

Jaffar Shayeb, one of the sheikh's political advisers who was pursuing his studies in the United States, opened a Saudi human rights office in Washington, where he organized a roster of articulate young Shia Saudis who were available to present their case on radio and television. Using this data, the Minnesota Lawyers Human Rights Committee produced *Shame in the House of Saud,* a scattershot dossier that set out the charges, some true, some exaggerated, detailing the Kingdom's mistreatment of Shias, women, and foreign laborers. But the movement's greatest triumph had come in the early months of 1990, when a government propaganda exhibition, "Saudi Arabia Between Yesterday and Today," toured Washington, New York, and a series of other cities. At several of the openings, a dozen Shia demonstrators, their faces swathed in red and white Saudi headdresses, invited visitors to sign anti-Saudi petitions and shouted aggressive slogans loudly through their bullhorns, taking the chance they would never have at home to confront Saudi worthies such as Prince Salman, the governor of Riyadh, who was accompanying the tour.

"Salman! Ya Salman!" shouted the young Saudis angrily. *"Fain hugoog al-insaan?* Where are our human rights?"

"It was electrifying, and also scary," remembers Faiza Ambah, one of the Saudi journalists covering the official party, looking out at the demonstrators. "It was a first. We knew they were Saudis behind the *shomagh* [headdresses]. We'd never seen Saudis demonstrating before."

Local TV crews asked for interviews, the official Saudi delegation looked pompous as it refused to comment, and a multimillion-dollar PR initiative had the opposite effect.

"Then we jumped into our VW bus," remembers one of the demonstrators happily, "and drove on to wait for them in the next city. They were trapped. They couldn't cancel or refuse to appear, and they knew what was waiting for them when they arrived in town. It must have been a nightmare for them."

. . .

That summer, however, the Gulf War brought a pause to the movement. The Shia exiles, like all other Saudis, were confronted with the prospect of Iraqi troops overrunning their homeland, and when they considered the options, Sheikh Hassan and his followers decided they were as patriotically Saudi as anyone else.

"We are ready to defend the nation and the independence of the nation," declared a spokesman in response to Saddam's invasion, adding that the sheikh and the movement's leadership "urged Shia citizens to join military service for the purpose of defending the country."

There was a little mischief in this second comment, since there were no Shia in the Saudi military, because the Saudi government had always refused to recruit them. But, in or out of the army, there was more than enough work to do, and the eight hundred thousand or so Shia of the Eastern Province set about it with gusto. They dug themselves in under the threat of Scuds and poison gas, and worked tirelessly providing food and shelter for the influx of half a million foreign fighting personnel. Meanwhile the Committee for Human Rights shut down its criticism outside the Kingdom for the time being, and supported Riyadh's controversial alliance with America. The victory, when it came, owed not a little to Shia staunchness at home and discretion abroad.

. . .

From King Fahd's point of view, the Shia support created a contrast that could hardly have been more stark. After a decade in which he had bet the shop on the Sunnis, lavishing money on the Wahhabis and giving them just about whatever they wanted, he found himself confronted by the petition-signing ingratitude of the Sahwah sheikhs and their criticism of the U.S. presence. He had financed his own opposition. Meanwhile the despised and supposedly untrustworthy Shia had committed themselves without reserve to the defense of the Kingdom. Occupying the most vulnerable part of the home front, they had not kicked up a moment's distraction.

The king and his son Mohammed had been trying to speak, off the record, to Sheikh Hassan and the Shia leadership for years. They had dispatched emissaries to Iran, Syria, and Washington, though never with a suggestion of apology.

"It always ended up," remembers one of their Shia interlocutors, "with the idea that the problem lay with *us* for being so extreme. As for 'sorry'—that's not a word you expect to hear from Saudi princes."

But following the Gulf War there was a change of attitude: "They seemed more ready," recalls Tawfiq Al-Seif, "to admit mistakes." And the Shia side also shifted.

"We did not want to become governors," says Sheikh Hassan. "It was not our target to remove the royal family. But we did want to eliminate racism and discrimination for the sake of our Shia people and for the sake of everyone in Saudi Arabia. We saw our movement like the antiapartheid campaign in South Africa. We felt that the time had come to talk."

"By then," says one government adviser, "they had worked out that, like a lot of minorities in this country, they would get a better deal from the Saudi monarchy than they would from any nonroyal government. The Al-Saud were the only horse to back. How could the Shia expect anything but oppression from the Wahhabis? The last thing they wanted was some sort of Islamist state with Sunni rule by the Sahwah sheikhs."

The talking took place in London, with the Shia side represented by Al-Seif and Hamza Al-Hassan, a long-serving activist in exile, and the government by Abdul Aziz Al-Tuwayjri, chief adviser to Abdullah, the crown prince. A lively-minded and cleverly string-pulling man with a penchant for history, Al-Tuwayjri was nicknamed "T-l" by Western diplomats in Riyadh to distinguish him from the other members of his talented family. Ahmed Al-Tuwayjri, the activist and framer of the Memorandum of Advice, was one of his nephews.

"He was an inspiring and very clever person to talk to," recalls Al-Seif, "and we were pleased to be meeting with someone we knew to be truly influential behind the scenes. He started by saying yes, he knew we had a problem, but that he did not want to raise our expectations. He was not certain he could deliver: we needed to realize that at that moment the government had a great deal on its plate."

The first meeting took place in 1992 at the Knightsbridge Holiday Inn, where the three men sat in the coffee shop, chatting things out as if in a majlis at home. When they wanted some fresh air, they walked out to Hyde Park and continued their discussions, strolling beneath the trees.

"We talked from twelve until seven," remembers Al-Seif, "and Al-Tuwayjri never took a single note. It was the first of several meetings, all of them pleasurable. He had a remarkable memory—every important detail we had agreed on was in the letters that he sent us later, after he'd reported to the crown prince, who had then gone to talk to the king."

The two Shia reported, for their part, to their committees in exile, conferring particularly with Al-Saffar in Damascus and Jaffar Shayeb in the United States. There was fierce controversy among the rank and file about compromising with the Al-Saud, but the leadership wanted a deal.

"We had come to the belief," remembers Al-Seif, "that being inside was better than being outside. Going home, we felt sure, would better enable us to bring about change."

Negotiations took a step forward in 1993 when Al-Tuwayjri was replaced as the Saudi interlocutor by Othman Al-Omair, the London-based editor of the newspaper *Al-Sharq Al-Awsat* ("Middle East"). The dashing editor, who had a playboy reputation, was a less substantial figure than Al-Tuwayjri, but he came to the Shia as the personal representative of Fahd. His job was to get Al-Seif and his fellow negotiators to Jeddah for a face-to-face meeting with the king.

• • •

"We had three preconditions before we would go," remembers Sadiq Al-Jabran, one of the four-man negotiating team. "The release of all political prisoners, the restoration of confiscated and canceled passports, and a general amnesty allowing all Shia exiles to come home without any further questioning or follow-ups. We couldn't believe it. They didn't bother to argue. They said yes to them all."

On August 10, 1993, a telegram to Saudi embassies around the world notified consular staff that "gracious royal directives have been issued to the Ministry of the Interior to pardon all those of the Shia denomination who have conducted oppositional acts of all kinds, and allowing those who are outside the Kingdom to return if they wish."

"We met in Damascus," remembers Jaffar Al-Shayeb. "We were all a little bit scared. We'd made sure the *New York Times* published the story about the amnesty as a sort of protection. But none of us had valid Saudi passports. We'd decided that the first thing we'd do when we landed in

Saudi Arabia was *umrah* [lesser pilgrimage], so we got off the plane in our towels. They let us in—they were expecting us—and we spent the first few days in Mecca, then Medina."

"How was Medina?" was the first question that King Fahd asked as he greeted the delegation in his palace beside the Red Sea in Jeddah on Wednesday, September 22, 1993—a question intended to show that he did not share the Wahhabi distaste for Shia going to Medina to revere the Prophet's tomb. The king clearly wanted to put his visitors at ease. He had taken off his *mishlah,* the dark, gold-trimmed cloak that Saudi royals only set aside socially when in the company of their family or the very closest of friends. He greeted his visitors wearing his simple white thobe.

"You are all welcome, my sons," he declared.

It was a virtuoso Fahd perfomance, full of jokes and personal confidences woven into his habitual soliloquy of words and reflections. His son Mohammed, governor of the Eastern Province, sat beside him respectfully, saying nothing at all. Bandar bin Sultan, visiting from Washington, was also there, uncharacteristically silent.

The king talked regretfully about his bad leg. By 1993, looking more than his sixty-nine years, he was scarcely mobile, walking with difficulty. He was scornful on the subject of Yasser Arafat and Hussein of Jordan, the two former "friends" who had tried to kick the Kingdom when it was threatened by Saddam Hussein. Now, his implication seemed, he was talking in the company of *true* friends—"We need *all* our sons," he said.

"I remember when I was minister of education and minister of the interior," he reminisced, beginning to approach the issue. "I always made it a point to have good information on the Shia population. The Shia are equal citizens like everyone else. They are very hard workers. Every country in the world has problems, but they can always be resolved if people are willing to talk and listen."

Tawfiq Al-Seif had been appointed spokesman for the delegation and explained that, in the long years of exile, many of the Shia had married foreign wives.

"The women will be given the choice of Saudi nationality if they want it," said Fahd without ado.

To whom in the government could they come back and talk, asked Tawfiq, when it came to settling the details of this and other practicalities?

"I am taking charge of this entire matter personally," said the king with a smile. "It is very dear to my heart."

Fahd felt confident enough to play a little joke. One of the Shia complained that whenever a Saudi customs officer discovered Shia books in a suitcase, the books would get impounded and the Shia traveler would also be detained for questioning—in contrast to travelers who tried to smuggle *Playboy,* who simply had the magazine confiscated before being sent on their way.

"What's this *Playboy* magazine?" asked Fahd, pretending ignorance.

Having compelled his visitors to describe the nature of *Playboy* to him with some embarrassment, the king then assured them that there was no problem. Readers of Shia literature would, in future, be treated with no less sympathy than the readers of girly publications.

After an hour and a half the audience was over, and the four Shia were out of the palace, surrounded by the nighttime picnickers and donkey riders of the Jeddah Corniche, wondering if the whole thing had been a dream. For the first—and last—time in their lives they had been tête-à-tête with their king. They had made Saudi history. It was the first time that Fahd had ever sat down with his opposition face-to-face. And on top of it all, they were home!

As the days, months, and years went by, the details of the Shia reconciliation took a long time to work out: a decade later many elements of the deal are still being worked out. The king's grand promise to take care of the matter personally meant, in reality, that no one took care of it, and voices in the Shia community were soon complaining that Sheikh Hassan had given up the leverage afforded by masked young demonstrators in Washington too rapidly and for too slight a price.

"Since His Majesty gave you his promise," said Prince Nayef, straining a smile when the Shia leaders finally got to see him, "we shall investigate the best way to carry these things out."

Nayef had seen the intelligence reports of Iranian aid to Shia movements inside Saudi Arabia, and he viewed his brother's demarche with some reserve.

"In the end," says Ali Al-Marzouq, "all we really got was our passports back. But that's all right. We knew we could build on that."

CHAPTER 19

Change of Heart

The pardon and return of the Shia provided an unexpected dividend for Mansour Al-Nogaidan and his fellow video-store bombers—an early release from jail. King Fahd's blanket pardon of the long-imprisoned Shia rafada (rejectionists) offended many of the Kingdom's hard-line ulema and sheikhs. So the king ordered that a comparable batch of Salafi prisoners should be freed. It was the classic Al-Saud balancing act. At the end of September 1993 Mansour found himself at liberty, having served less than two of his sixteen years.

Ever questioning and reflecting, the young Salafi, still only twenty-two, had started to change his opinions inside prison—though this was no thanks to the efforts of the prison authorities to "reeducate" their charges.

"One day they brought us together to listen to a lecture from Faleh Al-Harbi—he was a [Prince] Nayef guy. We just laughed at him in front of all the officers. None of us would accept being 'fed' with any government ideas. Before they took us to court, we spent days preparing our arguments, because a lot of the hard-liners refused to accept the court's jurisdiction. One of them—his name was Ali, I remember—said, 'I want to declare that King Fahd is kafir, an infidel—and may God bless his soul.'"

Mansour knew it was unsafe to admit his personal softening to his hard-line fellow prisoners, who, in the pious Islamic tradition of "advice," were busy encouraging the good and discouraging the bad. They had taken it on themselves to go through and censor the newspapers being read by their fellow prisoners.

"They tore out every single picture and photograph of any sort—which didn't leave very much to read. They believed that the newspaper images would kick out the angels who were looking after all the godly ones in their cells."

Gradually Mansour identified two friends who shared his growing moderation—though none of the trio would admit their personal uncertainty as to whether an angel was actually keeping them company in their cell. The three "freethinkers" would talk together in the exercise yard, exchanging uncensored newspapers and cautiously swapping opinions derived from non-Salafi books.

"We knew that we were wandering outside the 'red lines,' but we did not want to risk admitting it."

The process continued when Mansour got out of jail.

"I went to visit a half brother in Buraydah who was quite an intellectual. 'I have a book for you,' he said. It was by Mohammed Abid Al-Jabiri, *Construction of the Arab Mind,* a work of philosophy, which I would not normally have touched. But my brother told me that Al-Jabiri was a scholar at Al-Azhar [the ancient religious university] in Cairo, so I decided to find out what he said."

This was not an action to be taken lightly. Since philosophy does not accept the overriding authority of a God and his law, the entire process of open-ended philosophic reasoning is *haram* (forbidden) to pious Muslims.

"Shame on you," said one of Mansour's friends when he caught him reading Al-Jabiri. "That man is the root of secularism."

But by this time Mansour was hooked on the wide-ranging vision of Al-Jabiri, with his comparisons between the Koran and the big ideas of Hellenic, Christian, and Persian cultures.

"I can take what I want," he told his conservative friend, "and I can leave the rest."

One book led to another. Mansour found himself reading more philosophy, some works on European thinking, and even Egyptian novels. Early in 1995 he attended a discussion group in Mecca, where he tentatively aired some of his developing ideas—and aroused general hostility. One of his friends reached out and squeezed his hand sharply to get him to stop. Orthodoxy was still very much the order of the day. A few months earlier the eloquent Sahwah sheikhs Safar Al-Hawali and Salman Al-Awdah had been arrested, having refused to sign letters promising to tone down their sermons, while Saad Al-Faqih and Mohammed Al-Masari, the exiled dissidents in London, were stepping up their anti-Saudi rhetoric.

In November 1995, a huge bomb tore apart the National Guard training center in Riyadh, killing five Americans and two Indian officials. The Mabahith hurried to round up the usual suspects—and Mansour Al-Nogaidan was one of them. He was a convicted firebomber, after all.

"I've changed my opinions," he told his interrogating officer.

"We have evidence," came the reply, "that in a Mecca discussion group earlier this year you told people to stand up and criticize the government when it does wrong."

"Perhaps I did," replied Mansour. "That's what I believe. But I certainly did not tell people to try to change things with bombs."

The distinction was lost on his interrogators, and Mansour went back to jail again—this time for more than two years.

• • •

The 1995 bombing of Riyadh's National Guard center was the first act of terrorism in Saudi Arabia since Juhayman's seizing of the Grand Mosque, and Osama Bin Laden praised it loudly from his base in the Sudan. It was evidence, he told a Pakistani interviewer, of a movement that would soon eliminate the House of Saud from the Arabian Peninsula. He also endorsed the still more lethal truck bombing of the Khobar Towers residential complex near Dhahran that came eight months later. The entire front of the building was torn away in a massive explosion whose shock was felt in Bahrain, across the water, more than twenty miles away. Nineteen U.S. Air Force personnel were killed, with 372 wounded.

Bin Laden had no direct connection with either atrocity. The four Saudis who were tried and executed for the Riyadh bombing were jihadis who had fought in Afghanistan, but they listed Bin Laden as only one of several opposition figures whose ideas had influenced them. The Khobar Towers attack bore clear hallmarks of Iranian involvement, and after five years of investigations the FBI issued indictments against thirteen members of a pro-Iranian organization that went by the name of Saudi Hizballah ("Party of God"). Osama was not yet a serious terrorist, but his strident declamations showed how his move across the Red Sea to the Sudan had helped him develop a new role. He had appointed himself chief tormentor and nemesis to the House of Saud.

• • •

Bin Laden had arrived in Khartoum early in 1992, and he got started at a fast clip, buying up several small farms by the Blue Nile to create for himself a mini-estate. On the weekends he would go down to the river to ride his horses, the very model of the successful businessman relaxing on his country acres. Transferring assets from Saudi Arabia and Afghanistan, he set himself up in a nine-room office in the Sudanese capital, from which he ran a trucking company, a leather-tanning factory, a bakery, a honey and sweets-producing company, a furniture-making venture, and an import-export trading business. American investigators later discovered that many of these enterprises were registered in Luxembourg and Switzerland. Osama was still operating in the style of his brothers on the other side of the Red Sea—at the heart of his little conglomerate was a heavy-construction company.

The British journalist Robert Fisk came across the entrepreneur late the following year in a remote area that Bin Laden company bulldozers had connected to the highway running from Khartoum to Port Sudan. Dressed in a white thobe and gold-trimmed cloak, with the local children dancing in front of him and the grateful villagers slaughtering chicken, goats, and sheep, Bin Laden looked for all the world like a philanthropic Saudi sheikh.

"We have been waiting for this road through all the revolutions in Sudan," declared one of the elders. "We had waited till we had given up on everybody—and then Osama Bin Laden came along!"

Osama enjoyed playing bountiful magnate in the land to which his father had come as a penniless Yemeni laborer in the 1920s. Sudan was where Mohammed the Builder had lost his eye playing soccer. Now his son was filling the role that his father had enjoyed with Ibn Saud, serving as constructor-in-residence at the court of Hassan Al-Turabi. Osama built highways and developed other business projects, not all of them successful, while secretly contributing to Al-Turabi's plans for international jihad. For several years he was doing everything in Sudan that he might have hoped to accomplish in a properly directed Islamist Arabia.

Then in April 1994 the Saudi government publicly stripped Osama of his Saudi citizenship. All his bank accounts and Saudi assets were frozen, and Fahd also put pressure on his family. The Bin Ladens could not go on garnering the cream of government construction contracts while they included—and effectively provided shelter to—the government's number one critic. They would have to decide. Within days of the government announcement, the brothers gathered in a solemn family conclave in Jeddah to issue a statement of "regret, denunciation, and condemnation of all acts that Osama Bin Laden may have committed." They formally renounced him as a member of the family, and confiscated his share of the family fortune, which they placed in a supervised trust for his children.

In his subsequent accounts of his life, Osama Bin Laden would frequently refer to 1994 as a turning point, focusing on the arrests in Saudi Arabia that September of the Sahwah preachers Safar Al-Hawali and Salman Al-Awdah. It was the imprisoning of these two good and religious men, he would say, that convinced him of the Al-Saud's perfidy. He made no public reference to the removal of his citizenship, nor to the statement by his brothers, but the renunciation must have hurt. For one thing, it cut him off from the source of his funds. Osama was compelled to scale back his businesses severely, firing dozens of his brightest young workers.

His thoughts began to turn homeward, encouraged by visits from a succession of family members, including his mother—and by the pious young journalist Jamal Khashoggi, who had been asked by the Bin Ladens to see what he could do to get Osama back.

"One of his cousins rang me," recalls Khashoggi. "He told me 'Osama's changed, he wants to come back.'"

Khashoggi's task was to coax Bin Laden to give an interview in which he expressed some remorse and, ideally, renounced any commitment to violence. The family would then show that to the government in hopes it might prepare the way for a reconciliation.

"On the first evening, he started talking about Medina," recalls Khashoggi, "saying how much he'd like to go back and settle there. He had a wife who came from Medina."

The two Saudis were sitting around a sheet of plastic laid on the ground, leaning forward to pull chunks of lamb from a pile of rice, nostalgically enjoying *kabsa,* the Saudi national dish.

"We got onto the subject of the recent bombings," says Khashoggi, "and this time Osama said he disapproved of them. I got out my tape recorder at once. 'Shall I start taping?' I asked. 'No,' he said. 'Let's talk tomorrow.'"

The next day Osama was in a negotiating mood.

"What will I get in return," he asked Khashoggi, "if I give an interview?"

"I'm not here on behalf of the government," replied Khashoggi. "I'm here to break the ice."

During their time together, Khashoggi decided that Osama had become rather odd. He had forbidden his wives to do any ironing.

" 'Irons consume electricity,' he told me, 'and we must train ourselves to live without electricity. If the Israelis come and bomb the power plant here, we'll be without water and power.' "

The eccentricity reminded Khashoggi of Osama's home on Macarona Street, where the jihadi had once wanted to connect two rooms together.

"He just knocked a huge hole in the wall with a sledgehammer," remembers Khashoggi. "He took away the debris, but he left the hole all unfinished and jagged."

On the night before he was due to leave, Khashoggi tried to focus Osama's attention on the mission.

" 'My flight is at eight tomorrow evening,' I told him. 'And I'll be leaving for the airport at six. You can contact me anytime tomorrow and I'll come over—right up until six. If you want to do the interview, I'll forget about the flight and spend as much time with you as you want.' "

Khashoggi waited all the next day at the hotel. But the call never came.

CHAPTER 20

Enter the Crown Prince

On November 19, 1995, a few days after the terrorist bombing of the National Guard training center in Riyadh, King Fahd suffered a stroke. He was seventy-four years old. Like many a Saudi, he was overweight and he smoked. His deputy, Crown Prince Abdullah, now stepped forward to take over the day-to-day running of the Saudi government, and while his position in the family meant he had to be accepted, many outsiders feared the worst.

Throughout Fahd's reign the black-bearded Abdullah had been kept in the background by the king and the Sudayri brothers, making few public pronouncements, in part because of his notorious stutter. Abdullah's lips would struggle silently beneath his thick black mustache, then he would lift his hand high and slap it down hard on his thigh: out would come the words in a rush. The story in the National Guard—which, several said, they had been told by Abdullah himself—was that the stutter went back to an occasion when the prince got on the wrong side of his father. The angry Abdul Aziz had his errant son locked up in a cell without light, so when the boy eventually emerged, his speech was permanently impaired.

The gap between intention and performance could be embarrassing. It caused some who met Abdullah to dismiss him as a simple man, and he rather cultivated the image of simplicity. Every Sunday evening he held a majlis to which the bedouin streamed by the hundred—"right out of the desert," remembers Walter Cutler, who was U.S. ambassador to Riyadh twice in the 1980s. The crown prince sat in an ornate chair, the paramount chieftain gravely listening to his petitioners for more than an hour. Then he would kneel down to pray with all his guests, adjourning to the banqueting hall for a huge communal supper.

It was like the majlises organized every evening around the country by the Al-Saud—with one important distinction. As the years went by petitioners had come to adopt ever more extravagant forms of deference to their princes, trying to kiss hands and even weeping and crying out in supplication. Abdullah would have none of it. Nick Cocking, head of the British military mission to the National Guard and military adviser to Abdullah through the 1980s, noticed, as the petitioners lined up in front of him, that the crown prince was carrying a slender bamboo camel stick. Whenever he detected an obsequious kiss or prostration in the making, Abdullah would reach out and tap the offending head, hand, or body part.

"You're a man," he would growl at the culprit, who was usually a besuited Lebanese, not a Saudi. "What are you doing groveling on the floor?"

In the bedouin tradition, Abdullah was profoundly egalitarian, and among those in the know he was reckoned to be both honest and reform-minded. It was remarkable how many of the fiercest opposition tracts of the 1990s exempted him from their attacks. Osama Bin Laden even had a dream about Abdullah, which he described to Abu Rida Al-Suri, one of his longtime jihadi companions. Walking in his dream around the Prophet's city of Medina, Osama had heard the sounds of popular celebration and looked over a mud wall—to see the Saudi crown prince arriving to the joy of a happy and cheering throng.

"It means that Abdullah will become king," said Bin Laden. "That will be a relief to the people and make them happy. If Abdullah becomes king, then I will go back."

FRUIT OF RECONCILIATION

Crown Prince Abdullah was born of "enemy" stock. When, in 1921, his father, Abdul Aziz, finally captured the northern town of Hail, the power base of his greatest adversaries, the Rasheeds, he gave out food to the inhabitants and forbade all looting or killing. But the Rasheedi leader, Mohammed bin Talal Al-Rasheed, expected no such kindness, for he had refused to surrender with the citizens. He had withdrawn to Hail's fort to keep on fighting, and he had heard the tales of Ibn Saud's vengeance when he was crossed.

So when, after his capture, servants came telling him to wash and bathe for a great occasion, the Rasheedi chieftain feared that this must be for his own execution. He put on his best robes to meet his death with dignity, but he found himself being led into Ibn Saud's majlis and being set in the place of honor.

"Sit here beside me," said Abdul Aziz, rising to embrace and to kiss his former enemy. "The time for death and killing is past. We are all brothers now. You and yours will come to Riyadh to live with me as part of my own family."

So the Rasheedi princes came to live in Riyadh where they had once ruled, and from which they had been expelled in 1902 by Abdul Aziz. Conciliation was a controlling technique at which the Al-Saud excelled.

"Let us treat our foes with mercy," the Saudi ruler used to say. "When *they* punished *us,* it stirred us to revenge."

It also made sense, of course, to keep such bitter enemies close at hand and under supervision.

Three Rasheed women had been widowed by the fighting, and Abdul Aziz took special care of them, giving one to his younger brother Saad, and the second to his eldest son, Saud bin Abdul Aziz. He took the third widow, Fahda bint Asi Al-Shuraim, of the Shammar tribe, as a wife for himself. Fahda came to live with him in Riyadh, and two years later, in 1923, she gave birth to a son, on whom his proud father bestowed the name Abd'Allah—"Slave of God." The boy was the fruit of reconciliation.

• • •

It was as a reconciler that Abdullah bin Abdul Aziz first made his mark on his family. As the Al-Saud splintered in the late 1950s under the challenge of Arab nationalism and the charismatic Gamal Abdul Nasser, a group of radical young princes flew to Cairo and called for constitutional democracy.

"In our country," complained their leader, Talal bin Abdul Aziz, "there is no law that upholds the freedom and rights of the citizen."

Idealistic and liberal, Talal was the family maverick—the Ralph Nader of the Al-Saud. He had served as communications minister in the 1950s and later as finance minister under the controversial King Saud. Subsequently he would serve as a special envoy for UNESCO. Abdullah was close to Talal both in age and ideas, and there was a sense in which, as the elder half brother, Abdullah had played godfather to the rebellious "Free Princes."* He had a deep, almost simplistic radicalism about his politics, and while in religion he had to be rated a solid Wahhabi (one of Abdullah's strengths as a reformer was that he could never be dismissed with the damning putdown of "secular"), he sniffed at extreme ideas that came, as he put it, "from the dryness of the desert."

Abdullah was not prepared to break family ranks. For much of the 1950s he had steered clear of his siblings' squabbling, effectively exiling himself to Beirut, where he had picked up a love of card games and playing boules, along with some passable French. So when the quarrels reached their climax, it was to Abdullah that the family turned. Faisal and Fahd persuaded him to use his closeness to Talal, and also his neutrality, in the cause of peace.

"I wish Talal had never left," said Abdullah in Beirut in 1962, "and now I wish he would return."

He sympathized with many of his half brother's complaints, but he placed family unity above them.

"Talal knows full well," he said, "that Saudi Arabia has a constitution inspired by God and not drawn up by man. . . . True socialism is the Arab socialism laid down by the Koran."

The early 1960s were perilous years for the Al-Saud. Ten years after the death of Abdul Aziz, a succession of family disputes was threatening to tear his achievement apart. A century earlier the so-called Second Saudi State had disintegrated in dynastic quarreling, creating the vacuum into which the Rasheeds had moved. Now the physical fruit of the Rasheed reunion made sure that the same did not happen again. The solidity of Abdullah played a crucial role in pulling the clan through. In 1959 he accepted the invitation of Faisal, then crown prince, to come home and take command of the National Guard, the tribal force of bedouin levies. Abdullah kept the Guard loyal in the power play that ended in November 1964 when Faisal replaced his brother Saud as king, and he then used his closeness to Talal to help negotiate the peaceful return of the Free Princes as well.

*The "Free Princes" were Talal, Fawwaz, and Badr bin Abdul Aziz, plus a cousin, Saad ibn Fahd. Abdul Muhsin bin Abdul Aziz expressed support for their protest, but did not go into exile himself.

• • •

Commanding the National Guard became the cornerstone of Abdullah's power and identity. With no full blood brothers, he was something of a loner in the family, many of whom viewed his radical soul mates like Talal with suspicion. But the National Guard was like a family in its own right, with military might and a patchwork of nationwide patronage that gave Abdullah the punching power of several princes—more than enough, as it turned out, to keep the Sudayri Seven on their toes.

At the time of this writing Abdullah ibn Abdul Aziz—King Abdullah since 2005—has been commander of the National Guard for more than forty-seven years, his tough public persona perfectly reflecting the character of a tough tribal force. The original function of the Guard was to enlist the loyalty of the tribes to protect the royal family against any threat—including, in the last resort, a threat from the country's other armed forces. The Guard was founded at a time of suspected military coups, so its first bases were sited close to Riyadh and the major cities. The idea was that the Guard could block hostile forces coming from the more distant army and air force bases on the borders. Its anti-aircraft weapons were designed to shoot down Saudi fighter planes. Its antitank rockets had to be good enough to take on the Saudi Army.

Nick Cocking tried to incorporate some of these basic but politically sensitive objectives into a National Guard mission statement that he drafted soon after he arrived in Riyadh in 1984—and received his only rebuke in eight years of happy collaboration with the crown prince. "Please tell the brigadier," came the message, "not to write about things that are not his business."

Without putting anything on paper, Abdullah had developed his own mission statement for his "White Army," whom he dressed in khaki. What the crown prince wrought with the National Guard over the years revealed a man of more complexity than his exterior suggested.

"He saw the Guard primarily as a way to develop and educate Saudis," says Abdul Rahman Abuhaimid, who supervised the Guard's civil works with the rank of deputy commander for twenty-four years. "Our hospitals, our schools, our housing, our training—everything had to be the very best. He would insist on testing the prototypes for the various housing units to make sure that families would be happy in them."

Under Abdullah the National Guard became a reasonably competent fighting force, but its military aspects often seemed less important to him than its civilian infrastructure and social development—the creation of his own ministate to standards that he could not, at that moment, extend throughout the country. The Guard's local, part-time territorial levies remained tribally based, but Abdullah insisted that tribes should be mixed inside the full-time professional Guard regiments, and that each base should feature active adult-education units. Today the hospitals of the Saudi National Guard are modern, clean, and bright—anything but tribal. One of them, in Riyadh, is the world's leading specialist center for the separation and rehabilitation of conjoined twins. It is an unpublicized hobby of Abdullah's to go to the center to spend time with the separated twins and their parents, whom he flies to Riyadh from all over the world at his own expense.

Abdullah constructed a double identity just as Fahd did—and, indeed, as all Saudi princes do—by presenting his people with the image of a traditional, stern, and formal desert authority figure, while acting totally otherwise in private. But whereas Fahd's private persona involved Mediterranean yachts and casinos, Abdullah's hidden world involved hours splashing in the swimming pool with his children. Struck by the elegant freestyle stroke of Abdullah's daughter Reema, Nick Cocking's wife, Anna, asked her the name of her swimming coach. With a smile, and a perfect accent, the little girl answered, "My father, of course." Abdullah made sure that all his children learned English.

He liked splashing in the pool by himself, swimming a daily set of lengths that was part of his self-improvement regime. Another aspect involved speech-therapy lessons with a series of specialists who were flown to Riyadh and worked with him on exercises that eventually all but eliminated his stutter.

"I remember a speech that he gave [in Arabic] in London at the Mansion House," says Nick Cocking. "Now that's a pretty intimidating venue. He was totally fluent—word perfect."

In his younger days Abdullah shared in the distribution of land grants and cash that Abdul Aziz, Saud, Faisal—and particularly King Khaled—spread around the royal family. But he did not elbow his way into profits in the way that many of his half brothers did.

"Abdullah never pocketed a direct government commission himself," says one insider. "Of that I am quite sure. He is not badly off. He lives like a prince. But he is certainly the least wealthy of the senior sons of Abdul Aziz—the brothers who are over seventy."

The crown prince was no innocent. He understood the temptations of patronage and he tried to channel them in constructive directions.

"He would study all the National Guard contracts very carefully," remembers Abdul Rahman Abuhaimid. "He always insisted, when it came to foreign governments, that they should be pushed to give something extra at their own expense—training or education to transfer skills to local Saudis. And he was constantly on the lookout to close all the doors and windows against corruption. 'Do you think,' he would ask, 'that there is anyone we know who is linked in on this?' "

Cracking down on corruption and overpricing became Abdullah's hallmark. *"Trop!"* "Too much!" he would say, deploying his best Lebanese French as he studied almost any contract, and the papers would go back to be renegotiated. Legend had it that the crown prince would allow his four wives a new car only every two years, and that he sat down with his sons once a week to go through their bank accounts. His sons deny the truth of that, but most of them are low-key in their appetites and spending patterns.

"I was in first class, going from Riyadh to Jeddah," remembers a Saudi newspaper editor, "when I saw one of Abdullah's sons walking through, going back to sit in the business cabin. I offered him my seat and he refused. Imagine one of Fahd's sons not traveling right up front with an entourage of ten. Few people know who Abdullah's sons are—and he tells them to keep it that way." (The same is true of Abdullah's daughters.)

Abdullah has tried—with varying success—to apply that principle across the entire royal family, and certainly today the British staff who work for Saudia, the national airline, at London's Heathrow Airport bless his name. Gone are the last-minute crises as princes—and friends of princes—turn up at the check-in desk without reservations, requiring that ordinary mortals get turfed off the flight. Abdullah ended the special flying privileges for most of the royal family soon after he took power.

• • •

Abdullah's proper taking of power, however, took time and involved quite a fight. Until 1995 the crown prince's stutter was symbolic of his limited influence at the top of the family. Fahd and his eldest Sudayri brothers all got on with running the country as they wished. Abdullah was never part of their inner circle and the brothers found it hard to change their ways after Fahd's stroke.

"They could make things difficult for Abdullah," recalls a royal adviser. "They might 'forget' to tell him things and just go on running the show in their own way."

Fahd made something of a recovery, and the Sudayris forced Abdullah formally to return the powers of regency he had assumed. When the king had a second and more severe stroke in 1997, they played down its significance, but the sad truth of Fahd's condition was difficult to ignore. The king could speak only haltingly, and it was embarrassing when he was wheeled in to preside over family dinners.

"Poor guy," remembers one of his female relatives. "He'd give you that smile. It was sort of pathetic. He was only just hanging in there."

The king's health depended on the drugs administered to him that day. A European ambassador remembers escorting a visiting minister from his country for a courtesy call. As they walked into the royal presence, a strange and indecipherable sound emanated from Fahd's throat.

"His Majesty is delighted that you have come all this way to visit him," said the interpreter brightly.

Another croak ensued.

"His Majesty welcomes the chance to strengthen the ties that have always connected our two nations."

For television appearances the king was whisked around in a wheelchair that was hidden away when the cameras started rolling. It was an Orwellian pretense, but it reflected the mystique at the heart of any monarchy, and the particular reverence for seniority to which the Al-Saud had always subscribed.

Abdullah chafed at the limits within which he had to operate, but as in the Free Princes crisis of 1962, he remained a loyal supporter of the family way.

"If you're staying in your brother's house," he would say, "you don't change the curtains."

The crown prince had long been developing his own very definite ideas about what was needed to right the wrongs of the country—and they were very different from some of Fahd's.

"If you could have read the letters that he sent privately, brother to brother, to the king," confided Abdul Aziz Al-Tuwayjri, Abdullah's closest adviser, talking of the years before Fahd's illness, "you would have thought that the crown prince was leader of the opposition."

But there was no hint of this in public—quite the contrary. In the autumn of 1998 Abdullah reached out to Azouzi, the twenty-five-year-old Abdul Aziz bin Fahd, to bring the young prince into the Saudi cabinet as a "minister without portfolio." By virtue of the soothsayer's prophecy, Azouzi effectively controlled access to his ailing father, and he became the crown prince's direct channel to the king, securing Fahd's signature on especially important documents. Whenever Abdullah undertook the presentation of ceremonial orders and medals to visiting heads of state, he would make clear that he himself did not belong to the ultimate, elevated level to which the visitor was being admitted. That honor was reserved for his beloved elder brother, the king.

In the absence of fathers and mothers, elder brothers command absolute deference in Saudi society; respect for age is one of the pillars on which a tribal society rests.

"After Saud became king, in 1953," recalls a friend of the family, "Faisal would scamper to bring him his shoes, even though he felt contempt for what his elder brother was doing."

One of the sights to enjoy when Saudi princes get together is to observe how they shuffle instinctively into their order of precedence: they know their rank in the hierarchy and they stick to it, even where seniority is a matter of having been born only days apart. It would have been disrespectful for Abdullah to significantly alter his brother's council of ministers while Fahd remained alive, and in any case the kingdom's two most important ministries, Defense and the Interior, were operated as personal fiefdoms by Fahd's full brothers, Sultan and Nayef—as, indeed, Abdullah retained permanent control of the National Guard.

In this respect, Abdullah was complicit in his own helplessness. As the 1990s drew to close, the king and the crown prince were each handicapped in their different ways. Neither could give of their best—and the Saudi curtains were in sore need of changing. Having briefly surged above twenty dollars per barrel at the time of the Gulf War, oil prices tumbled downward for the rest of the decade—in 1998 the price of a barrel of oil would sink to nine dollars.

"We must all get used to a different way of life," declared Abdullah in January 1999, proclaiming that the days of easy oil money were history. He announced a stringent austerity budget, cutting government spending by 16 percent, and urged Saudis to seek a way ahead "which does not stand on total dependence on the state."

"This was the first and only time in my life I saw a suicide," remembers Dr. Ahmad Gabbani, a human resources director in Jeddah. "It was on the Medina Road. There was a wooden bridge over the road, and some poor guy had put a rope round his neck and jumped. I saw the body hanging there. People said that he was crazy. It is a deep sin if you are a Muslim to take your own life. But it turned out that the man could not find a job. He could not provide for his family."

The Ministry of Finance refused to pay up on massive contracts that were long completed without dispute. Local businessmen trekked cap in hand around the ministries for month after humiliating month trying to secure payment for themselves and their foreign partners.

"You've made enough money in the past," they were told dismissively.

• • •

In the middle of this recession, an acerbic and humorous little economist was trying to reform the Saudi telephone system. The pixielike Dr. Ali Al-Johani had been appointed minister of posts and telecommunications (PTT) three months before Fahd's stroke and had concluded that the only way to improve was to privatize.

"The PTT was a bazaar," he remembers. "So many people were for sale. There were simply not enough lines to go around. Every new line, every new number went across the desk of somebody in the ministry and they put whatever price they wanted on it."

Al-Johani identified twelve senior officials who had to go. Six accepted his offer of a golden handshake, but six refused to budge, so he took their names to the crown prince, requesting their immediate dismissal.

Abdullah was astonished.

"Six?" he asked. "Just six? I'll sign for six hundred."

Abdullah had long held a profound contempt for civil servants. Bureaucracy pressed his buttons. To suggest that a committee might be formed was a sure way to trigger the ire of the crown prince.

"Prince Abdullah," says Al-Johani, "can smell reform from miles away. He might not have known, at the time, the detailed economic benefits of privatization. But he knew that it meant giving greater freedom to Saudi citizens, and that it would give me greater freedom to change things for the better. That was good enough for him. Some of the nonroyal ministers complained that the government should not be surrendering control over such a major area of information, but that was not an issue for him, nor for Prince Sultan either. In every battle I have to say that those two men gave me their total backing."

The new minister soon discovered that he needed it.

"I had opened the gates of hell. To start with, everybody wanted to be my best friend. Then when I did not give them what they wanted, they became my worst enemy—the tribes, the merchants, the families. They accused me of corruption, of course, but let me tell you, there are three hundred thousand Al-Johanis and not one of them got a job or a phone line because of me.

"So that made enemies out of *them,* of course, my own people. They said I was a traitor, that I was not looking after my own. I came to feel I could trust no one. If I had an important document to take to the Council of Ministers, I would carry the draft myself down to the basement of the ministry building. There was one typist there I knew. I could rely on him to type it promptly without phoning someone or sneaking an extra photocopy."

The new minister held twice-weekly majlises, royal style, so customers could come and present their complaints. Discovering that the ministry had been holding back a huge stock of lines for its own purposes, Al-Johani gave away all but fifteen. He published a priority entitlement code for securing telephone service, starting with doctors, emergency workers, and sick children. Most daring of all, he got the crown prince's backing to cut off the mobile service of princes and princesses who did not pay their bills.

"They could not believe it, and they went to complain to the crown prince. He just told them they must pay their bills like everyone else."

It was a crucial change. Elite Saudis—royal and nonroyal—might take as many as a hundred mobiles to London for their family and entourage to use, calling freely, day and night, all over the world throughout their holiday.

"We, the Saudi PTT, would have had to pay out tens of millions of dollars in foreign service charges," remembers Al-Johani. "It would have been impossible to privatize if we had not made that reform."

A team of foreign consultants to the ministry told Al-Johani it would take twelve years to privatize the telephones.

" 'So how come,' I asked them, 'Mrs. Thatcher did it in two?' "

"You meet with the senior partners of these foreign consultants," adds the sharp-toothed former minister, "and they shower you with wisdom that is music to your ears. You sign a contract to tap their expertise, and then you never see them again. They send you out beginners who can't speak proper English and who serve you outdated information from the Internet."

In the middle of all this, Al-Johani started feeling feverish as the day wore on. He was diagnosed with leukemia—bone-marrow cancer. He flew to Seattle for chemotherapy, leaving the PTT in the hands of a succession of other ministers who had little time or inclination to do Dr. Ali's job.

"In fact," he recalls without too much malice, "one of them certainly *wanted* my job." On his return, he resumed his battle, couriering bone-marrow samples to Seattle every week or so.

"The chemo and the immune drugs had a very bad effect on my temper. I've never been easy to work with. I can't tolerate fools gladly, and I hate being obstructed—I have to admit it. There was only one way to do things, and I was the only person who knew what that was."

In the end, the academics and administrators who made up the board of the newly privatized Saudi Telecoms Company said they could not work with Al-Johani anymore. He treated them like the petty bureaucrats he believed them to be, and they had no further wish to be snapped at. They presented their combined resignation to the crown prince, and Abdullah summoned Dr. Ali. The battle was over, he said; the day had been won. The prince made Al-Johani a minister of state with cabinet responsibilities for three years, while Prince Sultan made him a present of his most valuable and handsome white bull camel.

Saudi telephone lines had been liberated, blazing a fresh trail for the congenitally centrist and risk-averse Saudi government, which now edged toward a new economic style. Fahd's long-serving finance minister, Mohammed Aba Al-Khail, had started slow negotiations for Saudi Arabia to join the World Trade Organization, but the economic team that Abdullah recruited brought fresh energy to the bid.

"We saw WTO accession as a vehicle for domestic reform," recalls one of the team. "We could use the new regulations as a pretext. The business establishment was wary of change. But now we could go to them and say, 'Look guys, sorry. These are the rules. They come from the outside.' It was a whole change of philosophy."

Abdullah announced the creation of a new Supreme Economic Council to streamline economic decision making. But this could provide no immediate help to the growing numbers of young Saudis who could not find jobs at the end of the 1990s. Youth unemployment was a tragedy. The unrestricted entry of cheap foreign workers had flooded the Saudi labor market with millions of third-world workers who were willing to live in primitive camps and to work for seven hundred riyals ($190) per month. This was a third of the amount on which a Saudi could survive, and the logical solution—that young Saudis should be trained to work as managers—was handicapped by the rising generation's embarrassing deficiencies in education, particularly when it came to practical knowledge and independent reasoning skills. The teaching of math, science, and English in Saudi schools had been drastically reduced in the early 1980s to make room for the extra religious classes that featured learning by rote—the post-Juhayman backlash had almost guaranteed the production of more Juhaymans.

The days of the oil boom seemed very distant. Most young men leaving school or graduating from university took it for granted that the next two or three years of their life would be "dead," with no prospect of work. Hanging out in shopping malls or driving aimlessly around the streets of Jeddah or Riyadh without the cash to buy new clothes, let alone to finance marriage, was a depressing existence. Small wonder that the vision of jihad in foreign lands offered purpose and excitement that attracted many a frustrated young "Angry Face."

CHAPTER 21

The Students

Islam's triumphant ousting of Communist Russia from Afghanistan in 1989 did not bring peace to the Afghan people. On the contrary. Scarcely missing a beat, resistance to the foreign enemy morphed into a bitter and bloody civil war.

"After the Russians left, they just turned on each other," recalls Ahmed Badeeb, chief of staff of Prince Turki Al-Faisal's General Intelligence Department, the Istikhbarat. "There seemed no way that we could stop them fighting. They were all as bad as each other. We cut off the payments we had been making to them, but they just went on feuding. I remember that we once made a really major effort. We put all the leaders on a plane and flew them to Mecca for a peace conference. We actually opened up the Kaaba and took them inside so they could swear reconciliation to each other—right in the very heart of Islam. It was a truly exceptional gesture, very moving, with lots of embracing and tears. Then, as they were coming back out down the ladder—before their feet had even touched down on the floor of the mosque—I got a call saying that one of them must have given orders to shell Kabul because the electricity station had just been hit. 'Shame on you,' I said, as I took them all out to the airport. 'You are devastating your own country.' "

After a decade of armed struggle, conflict had become a way of life for Afghanistan's mujahideen. The country was awash with weaponry, and the competing regional and ethnic factions fought ruthlessly for supremacy.

"They inherited big problems, but they kept creating new ones," says Badeeb. "I told my people to leave the bastards alone for a bit. We kept out of the politics and just did what we could to help the ordinary people."

Badeeb had a personal project that he had started in the 1980s, a technical school for handicapped Afghani children and orphans.

"There were a lot of children," he remembers, "without an arm or a leg because of the land mines. I wanted to help them, so I financed this school with some Saudi friends as a charity. It was on the Pakistan border. We raised a lot of money from Mecca. We hired local teachers and taught them rug making, sewing, electrical work, and plumbing—practical, peaceful things that were an alternative to fighting."

Badeeb had founded a madrasa, or school, but not in a narrowly religious sense—nor for the unashamedly militaristic reasons that some of these schools were created.

"We have to remember and admit," says one Saudi diplomat who can recall discussing the funding and promotion of the Afghan madrasas with the CIA in the 1980s, "that the original purpose of these schools was strategic. The fighting with the Soviets had tragic consequences—it was creating a lot of orphans. So some of us in Washington did some brainstorming. 'What better source of future fighters,' we said, 'than these boys whose fathers have been killed by the Russians?' The plan was to find them, clothe them, put them through school—then ship them to the front. The Saudis get the blame for the madrasas now, but let's not forget that many of them were part of a joint U.S.-Saudi project to take these poor kids and make them warriors for the West."

"There were a lot of religiously focused madrasas along the Afghan-Pakistan border and in the Pakistan tribal areas," recalls Ahmed Badeeb. "Some of them were financed by charities in Riyadh, and Prince Turki was not happy with that. He said the money should go on more practical education. But how can you stop people who want to spend money promoting their religion?

"Let's face it, we all made mistakes. America just walked away from Afghanistan. After the Russians left, I went to the States and Europe and to Eastern Europe trying to organize some sort of reconstruction. I went to Turkmenistan and also Iran. I got nil response. The only person who did anything serious was King Fahd. He allocated $300 million to be spent through the various Saudi ministries—so much on electricity and power, so much on religious guidance, but always on peaceful, humanitarian projects for the people."

Fahd was adamant that funds should no longer go to the feuding mujahideen.

"Stopping the funds was intended to show disapproval, but also as an incentive," remembers Prince Turki Al-Faisal. "We kept telling them we were ready to provide support if they were willing to make peace—if they could find a way."

The way eventually came from an unexpected source, from the south of the country, the area dominated by the Pashtun tribes, and it grew out of the madrasas. Focusing their studies on the Koran and its picture of the just and perfect society that Mohammed was able to create in the midst of warfare fourteen centuries earlier, the young Pashtun pupils in these schools could not help but see a lesson for their own benighted country in the simple, black-and-white rules of fundamentalist Islam.

"We would discuss the terrible plight of our people living under these bandits . . ." the one-eyed Taliban foreign minister Mohammed Ghaus would later explain to the Pakistani writer Ahmed Rashid. "We only had a vague idea what to do and we thought we would fail. But we believed we were working with Allah as His pupils."

The Arabic for pupil or student is *talib.* In Pashtu, a group of talibs make up a *taliban*—and in the mid-1990s the idealistic talibs in the Kandahar area started taking their destiny into their own hands. Going from village to village, the long-bearded, turban-wearing young tribesmen carried a Koran in one hand and a Kalashnikov in the other.

"Put down your weapons for the sake of the Koran," they said to the bandits and warlords, brandishing the holy book in their faces. If anyone resisted, the young students shot them dead on the spot. It was traditional, rough Pashtun justice, turned into a jihad by the Salafi teachings that the talibs had absorbed in their madrasas.

"We want to live a life like the Prophet lived fourteen hundred years ago," one Taliban leader explained to Ahmed Rashid, "and jihad is our right. We want to re-create the time of the Prophet, and we are only carrying out what the Afghan people have wanted for the past fourteen years."

The war-weary population of Kandahar welcomed the simple and direct methods of the young students. They might be as violent as any other Afghan faction, but they seemed to be untainted by corruption and they were of local stock. Within a matter of months much of the Pashtun south, including Kandahar itself, Afghanistan's second largest city with a population of over four hundred thousand, was under Taliban authority. Driving to Kandahar the previous year through the Khojak Pass from Pakistan, Ahmed Rashid had been stopped twenty times or more by armed bandits who had strung chains across the road, demanding tolls for safe passage. By the end of 1994 the 130-mile stretch of road was clear of obstructions. Local trucking companies—including heroin merchants who were transporting their share of the opium harvest—willingly paid their dues to the Taliban.

. . .

Prince Turki was introduced to these holy liberators early in 1995 in the course of a visit to Pakistan—which was no coincidence, since the spectacular advance of the Taliban had not been the work of God alone. The students had received crucial funding and armaments—particularly in the clearing of the road to Kandahar—from Pakistan's ISI (Inter-Service Intelligence) who had masterminded the campaign against the Soviets and had become as frustrated as anyone else by the subsequent conflicts between their protégés.

"These are my boys," declared General Naseerullah Babar, the Pakistani interior minister, beaming proudly as he welcomed the Saudi intelligence chief to Islamabad and introduced him to a group of Taliban headed by a young mullah, Mohammed Rabbani.

"We're totally devoted to bringing peace to our country," said Rabbani (no relation to the Afghan president Rabbani), who acted with extreme humbleness toward the prince. "Anything that comes from Saudi Arabia, we will accept."

The young man seemed genuine to Turki, but naïve.

"He was not well educated," remembers the prince of Rabbani. "He was a country boy. I don't think he really understood what was going on. But just the same he was at that time the number two man in their hierarchy."

Sometime afterward Ahmed Badeeb met the Taliban's number one—thanks again to the Pakistanis.

"Afghanistan, Pakistan—they're almost like one country," says Badeeb, explaining why Saudi intelligence, which had operated hand-in-glove with the ISI throughout the war of the 1980s, was now following the Pakistani lead again. "They kept telling us about these young men who were protecting their local areas in the south, working to make them more safe and decent, and eventually they arranged a meeting with the chief. I shall never forget. These two strong young men appeared with big beards, two Taliban, carrying a third. 'Our guy is suffering,' they said. He had lost an eye and was without a leg."

Badeeb was being introduced to the Taliban's mysterious and reclusive leader, Mullah Omar. Aged around forty-four in 1995, Omar was already the stuff of legend. When exploding shrapnel had damaged his face five years earlier, it was said, he had taken a knife and cut out his right eye himself. He had a reasonable command of Arabic, which he spoke in a low and modest voice, and he issued only rare public statements. His group, he explained, was "a simple band of dedicated youths determined to establish the laws of God on earth. . . . The Taliban will fight until there is no blood in Afghanistan left to be shed, and Islam becomes a way of life for our people."

The Saudi intelligence envoy was impressed.

. . .

A few months later Badeeb was coming in to land at Kandahar airport in a Saudi intelligence G-2 corporate jet, when he spotted a cow wandering across the middle of the runway. His pilot zoomed upward and circled once or twice while the welcoming committee of Taliban shooed the animal away. King Fahd had liked what he heard about Kandahar's pious and militant students. They seemed the best hope of restoring some order to the enduring chaos of Afghanistan, and Prince Turki's chief of staff had been dispatched to find out more.

"Don't you remember us?" asked some of the bearded young warriors as they crowded around Badeeb on the tarmac. "We were pupils at your school!"

It was a genial, almost fraternal reunion. Meeting up again with Mullah Omar, Badeeb found himself greeted with a warm hug. Returning the gesture, he presented the one-eyed leader with a copy of the Koran.

"Whatever Saudi Arabia wants me to do," declared Omar, repeating the homage that his number two had paid to Prince Turki, "I will do."

The Taliban were effectively placing themselves under Saudi sponsorship, asking for Saudi money and materials, and according to Ahmed Rashid they received it. "The Saudis provided fuel, money, and hundreds of new pickups to the Taliban," he wrote in his book *Taliban,* published in 2000, the first significant history of the movement. "Much of this aid was flown in to Kandahar from the Gulf port city of Dubai."

Prince Turki Al-Faisal flatly denies this.

"The Saudi government gave no financial aid to the Taliban whatsoever," he says. "Not one cent. I can say that categorically. When I read later of the alleged pickup trucks from Dubai, I had the matter investigated. There was absolutely no truth to the story. We certainly provided some low-cost fuel to the Rabbani government in Kabul for humanitarian purposes. That was kept in Pakistani depots. And we were also encouraging the project of a pipeline to bring fuel from the north. That was all. We kept receiving aid requests, and we always said, 'No. Not until the fighting stops.' The Taliban got their assistance from Pakistani intelligence and also from outside businesspeople and well-wishers. Some of those came from the Gulf—from Kuwait and the Emirates—and some of them may have been Saudis."

Here was the loophole. As news of the Taliban's godly reformation arrived back to Saudi Arabia, it had been greeted with general delight—the Afghan jihad was being fought over again, with pure, young Salafi warriors. The collection boxes reappeared in mosques and supermarkets, re-creating the charity chain of the 1980s, only now transmitting much larger sums of money. The Friday preachers had a theme on which to wax lyrical, with Abdul Aziz Bin Baz, grand mufti since 1992, a particular enthusiast. The man who had sponsored and protected Juhayman now urged the holy cause of the Afghan students with the ulema, and more potently still with the senior princes to whom he had private access. It is not known—it will never be known—which of the family of Abdul Aziz privately parted with money at the venerable sheikh's request, but what was pocket money to them could easily have bought a fleet of pickup trucks for the Taliban.

"I know," says Ahmed Rashid, "that whenever I saw pickup trucks, especially new shiny ones, and asked the Taliban where they came from, the answer was always from the Saudis or the Emiratis. They were very specific about which country gave it to them, because they wanted to show they had international support, although they didn't distinguish between government, personal, or charitable aid. In the [British] Foreign Office I was told of specific instances of Saudi aid. Some of it was from the government—in the early days there was a lot of official sympathy and support for the Taliban. But some of it was certainly from private individuals and charities."

Saudi charities became high profile in Afghanistan. By the end of 1995 the student warriors were operating with more resources than they could possibly have received from their relatively poor Pakistani patrons, and they made particularly effective use of their Datsun 4x4 pickups. They bolted machine guns onto the rear platforms to convert the vehicles into gunships, then deployed them as a nimble, mechanized cavalry—updated versions of the gun-mounted Chevrolets with which Abdul Aziz slaughtered the Ikhwan at Sibillah. As winter closed in the Taliban took control of the entire south, center, and west of the country and soon found themselves at the gates of Kabul. In the spring of 1996 Mullah Omar summoned to Kandahar more than a thousand religious leaders from the territories he controlled to have them proclaim him Amir-ul-Momineen, the "Commander of the Faithful."

Kandahar's most sacred shrine houses a silver box containing a unique relic, an ancient robe that is said to have been the cloak of the Prophet Mohammed. It is removed only at moments of special emergency—the last occasion had been more than sixty years previously during a cholera epidemic. Now, on April 4, 1996, Mullah Omar had the Prophet's Cloak brought to the top floor of a mosque in the center of the city, stuck his hands into the sleeves of the holy garment, and proceeded to parade around the roof, wrapping and unwrapping the sacred fabric for half an hour as the mullahs in the courtyard threw their turbans in the air and shouted out their homage.

By Wahhabi standards, Omar's gesture was doubly un-Islamic—relic worship magnified by an act of theater. But the Taliban's Saudi benefactors took a tolerant view. These were the excesses of a young movement that would mellow, they felt sure, and the spinning mullah had certainly energized the madrasa graduates. By the end of September 1996 the Taliban had conquered Kabul and had extended their rule to twenty-two of the country's thirty-one provinces. They announced that their godly government would be known as the Islamic Emirate of Afghanistan, and while most of the world prudently stepped back and waited, three countries granted this unusual entity official recognition: Pakistan, the United Arab Emirates—and Saudi Arabia.

• • •

There was a dark side, however, to the students' rapid and unlikely triumph. On the night that they occupied Kabul, the Taliban flouted the diplomatic immunity of the United Nations compound to kidnap Mohammed Najibullah, the last Communist president of Afghanistan, who had lived in UN custody since his deposition four years earlier. In what would become a pattern of brutality, they beat Najibullah and his brother senseless, castrated both men, dragged their bodies behind a jeep, then hanged them by wire nooses from lampposts.

The next day they started issuing the prohibitions for which the Taliban would become notorious: no kite-flying, no pool tables, no music, no nail polish, no toothpaste, no televisions, no beard-shaving, no "British or American hairstyles," no pigeon keeping, no playing with birds. Less comically, the Taliban also imposed the wearing of the head-to-toe veil, the burqa, closed all girls' schools and colleges, and banned women from working—a particularly savage blow to the tens of thousands of Afghan war widows who had to work to keep their children alive.

"Women, you should not step outside your residence," instructed a Taliban decree of November 1996. "If women are going outside with fashionable, ornamental, tight and charming clothes to show themselves, they will be cursed by the Islamic sharia and should never expect to go to heaven."

These draconian regulations were enforced by religious police squads, local Committees for the Promotion of Virtue and Prevention of Vice that were built directly on the Saudi model of fundamentalist vigilantes and drew support from Saudi religious charities. Bin Baz's energetic support for the Taliban was matched by other members of the ulema.

"I remember," says Ahmed Rashid, "that all the Taliban who had worked or done hajj [pilgrimage] in Saudi Arabia were terribly impressed by the religious police and tried to copy that system to the letter. The money for their training and salaries came partly from Saudi Arabia."

Ahmed Rashid took the trouble to collect and document the Taliban's medieval flailings against the modern West, and a few months later he stumbled on a spectacle that they were organizing for popular entertainment. Wondering why ten thousand men and children were gathering so eagerly in the Kandahar football stadium one Thursday afternoon, he went inside to discover a convicted murderer being led between the goalposts—to be executed by a member of his victim's family.

The roots of Taliban practice were not Wahhabi—their ideas stemmed from the local Deobandi school of Islam. But the two fundamentalisms were soul mates. Not for the first or last time, Saudi favor to Islamic purists had helped give birth to a monster—and as if to emphasize the point, on May 19, 1996, Osama Bin Laden flew into Afghanistan from Sudan.

• • •

Bin Laden knew next to nothing about the Taliban. They were a phenomenon of the 1990s. But he could plainly see what they were doing to his friends, the now discredited mujahideen. Soon after arriving in Jalalabad he made it his business, according to Huthayfah, the son of Abdullah Azzam, to contact Mullah Omar and ask for his protection. *"Ahlan wa sahlan,"* came the warm and positive answer, as Huthayfah later reported it. "You are most welcome. We will never give you up to anyone who wants you."

It sounds oversimplified. Bin Laden's protector in Jalalabad was Younis Khalis, a mujahid friend from the old days. But Khalis would soon join forces with the Taliban, and as events unrolled, Mullah Omar's promise came to pass. There were many Western-style reasons, from personal rivalry to realpolitik, why it made sense for the Taliban leader to be wary of the uninvited Osama—both men had toweringly grandiose visions of their purpose in life. But those visions also locked them firmly into the same Islamic mission. The two holy warriors needed to coexist, and they found a way to do so. Breaking off from a sermon one day, Mullah Omar singled out Bin Laden in the congregation and praised him to the worshippers as one of Islam's most important spiritual leaders. Osama returned the compliment, telling the world that his fatwas were now being issued from Khorassan, the great Afghan-based empire of the Prophet's time, from which, according to certain hadiths, the armies of Islam would emerge in the final days, wearing black turbans and unfolding black banners, like the black flag of the Taliban, to defeat the kuffar and march in triumph to Jerusalem.

It was fortunate, perhaps, for the two partners in this messianic alliance that Saudi Arabia could not, for the moment, see a way to break them up. In 1996 the Al-Saud were severely annoyed with Bin Laden, but they had no ready means to implement their displeasure. If they brought Osama back to the Kingdom, he could only be a source of trouble, whether at liberty or in jail. At that date his crimes were matters of inflammatory words, not proven misdeeds for which he could easily be punished—nor, at that point, had he accomplished anything to suggest he would go much beyond words in the future. He seemed, as Bandar bin Sultan later put it, just a "young, misguided kid" with a big mouth and lots of money—"not a threat to the system; not a threat to anyone." The Saudi government had deliberately passed up on chances to extract Bin Laden from the Sudan in the early 1990s, and in Afghanistan he seemed even more safely out of the way.

In 1996 the Taliban took full control of the Khyber Pass areas where Younis Khalis had been operating and sent a message to Prince Turki Al-Faisal.

"We've taken over Jalalabad," they told him, "and Bin Laden is here. We have offered him sanctuary and we can guarantee his behavior."

The prince recalled his reply in an interview he gave to the U.S. TV show *Nightline* in December 2001. "Well, if you have already offered him refuge, make sure he does not operate against the Kingdom or say anything against the Kingdom." At that moment Turki felt quite confident, he explained, that the Taliban would take charge of "keeping his mouth shut."

Viewed from the other side of 9/11, this seems an incredibly casual, even negligent, attitude to adopt toward the man who would become the world's most notorious terrorist. But that was not the position that Bin Laden occupied at the end of 1996. The terrorism expert Peter Bergen has assembled the memories of journalists who went to Afghanistan to interview Osama at this time, and while their stories all play up their own personal sense of risk and danger, none of them presented the lone Saudi exile as a man who could flatten Lower Manhattan. Several of them painted him, even, as faintly mad. Railing at the world windily from remote tents and caves in the Hindu Kush, Bin Laden sounded like a crazed Don Quixote.

"Oh William," he declared that August, addressing William Perry, the U.S. secretary of defense at the time, "tomorrow you will know which young man is confronting your misguided brethren. . . . These youths will not ask you for explanations. They will sing out that there is nothing between us that needs to be explained—there is only killing and neck smiting."

Bin Laden titled his eight-thousand-word diatribe "Declaration of War Against the Americans Occupying the Land of the Two Holy Places." It sounded ludicrous. In the context of his flight from the Sudan and his hand-to-mouth survival in Afghanistan, his antique rhetoric seemed especially full of bluster—particularly to Prince Turki, who knew just how little actual fighting "Abu Abdullah" had actually done in the 1980s jihad for which he was now claiming such credit. In the Sudan, Bin Laden had fulminated indignantly for four years and had organized training camps to little effect. Now that he was back in the chaos of Afghanistan, it did not seem to make much difference if he fulminated some more—or even opened up his camps again.

CHAPTER 22

Infinite Reach

By the spring of 1997 Osama Bin Laden had been living in Afghanistan for nearly a year. He had been working with the Taliban to set up a new generation of multinational jihadi training camps, and the recruits were flowing in—including a young electrical engineer from Jeddah, Khaled Al-Hubayshi.

"Go to Afghanistan," Al-Hubayshi had been told by all the veterans he consulted. "That is the only place you can learn the real jihad." The twenty-year-old had already tried the Philippines. In 1996 he had sold his car to finance a trip to the southern island of Mindanao, where he spent several months with Muslim separatists who were training at "Camp Vietnam."

But the Filipino rebels were too casual, in Khaled's opinion. They did not practice with live ammunition. Having studied electricity, he wanted to develop his expertise in the field of bombs and explosive circuits—and he found all he hoped for when he made his way the next year to Khost, in southern Afghanistan, near the border with Pakistan. It was May 1997.

Bin Laden had been a hero of Khaled's since his Afghan exploits were reported in the Saudi press in the late 1980s, which got the boy thinking that he might follow in the great man's footsteps. While studying at technical college, Khaled had been enraged by videocassettes that showed Muslims suffering at the hands of the Serbian army in Bosnia.

"Women were being raped and children killed just because they were Muslims," he remembers. "I had that young man's feeling that I had to do something myself. It was genocide. I could not sleep for the thought. Our religion tells us that Muslims must help each other, and the idea of jihad lifted my feeling of helplessness. When I finally got to camp and started training I slept well for the first time in months."

Khaled Al-Hubayshi's Guantánamo interrogation sheet sets out the formidable list of terrorist skills that he acquired from 1997 onward under the patronage of Al-Qaeda and the Taliban: "The detainee attended three courses at the Kaldan Camp; the Basic, the Gunnery and the Tactics. . . . The detainee's Basic Course consisted of training on the AK-47 Kalashnikov 7.62 assault rifle, the Seminov SKS/Type-56 7.62 mm semiautomatic rifle, the RPD 7.62 light machine gun, the PK 7.62 mm medium machine gun, the Dushka Dshk-38 12.7 mm heavy machine gun, the RPG-7 (antitank rocket propelled grenade), and the Grenov (RPG-18)."

The mind-boggling array of Russian weaponry is a reminder of the very practical ways in which Al-Qaeda's war on the West was built on the West's secret war against the Soviets ten years earlier. It also showed how comprehensively the late-twentieth-century jihadists went about their training.

"We woke before sunrise for Fajr [the dawn prayer]," remembers Khaled. "Then we paraded, all in lines—there must have been 150 of us at Kaldan. We did a warm-up, some physical training, before we went off for two hours running in the mountains, carrying our weapons. Every so often we would stop to do press-ups. We got very fit. I discovered that you're gonna lose weight if you train with Al-Qaeda!"

Back in civilian life today, the comfortably padded Al-Hubayshi grins wryly at the memory.

"Breakfast was eggs, bread, and *ful medames* [Arab baked beans]. The food in the Al-Qaeda camps was good and healthy. Then through the day we did our classes. There was a lot to learn: map reading, camouflage, urban warfare, weaponry, explosives—how to blow up a building, a tree, a bridge, a person. Each subject had a different instructor. I remember our explosives instructor, in particular. He was an Egyptian with blond hair, Ahmed Abdullah."

None of the jihadis used their real names, usually adopting nicknames in the style of Bin Laden's "Abu Abdullah" ("Father of Abdullah"). Khaled had no children, so he called himself "Abu Sulayman" ("Father of Solomon"), using the name of his own father on the assumption that he would one day pass on that name to his firstborn.

"We looked at all newcomers very suspiciously," he remembers. "We knew that the Saudi government, the Egyptians, and the Yemenis were all sending spies. So new arrivals had to prove themselves."

There was a hierarchy among the jihadis.

"The Yemenis were at the bottom," remembers Khaled. "They were so poor, they were sort of stuck. They were probably better off in Afghanistan than they were at home, and they couldn't travel anywhere in any case. They couldn't get the visas. The Egyptians couldn't travel much either, and they certainly couldn't go home. They were wanted men, without much money. The Saudis were top of the heap because we had money. A Saudi wasn't desperate for $150. His family could wire him $500 anytime. He had a car in his country. He could go home anytime. So if he was here, he'd come to die. He could do the big job."

It has been said that Osama Bin Laden deliberately chose Saudis to fill the planes on 9/11 in order to drive a wedge between the Kingdom and its American supporters, and that makes perfect sense. But there was also a practical element. Until 9/11 citizens of Saudi Arabia—unlike Egyptians, Yemenis, or most other Arabs—could travel in and out of America with relative ease, since it was assumed that, sooner or later, they would end up back at home.

"You would buy the ticket," remembers one frequent traveler of those days, "and your travel agent would get the U.S. visa automatically. You didn't even have to go to the embassy."

In the 1990s the Saudi government did not allow young Saudi males to travel directly to Afghanistan, but it did not make much effort to stop those who traveled to the camps via Pakistan. Islamic charity workers came and went freely. Using a false passport, Khaled Al-Hubayshi was able to break off his training and resume his job in Jeddah for a spell before going back to Afghanistan to an Al-Qaeda-sponsored camp.

"Each camp," he recalls, "had its own private sponsors and supporters—a lot of them were funded by charity money. Al-Qaeda camps were for the elite: they had the best training."

Pakistani support for the camps was indicated by the numbers of young men who were sent off to fight in Kashmir in the campaign against India, while Bin Laden dispatched some of his graduates to stiffen up the Taliban's military efforts against the Afghan Northern Alliance. It was rent for the hospitality he was receiving from Mullah Omar. But there was not much love lost between the visiting Saudis and local Afghanis.

"We traveled everywhere with a hand grenade," Khaled remembers. "It was much better protection than a pistol. If there was any trouble with an Afghan, you'd just remove the pin and wave it in front of them. 'I came here to die,' you'd say. You could see the fear in their eyes. They would kill you for a hundred dollars—so you had to scare them by acting crazy."

Khaled was devout, but he had little respect for the religiosity of the Taliban.

"It was just a mask," he says today. "And, in my opinion, a mask for racism. They believed that their people, the Pashtun, should be rulers of all Afghanistan, so they used religion to control the people. I remember one taxi driver who played music in his cab. The Taliban beat him up and took his car for a week. That was their technique—to scare people, so everybody kept in line. And most of the time it worked pretty well. Nobody fucked up."

It made for difficulties, however, when the video machine broke down in Khaled's camp.

"We'd been using the machine to play videos in our lessons about jihad and military techniques. It was not illegal. But when the repairman came, he came creeping in with his tool case, looking everywhere around him like he was on a secret mission."

Khaled rose through the ranks and graduated to more elite and specialized training programs. By the beginning of 1998 there were some eight thousand non-Afghans stationed in and around the jihadi camps, according to one estimate by Saudi intelligence. It is not known how many of these were trained fighters directly loyal to Bin Laden, but there were enough for him to start putting his lofty dreams into practice—his bombast was no longer so empty. That February he called on Muslims around the world to support his "International Islamic Front for Jihad Against Jews and Crusaders." Signed by militant leaders from Bangladesh, Egypt, Kashmir, and Pakistan, the manifesto reflected the wide-ranging coalition of radicals that had gathered in Afghanistan since the triumph of the Taliban, and it extended Bin Laden's previous declaration of war on America to civilians.

"We believe that the worst thieves in the world today, and the worst terrorists, are the Americans," he told PBS's *Frontline*. "Nothing could stop you, except perhaps retaliation in kind. We do not have to differentiate between military or civilian. As far as we are concerned, they are all targets."

The manifesto made clear that Bin Laden's basic quarrel still derived from the role that America was playing in his own country. The Gulf War had ended in 1991, but U.S. Air Force planes remained stationed in Saudi bases and the military cities, backed up by large and obvious contingents of U.S. personnel. It was difficult to deny the accusation that Osama lodged in his quaintly biblical language: "Since Allah made it flat, created its desert, and surrounded it with seas," he declared, "the Arabian Peninsula has never been stormed by any forces like the Crusader armies spreading in it like locusts." He had no need to add that these infidels had come to Arabia—"stealing its resources, dictating to its leaders, [and] humiliating its people"—at the invitation of the House of Saud.

. . .

"Finish this!"

Crown Prince Abdullah issued the order with his customary bluntness. Osama Bin Laden's insulting and defiant February declaration of jihad had been bad enough, but a month or so afterward the Mabahith had picked up some Bin Laden followers transporting missiles that were intended for use *inside* the Kingdom. They had planned to attack the U.S. consulate in Jeddah.

"We had kept complaining to the Taliban," remembers Turki Al-Faisal, "but here was solid evidence that Bin Laden was doing fieldwork at home, in Saudi Arabia itself. Enough was enough."

The Al-Saud could no longer allow Bin Laden to roam free in Afghanistan, and in June 1998, Prince Turki flew off to Kandahar. As his plane banked over the airport, the intelligence boss could clearly make out Tarnak Farms, the huddle of mud-walled buildings, where, his agents reported, Osama had been living for some time—the new headquarters of his campaign to mount global jihad.

The Taliban leaders were waiting, grouped around Mullah Omar—a remarkable sight with their collection of missing eyes, arms, and legs. They were easily the world's most physically disabled government.

"I can't just give him to you to put on a plane," was Omar's response to

Turki's opening argument, which had been a reproachful reminder of the mullah's original undertaking that he would prevent Bin Laden from operating or speaking against the Kingdom while he was in Afghanistan. Bin Laden had scarcely stopped talking and giving interviews since his arrival, and that was clearly in breach of what the Taliban had promised.

"We provided him shelter," responded the Taliban leader, launching into a long lecture on the Pashtun code of hospitality and its strict rules against betraying guests.

The prince was prepared for some such tactic. To back up his own arguments, he had brought from Riyadh the learned Sheikh Abdullah Turki, a scholar of Islam-wide renown and one of the Saudi ulema, who now pointed out to the Taliban how a guest who repeatedly broke his word, as Bin Laden had done in giving so many aggressive and troublemaking interviews to the world's press, forfeited his claim to his host's protection. As a former Saudi minister of religious endowments, Sheikh Abdullah also provided a not-so-subtle reminder to the Afghans of the Saudi charities that were financing their revolution so generously—but whose spending ultimately depended on a certain give-and-take.

Mullah Omar seemed unmoved by either consideration. Offering a face-saving compromise, Prince Turki suggested the formation of a joint Saudi-Taliban commission that would negotiate an Islamic mechanism to hand over the jihadist, and he recalls leaving them with a final question: "Are you agreed in principle that you will give us Bin Laden?"

Prince Turki is quite adamant that Mullah Omar's answer was a firm "Yes"—and that no money or aid changed hands. Observers have suggested that the arrival of several hundred new 4x4 pickup trucks in Kandahar later that summer was a Saudi down payment on the deal, but Prince Turki denies this.

"The trucks," agrees Ahmed Rashid, "could have come from any of the talibs' Gulf sponsors."

At the end of July the Taliban used their new trucks, enhanced with machine guns, to finally capture the northern town of Mazar-e Sharif. This historic center of Shia worship, the "Noble Shrine," had resisted Taliban attacks the previous summer and was now punished with a series of ghastly reprisals. Ahmed Rashid later estimated that six thousand to eight thousand Shia men, women, and children were slaughtered in a rampage of murder and rape that included slitting people's throats and bleeding them to death, halal-style, and packing hundreds of victims into shipping containers without water, to be baked alive in the desert sun.

The massacre of Mazar-e Sharif was the Taliban's most gruesome atrocity yet. But it was overshadowed in the world's headlines by news from Africa. On August 7, 1998, the eighth anniversary of the arrival of American troops in Saudi Arabia in 1990, two teams of Al-Qaeda suicide bombers launched onslaughts against America's embassies in Nairobi, Kenya, and Dar es Salaam, Tanzania. Two hundred twenty-four people died and more than forty-five hundred were injured in attacks that were coordinated to within eight minutes of each other. The double campaign had been organized on the ground by Ahmed Abdullah, Khaled Al-Hubayshi's blond-haired Egyptian explosives instructor, whose final act was to press the detonator he had wired into the dashboard of the truck that he drove into the U.S. embassy parking lot in Dar es Salaam.

It was the first of Al-Qaeda's international spectaculars, and a chilling demonstration of the organization's ability to orchestrate histrionic attacks at a distance of thousands of miles. Osama Bin Laden's string of threats from Afghan tents and caves no longer seemed so windy or rhetorical.

• • •

The atrocity demanded a response from the American government, which had been virtually paralyzed that summer by the revelations of the affair between the president, Bill Clinton, and Monica Lewinsky, a White House intern. When Crown Prince Abdullah went to Washington in 1998 for his first visit as the de facto Saudi ruler, he was dismayed that two-thirds of his meeting with the president was consumed by talk of the scandal. Abdullah could not understand how the leader of what was now the world's only superpower could be in such straits over an extramarital affair.

"You are the rock," he said with concern as the two men parted. "The mountain is not swayed by the breeze."

Many Saudis saw significance in the fact that Ms. Lewinsky was Jewish. The intern's relationship with the president had involved Clinton unzipping his trousers to receive oral sexual favors from Ms. Lewinsky, and this impressed many as neatly symbolizing Jewish influence on the American centers of power.

On August 20, 1998, Operation Infinite Reach launched thirteen Tomahawk missiles against a suspected chemical weapons factory in Sudan, which turned out to be an innocent pharmaceutical plant, while seventy-five cruise missiles were fired from U.S. warships in the Indian Ocean in the direction of the recently built terrorist training camps in Afghanistan. The error of intelligence concerning the factory, coupled with the total failure of the missiles to reach a single member of the terrorist leadership that was their target, showed how ill-prepared and ill-equipped the United States was for the challenges of the new age of terrorism. It also gave Bin Laden the international stature he had sought for so long.

"By the grace of God, I am alive!" he exulted in a crackling wireless transmission.

As he gave thanks to God for his escape, however, Osama read out the name of one Saudi who was not so fortunate—Saleh Mutabaqani, a young man from a prominent Jeddah family who had been training fighters in one of the camps. Saleh was the solitary Saudi casualty, and Bin Laden proclaimed the young man a martyr.

"I remember meeting Saleh after he first came back from the war against the Soviets," recalls his cousin Mustapha. "He was a very cool guy, very peaceful. He seemed very soft—and also holy. I told him the bad jokes that I liked to say in those days, and he just did not react. It was like he was from another world. Later we heard that he was the head of a group, that he could make bombs, that he could strip and fix a machine gun in the dark—that he could do things you would never have guessed. Lots of people *talk* about fighting for God. Saleh really did it. The government took away his passport around that time, but somehow he went back.

"It was a shock to all of us when Bin Laden announced Saleh's name as a martyr on CNN. The press came asking questions. But the family said it must have been some mistake of spelling—they said they didn't know who he was."

. . .

In the middle of September 1998, Prince Turki Al-Faisal was once again circling in a plane over Kandahar airport. Three months earlier he had brought a religious sheikh to reinforce his mission. This time he brought along more earthly "muscle"—General Naseem Rama, the head of Pakistani intelligence. If Mullah Omar got awkward, he would have to face down his principal boss and official paymaster.

"We've been waiting for you," said the prince as he picked up his tea in the same Kandahar guesthouse he had visited in June. "You gave us your word that you were going to deliver Osama Bin Laden to us."

Unfailingly gentle in his speech, Prince Turki Al-Faisal can also direct his gaze with an intensity that is intimidating. He has the hawklike features and piercing eyes of his father, King Faisal—and he evidently disconcerted Mullah Omar, for the Taliban leader gave him no answer. Instead he stood up abruptly and left the room.

It was a long twenty minutes before he returned, and as the intelligence chief waited, sipping tea with his fellow spymaster, he wondered who the Taliban leader was talking to behind the door—the cohorts, he later concluded, of Omar's shura (advisory council).

"There must have been a translator's mistake," said the one-eyed mullah unapologetically as he reentered the room. "I never told you we would hand over Bin Laden."

Now it was Prince Turki's turn to be disconcerted.

"But, Mullah Omar," he expostulated, "you did not say this only one time!"

Only six weeks previously, he pointed out, in the month of July, Omar's principal adviser, Mullah Wakil Ahmed Mutawwakil, had traveled to Saudi Arabia for the express purpose of working out the Islamic formalities of Bin Laden's return with the Saudi government and to negotiate the terms of the handover.

It was just two weeks after that, however, on August 7, 1998, that Bin Laden had launched his lethal attacks on America's East African embassies, and that had clearly changed the situation. By several accounts, Mullah Omar had been furious with his guest for taking such drastic action without even extending the courtesy of informing him. But the Taliban chief was trapped by the enthusiasm with which the community of radical Muslims around the world, and particularly in Kandahar, had greeted the twin attacks. How could the leader of Afghanistan's Islamic revolution now disavow the man who had become the most admired jihadi on earth?

"Why are you doing this?" he blustered angrily at Prince Turki. "Why are you persecuting and harassing this courageous, valiant Muslim?"

As he played for time, the Taliban leader was effectively admitting his lack of maneuvering space over the surrender of Bin Laden—and that

America's attacks on Afghan targets had cornered him still further. At least twenty Afghans had been killed by the Tomahawk missiles. Omar could not now do a deal with their murderers. Nor could he meekly present Turki, America's surrogate, with the jihadi hero that America had tried, and failed, to assassinate.

Turki wondered if the Taliban leader was on drugs as Omar sweated and his voice grew ever shriller.

"He looked ill," remembers the prince. "It was clearly the strain of the moment. He was being called to account—and in front of his patron in the Pakistani ISI. I have thought about that moment a lot, and I am sure it was the American action that had pushed him to go back on his word."

Bin Laden, exclaimed Omar, was "a man of honor, a man of distinction." There had always been an element of awe in the simple mullah's attitude toward the wealthy, world-traveled Saudi warrior—gratitude, almost, that this Islamic champion should have chosen Afghanistan for his base. "Taqwa," the code name that the Taliban would later assign to Bin Laden, means fear or reverence for God.

"Instead of seeking to persecute him," proposed the Afghan leader, "you should put your hand in ours and his, and fight against the infidels!" America, he insisted, was the great enemy of the Muslims.

This was getting into dangerous territory, and, sure enough, the mullah stumbled over the boundary. The hospitality that Saudi Arabia gave to U.S. forces, he declared, meant that the Kingdom was, in effect, "an occupied country." Bin Laden himself could not have put it more offensively—and as he heard it, Prince Turki felt sure that Bin Laden himself must have fed this sort of thinking directly to Omar.

"I am not going to take any more of this," the prince announced furiously, rising to his feet and making for the door. "But you must remember, Mullah Omar, what you are doing now is going to bring a lot of harm to the Afghan people."

Within days the Saudi chargé d'affaires was withdrawn from Kabul—it was the end of official Saudi relations with the Taliban. But it was also the end of the last and best practical chance to protect the world from the destructive anger and ambition of Osama Bin Laden.

CHAPTER 23

New Century

For long periods in the 1990s, according to Prince Bandar bin Sultan, relations between the United States and Saudi Arabia had lapsed into stagnation. "Autopilot" was how the former F-5 squadron leader described the condition. Even before the paralysis induced by the Lewinsky scandal, Bandar told David Ottaway of the *Washington Post*, the United States and the Kingdom were largely ignoring each other. The two countries just shrugged their shoulders and got on with "doing their own thing."

The Saudi ambassador blamed the problem on the elusive and political character of Bill Clinton himself. Dealing with this U.S. president, he complained, was like dealing with Yasser Arafat—you never knew if he was saying yes or no. The Saudis had devised the word *la'am* to characterize the slipperiness of the Palestinian leader, a running together of the Arabic words *la* (no) and *nam* (yes) because Arafat was forever saying both at the same time. The same went for President Clinton, in the opinion of Bandar—who was speaking, by the mid-'90s, with the authority of the longest serving foreign ambassador to Washington, the dean of the diplomatic corps.

Clinton had also perfected the Arafat trick of extracting large sums of money from the Saudis while giving little or nothing in return. In 1989, as governor of Arkansas, long before his plans to run for president were even guessed at, Clinton approached Bandar for the unprecedented sum of $23 million to help the University of Arkansas establish a Middle East Center. To the surprise of Bandar, whose largest charitable contribution to that date had been $1 million to Nancy Reagan's "Just Say No" anti-drugs campaign, King Fahd agreed, and the money was eventually paid.

But the Kingdom had to wait two years after the departure of U.S. ambassador Chas Freeman in August 1992 for Clinton to appoint a replacement (the former governor of Mississippi, Ray Mabus)—and money was never far from the top of the president's agenda. When Louis Freeh, the FBI director, attended a key meeting with Prince Abdullah convened in Washington in 1998 to pressure the Saudis into providing more help with the investigation of the Khobar Towers bombing, he was astonished that the president "raised the subject [of the investigation] only to tell the crown prince that he understood the Saudis' reluctance to cooperate. . . . Then he hit Abdullah up for a contribution to the Clinton Presidential Library."*

Wyche Fowler, the former U.S. senator from Georgia who had become ambassador to Riyadh in 1996 and was present at the meeting, contradicts this account. "Louis Freeh did a great job building up our intelligence links with the Saudis," he says. "But in my opinion, his recollection on this is incorrect. President Clinton made no such request of the crown prince in our presence."

As the Americans saw it, the problem lay in quite the opposite direction. It was a matter of Prince Bandar falling down on the job. By his own admission, the ambassador went into an emotional decline when his friend George H. W. Bush failed to secure reelection to the White House in 1992. That in itself was enough to create distance between Bandar and the new president. Foreign diplomats, and particularly senior diplomats like Bandar, were not expected to take sides in U.S. elections—let alone travel, as Bandar did in November 1992, to spend election night in Houston close to his friend George with the deliberate intention of demonstrating his personal support.

Bandar was unapologetic.

"There's nothing more bonding than going to war together," he said nostalgically of his Desert Storm days with Bush, Baker, Scowcroft, and Cheney. "I did have a very special relationship with President Bush."

Bandar had medical problems. Two of his vertebrae had been crushed in a crash landing in his fighter days, resulting in nerve damage that nearly

*In December 2007 the *Washington Post* reported that the Saudi royal family contributed about $10 million to Bill Clinton's presidential library—"roughly the amount it gave to the presidential library of George W. Bush, according to people directly familiar with the contributions." It is believed that the Al-Saud routinely contributed to the libraries of retiring U.S. presidents from Jimmy Carter onward, if not earlier. However, the size of all donations remains confidential, owing to the status of the libraries as charitable foundations.

lost him the use of his right leg. He had to walk with a stick for a time. And in contrast to his ebullient exterior, the prince also suffered, Churchill-style, from bouts of "black dog" depression that kept him away from Washington for months at a time. In the late 1990s the ambassador became known as "the invisible dean" for his failure to attend the functions that went with his diplomatic duties. He even failed to appear at his own embassy for Saudi National Day.

So through the crucial, final years of the twentieth century, when, we now know, Saudi Arabia's terrorist mastermind was building up the infrastructure to launch his spectacular twenty-first-century attacks on America, the principal channel in U.S.-Saudi communications was out of action—or, to say the least, operating only intermittently.

This tale of failed potential should have ended with the success of George H. W. Bush's son George W. in the election of November 2000. "Talk about a replay!" declared the delighted Bandar as he sat down again with David Ottaway to tick off the names of old friends returning from previous administrations—as vice president, Dick Cheney; secretary of state, Colin Powell; national security adviser, Condoleezza Rice; and even Paul Wolfowitz, whose Defense Department efforts in the Gulf War had made him, in the prince's opinion, "more pro-Saudi than us." After eight blank and largely wasted years, it was back to business as usual for "Bandar Bush." Yet even as he celebrated, the ambassador had a nagging sense that it was all "too good to be true."

1945: ZIONIST CONNECTION

In the autumn of 1945, a few months after he came into office, President Harry Truman held a meeting in Washington with William Eddy, the U.S. chief of mission in Saudi Arabia, and with other U.S. diplomats to the major Arab countries. There had been widespread anger in the Arab world at the favor that America was showing toward the Zionist effort to create a Jewish state in Palestine, and the diplomats had been assembled to explain the reasons for Arab opposition.

But nothing he heard appeared to change Truman's mind.

"I'm sorry, gentlemen," said the president, summing up his position with the utmost candor, "but I have to answer to hundreds of thousands who are anxious for the success of Zionism. I do not have hundreds of thousands of Arabs among my constituents."

• • •

Truman was not quite correct. The U.S. Census of 1940 showed 107,420 individuals classified "white" who gave their "mother tongue" as Arabic, and census analysts reckon the real count of Arab-Americans at three times that. But the president's political point remained. By the 1940s the Jews were organized politically in America in a way that the Arabs never were, and, to date, have never chosen to be. Today there are some 3.5 million Arab-Americans (a good number of them Christian), and their political clout does not begin to match that of the 6.4 million U.S. Jews. Following the hard-fought creation of Israel in 1948, every successive crisis in the Middle East would increase pro-Israeli feeling inside America—and then came the emergence of so-called Christian Zionism in the 1980s. Popular evangelists like Jerry Falwell and Pat Robertson preached that the return of Jews to the Holy Land had happened in accordance with biblical prophecy—"to stand against Israel is to stand against God," proclaimed Falwell in 1981.

These Christian Zionist teachings were the foreign policy equivalent of "right to life"—a litmus-test issue by which American evangelicals made their decisions in the voting booth—and the support of Falwell and other Christian fundamentalists proved crucial to George W. Bush's disputed election as president in 2000. Bush the Younger never endorsed Christian Zionism in so many words, but, as he came into office in 2001, the born-again Christian acted as if he believed it. One of his earliest and most warmly welcomed guests in the White House was Ariel Sharon, the hard-line Israeli prime minister notorious for turning a blind eye to the massacre of Palestinians when he was a general during the 1982 war in Lebanon. It was Sharon's aggressive visit to Jerusalem's Temple Mount in September 2000 that had largely provoked the new, bitterly violent Palestinian intifada, and the Bush administration appeared to endorse Sharon's shoot-from-the-hip style. Asked about Israeli attempts to assassinate Palestinian leaders, Vice President Cheney said he saw "some justification in their trying to protect themselves by preempting."

Such unconcealed favoritism was not what the Saudis expected of any U.S. administration—and certainly not from the son of the man who had come to their rescue in the Gulf War. In London, the Kingdom's acerbic ambassador Ghazi Algosaibi wrote a column in the newspaper *Al-Hayat* speculating on the psychological complexes that "Little George" was evidently feeling toward "Big George." These hang-ups had made the new president a menace to the whole world in record time, wrote the ambassador in comments that made it to the top of Fox News: "Little George" deserved a special medal—"the Prize for Turning Friends into Enemies Without Effort."

The blunt speaking of Algosaibi had been disavowed in the past by his more diplomatic superiors, but not on this occasion.

"I did not make him a writer, I found him a writer," Abdullah responded to the White House when it lodged a formal, high-level protest at the ambassador's comments.

The crown prince was losing his patience with America.

. . .

The image on the TV screen was painful. An Israeli soldier was placing his boot on the head of a Palestinian woman, pinning her down to the ground. When he saw it on the night of August 23, 2001, Crown Prince Abdullah went ballistic.

"A woman being beaten by a man?" recalls one senior Saudi official. "He just felt this was the ultimate insult."

Abdullah was sitting in the elegant, dark-paneled study of his home beside the Red Sea in Jeddah. On the walls were pictures of his father, some Koranic inscriptions, and a selection of the Orientalist paintings that he loved. Unusually for a Saudi palace, there was not a trace of gold, nor a chandelier in sight.

The crown prince's rage boiled over.

"Is the blood of an Israeli child more expensive and holy than the blood of a Palestinian child?" he asked.

Like his subjects, Abdullah had been watching the cable news channels' coverage of the Palestinian intifada, and he was dismayed at the round-the-clock images of tanks, tears, and suffering. Some people called it the "Al-Jazeera" or "CNN" effect, but it could also have been called the CPA (Crown Prince Abdullah) effect. The new American president had expressed the hope that the Saudi leader would come to visit him soon, but Abdullah refused to consider the idea. He was personally indignant, and he had little doubt what ordinary Saudis would think of him if he went.

Bush invited the crown prince to the White House, to Camp David, to the Kentucky Derby, and, the ultimate honor, to his ranch in Crawford, Texas, but Abdullah rebuffed every offer. In desperation, Washington suggested the Franklin D. Roosevelt Library in Hyde Park, New York—a flattering reference to the 1945 meeting between FDR and Abdullah's father that had established the famed "special" relationship. Abdullah was unimpressed. He even declined to be shifted when George W.'s father put in a personal phone call to reassure him that his son's "heart was in the right place."

The crown prince had been stoking his anger since the spring.

"Don't they see," he had asked in a visit to Morocco that June, "what is happening to Palestinian children, women, and the elderly?"

Now his message was complete, and the time had come to deliver it. "I reject people who say that when you kill a Palestinian, it is defense; when a Palestinian kills an Israeli, it's a terrorist act."

The crown prince picked up the phone and asked to be put through to his ambassador in the United States.

...

As it happened, Bandar bin Sultan had been away from the phone that warm August night—he was taking a break at his home in Aspen—and by the time he got the message it was too late for him to call Riyadh. When uncle and nephew spoke the next day, George W. was on television, handling questions on the Middle East at a news conference. The two Saudi princes, one in Riyadh, one in Colorado, watched the president speaking in Texas—and Abdullah grew angrier than ever at the American's total acceptance of the Israeli point of view.

"If the Palestinians are interested in a dialogue," said the president in the apparently reasonable tone he reserved for his most provocative statements, "then I strongly urge Mr. Arafat to put 100 percent effort into solving the terrorist activity, stopping the terrorist activity. And I believe he can do a better job of doing that."

The disdainful use of "terrorist activity" to describe the battle that Arabs saw as a fight for justice caused Abdullah to explode for the second time in twenty-four hours. He characterized this phrase in the same way as he did "Israel's right to defend itself"—as a disingenuous simplification.

Bandar must get to see Bush at once, instructed the crown prince, and within hours the ambassador had managed to get a message to Colin Powell, the secretary of state, and to Condoleezza Rice, the national security adviser.

"We believe," went the message, "there has been a strategic decision by the United States that its national interest in the Middle East is 100 percent based on [Israeli prime minister] Sharon."

If this was America's decision, it was her sovereign right to make it. But it was Saudi Arabia's sovereign right, declared the crown prince, to pursue her own course in response to that.

"Starting from today, you're Uruguay, as they say." This particular phrase was contributed by Bandar, deriving from his version of a knock-knock joke that ended with the punchline, "You go Uruguay, and I'll go mine." He had taken notes while Abdullah spoke to him on the phone, then amplified his uncle's thoughts, as he used to do with Fahd's, to craft a message that would, in his opinion, press the particular buttons of his listeners.

"A government that doesn't keep its finger on the pulse of what its people are feeling will not survive," continued the message, which ran, in the end, to twenty-five pages of Bandar's notes. "Look at what happened to the Shah. Sometimes we come to a crossroads; we have to make choices, and we are not afraid to make the strategic shift that our own interests dictate."

It was a firm and extensive warning, and to emphasize the point, Abdullah picked up the phone again. He ordered General Salih bin Ali Al-Muhayya, the Saudi chief of staff, who had arrived in Washington the previous day for the annual review of Saudi-U.S. military collaboration, to return to Riyadh immediately. The general was instructed not to meet with any Americans. A delegation of some forty senior Saudi officers who were flying to join Muhayya were ordered off their plane. The annual review was canceled.

"That's the moment the U.S. knew they had a problem," remembers one of the Saudis involved.

"Hey, you guys scared us," said Powell to Bandar.

"The hell with you," replied the prince. "We scared ourselves."

• • •

The Saudis had expected that the White House would take four or five days to get back to them. In the event, George W. Bush's personal, two-page letter of conciliation arrived in less than thirty-six hours—and it was a revelation.

"What came through," commented one surprised Saudi, "was the humane part of George W. He was very, very positive."

Writing warmly, the president totally accepted Abdullah's point about the blood of innocent people—"Palestinian, Israeli, Jewish, Christian, or Muslim"—and he told the crown prince that he rejected the humiliation of individuals, which the Saudi leader took to be a response to his complaint about the Israeli soldier's boot. Most important of all, the president set down quite explicitly his acceptance of the "Two-State Solution"—the creation of a viable Palestinian state on the West Bank and Gaza Strip.

This was new—"groundbreaking," felt the Saudis. No U.S. president had given such a strong commitment before, and it staked out a U.S. position that was clearly different from that of Sharon. Bush's letter had "things in it," according to someone who saw it, "[that] had never been put in writing. He wrote constructively about the status of Jerusalem and the settlement of the refugee issue. He actually said, 'I support two states.' "

The letter offered the prospect of a peace settlement with which the Saudis could live, and Bandar carried it back to Riyadh to discuss its contents personally with Abdullah. The U.S. president had even expressed a willingness to take a more active role in the peace process himself.

In the days that followed Abdullah got in touch with other Arab leaders—the presidents of Egypt and Syria and the king of Jordan—to share the good news. He briefed them on his message, and on the personal reply that his protest had prompted. He summoned Yasser Arafat from a visit to South Africa to come and read both documents: when Abdullah felt stirred to action, nothing much stood in his way. He got Arafat to give a written pledge that he would meet Bush's conditions for restarting peace talks.

" 'This is your last chance,' we told him," according to Bandar. " 'You can't screw it up like you did with Clinton.' "

Arafat's pledge was sent to Washington with the crown prince's own response to Bush's letter, and by early September Bandar was back in

Washington, working out the details. On Friday, September 7, his U.S. counterparts seemed ready to move on a peace initiative, and over the weekend he discussed definite steps—a speech by Colin Powell, by Bush himself (the Saudis' preferred option), or possibly both. Yasser Arafat was coming to the UN later in the month; Would Bush agree to meet him? The president did not like the idea.

"Arafat is a liar," he complained.

"We know that he's a liar," responded the Saudis. No one in Riyadh liked Arafat. Cabinet members knew they were in disfavor when the king assigned them to escort the Palestinian leader on one of his regular fund-raising trips—"I had him once for nearly a week," recalls one minister with a shudder. "All those kisses and licks!"

Bush should hear out what the Palestinian said, the Saudis counseled, then hold him to whatever he promised

"If he goes back on himself," said Bandar, "we won't trouble you with him again."

"Suddenly," remembered the Saudi ambassador, "I felt . . . that we really were going to have a major initiative here that could save all of us from ourselves—mostly—and from each other. . . . The happiest man in the world on Monday night was Bandar bin Sultan. I was in the swimming pool [of his palatial residence in McLean, Virginia] smoking a cigar. I gave myself a day off because I had worked the whole weekend. I had been to Saudi Arabia . . . out with the [Bush] response, back with our response. I worked on the weekend up to three o'clock, four o'clock in the morning . . . I worked all Monday. And I said to my office, 'Tuesday, I'm taking the day off.' "

Tuesday was September 11, 2001.

PART THREE

AL-QAEDA COMES HOME

A.D. 2001–2009 (A.H. 1422–1430)

If we want things to stay as they are, things will have to change.

—Guiseppe di Lampedusa, *The Leopard*

CHAPTER 24

Fifteen Flying Saudis

Prince Khaled Al-Faisal saw the smoke from the first hit pouring out of the tower on television.

"I was in a meeting in Riyadh with three other people," he recalls. "The TV was on CNN, and when I saw the smoke coming out, I put the sound up higher. The commentator said that a small plane had hit the twin towers. I was just thinking that it looked like a lot of smoke for a small plane to make, when suddenly—Oh my God, what's this?—I saw the second plane, a huge airliner, come flying sideways into the picture. I actually watched as that second plane flew straight into the tower and exploded."

The broadcaster's tone changed.

"It was quite clear to me," says the prince, who was then governor of the southern region of Asir—from which, it turned out, four of the hijackers came—"that this could not be an accident. It was a deliberate attack. I turned to my companions and said, 'Look at your watches. What's the time? Everything is going to change. We live now in a different world from the one we inhabited an hour ago.'"

Then he added—"I only hope these men are not Saudis."

. . .

Khaled Al-Hubayshi hoped the very opposite. On September 11, 2001, the young Jeddah-born jihadi was staying in an Al-Qaeda guesthouse in Kabul, holding his little Sony portable radio clamped against his ear. Like hundreds of other young extremists then training in Afghanistan, he was listening as reports came in of the very *first* plane hitting its target. They had all been told that "something" was about to happen.

"The leader of our guesthouse had told us to start listening to our radios a couple of hours before it happened," he recalls. "He knew something was coming, but he did not tell us what it would be. He probably did not know himself. I later heard that the guys on the first Boston plane [Mohammed Atta and his team] sent back a message to report they had gotten through the airport security and were getting on board. So Bin Laden knew that the operation had started. As the news came through we could not believe it. Everyone was around the big radios cheering. We had never imagined that we had the power to hit America like that.

"But after a time, as I heard the stories of people jumping out of the towers, I began to wonder. All those thousands of civilians dead. What had this got to do with defending the Muslims? And then I started to think about my own survival—Am I going to stay? Am I going to fight?"

Like Prince Khaled in Riyadh, Al-Hubayshi realized that life could never be the same again.

"The moment we heard about the attacks on New York we knew, sure as hell, that the *Yanqees* were not going to take it lying down. They were going to come after us.

"Shit! I wondered. What's going to happen next?"

. . .

Fouad Al-Farhan, a young student in Jeddah, had little doubt that the hijackers were Saudis, and when the names were released he tried to find out more about them—particularly the Al-Ghamdi boys, Ahmed, Hamza, and Saeed from Al-Baha, north of Asir.

"I had heard strange things about them," he recalls. "One of them slept in a room with a view of a graveyard right outside his window—now why did he do that? It's not natural. And the other was famous for coming out of evening prayers and pointing up at the sky. 'You see that star?' he'd say. 'I can tell you that it's not a star. It's an American spy satellite. It's looking down on us. It's filming us right now.'

"So, based on what I can discover, my explanation of 9/11 is down to defective human mechanisms—wackos. And every human society has wackos. But we have to accept that most of them were Saudi wackos. Fifteen out of nineteen. We cannot shift the blame. If you subject a society to all those pressures—the rigid religion, the tribe, the law, the traditions, the family, the police, and, above all, the oppressive political system in which you can't express yourself—you are going to end up with wackos.

And if you then present them with the doctrine of takfeer, the idea that all their problems come from outside themselves, and that you should try to destroy people who do not share your own particular view of God, then you are going to end up with some folks who are very dangerous indeed."

. . .

As someone who had himself committed terrorist acts, Mansour Al-Nogaidan knew the perils of takfeer. He had been speaking out against it for months. After his latest release from jail, his friends had found him a mosque in Riyadh where he was well looked after. It was a cushy billet. But Mansour had a new gospel to propagate. While reflecting in jail on the rigidity of the Wahhabi religious establishment, he had come to be offended by their refusal to accept any questioning—and that was not a criticism that the elders of his local community wanted to hear. They forced him out. Moving on to a career in journalism, the ex-imam was similarly outspoken. Not content with reading outside the red lines, he insisted on writing outside them and started to make a name for himself as an outpoken columnist.

When it came to 9/11, however, Mansour had to confess that he was nonplussed. He was visiting his family in Buraydah when he saw the strike against the second tower live on television, and he found himself lost for words. He just stared blankly at the horror on the screen, appalled and silenced by the biblical smoke and destruction.

"I was shocked to my core. I didn't know what I thought for three days. Where had it come from? It just defied human thinking."

. . .

The demon center forward had scored a goal the crowd would never forget. Like Juhayman Al-Otaybi, Osama Bin Laden astonished his enemies with a coup for which no one was seriously prepared. Twenty years earlier Juhayman's anger had transformed the Kingdom. Now Osama Bin Laden's astonishing assault on America's sovereignty and sense of security would transform the world—and America in particular.

"When I was coming up, it was a dangerous world," George W. Bush had declared to the voters of Iowa the previous year. "It was Us versus Them, and it was clear who 'them' was. Today, we are not so sure who the 'they' are."

Clarity was restored by 9/11. Once more there was something of which

America, the greatest power in the history of the world, could feel comfortingly afraid. As Gore Vidal remarked, "We desperately want a huge, dangerous enemy."

Bin Laden attacked America for playing two ends against the middle. By financing Islamic extremism in Afghanistan in the 1980s and allying with the House of Saud while also supporting the Israeli cause at the expense of the Arabs, Washington had sent a conflicted foreign policy message that managed to provoke more death and destruction in the mainland United States than forty-five years of Cold War. America was the "far Satan," in Osama's eyes, because it was the patron and supporter of the Al-Saud, the "near Satan" that was his ultimate target. Understandably wounded and angry as they surveyed the smoking ruins of downtown Manhattan, few Americans could see that it was through the selection of contradictory friends that their successive governments had picked themselves this lethal foe.

• • •

Riyadh was suffering from an equivalent denial, as Robert Jordan, George W. Bush's Texas lawyer, discovered when he arrived a few weeks after 9/11 to take up his post as U.S. ambassador.

"Many senior princes believed it was a Jewish plot. Nayef [the interior minister] actually *said* it was a Zionist conspiracy in a public statement. Even Abdullah was suspicious. They had latched onto this report that three thousand Jewish employees had not gone into work that day. It was an urban myth that has since been discredited, but at the time it was the only way they could make sense of it."

"Ana ma talabtah, bas Allah jabha"—"I didn't ask for it, but God brought it," was the attitude of many Saudis.

"To accept that Saudis were major players in 9/11," remembers the *Arab News* editor Khaled Al-Maeena, "was like accepting that your son was a serial killer. You had to refuse to believe it."

The irony of the Jewish conspiracy theories was that a group of Arabs—and no one but Arabs—had finally hit the enemy in a way that was quite extraordinary. In terms of organization, surprise, and daring, 9/11 was an aggressive and murderous stroke of sheer brilliance. Why, if you were a proud and upstanding Arab, would you want to hand the credit to the Zionists?

The close relationship of Prince Bandar bin Sultan with George H. W. Bush (here at the White House in 1989) was strengthened by the joint challenge of ousting Saddam Hussein from Kuwait in 1991.

Not attaining such intimacy with the Clinton administration, the Saudi ambassador presumed the good times would return with George W. Bush in the White House. Then came 9/11.

كارثة أمريكا: خسائر الأسهم بمئات المليارات ومخاوف على 700 مليار دولار عربية وارتفاع أسعار النفط والذهب

الوطن
AL-WATAN

36 صفحة

ريالان

دهانات الجزيرة
جودة وجمال

المجتمع 33	الرياضة 27	الثقافة 26	الاقتصاد 16	المحليات 11
50% من مجموع الوفيات في العالم سببها ضغط العمل	لاعب الرجاء المغربي (القاسمي) للهلال السعودي بـ150 ألف دولار	سعد نعمر لـ(الوطن): الدعاية وعدم المشاركة في المهرجانات العربية عطلا الفن السعودي	البنوك السعودية قادرة على المنافسة عالمياً	انطلاقة المرحلة الأولى الميدانية لأعمال التعداد العام للسكان والمساكن الأسبوع المقبل

انتحاريون يخطفون طائرات ويهاجمون مركز التجارة العالمي والبنتاجون والخارجية وتساؤل عما إذا كان المنفذون قتلوا الطيارين وقادوا الطائرات بأنفسهم

أكبر هجوم انتحاري منسق يستهدف أمريكا ويهز العالم

"الثلاثاء الأسود" يشهد كارثة ضرب العصب الأمريكي عسكرياً واقتصادياً وسياسياً

خادم الحرمين وولي العهد يستقبلان الرئيس السوداني

السعودية تدين الهجمات لأنها تتعارض مع القيم الدينية والمفاهيم الحضارية

Front page of the *Al-Watan* ("The Nation") edition for September 12, 2001, reports 9/11 to Saudi Arabia: *"Suicide bombers hijack planes and attack the World Trade Center and Pentagon—Did the hijackers kill the pilots and then fly the aircraft? The biggest suicide attack against America shakes the world. Saudi Arabia condemns the attack—'In conflict with our religious and civilized values.'"*

Right: Khaled Al-Hubayshi muffled against the cold as a jihadi (holy warrior) in Afghanistan in 2001. *Far right:* Khaled today, after three and a half years in Guantánamo Bay and fifteen months in a Saudi jail, followed by a marriage arranged with the help of the Interior Ministry.

Left: Mansour Al-Nogaidan in 1995, jailed four times for his extremist views and once for firebombing a video store. *Right:* Mansour in 2008 with his wife Muna, son Yoseph, and daughter Laila.

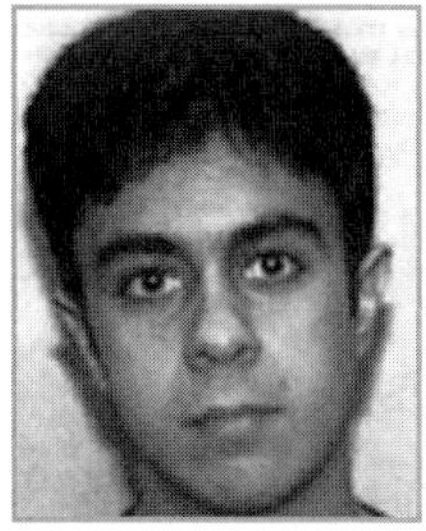
Saeed Al-Ghamdi

Ahmad Al-Ghamdi

Hamza Al-Ghamdi

Hani Hanjour

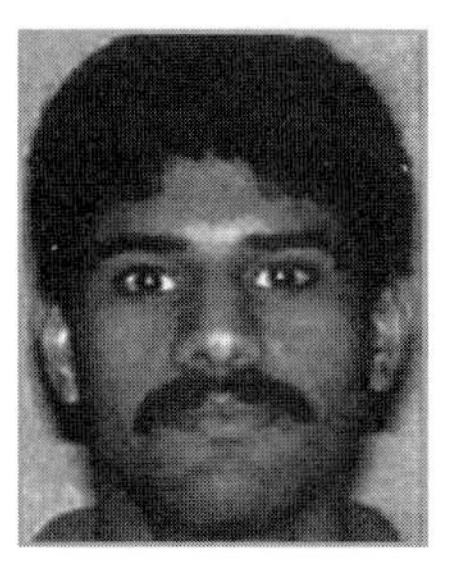
Nawwaf Al-Hazmi

Salem Al-Hazmi

Ahmad Al-Haznawi

Khaled Al-Mihdhar

Majed Moqed

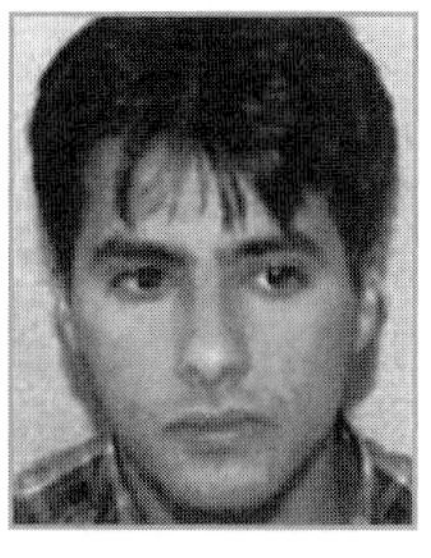
Ahmad Al-Nami

Abdul Aziz Al-Omar

Mohanad Al-Shehri

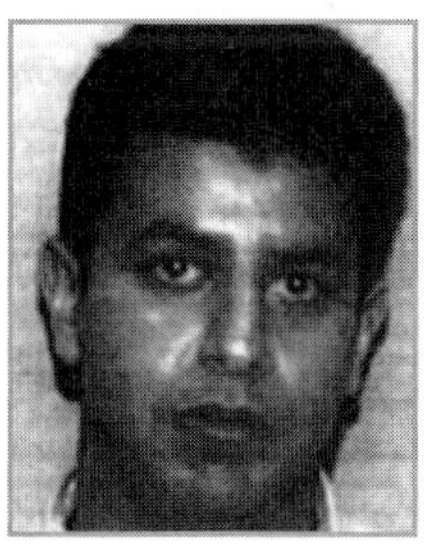
Wail Al-Shehri

Waleed Al-Shehri

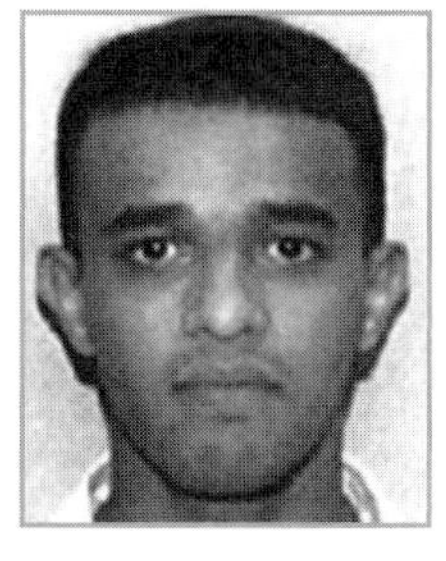
Sattam Al-Suqani

The fifteen Saudi hijackers of 9/11

5. MESSAGE

نص الرسالة

Family and/or private news only

أخبار شخصية أو عائلية فقط

بسم الله الرحمن الرحيم

٢٧/٩/١٤٢٣هـ

6.

Date .... التاريخ Signature .... الامضاء

Yasser Al-Zahrani's letter to his father, at the end of his first year in Guantánamo: *Family and/or private news only:*

"My dear Father, Peace be upon you, with God's mercy and blessings, and may you be well every year. I ask God to give us the chance to celebrate Ramadan with His blessings to you and to us with His gift of health and well-being, and to give you the help and support you need. And may God forgive us for all our sins that we have already committed or might commit. I write to you with all trust that God will get us together soon—not meaning that I know what God will do, but trusting the promise of God and His Prophet. If you receive this letter, please let me hear back from you, and please say 'Hello' to all my beloved ones, sisters, brothers, and relatives." —Dated 27/9/1423 AH (December 2, 2002 A.D.)

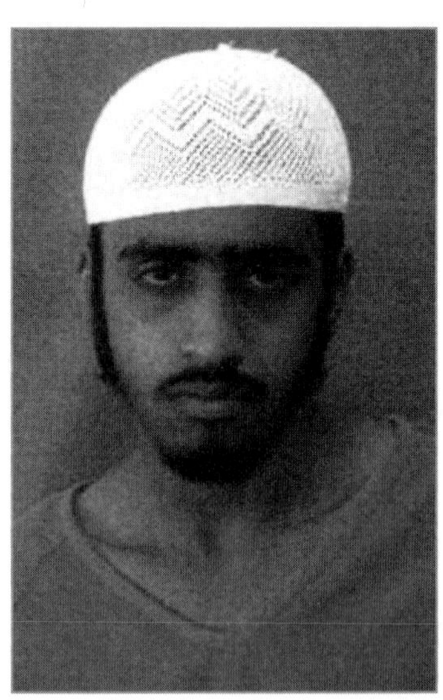

Left: Yasser Al-Zahrani as a teenager in Saudi Arabia, several years before he left to join Al-Qaeda's battle in Afghanistan. *Right:* Yasser in his Guantánamo uniform, some time before his mysterious death by hanging in his cell in June 2006.

BBC security correspondent Frank Gardner lies wounded in a Riyadh street, shot six times by Al-Qaeda gunmen who came across him filming with his cameraman Simon Cumbers on June 6, 2004. Cumbers was shot dead.

Frank Gardner at Buckingham Palace, October 13, 2005, having received the OBE (Order of the British Empire) from Queen Elizabeth II.

Religious sheikhs work with former Guantánamo inmates and other captured extremists to try to map a more moderate way of life at the Mohammed bin Nayef Rehabilitation Center north of Riyadh, November 2007, and to view jihad (holy war) in a new light.

Crown Prince Abdullah (shown here as commander of the National Guard in the 1960s) took over day-to-day management of the Kingdom after King Fahd's health worsened in the late 1990s.

In March 2002, the tragic deaths of fifteen girls in a fire in a cleric-supervised girls' school in Mecca prompted a widespread outcry. Crown Prince Abdullah abruptly removed control of Saudi girls' education from the religious establishment, harnessing the indignation to his program of national reform.

Shortly before his accession as king in August 2006, Abdullah became the first royal to be photographed visiting the shack of one of the Saudi underclass. His other initiatives have included greater press freedom, the creation of human rights commissions, the establishment of a "National Dialogue" to air controversial social issues, and the reform of intolerant Saudi textbooks. He introduced municipal elections in 2005 but has postponed the second round due in 2009.

In November 2008 Abdullah bin Abdul Aziz went to New York to inaugurate his dialogue on religious understanding at the United Nations, then joined the other leaders of the world's top twenty economies for the G20 economic crisis summit in Washington, the only king and the only Arab.

Elvis and his fan club: Custodian of the Two Holy Mosques, King Abdullah bin Abdul Aziz, at the National Dialogue held in Abha, southern Saudi Arabia, April 2008, to discuss the status of women. The king has worked hard to deliver more rights to his female subjects—though not, as yet, the right to drive a car, or to make almost any significant decision without the consent of a male relative.

"That was typical Arab victim talk," says the Jeddah journalist Somaya Jabarti. "When we engage in conspiracy theories we are disempowering ourselves. We are guilty of passive thinking, saying that someone else is always responsible."

"Bin Laden was evil and murderous," says Prince Amr Al-Faisal. "As a Muslim I fiercely and totally condemn what he did. But the Saudis are daring people, and it is not surprising that one of the most daring terrorists in the world should be a Saudi. As many Muslims saw it, the falling of the twin towers was a lesson to the pride and complacency of the Americans. It gave them just a little taste of what the Muslims have been going through."

. . .

Out in the Saudi heartland most people agreed. When Mohammed Al-Harbi, then a twenty-five-year-old chemistry teacher, went into school in Buraydah on the day after 9/11, there was a happy buzz in the staff room.

" 'The jihad has started,' they were saying. 'There is more to come.' They were all very supportive and content with the attack on New York, and were clearly very happy that it had been done by Saudi hands—or so they assumed. It was like their football team had won."

Mohammed, a small, neat-bearded man, rather enjoyed tweaking his colleagues and provoking arguments with them, particularly on religious matters.

"They used to tell me that I was not qualified to discuss religion. 'You have no marks of a religious person,' they'd say—meaning that I trimmed my beard instead of letting it grow long and bushy, Salafi-style. They were all quite nice and friendly about it in those early days. They gave me books and tapes to educate me."

But now the argument grew more pointed.

"Let's put religion on the side, for the moment," Mohammed would argue. "Let's agree that an educated nation like America should be respected. Think how much money it took to build those towers. It is haram [shameful] to wreak such destruction."

His colleagues shrugged their shoulders.

"That is the money of kuffar [infidels]," they replied.

"Don't three thousand lives count for anything?" Mohammed asked.

"They're not Muslims."

"But don't you feel sorry for all those people?" the chemistry teacher persisted. "I feel very sorry for them."

"Why don't you ever express sorrow for the Palestinians?" came the reply.

"Because the Palestinians have had a hand in their own destiny," replied the chemistry teacher. "Those people in the towers were helpless."

When he got into the classroom, Mohammed continued the discussion with his pupils and found them apparently accepting of his arguments. But in the weeks that followed, he discovered that his teaching colleagues were going behind his back to cross-examine his students, taking notes of what he had said.

"'What did he tell you?' they'd ask my pupils. 'Don't listen to him. He's not in the correct path.'"

A little less than a month after 9/11, U.S. and UK forces invaded Afghanistan. At once feelings in the Buraydah staff room grew more strained. As news reports came in, Mohammed openly celebrated the defeat of the Taliban, whose intolerance he had always deplored.

"I am getting worried about you," said one of his bearded colleagues with feeling. "I am getting very worried about the secular thoughts in your head."

Mohammed understood the coded message.

"He was trying to sound friendly and concerned. But I knew that he was issuing a warning—a very serious warning. If an Islamic court finds that your thoughts are 'secular,' they take that to mean that you're a Muslim who has renounced the faith, that you're an 'apostate.' And the penalty for apostasy is death."

. . .

Robert Jordan, meanwhile, was trying to get established as America's ambassador to Riyadh—which included the presentation of his credentials in a bizarre ceremony at King Fahd's palace beside the Red Sea.

"I had three hours' notice to get to the airport with my documents. When I got there, I discovered sixty or seventy other ambassadors, the majority of the diplomatic corps, none of whom had been officially presented. We all flew down to Jeddah on the plane together—what a target *that* would have made for Al-Qaeda.

"King Fahd was pushed out in a wheelchair with a great deal of pomp and ceremony. It was a cool winter's afternoon. The ceremony was out of doors, and we each went up to meet him, one by one, to present our papers. It was very sad to think that at this critical moment, Saudi Arabia should be looking to an invalid as its king."

March 2002 was the twenty-year anniversary of Fahd's accession, and all Saudi schoolchildren were instructed to compose a letter of thanks to him. Ahmad Sabri, fifteen years old, sat in his Jeddah classroom, determined not to be a puppet. Suddenly he knew what to write: "Thank you, oh great and kind King Fahd, for the Kingdom's many wonderful things that improve the quality of our life—for the beautiful roads without potholes or repair sites, for the good schools, for the planes that always arrive on time . . ."

His teacher picked up the sheet of paper and studied his bright young pupil's list of sarcasms.

"Ahmad," he asked, "do you want to get into trouble?"

Ahmad pulled back his paper hurriedly and started to scribble the flattery that was required.

. . .

It was certainly the worst of moments to have a head of state who was incapacitated. But one of the several good things that emerged from 9/11, for Saudi Arabia at least, was that Abdullah bin Abdul Aziz finally became a ruling crown prince—if partly through default. Refusing to accept Saudi responsibility for what had happened, some of Fahd's Sudayri brothers literally lost the plot in the dark undergrowth of their conspiracy theories.

"It is enough to see a number of congressmen wearing Jewish yarmulkes," remarked Sultan, the deputy crown prince in June 2002, "to explain the allegations against us."

"We still ask ourselves," added his brother Nayef a few months later, "who has benefited from the September 11 attacks? I think that they [the Jews] were the protagonists of such attacks."

Crown Prince Abdullah was not averse to blaming the Zionists. But he was first among the senior sons of Abdul Aziz—the topmost princes who mattered—to accept the Saudi role in 9/11.

"We showed him the dossiers," remembers Robert Jordan, "with the details of who was on the planes, the actual comings-and-goings of all these young Saudis, their photographs, the shots from the airport security cameras. I suppose you could dismiss all that documentation as the most incredible hoax. Otherwise you had to take it seriously."

Abdullah did. As commander of the National Guard, he knew the exact significance of each tribal and family name on the 9/11 roll call: Al-Ghamdi, Al-Hazmi, Al-Haznawi, Al-Mihdhar, Al-Nami, Al-Omari, Al-Shehri, Al-Suqami, Hani Hanjour, Majed Moqed.* Abdullah knew the heads of many of these families. He made phone calls to check. He spoke to the relatives. He took it all very personally. In his simple, emotional way he looked on each of the young men as one of his sons, and his eyes welled up as he looked at their photo-booth photographs.

The crown prince was convinced. Saudi Arabia had a problem, and as the crisis evolved, the need for rapid decisions also solidified his power. On 9/11 itself he had gone into a huddle with Ali Al-Naimi, the long-serving oil minister, to agree that Saudi oil production be increased to its ceiling to avoid an energy crisis—the most important decision that the Kingdom could take that day, and perhaps, in itself, a certain signal of remorse. In his pre-9/11 jostling with Bush, Abdullah had taken decisive control of Saudi foreign policy. Now he took firmer charge of domestic policy as well.

Robert Jordan was impressed. Unlike any other ambassador, America's envoy had a standing appointment to sit down with the Kingdom's ruler on a regular basis, when the two sides went through a comprehensive state-of-the-relationship discussion through translators, with a TV camera and microphones recording every word.

"I found Abdullah rather austere, and also slow to speak," he recalls. "But he was always listening. He was learning. He was clearly seeking to make wise choices. He was a surprisingly emotional person. He seemed to form a lot of his judgments on the basis of how much he liked the person with whom he was dealing. And he was also, obviously, getting besieged with conflicting advice from different sections of the family."

Much of Jordan's time was spent shepherding a succession of worried officials sent from Washington to locate and plug the holes through which the United States felt that her principal Arab ally had let her down.

"They were difficult days," recalls Jordan. "Very painful. *They* were so

*There were three Al-Ghamdis (unrelated to one another), three Al-Shehris (a pair of brothers and one unrelated), and two Al-Hazmis (unrelated).

angry that *we* were so angry with them. I remember George Tenet [head of the CIA] came out to Riyadh. He was furious, very aggressive. I remember one meeting with Mohammed bin Nayef. He really got in the young prince's face."

Mohammed bin Nayef, the studious son of the interior minister, had been given the responsibility for counterterrorism.

"In the very earliest days," says Jordan, "the Saudis wouldn't share the 'pocket litter' with us—the debris found in the suspects' pockets, the speed-dials and such like, the messages on their mobile phones. That was back in the days of the Al-Khobar [Towers] bombing. Eventually they relaxed enough to let us listen in on their interrogations. Our people were allowed to look through a one-way mirror and pass along the questions we needed to be asked."

The trouble was that the FBI, which was charged with taking the lead in all this, was not really in a position to conduct many direct interrogations.

"On the day of 9/11," says Jordan, "the bureau had just five fluent Arabic speakers on its books, all of them prosecuting lawyers. 'Legal Attaché' is the title carried by the FBI man in any U.S. embassy. But the legal attachés exist to investigate and to set up prosecutions after the event. They are not there for prevention, or to gather intelligence—they are not detectives. I felt there was a profound need for a complete culture change."

There were many areas for improvement, Jordan discovered. The FBI and CIA representatives in his rambling, sand-colored Riyadh embassy compound were scarcely speaking to each other.

"The CIA would ask me to chase the Saudis for the cell-phone records of some local suspect. They'd complain that they couldn't get anything out of the Ministry of the Interior. So I'd go down to the ministry to jump up and down and make a lot of fuss, to be told that they had given that particular set of phone records to somebody in the embassy months ago—to the FBI man, who had kept the papers to himself! And this was happening twelve months after 9/11."

When he went back to Washington, the ambassador raised the problem with the CIA's George Tenet and Robert Mueller, the FBI director. The two men promised better cooperation between their agencies, but below them the institutional disdain of their respective hierarchies was almost impossible to overcome.

"The FBI simply was not committed to sending its best and brightest overseas," asserts Jordan. "The high-fliers stayed at home. They wanted to make their names in the domestic prosecutions. That was another part of the culture. As I was leaving Riyadh toward the end of 2003, one attaché was being disciplined for not being a very good officer, and his substitute only lasted two months."

Another FBI man in Riyadh, the deputy legal attaché Gamal Hafiz, an Egyptian by birth, was accused of being "pro-Muslim" when he refused to go into a mosque wearing a surveillance wire. He resigned his position and sued the bureau.

"After 9/11 we made a lot of noise," says Jordan, "but you could argue that the Saudis did a better job on what really mattered. In the end I think that they were quicker than us in getting up to speed on the true priorities of counterterrorism. It was fairly soon after 9/11 that Prince Saud Al-Faisal [the foreign minister] suggested to Washington that we should set up a joint U.S.-Saudi task force to cooperate on terrorism—and he received absolutely nil response from the White House. Deaf ears. Quite extraordinary! It wasn't until May 2004 that the president finally appointed Frances Townsend, and that was largely the result of Prince Saud doing the pushing."

• • •

Meanwhile the crown prince took the issues raised by 9/11 to the country—or rather, to the country's elite.

"We must pay careful attention," Abdullah declared in a series of televised gatherings to which he summoned the religious sheikhs, the tribal leaders, the media, and the business community. "Something serious has gone wrong here, and we have to put it right. Those who govern [wali al-amr] need to work out a strategy for what has to be done."

Each majlis nodded gravely, made some cautious suggestions, and went away to think. But one of the religious sheikhs came up with an extra point. Dr. Abdullah Turki, the learned member of the council of the ulema who had accompanied Prince Turki to Afghanistan to try to convince the Taliban to hand over Bin Laden, fastened on Abdullah's use of the term *wali al-amr.*

"Those who govern," he pointed out, included not only the king and the government, but also the senior ulema. From its earliest days the Saudi state had been a partnership between the political and the religious, and

Dr. Turki suggested that at this moment of crisis the religious sheikhs needed to have more say in how the country was run.

It was a controversial claim, but it had a historical basis. In the very earliest years of the Saudi state, according to the Nejdi historian Ibn Bishr, it was the religious leader Mohammed Ibn Abdul Wahhab—"the Sheikh"—who had exercised ultimate authority, not Mohammed Ibn Saud, the secular ruler. "No camels were mounted and no opinions were voiced," wrote the historian of the 1750s and '60s, without the approval of the Sheikh. He meant Abdul Wahhab.

In 2001 the House of Saud no longer saw it that way.

"I was watching the meeting on television," recalls Prince Turki Al-Faisal, "and when I heard that remark I wanted to shout out at the screen, 'You are totally wrong! Will someone please stand up and tell him so!' "

No one spoke, so the prince sat down immediately to lay out his views in an article that was published a few days later.

"I wanted to explain," he says, "how, from the very first caliphs, the secular rulers have always been the executive rulers in Islamic history—the ultimate boss. It has been their job to exercise the power, while the job of the religious men—the sheikhs and the mufti—has been to give them advice. *Never* to govern. That is where Khomeini and the Iranian ayatollahs departed from true Islam. They put themselves in the position of supreme governmental authority, which is a totally new thing—completely un-Islamic and un-historical."

A few days later another article appeared delivering the same verdict. Prince Talal bin Abdul Aziz, the former Free Prince, had a maverick reputation, but he ranked high in the brotherly pecking order. Younger than Sultan, Talal was actually senior to Nayef and Salman. More important, he was close to Abdullah and was known to share the crown prince's view that too much undigested religion had led to takfeer, and to impressionable young Saudis committing mass murder in the name of Allah. The sheikhs and the ulema had very valuable advice to offer, wrote the prince, but it was no more than that—advice. They should *not* consider that they were among "those who govern." Dr. Turki's bid for a direct religious role in Saudi government was firmly slapped down, and the reverend doctor did not argue back.

So 9/11 finally settled who ruled whom in Saudi Arabia. After Juhayman, the 1980s had seen the clerics dictating the agenda in an almost

Iranian fashion, with the Al-Saud anxious to appease them—no prince would have dared stand up in those days to contradict the say-so of a religious figure. In the 1990s the Sahwah (Awakening) sheikhs had claimed the right to lecture the government and to demand changes in accord with their religious beliefs, though that had landed some of them in prison. Now the arguments were over—so far as Crown Prince Abdullah was concerned. September 11 had shown what happened when religion got out of hand. Rulers must rule, and the religious must go along with that. The days were gone when no camels could be mounted and no opinions voiced without the say-so of the Sheikh and his successors.

CHAPTER 25

Fire

On March 11, 2002, a fire broke out at a girls' school in Mecca, and as the flames spread, the girls and their teachers started running for the street. The girls were dressed in their school uniforms, but in their haste they did not have time to collect their abayas, their black outer gowns.

Guarding the entrance to the school were some bushy-bearded members of the religious police. When female education started in the early 1960s, King Faisal had surrendered girls' schools to the supervision of the religious scholars—it was part of the bargain he had struck to get the innovation accepted. So all Saudi girls' schools came under the Directorate of Girls' Education, staffed predominantly by religious men, and this Monday morning, the men were not prepared to let their charges out unless they were wearing their abayas and veils. The long, antique, Victorian-style skirts and long sleeves of the girls' school uniforms were modest by most people's standards, but that was not good enough for the male guardians of their morality. They kept the doors barred—it was standard directorate practice to keep their charges locked inside their buildings throughout school hours—and, according to eyewitnesses, three of the "holy ones" actually beat some of the girls who tried to force their way to safety.

As the panic-stricken pupils turned and headed back to their smoke-filled classrooms to retrieve their gowns, they jammed the route of the girls who were trying to escape. Confusion and terror reigned behind the blocked doors. To the disbelief of firefighters who arrived from Mecca's

Civil Defense Department, girls who escaped by one door were being bundled back inside by the mutawwa through another. They even prevented the firefighters from entering the building.

"We told them the situation was dangerous, and it was not the time to discuss religious issues," said one Civil Defense officer, "but they refused and started shouting at us. Instead of extending a helping hand for the rescue work, they were using their hands to beat us."

Desperate parents who tried to help were also turned away. Meanwhile, trapped inside the burning building, fifteen girls died and more than fifty others were injured.

• • •

The Saudi press has a long and dishonorable tradition of averting its gaze from unpalatable facts—and, to be fair, of having its gaze forcibly averted by the authorities. But the scandal of the Mecca fire was too much. *Al-Watan* ("The Nation") had set up an incident team to cover precisely such emergencies: five reporters zeroed in on the officials and their flustered stonewalling, while another five gathered stories from survivors and eyewitnesses.

"They really brought in the information," recalls Qenan Al-Ghamdi, *Al-Watan*'s founding editor. "Well before the end of the day it was clear that the death of those fifteen girls was the fault of no one but the Directorate of Girls' Education—so that is what we wrote."

Other newspapers and TV reported similarly, their spontaneous outrage spiced with resentment at decades of busybodying by the religious police. Here was the ultimate example of how distorted the priorities of the mutawwa could be.

"It was the chance to get revenge," recalls Dr. Saud Al-Surehi, an editor on *Okaz*.

For the crown prince it was a chance to institute change. His half brother, the governor of Mecca, Abdul Majeed bin Abdul Aziz, was one of the progressives in the family. He visited the burnt-out school, interviewed the firefighters himself, and confirmed the truth of the story. Within a week Abdullah had summarily removed all Saudi girls' schools from the care of the religious authorities. The Kingdom's schools for girls would henceforward be supervised like those for boys, by the Ministry of Education—and as this book went to press in the spring of 2009, Abdullah appointed a woman, Norah Al-Faiz, a long-serving teacher and educational administrator, as deputy minister in charge of girls' schooling. She is Saudi Arabia's first woman to hold ministerial rank.

• • •

With the tragedy of Mecca coming just six months after 9/11, Crown Prince Abdullah finally took full control of the Saudi government. Removing the girls' schools from the hands of the clerics was the blunt assertion of a new direction. His other brothers and rivals had never defied the sheikhs so directly. But Abdullah had a long-standing religious and tribe-friendly reputation. His conservative credentials were impeccable.

Another sign of his enhanced power was the appearance in the cabinet of Dr. Ghazi Algosaibi, the outspoken ambassador who had derided "Big George" and "Little George" the previous year. A poet and novelist whose books were regularly banned for their skeptical, "secular" attitudes, the jovially rotund Algosaibi was never afraid to take on the religious establishment. The clerics had been delighted when, after a short spell as minister of health, the liberal technocrat was dispatched by Fahd to foreign service, first to Bahrain and then to London, where he managed to ruffle Jewish sensibilities by publishing an ode of heartfelt mourning for a female Palestinian suicide bomber. In 2002 Algosaibi's return as head of the newly created Ministry of Water was greeted with a howl of outrage from the conservative websites.

It was a step too far for the ulema, and they mounted a counterattack. They had been complaining for some time about the minister of education, Mohammed Al-Rasheed, who had introduced technology into Saudi schools and had been giving more time in the curriculum to science and math, which had meant a cutdown in the number of religious lessons. Al-Rasheed had also stirred controversy in the past by proposing that girls' schools should have exercise facilities for sports and physical education. Girls were like boys, he suggested, in their need to develop "a healthy mind in a healthy body." This was taken as the ultimate proof of the minister's degeneracy, and a campaign developed to remove him from his job. How could such a dangerous "atheist" be entrusted with the upbringing of Saudi womanhood?

In vain did Al-Rasheed, who had started his education in a religious school in the pious Nejdi town of Majmaa, go on television to reassure people that Islamic traditions would not be changed. When it was discovered that he had traveled to a Beirut conference that was attended by female delegates from Saudi Arabia, lurid website stories depicted the minister as a lothario who had lured innocent Saudi women out of the Kingdom by plane—"May He Be Cursed by God!" ran one headline. Thousands of telegrams addressed to "Crown Prince Abdullah, the Royal Court, Riyadh," protested against the presidency of Girls' Education being surrendered to someone who had "no ethics."

The crown prince gave way.

"It's time for you to relax," he told Al-Rasheed at a gathering in which the royal family convened to show their sympathy and support for him—but also their helplessness in the face of the concerted efforts of the country's fundamentalists. Abdullah handed the education portfolio and its new responsibility for girls' education to Dr. Abdullah Al-Obaid, a former rector of the Islamic University of Medina.

Al-Obaid's track record was, in fact, little less "progressive" in Saudi terms than that of his predecessor. He had started his educational career in the 1960s opening up girls' schools for King Faisal with detachments of armed troops. He can recall supervising one school where there were only two pupils for an entire year—the little daughters of the headmaster and the school caretaker. "Then suddenly," he remembers, "*everyone* wanted to get their girls educated." He was also well qualified to supervise modern curriculum reform, having gained a Ph.D. in the subject from the University of Oklahoma.

Unlike his predecessor, however, Abdullah Al-Obaid sported a long beard and chose *not* to wear an agal, the double black rope ring of the camel herder, on top of his headdress. Going agal-less is one of the trademark signs of a Salafi, based on the belief that the Prophet never wore the camel-rope rings of the bedouin on his head. It is a generally recognized signal of piety and "Wahhabi-ness." So the religious community concluded that Dr. Al-Obaid was one of them, and that, for the moment, the education of Saudi womenfolk remained in safe hands. As minister of education for seven years Al-Obaid began a number of new teaching initiatives before being replaced in Abdullah's cabinet reshuffle of February 2009. His successor was Faisal bin Abdullah bin Mohammed, a sparky and original-minded prince who founded Al-Aghar ("The Forehead") think tank to investigate ways of making Saudi Arabia a knowledge-based society. The prince happened also to be Abdullah's direct nephew and son-in-law, the clearest possible sign of the importance the Saudi king placed on the formidable task of modernizing his country's educational system.

• • •

In the months after 9/11 Mansour Al-Nogaidan discovered what the religious establishment could do to someone who incurred their wrath. In his post-Salafi career as a journalist he had been attacking his former mentors with all the bile and bite that he had deployed when he was one of them—and now they bit back. A Salafi website published his mobile phone number, and he was inundated with insults and threats that ranged from beatings to murder. Day after day, by day and by night, the poisonous text messages came flashing up on his screen, till he cracked.

"It was a bad message on a bad day," he recalls. "I can't remember exactly what it said—'You enemy of God. You miserable gay. You homosexual.' It was something like that, and I'd had enough. 'Go to hell!' I thought. So I texted back, 'You whore.'"

Three days later Mansour found himself summoned to attend an immediate court hearing. Insulting someone is an offense under Islamic law, and his phone correspondent, a religious teacher whom he did not know, had filed a charge that enabled a local religious judge to give effect to all the angry website promises of punishment.

"You are anti-God," the qadi (judge) declared indignantly, gesturing at a thick file of Mansour's recent writings.

"I just received a bad text message," replied Mansour, "and I replied."

Saudi judges are trained essentially as religious scholars, and Mansour understood the capriciousness with which they feel free to interpret the religious law. The "insult" charge was clearly just a pretext for some angry clerics to get their hands on him. But he was not expecting what came next.

"Seventy-five lashes," said the judge.

Mansour left the courtroom not knowing whether to laugh or cry.

"I did you a favor," said the judge. "I usually give eighty."

In the weeks that followed Mansour wrote letters to the senior princes. One powerful brother was willing to have the sentence wiped, he was told, if Mansour was willing for his part to compose an *isterham,* a plea for mercy. But the condemned man did not feel inclined to beg. His religious enemies were clearly exploiting a technicality to get their revenge for his criticisms of them—and if they were exploiting their power, then he could exploit his. Hearing of his plight, the *New York Times* had offered Mansour the platform of the Opinion page, and late in November 2003 he wrote an article, in Arabic, which the paper translated and presented under the headline "Telling the Truth, Facing the Whip":

> A week ago yesterday I was supposed to appear at the Sahafa police station [in Riyadh] to receive 75 lashes on my back. . . . At the last minute, I decided not to go to the police station and undergo this most humiliating punishment. With the nation at a virtual standstill for the holiday Eid al-Fitr, the sentence remains pending. I will leave this matter to fate.

In the paragraphs that followed Mansour hit out at "our officials and pundits who continue to claim that Saudi society loves other nations and wishes them peace." How could this be true, he asked, "when state-sponsored preachers in some of our largest mosques continue to curse and call for the destruction of all non-Muslims?" The Kingdom must change course. "To avert disaster we will have to pay the expensive price of reforms."

For two days Mansour heard nothing, then he was contacted by an official. The wali al-amr, he was told, had a message for him. He had made a very grave mistake in going public, and in a foreign newspaper at that. This was not the Saudi way. Mansour had aggrandized himself, and had also harmed the reputation of the country.

"Well, I have a message for 'those who govern,'" shot back the fiery young reformer. "If they leave the mosques and the law courts of this country in the hands of those religious extremists, then both the country and its reputation will be harmed still more."

Mansour Al-Nogaidan never received his seventy-five lashes. After a succession of inconclusive meetings—in which one official angrily accused him of writing for "the newspaper of the enemy"—he was finally brought face-to-face with his accuser in the presence of witnesses.

"Do you accept the truth of religion?" he was asked.

"Yes," Mansour replied—and before the combative ex-jihadi could say another word that might complicate his statement, his case was declared closed. "Those who govern" were desperate that he should not be lashed. By the end of 2003 the main thrust of Mansour's argument, that "deep-rooted Islamic extremism" had made Saudi Arabia "a nation that spawns terrorists" had come tragically true. The proof was out there to be seen in the streets.

CHAPTER 26

Al-Qaeda in the Arabian Peninsula

May 12, 2003, was a hot night in Riyadh, and the capital's smokers were out puffing on their hubbly-bubbly pipes, lounging on the raised sofas of the open-air cafés near the camel markets. There seemed nothing unusual about the four vehicles—two cars, a pickup truck, and an SUV—that drove out of town through the warm darkness toward the residential area of Al-Hamra: their drivers were ordinary-looking, bearded young Saudis. But the young men were armed, and their vehicles were packed with weapons and explosives. Their targets were three of the many compounds in the city that housed Westerners—and Americans in particular.

Sometime before midnight one of the cars attempted to gain entry to the back gate area of the Jadawel compound. As the compound's security guards approached to inspect the vehicle, the terrorists suddenly opened fire, killing one policeman and an unarmed Saudi civilian. The attackers sprayed gunfire wildly as they assaulted the inner gate.

"You infidels!" they screamed. "We've come to kill you!"

As they were attempting to fight their way inside the compound, the attackers' massive explosive charge detonated, killing all of them.

A few miles away at the Oasis Village and the Vinnell Corporation compounds, the terrorist assault teams similarly shot down the security guards from outside the barriers, then opened the gates to admit a second group. As they fired wildly, the gunmen called out to God, then detonated both their bombs, bringing the death toll that night to twelve terrorists and twenty-seven foreigners—nine of them Americans. Later that year eighteen more would be killed when the bombers targeted a compound for expatriates who were largely from Arab countries. The following May terrorists in Yanbu murdered five petrochemical workers, tying their victims' bodies to the backs of their pickup trucks and dragging them triumphantly through the streets. Foreigners got in the habit of looking under their cars every morning for bombs and checking their license plates for chalk markings—signs that they had been identified and targeted.

. . .

The attacks were the work of Saudi jihadis who had been driven out of Afghanistan by the U.S.-UK invasion in the months following 9/11. The demolition of their Afghan training camps forced several hundred extremists back to the Kingdom, where they regrouped in safe houses as "Al-Qaeda in the Arabian Peninsula," taking orders via coded phone messages from their leaders, who had gone into hiding in the tribal territories along the Afghani border. Osama Bin Laden may have retreated, but he saw the enforced return home of his Saudi followers as a blessed opportunity. He ordered them to take the battle to the Al-Saud on their home territory, and the young zealots went out in the desert to continue their target practice. It was easy for them to find local weaponry, much of it from Yemen and some of it left over from the 1991 Gulf War. After Saddam's retreat from Kuwait, the local bedouin had wasted no time looting the Kalashnikovs from the corpses of the Iraqi dead and bumping them in for sale on the Riyadh black market. Thus equipped, a mini-army of young extremists had stormed the Oasis Compound in the Eastern Province, killing no less than twenty-two, mainly expatriate, workers.

In June 2004 the BBC's Arabic-speaking terrorism specialist, Frank Gardner, flew in to cover this dramatic escalation. Sitting on the plane beside his Irish cameraman, Simon Cumbers, Gardner leafed through his research notes on Abdul Aziz Al-Muqrin, the thirty-two-year-old leader of the Al-Qaeda campaign on the ground, who had left school at seventeen to fight in Afghanistan, Algeria, Bosnia, and Somalia. Captured and extradited to Riyadh, this hardened jihadi had been jailed for four years, but had taken advantage of the Saudi prison regulation that enables prisoners to halve their sentence by memorizing the Koran.

"Crikey," thought Gardner, reading of Al-Muqrin's bloodthirsty exploits as his plane came in to land, "I hope I don't come across *him!*"

A few days later Gardner was finishing a piece-to-camera at the edge of Al-Suwaydi, the fundamentalist Riyadh neighborhood where Mansour Al-Nogaidan had plotted firebomb attacks in his Salafi days. The journalist knew he was close to dangerous territory. As he strolled across a dusty piece of waste ground, he was pointing out the spot where police and militants had traded fire a few months earlier. His Saudi minders from the ministry had authorized the location and were supposed to be protecting him, but they vanished within seconds of what happened next. A car pulled up and a young Saudi got out.

"*Assalaamu alaykum* [Peace be upon you]," said the young man with a smile, then without warning and with no haste, he reached into the pocket of his white thobe and drew out a gun.

"No! Don't do this!" shouted Gardner in Arabic, as he turned and sprinted away down the street. He felt a shot sting his shoulder, but he kept on running, and was just thinking that he had outpaced his attacker when he heard a loud bang and fell down on the tarmac, felled by a bullet in his leg. His escape route had been blocked by a minivan whose side door slid open to reveal a group of mean-eyed, wispy-bearded gunmen, each with a pistol in his hand. The BBC's terrorism correspondent had come face-to-face with his subject—their thin, pale features consumed, he would never forget, "by pure hatred and fanaticism."

Frank Gardner and Simon Cumbers had had the misfortune to be spotted by Abdul Aziz Al-Muqrin himself as he was driving past in a convoy with half a dozen followers. Seeing the camera on its tripod, the Al-Qaeda leader had halted immediately and given orders for a two-winged attack. By the time Gardner was cornered, Cumbers, the cameraman, had already been shot dead.

Gardner pleaded for his life as his assailants in the van chattered briefly about what to do with him. Then they cut short his pleas with a fusillade of shots into his body.

"Bloody hell," thought Gardner as he lay on the ground, feeling the bullets thump into his abdomen, "I'm really being shot. I'm taking a lot of rounds here."

In fact, the Saudi shooting was so erratic that only six bullets actually lodged in him. But they smashed bones and cut nerves so severely that the BBC man was left with eleven major wounds that would paralyze his lower body for the rest of his life. It was a miracle—and something of a mystery—why Al-Muqrin's team did not kill Gardner outright. One more bullet to the head would have finished him. But as the journalist lay on the ground, he heard the firing stop and footsteps approaching. One of the terrorists had stepped down from the van to rummage in the back pockets of his trousers, discovering a radio microphone in one, and a miniature Koran in the other. Gardner had a stock of these small Korans, inscribed with intricate calligraphy, that he gave away as presents.

Did that little Koran save his life? In their last attack Al-Qaeda had hitched their victim's body to the back of their vehicle. A week later Al-Muqrin would personally behead Paul Johnson, an American helicopter technician, filming his execution and placing his head in the family freezer as a trophy. As it was, the helpless Gardner heard the attackers revving their engine and driving away.

Just over a year later, after months of agonizing and highly skilled surgical repair and reconstruction in Britain, Gardner was invited to New Scotland Yard to meet a group of senior Saudi Mabahith officers who had flown to London to present him with their evidence. They had one of the attackers in custody, they reported; he had been wounded in a recent gun battle, and they believed he was Simon Cumbers's assassin. As for the other five, they handed Gardner a set of gruesome, almost life-size prints of bloodstained faces, bruised and puffed-up, their eyes closed in death. DNA tests, said the detectives, had confirmed the identity of all the corpses, including that of Abdul Aziz Al-Muqrin, killed in a shootout just a week or so after he drove through Al-Suwaydi and happened on his two infidel victims in the street.

It was small consolation to Frank Gardner—and still less to Louise Cumbers, the widow of Simon—but the Saudis were very proud of their roundup rate. Early in the troubles, in December 2003, they had published the names of the twenty-six most-wanted terrorists, and within a year they had killed or captured twenty-three of them.

• • •

Intelligence later revealed that Abdul Aziz Al-Muqrin and the other leaders of Al-Qaeda in the Arabian Peninsula had not wanted to attack Riyadh in May 2003. Their local cells were not ready, they had argued in their intercepted phone calls back to headquarters: their men were not sufficiently trained, nor were they sufficiently numerous. But from his refuge in Waziristan, Osama had insisted.

It was a grievous mistake, for the attacks of May 2003 turned a complacent giant into an implacable enemy. Girding his loins for a modern Sibillah, Crown Prince Abdullah angrily swore that every single "monster" would be brought to justice. Any that resisted would be killed out of hand. Prince Nayef may have blamed 9/11 on the Zionists, but now his Ministry of the Interior went for the terrorists with ruthless efficiency. Following the inroads they had made in their most-wanted list, they rounded up another six hundred or so terrorist suspects, along with their bomb-making equipment, bomb belts, and thousands of weapons that had been stockpiled for a major campaign around the Kingdom.

The same went for the general population. Until May 2003, the bearded, short-thobed young men who turned up and prayed so zealously in the local mosque had been viewed with benevolence and even approval by their neighbors. Their jihad in Afghanistan was generally supported. But their bombings on home territory changed all that. May 2003 was the Kingdom's 9/11. Ordinary Saudis looked at their salaries, their housing, and their children at school, and had no difficulty deciding on which side their interests lay. Feelings intensified after the attacks of November 2003, in which many of the victims were Arabs. Images of Muslim blood soaking black abayas were the final nails in the coffin of Al-Qaeda's Arabian campaign.

"That was when the Saudis really 'got religion,'" says the U.S. diplomat David Rundell.

Until the attacks inside the Kingdom, the attitude of the general population toward Al-Qaeda had been that of the Americans who let the IRA raise funds in Boston—"It's not really our problem."

"They were not strongly in favor of what Al-Qaeda was doing in the wider world," says Rundell, "but if three young guys with long beards moved in down the street, coming and going at odd times, no one thought to tell the police. That changed overnight. You had fathers taking their sons in to see trusted princes if they thought that the boy was going off the rails. This was partly to help the boy and partly to protect the family's reputation. Family reputation counts for a lot here. Launching attacks inside the Kingdom—that was Bin Laden's 'own goal.'"

The attacks also emboldened the government's attitude toward the fundamentalists. So this was the worst they could do? There was a new toughness in official pronouncements. Appeasement was over—and that gave strength to those who would modernize. People were no longer so scared to be secular and started to hit back at those who had sought to bully them.

"Get lost, you terrorists!" indignant women were heard to shout at religious policemen who ventured to correct their style of dress.

• • •

Up in Buraydah, Mohammed Al-Harbi, the short-bearded chemistry teacher, felt encouraged to speak out again. When school convened on the Saturday following the first Al-Hamra bombing in Riyadh, he took the microphone at morning assembly to read out a government statement. Three of the bombers had already been identified, according to the Ministry of the Interior: they were connected to Osama Bin Laden, a force for evil whose followers were cancer cells in the body politic.

The next day another teacher, long-bearded and short-thobed, took the microphone to address the assembled students. They should not waste their time listening to the news these days, was his message—nor should they listen to those who might offer their opinions on the news. People who presumed to judge and brand others as "evil" should be considered evil themselves. There was a certain hypocrisy in this, coming from an adherent of the fierce takfeer (excommunication) school, but the other long-bearded teachers all nodded in sage approval.

In the days that followed, the Ministry of Education sent a circular to all schools. It was important to teach pupils about the dangers of extremism, it stated: pupils must understand the need for tolerance and the acceptance of others. So in the spirit of the circular, Mohammed posted an article on the school notice board—"The People of the Caves Are Going to Hell" by the liberal columnist Hamad Al-Salmi. By "People of the Caves" Al-Salmi meant the members of Al-Qaeda in Afghanistan who were now sending gullible young followers to their deaths inside the Kingdom.

But next day Mohammed found the article torn into pieces on the floor, and he was confronted aggressively by the teacher who had done it. The writer of the article, Al-Salmi, was a "secular," said the teacher—no one but God was entitled to sentence anyone to hell. When Mohammed's mobile started ringing day and night with threatening messages, he thought it was so much bluster—until he came into school one morning and found a neat bullet hole drilled through the window of his office.

This was the point at which the young teacher decided to go to his headmaster and ask permission to bring in the police. But he discovered that his conservative opponents had already acted: they had framed charges that accused him of "mocking religion," the first step toward an indictment for apostasy—for which the sentence was death.

There were more than a dozen accusations that had clearly been gathered by his enemies on the teaching staff. He was accused of consuming alcohol in his chemistry laboratory and also of taking drugs. He was said to have talked positively about infidels and disrespectfully about religion. He had closed the classroom windows during a prayer call; he had refused to allow his pupils to leave the class to perform their preprayer ablutions; he had told them to shave their beards.

"How could I do that?" Mohammed protested at his trial in the local shariah court. "I've got a beard myself."

"You call that a *beard*?" scoffed the hairy qadi, looking at the teacher's neatly clipped goatee with scorn.

Mohammed had not helped his cause by ridiculing the revered Abdul Aziz Bin Baz. "How does he know the earth's flat if he's blind and can't see anything?" he was accused of saying, and he did not deny that he had said it. Nor did he deny having praised the kindness of Shia folk after a Shia had stopped to help him fix a flat tire on his way to school. He managed to fight off the accusation that he had learned to be a magician—certainly a death sentence, since practicing magic is held to be incompatible with Islam. But in the end his sentence was severe enough for the crime of "mocking religion": forty months in prison and 750 public lashes in downtown Buraydah.

The liberal media came to the rescue. Riyadh newspapers ran mocking coverage of the prosecution and ridiculed the verdict. Within days Prince Nayef had instructed the local governor to shut the case down—to the fury of the judge.

"You were supposed to be killed," he protested as he reluctantly let Mohammed go.

. . .

As the bombs were going off in the Saudi capital, the columnist Hussein Al-Shobokshi wrote of his dream of a better place—of how, twenty years or so in the future, these dreadful shootings would be a distant memory. He imagined himself flying into Jeddah from Riyadh on Saudia Airlines (since this was a dream, the airline was privatized and the plane landed on time) to be met by his daughter, who would then be twenty-seven, qualified and working as a high-powered trial lawyer (female lawyers cannot at present appear, let alone speak, in the courts of Saudi Arabia).

"How was the trip, Daddy?" his daughter asked, as she drove her car smoothly through the Jeddah traffic.

"Great," replied Hussein. "I attended the World Conference of Human Rights in Riyadh, where the Kingdom received a special award for the fairness and efficiency of its judicial system."

It was at this point that Shobokshi's readers realized, if they had not before, that the dreamer had to be joking. Hussein Shobokshi is a larger-than-life character in his midforties, almost as broad as he is tall, his features adorned with black designer stubble. His father, Ali, was the enterprising journalist who rented his floodlights to assist the recapture of the Grand Mosque in 1979. In July 2003 Hussein was the host of his own popular cable TV show, with an equally popular newspaper column to match.

"I went to congratulate our neighbor Fouad Tarshlo on his marriage to the daughter of Sheikh Golehan Al-Otaybi," Hussein imagined himself saying from the passenger seat. "Then I flew up to Buraydah to meet the mayor, Reza Baqir."

The satire lay in the surnames. It was quite impossible to imagine a Hijazi (Tarshlo) being accepted into the family of a Nejdi Sheikh (Al-Otaybi); while a Shia (Reza Baqir) could not hope to get work in a Wahhabi stronghold like Buraydah as a street cleaner, let alone become mayor.

"I had dinner," wrote Shobokshi, "in a smart new restaurant in Al-Shumaysi." This was the puritannical Riyadh neighborhood next door to Mansour Al-Nogaidan's Al-Suwaydi, now notorious as the site of Frank Gardner's shooting.

"Hurry up," Hussein told his daughter. "I want to get home to watch the television. The minister of finance is on tonight, getting grilled by the Shura members on all the details of the budget."

Perhaps it was this final fantasy that went a step too far. When the Saudi budget is published every year, no less than 40 percent (166.9 billion riyals in the budget for 2008) is labeled "Other Sectors," which includes defense, national security, intelligence, direct investment outside the country, and, most interesting of all, how much of the national pie is paid into the coffers of the royal family.

Hussein Shobokshi himself reckons it was his religious imaginings that got him into real trouble. Toward the end of his "dream" he expressed his intention of going to the Grand Mosque in Mecca to listen to the teachings of a learned member of the supreme ulema, Sheikh Taha Al-Maliki. With a name like that, the sheikh could only be a Sufi.

The call came within hours—from Hussein's editor in chief.

"I've had ten calls already," he said, "from the Ministry of Information."

Shobokshi was banned from being published, with immediate effect, and when he got to the TV studio, he discovered a message canceling his talk show—plus an in-box jammed with angry e-mails.

"Know your limits or you will be punished by God and by his followers on earth," threatened one. Others called him a goat and a cow—and one wished him cancer. This was clearly not the moment to be jumping too heavily on the toes of the Kingdom's religious and social prejudices. Bombs were still going off in Saudi streets, and there was also a practical legacy of the many young terrorists who had been captured—a lost generation with which both America and the Kingdom had to deal.

CHAPTER 27

Prodigal Sons

By the autumn of 2003, Khaled Al-Hubayshi had been imprisoned for twenty months inside the wire cages of Guantánamo Bay, Cuba. As he had feared two years earlier, listening to the 9/11 attacks on his little Sony portable in Kabul, the Yanqees had hit back.

"The Afghans threw the foreign jihadis out of town almost at once," he remembers. "They could see what was coming—in fact, they saved our lives. We were across the river, watching the bombs fall on the town. The explosions were like fireworks, but incredibly loud. It was overwhelming. There were missiles coming in as well as bombs. The Americans knew exactly what they were aiming for. When we got up next morning and went into town, our guesthouse had simply vanished. All that was left was a crater. It makes you wonder why, if they knew things like that, they didn't send in special forces quietly to capture Bin Laden and take out the camps. As it was, they made their all-out attack and they missed him."

Al-Hubayshi joined the hundred or so Al-Qaeda loyalists who retreated to Tora Bora, Osama Bin Laden's fortified cave complex in the mountains southeast of Kabul. The general presumption was that the holy warriors would load up their guns, rally round their leader, and defend this last stronghold to the death. But on December 7, 2001, Osama announced that he was leaving.

"He deserted us," remembers Al-Hubayshi bitterly. "After five weeks his people came round telling us to make our way to Pakistan as best we could and surrender to our embassies there. We had been ready to lay down our lives for him, and he couldn't make the effort to speak to us personally. Today I think that I was made use of by Bin Laden—exploited, just like all the young kids who went to jihad. What did he care when he sent us over the horizon to die? He was as bad as the religious sheikhs back in Saudi who preached jihad in their sermons every Friday. How many of them ever sent their own sons to Afghanistan?"

For six days the young Saudi and some thirty companions—Saudis, Algerians, and Moroccans—wandered through the desolate mountains of the Hindu Kush, barely surviving on dates and melted snow.

"I had just three hunded dollars in cash left, and my Kalashnikov. Then I threw away my weapon. I knew that we had lost. The Americans had been dropping leaflets offering big money for captured Arabs, and that's what happened. Some Afghan villagers sold us to the Pakistanis, who passed us on to the Marines. They shackled us and put blindfolds round our eyes, then they kicked the shit out of us. They took us to Kandahar. And that was the end of Khaled James Bond."

Several weeks later and still shackled, Khaled looked around as his captors removed his blindfold at the end of a long plane journey through the night. It was January 16, 2002.

"The weather was humid and the sun was high in the sky," he remembers. "And we all asked the same question—'Where is this place?' Was it Turkey? Or Morocco? Were we somewhere in the Gulf? We knew that the plane had come down once to land in the course of the journey, and then had taken off again. The Marines were under orders. Straightaway they told us the line of the *qibla* [the direction of Mecca] so that we knew which way to pray—and we could work out north, south, east, and west from the sun. But they would not tell us where we were. So we searched for clues everywhere. We saw these strange white birds with webbed feet, and we noticed that the Hummers were painted the color of sand. We asked the Red Cross when they came after a month, but they said they were not allowed to give us information like that."

In the end a British MI6 interrogator let Khaled in on the secret.

"When I asked where we were he pointed to the front of his hat, and I saw that it had 'Cuba' written on it.

"'You could have gotten that anywhere,' I said.

"'As you like.' He shrugged.

"'Cuba?' I said. 'Fidel Castro? Bring me some cigars!'"

Khaled Al-Hubayshi was one of 137 Saudis detained at the Guantánamo Bay detention facility, starting in January 2002, and he needed all his breeziness to survive.*

"At first it was all confrontation," he remembers, "—sheer, 100 percent aggression all the time. They hit us round the head and shouted. We went on hunger strike and threw shit at them from our buckets. But after a month or so most of us quieted down. I tried to work out how long I would be in this place. I reckoned four to six years—fifty, sixty, seventy months. It was no good hoping for a short time.

"So then I had to decide. Was I going to fight battles every day? You don't have to love your jailer, but why not be human? Once we got to know them, quite a few of the Americans turned out to be very decent people. I still have their e-mail addresses. A lot of them told us they thought the war in Iraq was a dreadful mistake. And as for the Puerto Rican guards, they really *hated* the Americans. They saw themselves as Yanqee slaves. On the second anniversary of 9/11, they gave us the thumbs-up. At mealtimes they would get us special spicy food. 'You are soldiers,' they said. 'You fought for your cause like anyone else.' "

The U.S. guards were replaced by rotation every six months.

"For the first week or so the new arrivals were always uptight and strict. Basically, they were scared. Then everybody mellowed out. In the end I was almost grateful for my time in Guantánamo. I developed this motto: 'You will find rocks and stones across your path in life, and you can trip over them if you choose. Or you can use them to build yourself a wall of success.' "

Along with his homemade self-help slogan, Al-Hubayshi retains two enduring memories of Guantánamo.

"All day long we heard the braying and mooing from the crazies in Block D, the mental-health block. It was the only way they could survive, poor things, to pretend they were cows and donkeys or whatever. They went quiet every night at nine o'clock exactly. That was when the orderlies arrived with syringes. Then I remember the day that Donald Rumsfeld came to visit. He walked right by all of us in the cages, but he never turned

*American figures show that some 759 prisoners were detained in Guantánamo from January 2002 to May 2006. The seven largest groupings by country of origin were: Afghanistan 219; Saudi Arabia 139; Yemen 109; Pakistan 70; Algeria 25; China 22; Morocco 15.

his head toward us once. The man did not look us in the eye. I could see it so clearly. He was too embarrassed. I reckon America's war director was ashamed of what America was doing."

If the shock of the 9/11 attacks brutalized official U.S. attitudes toward human rights, it had the opposite effect on the Saudi government.

"I had heard horror stories about Al-Haier," says Khaled Al-Hubayshi, referring to the notorious Ministry of the Interior prison south of Riyadh. "But when I got there I was amazed. It was a five-star hotel compared with Guantánamo."

After three and a half years in Cuba, Al-Hubayshi was included in one of the earliest batches of Saudis to be flown back to Riyadh, arriving in July 2005. He was driven straight from the airport to a cell in Al-Haier.

"The Americans kept us shackled and blindfolded till the minute we walked down the aircraft steps, and we dreaded what was waiting. But the Saudis were sort of soft and gentle. They made us feel welcome. I remember my first meal in Al-Haier: whole chicken legs! In Guantánamo they never once gave us meat with bones. They were scared we might shape the bones into weapons.

"In Al-Haier they let us phone our families, and mine came to see me a few days later. There were such tears. I scarcely gave a thought to my family when I went off to Afghanistan. But who stands by you when you're in trouble? In the end you learn what really matters. The Interior Ministry brought me a new thobe to wear to meet my mother, and they paid for the family to stay in a hotel as long as they wished."

Khaled was an early beneficiary of what would develop into a sophisticated Saudi government redemption program.

"I had to stand trial," he remembers. "I was sentenced to fifteen months for having a false passport and leaving the country without permission. But when that was over, I was free. 'We are going to help you,' they said. A month later the government gave me a Toyota Camry and they got me my old job back as an electrical engineer. I was living in the world again."

The architect of this surprisingly liberal and progressive reform program is the interior minister's son, the earnest and bespectacled Prince Mohammed bin Nayef. Resembling a combination of math professor and English vicar, the forty-eight-year-old prince does not look like a security director, but he has become something of a pioneer in terrorist redemption techniques. Bearded Guantánamo graduates flock beaming to the prince's Sunday majlis in Riyadh, while human-rights delegations fly in from around the world to study the rehab program that now bears his name.

"Everyone has a good thing inside him," says the prince. "These young people have been sick. We view their problem as a virus in the brain."

The prince is no softy.

"Security is a red line," he says, "and no one should cross it. If you do, you must take your punishment. Every extremist in our program has been tried and convicted and has served his sentence. Among our detainees we have about 20 percent who refuse to change. They are the hard nuts who cannot be cracked. They have to stay behind bars until they can satisfy a court that they have corrected all their false beliefs. But we try to help those who are willing to be helped. We bring in psychiatrists. We bring in clerics to show them where they have misread the Koran. They have a lot of religion lessons. We bring in all the family—father, mother, wife, brothers, sisters. We try to transform each detainee from a young man who wants to die to a young man who wants to live."

Whenever a young Saudi is killed in a terrorist incident or blows himself up, the prince receives the grisly DNA evidence, then gets on the phone to the dead man's family before the names are published.

"I give them my condolences and those of the government. I try to explain to them that their son was a victim. He was taken advantage of by abnormal ideologists. We don't want him seen as a hero, or any sort of idealized example to his family or tribe. They have lost a family member—we have lost a citizen. Some of them hang up. Sometimes they call back. We take care of all those families. We show an interest because those mothers and fathers are victims—and we know that if we don't take care of them, there are others who will try to step in."

The families are the focus of Prince Mohammed's program.

"This is how our culture operates," says the prince. "In the West a young man is independent of his family when he is eighteen. Here a man of thirty will do what his father or mother says, especially when the whole family is agreed. Some people say that our rehab program is too soft—that we should build a sort of Saudi Guantánamo to punish them. But that is just what Al-Qaeda would like. When people say we are spoiling these young men, that is music to my ears. If we used the old, harsh ways, then they would draw sympathy and the extremists would take advantage of that to try to get more people involved in terrorism."

The prince says he was saddened but not disheartened by the news in February 2009 that two of the graduates of the Saudi rehab program left the country soon after their release and went to Yemen to join active cells of Al-Qaeda in the Arabian Peninsula. The Ministry of the Interior has published a "wanted" list of no less than eighty-five radical young Saudis who are thought to be outside the Kingdom.

"Having Al-Qaeda in Yemen is obviously very dangerous," says Prince Mohammed. "It is like having Afghanistan along our southern border. There are four hundred miles of mountains where terrorists can slip across and be in Jeddah or Riyadh or Abqaiq [Aramco's principal petroleum processing plant] in a matter of hours. It is a major security threat. But we are ready for them. That is our job. The reason why they have all gone abroad is because our security is so tight at home. Nowadays they know that it is us, not them, who can count on the support of the community—and that is the battle that really matters. We are building a national consensus that extremism is wrong. In the last few months we have had nine young men surrender themselves because their families brought them in. Whoever wins society will win this war."

In fighting its war, the Ministry of the Interior has resorted to a novel tactic—marriage. No Saudi official will admit on the record that the Kingdom's terrorist problem might boil down to sexual frustration, but if a social system bans hot-blooded young men from contact with the opposite sex in their most hot-blooded years, perhaps it is hardly surprising that some of them channel this frustration into violence. One cornerstone of the extremist rehab program is to get the "beneficiaries," as they are called, settled down with a wife as soon as possible. The Ministry of the Interior pays each unmarried beneficiary 60,000 riyals (some $18,000), the going rate for a dowry, or bride price. The family arranges a marriage, and whenever he can, Prince Mohammed turns up for the wedding.

When Khaled Al-Hubayshi was released from Al-Haier prison early in 2007, he wasted no time finding himself a bride at government expense.

"The government has been good to me," he says. "So why should I not be good to the government?"

Today Khaled lives in Jeddah in a well-appointed apartment filled with stylish furniture, a flat-screen television, and a coffee machine on which his wife brews him a brisk cappuccino every morning. Afghanistan and Guantánamo are distant memories. He then gets into his government-purchased Toyota Camry and drives off to the electrical company, the very model of a settled, hardworking Saudi citizen.

But not every young Saudi who went to Guantánamo ended up so happily.

. . .

Yasser Al-Zahrani grew up on a rambling farm on the Taif Plateau, overlooking Mecca. There were sheep and goats; he learned to ride horses, and he loved playing football on the faded green Astroturf pitch in front of the house. His name came from the Arabic word for "easy," as he was an easy delivery for his mother, the elder of his father Talal's two wives.

"He was a funny guy," remembers one of his cousins. "He had a lot of friends. Yasser could make a stone laugh."

The boy was a good student, so his father had not expected the phone call he received in 2001, a few weeks after September 11. Calling from Karachi, Yasser explained that he had broken off his computer and English studies in Dubai. He wanted to help the Muslims. Like many pious young Saudis, Yasser saw 9/11 as the start of a new jihad. He was already on his way to Afghanistan.

"I was surprised," remembers Talal, a black-bearded colonel in the Mabahith, "but I was accepting. Yasser told me it was his duty to God. He knew that he had to go."

Then a few months later the phone rang again. It was a Saudi official calling to tell Talal that his son was being sent to Guantánamo—one of several dozen young Saudis who had been handed to the U.S. authorities by troops of the Northern Alliance following the epic battle of Janji.

"'Get up, you shit!' 'Shut the fuck up!' We learned a lot of English swear words," remembers Abu Fawwaz, a friend who was captured alongside Yasser after Janji. "The Americans seemed to enjoy waking us up in the middle of the night, or interrupting our prayers. I suppose they needed revenge for 9/11. They made us stand in line for an hour—forbidden from going to the toilet. Men peed where they stood. They tried to frighten us with dogs. Before we flew to Guantánamo they shaved off our hair and beards. That was the signal that told us we were going to travel—when the soldiers came round with the electric clippers."

Yasser and Abu Fawwaz arrived in Cuba in the same early weeks as Khaled Al-Hubayshi. The U.S. government records of Yasser's interrogations reveal that he misled his captors—he failed to tell them it was the attacks of 9/11 that inspired him to go and fight jihad. He told them he arrived in Afghanistan before 9/11.

"In four years of questioning, Yasser never told the Americans anything," says his father admiringly. "That's what his friends told me. He refused to speak unless he could have a lawyer. Nor could the Americans place a single charge against him. He was a person who had a will. Perhaps that is what brought him to his end."

In May 2006 Talal read a report about trouble in Guantánamo. Guards and prisoners had been fighting, and three prisoners had been injured. Two weeks later he received a call from Riyadh to tell him that Yasser was one of three prisoners—two Saudis and a Yemeni—who had "committed suicide."

"I just didn't believe it. The coincidence between the three injuries and then the three 'suicides' was ridiculous. His friends have told me that Yasser was calm and optimistic. There was a program for the release of Saudi prisoners. Quite a lot had left already, and he was hoping to be in the next batch. Why would he not wait for that? I know my son's personality—he would *never* commit the sin of suicide. He told me in his letters he was learning his Koran. 'You know me,' he wrote. 'I have a lot of faith.'

"The Americans claimed that the three men hanged themselves in different parts of the camp at the same time—but how could that be, with surveillance cameras everywhere twenty-four seven? We know that the guards were patrolling the cages every three to five minutes."

Abu Fawwaz, one of the numerous Saudis released and sent back to Riyadh before Yasser's death, agrees.

"There was no rope in those cages: there was no way you could hang yourself. Besides, Yasser went to Afghanistan seeking heaven. Suicide is the entrance to hell. He knew that."

When Talal got to Riyadh to claim his son's body, he was met by three high-level officials of the Interior Ministry (in 2002 he had taken early retirement from the Mabahith to go into business).

"They told me the American story that it was suicide, and they seemed to be telling me that I should resign myself to that—they made it very clear that they did not want a row. The government was working its hardest, they told me, to get the remaining Saudi boys home without a lot of fuss. I didn't blame them, but I told them I did not have any comment. I needed to see my son's body."

Talal went into the mortuary to say good-bye to his dead son, and what he saw there made up his mind.

"I kissed the boy on the forehead. I had had my doubts before I saw the body, and now I was quite sure. I said, 'I don't accept any of this. I accuse the Americans.'"

Yasser's larynx had been removed.

"Forensic doctors will tell you—if you hang yourself, you don't break your larynx. The rope cuts into your throat higher up. But your larynx *can* get broken if somebody strangles you."

An autopsy by a panel of five Saudi doctors found marks on Yasser's body that could have been signs of torture, and a wound to the chest consistent with some sort of fight. There were marks on the right shoulder from injections made while the young man was alive, but it was no longer possible to determine what had been injected into the body.

"We know how the Americans provoked and insulted their Arab prisoners at Abu Ghraib. It was the same in Guantánamo. Yasser's friends told me that the guards would stamp on their Korans and tear the pages. No wonder the Muslims were enraged. America has become an oppressor to us. They are as brutal and dominating as the Soviets."

Yasser's beard had been torn out on the left side, as if in a struggle of some sort, and there were strange, dark red marks on his skin. The Saudi doctors requested the American authorities to send them the toxicity report that should have been made at the time of death: they wished to determine the amount of poison in the body, and they wanted the evidence from the surveillance cameras.

For Talal and his family, there was even more compelling evidence that Yasser had not died by the sinful method of suicide.

"When I saw his body in Riyadh," says Talal, "he had already been dead for fifteen days, but he seemed like he was sleeping. He smelt fragrant. Then, at his funeral a week later, all his friends and family who went to kiss him said the same. He was not changed. By then his body had been cooled and warmed for two autopsies. Normally a body that old would smell decayed. My son did not commit suicide. He was a martyr."

Talal angrily discounts the idea that the fragrance might be from embalming fluid—and he also rejects the report on Yasser's death by the Naval Criminal Investigative Service (NCIS) that was finally released in August 2008.

"The report had three thousand pages," he says, "and that was three thousand lies."

The NCIS investigators described finding similarly worded suicide notes in the pockets of Yasser and of the two other men who died, as well as in the pockets of a number of other prisoners who did not die—proof, in the American view, of "a coordinated suicide pact."

"They have refused to show us this note that they say they found on Yasser," says Talal. "Until I see my son's handwriting, I will never believe that he took his own life. My family knows that he died fighting—he was a martyr."

The photograph that Yasser's mother keeps on her mobile phone provides strange support for Talal's faith. Lying on his stretcher beside the Prophet's Mosque in Medina three weeks after his death and a journey from the other side of the world, Yasser Al-Zahrani does not look like a corpse. On the small screen he seems to be sleeping. Every so often his mother switches on the digital image and kisses it.

"We prayed over him," remembers his cousin Mohammed, "then we buried him in the famous cemetery beside the mosque, where many of the Companions of the Prophet are buried. All the Prophet's wives, except Khadija, are buried there, and all his daughters. It was a distinguished funeral, with many hundreds of mourners."

The men fall silent at the memory, sitting on the patterned armchairs and carpet of the family majlis, quietly passing around the letters that Yasser wrote from Guantánamo—sheets of lined paper sent home via the Red Cross in Geneva. CLEARED BY U.S. FORCES has been stamped across the back.

"I know I cannot bring him back," says Talal. "But it will be his memorial if we can see Guantánamo Camp shut down. If there is no illegality there, as the Americans say, why have they situated the place in a foreign country?"

Soon after Yasser went to Guantánamo, he sent his father a letter, to which Talal replied.

"I told him, 'My son, please be patient and wait. Try to help the investigators and the guards and everyone to come to know Allah.' His friends told me he was doing that to the end. He was the imam—the leader of the prayers in his group. Whatever the Americans said to him, and whatever they did to him, Yasser always had one answer: 'There is no God but God, and Mohammed is His messenger.' "

CHAPTER 28

King Abdullah

On August 1, 2005, after years of disability and several months in intensive care, King Fahd finally expired. The career that started with such promise as the bright young technocratic prince had ended with a sad decade of lingering decline—and stagnation for his country. The partnership of brothers that has run Saudi Arabia since 1953 has always functioned best when there has been a strong leader to push the consensus along.

"The Angel of Death was not kind to His Majesty," says one of his kitchen cabinet. "Nor to the rest of us. He should have come for the king ten years earlier."

Wrapped in a sheet, Fahd's body was borne on a stretcher to the public cemetery, and buried there, according to Wahhabi custom, in an unmarked grave. Abdullah bin Abdul Aziz was finally king, and people exulted in the change of style.

The royal court had witnessed an amusing pantomime that summer as the princes had been preparing for their holidays.

"We are leaving very soon," they would say, informing Abdullah of their destination, to which Abdullah would respond with a graceful nod and the wish that they might have an enjoyable time. He knew exactly what they wanted. It had been Fahd's habit to hand envelopes containing literally millions of dollars to relatives heading on vacation, and following the old king's death, one daring family member took it upon himself to remind the new king of that tradition.

Abdullah gave him a withering look and said nothing. But a few days later a message went out to the family announcing the end of holiday handouts and urging the virtues of living within one's means. The fleet of royal jets was cut from fourteen to five, and the provision of free ticket vouchers on the national airline was also curtailed. Invited to pick himself his own brand-new private jet, King Abdullah said he would continue using the one that had served him as crown prince.

Journalists who caught wind of these economies naturally approved, even if it was not the sort of story that could possibly be reported in the Saudi press. Then the travel arrangements for the new king's first state visits were made public. As in the past, announced the Ministry of Information, editors, reporters, and photographers would be very welcome to travel with the government party on the official royal planes, but these journeys would no longer be free. Editors would be guests of the king, but other media passengers would be required to pay the equivalent of the full first-class air fare—in advance.

THE IMAM AND THE DATE FARMER

There was once a farmer who inherited an ailing and broken-down grove of date palms and who toiled long and hard to restore the palms to shape. He cut back dead branches, enriched the soil with camel droppings, and diverted a watercourse—to produce, after a year, a bountiful crop of luscious dates.

"What a glorious harvest God has provided!" remarked the long-bearded imam at the village, nodding his head in pious pleasure as he passed by the grove one day. "*Al-hamdu lillah!* [Thanks be to God!]"

"Al-hamdu lillah, indeed," replied the farmer. "You should have seen the harvest when God was the only one doing the work!"

. . .

Unlike his predecessor, who could "vanish" on occasions for weeks at a time, Abdullah bin Abdul Aziz works hard, on a timetable that is predictable, but also eccentric.

"We're all on the same schedule," says one of his young advisers, ruefully shaking his head.

The new king sleeps twice every day, the first time between ten or so in the evening and one o'clock in the morning, when he rises for a spate of hard work through the small hours. Then, following the dawn prayer, he goes back to bed for a second rest from which he awakes around

9 A.M. In his younger years a certain amount of his morning work had been done in his swimming pool, where he would plough stolidly up and down, doing the lengths that his doctors prescribed for his health, while pausing to execute official business from time to time. Aides would bring papers for his attention, and the crown prince would come to the side of the pool to study them, dripping gently in a mist of chlorinated water vapor while he considered his decision. As his duties grew more onerous, the practice stopped. Abdullah has learned the importance of keeping business and relaxation separate. But the young prince's poolside ponderings betrayed his inherent impatience: No delays, thank you, let's get the job done.

Under the influence of "T-1," the historically-minded Abdul Aziz Al-Tuwayjri, Abdullah had long been concerned with building up Saudi national feeling. Quietly rebutting Wahhabi claims that they were the core of the Saudi polity, Abdullah and Al-Tuwayjri had helped develop a folklore festival in the 1970s and '80s around the annual camel race at Janadriyya, to the northeast of Riyadh. Abdullah had a farm near the track, and as owners and tribesmen gathered every February for the camel equivalent of the Kentucky Derby, the crown prince started inviting them to linger for displays of cooking and craftsmanship and traditional dancing. The gathering proved a hit. It was quite hard to find legitimate, public ways to enjoy oneself in post-Juhayman Saudi Arabia, and crowds came from the most obscure corners of the Kingdom. Janadriya grew rapidly, and when Al-Tuwayjri started inviting some of Islam's cutting-edge thinkers to present their views the festival became seriously intellectual.

From the Wahhabi point of view, it was seriously subversive. The Moroccan philosopher Mohammed Abid Al-Jabiri, whose work changed the thinking of Monsour Al-Nogaidan came to argue for an empowerment of reason if Arab culture was to survive in the modern world. The Algerian Mohammed Arkoun was invited to advance his advocacy of Islamic humanism—another philosopher playing with ideas that were anathema to the Wahhabi establishment. On the unlikely basis of a camel track, the once stuttering crown prince was starting to provide a secular counterweight to the crushing domination that religion had come to exercise over Saudi culture, and it was difficult for the clerics to argue with his patronage. The festival was the only place in the Kingdom where girls and boys danced together in public, but they wore national costume, and T-1 explained how the music and dancing were prized examples of ancient tribal tradition. The local arts and crafts of Qateef were displayed at Janadriya by folk who might well be Shia rafada (rejectionists). But that was irrelevant to the values of the festival, where diversity, including religious diversity, was welcomed inside the cadre of national sentiment. Who could possibly disagree with that?

The one area where the religious had been able to check Abdullah's promotion of secular loyalties had been in the celebration of Saudi National Day, September 23, the anniversary of Abdul Aziz's proclamation of the Saudi state in 1932. Only God could grant holidays to Muslims, in the opinion of the ulema. A well-known hadith described how Mohammed had reproved his followers when he arrived in Medina to find them celebrating two local, secular festivals left over from the "days of ignorance."

"Allah has substituted what is better for you," declared the Prophet. "The Eid Al-Adha [the day of sacrifice, marking the end of the pilgrimage] and the Eid Al-Fitr [the breaking of the fast at the end of Ramadan]."

So these two Eid celebrations, both religious, were the only officially sanctioned holidays in Saudi Arabia, and for decades the sheikhs successfully resisted attempts to add September 23 to the short list of official congés. But with the accession of Abdullah the battlefield changed. If the king wanted a holiday, the king could grant it, and whatever the clerics might mutter, the people approved. Since 2006 the night of September 23 has become an occasion for national mayhem in Saudi Arabia, the streets blocked with green-flag-waving cars, many of them sprayed with green foam for the night.

The people were Abdullah's trump card. He was already the first Saudi ruler to have presided over elections. Admittedly the voting, held in the spring of 2005, was only for local, virtually powerless municipal councils—and then for only half the seats on those; women were not allowed to stand for office or to vote. But the male electorate got the chance to eat large quantities of mutton for three weeks, since Saudi electioneering proved to revolve around lamb and tents. As polling day approached, vacant lots and building land were taken over by gaudy and beflagged encampments where the candidates held court, inviting voters inside and plying them with mountains of rice and whole roasted sheep.

"It was rather a wonderful time," remembers one defeated liberal candidate fondly. "For three weeks the newspapers carried more photos and stories about nonroyal Saudis—us the candidates—than they did of princes and ministers. I felt for a brief moment as if I actually owned my own country."

The results of the voting proved the truth of what Fahd once prophesied about elections—it was usually the religious who won.* Candidates with Western sympathies or any suspicion of secularism lost out heavily to hard-line conservatives who were endorsed by the local religious establishment. Imams and holy men made their opinions felt through "golden lists" of religiously approved candidates, sent out to voters on their cell phones—text messaging was clearly not bidah (unacceptable innovation) if it served God's cause. The vote also provided statistical backing for the analysis that informed observers had long maintained—that for all their faults, and quite contrary to their stereotypical reputation, the House of Saud provided a minority force pushing for Western, secular change in a Kingdom of largely retrograde caution.

"How old is democracy in your country?" Abdullah asked a French reporter who sounded skeptical about the short-lived Saudi voting craze. "And how long did it take to reach its present stage? We too will get there by the grace of God."

The voting process for which Abdullah had to fight hardest was inside his own family, where he sought to bring transparency to the way that Saudi kings and crown princes "rose" to the top. From earliest times, and as in other princely families around the Gulf, the Al-Saud chose their leaders in the bedouin fashion: a conclave of elders would decide who was most fit for the job. There was no automatic right of blood succession. This was similar to the succession of England's Anglo-Saxon kings, in which a family council would consider the pool of available aethelings—those whose blood and family connections made them "throneworthy"—and would then decide who was throne-worthiest of all. Thus Alfred the Great, who saved Wessex and England from the Vikings at the end of the ninth century, was chosen over the sons of his elder brother Ethelred, because he was judged to possess superior leadership qualities.

In the same fashion, the Al-Saud family councils had skipped over fallible candidates like Mohammed, Khaled's cantankerous elder brother, and had actually deposed the controversial Saud in 1964. The one fixed

*In Qateef the Shia won handsomely, thanks to a grassroots campaign organized by Jaffar Shayeb and the other veterans of exile with Sheikh Hassan Al-Saffar.

rule, enshrined in the Basic Law with which Fahd had established the Majlis Al-Shura in 1992, was that the succession had to pass through the line of Abdul Aziz's thirty-five sons, their precedence being decided by their age, while their competence was judged on undefined grounds by their peers. This was where the shenanigans began. With seven active and powerful voices, the Sudayri brothers exercised a disproportionate sway in the process, and the new king sought a voice for the rest of the family. He also wanted to ensure that decision making could never again be paralyzed as it had been in the years of Fahd's decline.

Abdullah had worked out the shape of a family electoral council to be known as the Bayaa, or "Allegiance Council," named after the *bayaa* (oath of allegiance) that princes and all Saudis swore to the king. Each son of Abdul Aziz would have one vote, to be exercised by the son himself during his lifetime, then by one of his sons or grandsons after his death or in the event of his becoming king or crown prince. This meant that the council would have thirty-five members at the time of its formation, but would go down to thirty-four after the death of Fawwaz bin Abdul Aziz, since Fawwaz had no sons. The council's function was to meet after the death of a king or a crown prince to decide the succession—and to adjudicate on cases of medical disability in office. If Abdullah predeceased Sultan, Sultan would become king and would summon the Allegiance Council to approve a crown prince. If Sultan predeceased Abdullah, then Abdullah would summon the council. In each case the king would submit his own nomination for crown prince, but the members of the council had the power to reject this choice and to come up with one of their own.

The cut-and-dried functions of the council made perfect sense to Abdullah. But for that very reason, a number of the more traditional princes were not happy—the idea that the family's innermost deliberations should be semiexposed to popular scrutiny was demeaning. The brothers gathered one night during Ramadan to discuss the project, and as the dawn prayer approached there seemed to be a deadlock; then Prince Nayef spoke up. Often thought of as a conservative, the minister of the interior was cast in the popular imagination as an opponent of Abdullah's—but not on this occasion.

"It makes sense to me," said Nayef, echoing the king and brushing aside the suggestion that the discussion be continued on another occasion. "We should do it now."

So as the prayer calls were starting, the royal staff passed the news of the council's creation to the official Saudi Press Agency, where it hit the wires around 4 A.M. Insomniac television viewers were treated to the council's voting processes being explained by a hastily briefed reporter with dawn rising behind him.

A year later, on December 9, 2007, the Allegiance Council met for its founding session in a swirl of incense and dark, gold-trimmed robes. There was much nose kissing and shoulder nuzzling—when they get together, the male members of the Al-Saud kiss and embrace to a remarkable degree. Eighteen surviving sons of Abdul Aziz's were represented,* and the gathering watched as the sons of their nineteen dead brothers came forward, group by group, to announce which of their number they had chosen to exercise their late father's vote. It was a moving occasion. The sons of Faisal had chosen Khaled, the outspoken, reforming governor of Mecca. The sons of Sultan had chosen Khaled, the hero of the Gulf War. Mohammed bin Fahd represented the sons of the late king. Here were future kings and crown princes as yet unchosen—the proof that the House of Saud, in its own terms at least, could hang together and go on doing its job.

• • •

The question was, could Saudi Arabia? The Kingdom had weathered the enforced austerity of the Fahd years, but the extremist attacks of 2003 indicated the fault lines—several hundred young men who expressed their

*The eighteen surviving sons of Abdul Aziz were headed by King Abdullah (b. 1923) and Crown Prince Sultan (b. 1924), who are not members of the Allegiance Council (but are represented by their sons—see below). The council chairman was Mishaal bin Abdul Aziz, with fifteen council-member sons, in order of birth: Abdul Rahman, Miteb, Talal, Badr, Turki (living in Egypt), Nayef, Fawwaz, Salman, Mamduh, Abdul Elah, Sattam, Ahmad, Mashhur, Hadhlul, and Migren bin Abdul Aziz. Not present were three ailing brothers—Bandar, Musaed, and Nawwaf bin Abdul Aziz—who have delegated their council places and votes to their sons. Fawwaz died in 2008 without any sons, bringing the number of council members down to thirty-four. The nineteen grandson members of the council were: Mohammed bin Saud, Khaled bin Faisal, Mohammed bin Saad, Turki bin Faisal bin Turki the first (Abdul Aziz had two sons named Turki, the elder of whom died in 1919), Mohammed bin Nasser, Faisal bin Bandar, Saud bin Abdul Muhsin, Mohammed bin Fahd, Khaled bin Sultan, Talal bin Mansour, Khaled bin Abdullah, Mohammed bin Mishari, Faisal bin Khaled, Badr bin Mohammed, Faisal bin Thamer, Mishaal bin Majed, Abdullah bin Musaed, Faisal bin Abdul Majeed, and Abdul Aziz bin Nawwaf. In February 2009 the death was announced of Prince Turki bin Faisal bin Turki the first. As this book went to press, in May 2009, his replacement was still to be selected.

disagreement with other people by bombing them, backed up by a significant number of their elders who claimed to speak for God while issuing death threats and fatwas. Religion had caused misery. As King Abdullah later remarked, "Terrorism and criminality would not have appeared . . . except for the absence of the principle of tolerance." Saudi Arabia had handicapped itself grievously with its culture of accusation.

To try to change this culture Abdullah had convened in June 2003 the first National Meeting for Intellectual Dialogue. The Dialogue, which was endowed with a secretariat and a full constitution, was one of the fruits of 9/11 and held its first meeting, appropriately, a few weeks after the start of the Al-Qaeda attacks in Riyadh. Abdullah addressed the opening session, sternly admonishing the participants to speak courteously to one another, and to "respect the opinions of others." To pacify the ulema, always wary of any rival forum, this initial gathering consisted entirely of men who were clerics. But they were not all Wahhabis. Also invited were religious leaders of the Kingdom's Shia, Sufi, Ismaili, and Maliki Muslim communities*—which prompted Safar Al-Hawali, one of the Awakening sheikhs, to decline his invitation. He denounced the inclusion of these "deviants," to the fervent approval of the conservative websites. Yet his well known Awakening counterpart Salman Al-Awdah not only attended the Dialogue and listened respectfully to the other delegates—he offered Sheikh Hassan Al-Saffar, the Shia leader, a lift afterward in his car. The image of the two bearded clerics talking together, one in his agal-less headdress, the other in his turban, conveyed Abdullah's message precisely.

The king's aides spoke of their boss seeking to build up "the institutions of civil society." Democracy could not be conjured out of the air. Twenty years was the time frame Abdullah set for achieving a full adult, male and female franchise in the Kingdom, in the course of which period he hoped that people would gradually learn how to exercise their democratic rights with respect. Cynics responded that twenty years might as well be two hundred—they would believe the unlikely sight of the Al-Saud actually surrendering their power and profit when they saw it with their own eyes. But Abdullah persevered. In 2005 he set up not one, but two domestic

*To oversimplify greatly, Sufi Muslims are mystics, Ismailis revere the Aga Khan, and Malikis are one of the four schools of Islamic thought; they have their own style of prayer, looking straight ahead at certain moments, for example, when other Muslims lower their eyes.

human rights commissions, one an official government body, the other an "independent" NGO—its independence being compromised by the fact that its funding also came from the government—and invited both Amnesty International and Human Rights Watch to send their inspectors to Riyadh.

The king's most wide-reaching reform to date has been to complete the process started by Fahd before his stroke, the accession of the Kingdom to the World Trade Organization. In a trade context this has involved the removal of various preferential tariffs, notably the discounts to the U.S. oil majors who founded Aramco. More profoundly, it required the passing—and enforcement—of forty-two new laws to impose international standards of arbitration, fiscal transparency, legal process, and the protection of intellectual property on the previous jungle of Saudi business practice. As a result of these reforms, Saudi business efficiency as measured by the International Finance Corporation, a division of the World Bank, rocketed in three years from thirty-fifth in the world to sixteenth, the highest ranking in the Middle East. Foreign businessmen on the ground struggling with delays and bureaucracy wondered what criteria could possibly have placed Saudi Arabia above Germany (twenty-fifth) and France (thirty-first) as places to do business, but in Saudi terms the improvement was tangible.

The other consequence of joining the WTO (ahead of Russia or Iran, but behind all the other Gulf states) was the opening of Saudi Arabia to foreign investment. This has inspired a space-age plan to build six "economic cities" around the Kingdom, towering multibillion-dollar megalopolises of glass and steel that look for all the world like Dubai or Abu Dhabi. Many Saudis are uneasy that such gaudy, non-Saudi, and imitative projects should be made the focus of national progress. While the high-borrowing, high-spending "Dubai" model has been discredited by the economic problems of 2008–9, Saudi Arabia's conservative fiscal policies have been vindicated by the crash. Domestic public debt (there is no foreign debt) is a mere 13 percent of GDP, with $513 billion in managed foreign assets, placing Saudi Arabia third in the world rankings to China and Japan.

Still, the futuristic cities, if they are ever built, promise to be traditional in one sense at least—the land for the first one, King Abdullah Economic

City, on the Red Sea coast two hours north of Jeddah, was provided by members of the royal family, Azouzi and Prince Bandar among them, who all became partners in the project.

• • •

There is only so much that one reforming monarch can accomplish in a country of entrenched habits with eighteen million natives and ten million foreigners (five or six million authorized, the remainder illegal), but King Abdullah keeps on trying. One outspoken writer and thinker—a member of the Shura Council—was worried to be summoned to the royal presence after he wrote an article that criticized the slow pace of reform. There were too many obstacles to modernization, he complained—lazy bureaucrats, wasta (elite influence, meaning royal and business corruption), and also the religious establishment: the sheikhs were getting in the way.

"A good article," Abdullah informed him approvingly. "You should write more like that."

"Thank you, tal omrak (may your life be long)," replied the writer, relieved not to be bawled out. "But I have to tell you that I am getting very seriously threatened for what I have said."

Like Mansour Al-Nogaidan and anyone else who was perceived to be undermining religious orthodoxy, the columnist had received dozens of hostile and even murderous text messages on his mobile phone in the forty-eight hours since his article had appeared.

"I am happy to write more articles like that," he said hesitantly. "But if I write them, who will give me protection?"

There was a moment's silence, then Abdullah looked him full in the face, his black beard jutting fiercely forward.

"*Ana* (I)," he said deliberately, striking his right hand loudly against his barrel chest so that it echoed. "I—Abdullah bin Abdul Aziz."

Then Abdullah called for one of his private secretaries to hand over his name and an all-hours royal-switchboard telephone number.

CHAPTER 29

Girls of Saudi

Suzanne Al-Mashhadi works in one of Jeddah's well-appointed drug and alcohol rehab units. While Saudi law fiercely prohibits drugs and alcohol—drug dealers are routinely executed—the Saudi government today adopts a supportive attitude toward addicts who seek to break the cycle of their dependence. Suzanne Al-Mashhadi is one of a team of social workers who liaise with the female relatives of male patients.

"They would never dream of talking about their problems with a man," she says, "and it helps that I sound like an Egyptian."

The daughter of a Saudi father, Suzanne picked up her idioms from her Egyptian mother. Where, for example, a Saudi would say *"Ma arif"* ("I don't know"), an Egyptian says *"Ma rafsh."*

"When they hear me talk like a foreigner, the families relax. They open up. They tell me the secrets that they would never dare tell a fellow Saudi. The shame falls away, and sometimes we actually get to hear the truth about a situation."

Dealing with shame and hypocrisy in her professional life has fine-tuned Suzanne Al-Mashhadi's sense of the principal Saudi battlefield—the battle of the sexes. At the beginning of 2007 she published a column in the Riyadh newspaper *Al-Hayat,** "I Am Black and You Are White." Her title derived from the elegant white clothing that helps Saudi men stay relatively cool and composed in the local heat, while Saudi women are condemned to get hot and flustered in the frumpy black mourning gar-

**Al-Hayat* means "life." Since 1990 the newspaper has been owned by Prince Khaled bin Sultan.

ments that they wear—almost as if grieving the loss of their independence and identity.

"You are the first dream for every father, who wants a son to boast about," she wrote, addressing an imaginary male listener, "and the first love for every mother, who knows it is now less likely that her husband will look for another woman to produce the son he desires. They take your name for themselves and proclaim it in a proud tone—Umm-Mohammed or Abu-Mohammed [Mother or Father of Mohammed]. That is a pleasure which I can never deliver to my parents. Compared to you, I simply do not exist."

The black-white discrimination, wrote Suzanne, goes on from birth, through pro-male divorce rights and control of the children, until death itself.

"When I die, your friends will wish 'May God renew your bed.' But should *you* die first, no one would ever say that to *me.* I will be considered immoral if I should think to embrace another man—with my own children standing in the front line of those who would condemn me and give me grief."

Suzanne was expecting some criticism of what she wrote, but she was astonished at the source of it.

"Almost all the nasty e-mails, and certainly the really bitter ones, came from *women*—from other women who cursed me to hell: 'You are a liberal,' 'You are a secular,' 'You do not represent us.' I wondered if some of the notes had been sent by men pretending to be women. But the encouraging e-mails all seemed to come from men. When did Saudi men get so liberal, I wondered? I never noticed the change. This is the big problem, I've decided, in Saudi society. It's the only problem—men and women."

. . .

Khaled Bahaziq, the vacationing jihadi, had come to the same conclusion. As extremism gathered steam in the years after the Gulf War, the warrior who went to Afghanistan ten times had started to sense the limitations of jihad.

"Muslims are very good at being ready to die," he remarks. "They are not so good at being ready to live together in peace—at learning to accept and tolerate their differences."

Continuing to interest himself in Islam's oppressed, Khaled had traveled to Bosnia in the early 1990s. But he did not join in the fighting.

"There were other people trained and ready for that. By then I was starting to think about how people could learn to live together in harmony—and man-woman relations are the basis of that."

Back in Jeddah, Khaled started to volunteer in his spare time for an Islamic charity, Maktab Al-Dawah, the Cooperative Guidance Center, attending the domestic law courts to offer support to the victims of divorce and custody cases—who were invariably women.

"I used to cry as I watched some of those cases. Many women had asked their husbands for their rights, and had been given a violent answer. They had been battered. One woman had lost her sight in one eye. But the courts gave no redress. So far as I could see, everything in the legal process, and especially the prejudice of the male judges, favored the man."

Looking in Islam, Khaled could find no justification for this.

"Nowhere in the Koran does it say that the woman must serve the man. If anything, it is the other way around. That is how the Prophet acted. It is famous that he did all the work for his wives."

Feeling certain that he was dealing with a social, not a religious problem, Khaled started taking courses in counseling.

"I wanted to stop the cultural mistreatment of our women. Saudi men only talk sweetly to their wives when they want sex. So many of our problems come from the possessive, controlling attitude of Saudi men toward their women. And, of course, you cannot control another person—not in their hearts—except by love. Unconditional love."

As his reputation as a counselor grew, more and more patients came to him—almost all of them women.

"I never tell people what they 'should' do. I don't offer a magic solution. I just try to help them open their eyes. I ask them, for example, what advice they would like to give to themselves. I *always* ask to see the husband, but he hardly ever comes—I don't get the chance to talk to many men."

The counselor got the chance to change that to some degree when he was offered his own weekly TV show on a cable channel—*Go for Happiness.* His earnest advice turned out to be a hit, with extra programs screened during Ramadan. The Afghan jihadi had become marriage counselor to the Kingdom.

"On television," he explains, "my main emphasis is on teaching manners—to the men. The women don't need it. They have the manners already. It's the Saudi men who have to learn how to treat their womenfolk properly, and I tell them that if they manage to do that they will find themselves rewarded a thousandfold. When we become generous to our women, they become generous to us in return. If a man is good and kind to a woman, she will give him her life. If he does not, he will never taste her life properly—nor his own soul either."

. . .

Mashael (not her real name) got married when she was eighteen.

"I'd been seeing my husband secretly for about a year and a half," she remembers. "His sister was a good friend of mine, and she helped us get together away from the world. We spent hours on the phone. I was crazy about him. I forced my family to agree. It was so romantic."

But the romance melted within months of the couple getting married.

"I could not believe how quickly it happened. After the second day I thought, 'This man is weird.' He was so incredibly possessive. I was no longer my own person. He expected me to build every detail of my life around him, while he kept the right to do whatever he liked. He told me what to wear, how he wanted me to cut my hair—even what I should think and feel. That was his right. I was his new piece of property."

The world is full of possessive and domineering husbands, but in Saudi Arabia the law actually enshrines the principle that the male knows better than the female. A woman may not enroll in university, open a bank account, get a job, or travel outside the country without the written permission of a *mahram* (guardian) who must be a male blood relative—her father, grandfather, brother, husband, or, in the case of a widow or separated woman, her adult son.

"I had to agree completely with his opinions, what he felt about our family and friends. If I disagreed he'd fly into a temper, use ugly words, and threaten me. I knew that I had made a terrible mistake. I wanted to go back to my family, but my pride would not let me. I knew that they would blame me."

Mashael had been unwilling to accept the ancient tradition of family-arranged marriage, with its modest, not to say pessimistic expectations of personal happiness. Like a growing number of young Saudis, she had been tempted by the Western fantasy of fulfillment through "love," which Saudi TV and popular culture promote today as enthusiastically as any Hollywood movie. But Saudi taboos rule out the rituals of courtship and sexual experimentation by which young Westerners have the chance to make their mistakes and move on. Open dating, let alone living together, is unthinkable in a society ruled by traditions that judge families by their ability to keep their daughters virginal.

"My husband and I simply did not know each other," says Mashael, today an articulate and stylish woman in her late thirties, whose long black hair tumbles over the black silk of her abaya. "I'm not blaming anyone but myself. We married too young."

Having fallen victim to a common Saudi problem, she adopted what turns out to be a common Saudi solution.

"I found love with a woman. Before I was married, I never knew that a relationship between woman and woman could happen. I did not dream it was possible. Then I went to university, and I had my first love affair with a woman. It was soft. It was warm. It was like a painkiller."

Lesbianism is not hard to find on Saudi female campuses, according to numerous Saudi and Western women, with crushes and cliques and super-close friendships. These relationships may not always be sexual, but they are marked by the heightened emotions described by Jane Austen and other chroniclers of early-nineteenth-century England, where the Industrial Revolution was creating the world's first "modern" society, bringing new concepts of "romance" and individual choice into conflict with traditional family rules and rigidities.

"I was looking for consolation," says Mashael, "and I found it. I entered those groups. To start with you are curious, then you go with the flow. It is around you everywhere. A girl strokes your hand and you know she's trying to seduce you, but, in a way, you want to be seduced. You think, 'Why not?' Sex life is a disaster between Saudi men and women, and everyone knows that the men play around. The level of betrayal is extraordinarily high. So after a time you think, 'Why not with another woman?' It is a great way to have revenge."

And also a safe way.

"In this society you are mad if you have an affair with a man. With a woman it is safe. No one can question why you spend an evening at home together. You can go shopping or go out to eat with a woman. You can have a conversation. You can have friendship. You are two individuals with your own rights and personalities. You are not an object, the mere possession of someone else. There does not have to be sex every time. You can just hug each other or touch. And when there is sex, it is more romantic and slow. Even the kiss is different between woman and woman. It is more gentle. You are trying to give each other pleasure, not just take it, and you are sharing your feelings. You can be open together about your troubles and your problems. The love is generous. You can give each other quality time—because in Saudi Arabia a man spends very little time with his wife. It is in that separation that lies the pain."

Lesbian or not, many Saudi women spend immeasurably more time with other women—and their children—than they do with their husbands. Men routinely head out in the evening to dine, drink coffee, gossip, talk politics, and generally while away the time in masculine pastimes, much as Edwardian gentlemen did in their clubs. Even if he does not have much more than TV-watching on the agenda, the husband will go out to view, and usually eat, in the male section of a buddy's house, while the womenfolk gather in their own quarters—both sexes being catered for, even in quite lowly homes, by the ubiquitous Asian menservants, cooks, and maids.

"At the end of the evening," says one Saudi woman, "the husband will come home with one expectation. He's been chatting all night. It's not more conversation that he wants."

This segregated lifestyle is the rule in the royal family, so there is lesbianism inside the palaces as everywhere else.

"I'd hate to be a princess," says a woman who has royal friends, "because it is not easy for them to marry outside the family. Nowadays many of them are well educated, and they do not want to marry any self-indulgent idiot prince. Some were previously married briefly. So behind those walls there are a lot of clever, pretty women in their thirties who are single with no prospect of a man."

Tribes control their identity by controlling their womenfolk, and that is certainly the case with the Kingdom's top tribe of all. Rare is the princess who is able to marry a Saudi nonroyal, and should she wish to marry a foreigner, according to a Riyadh joke, she must be over forty, physically disabled, or the holder of a Ph.D.—preferably all three at once. Maybe it is not a joke, for there are an increasing number of royal women taking further education, and who like to be addressed as "Princess Doctor."

"The elite wear masks in this country," says Mashael. "They pretend they don't feel the pain, that empty-inside feeling of dissatisfaction with their life. Men and women are conditioned in this society to live separate lives, so they go on living separately. It's not questioned. If you're a woman and you want the happiness that goes with being part of a couple, you have to get that, in my experience, from another woman. And because you both want each other to be happy, that can help with your marriage. Often my girlfriend would give me advice to help me make things better with my husband. When things were difficult at home, I would give her a phone call just for two or three minutes and I would feel recharged."

Still married to the same husband, with several children and another child on the way, Mashael, like a growing number of middle-class Saudi women, now runs a successful small business. She does not consider herself a lesbian.

"In another society, I would never have gone with a woman. I would never have thought of it, or been offered it. And I would certainly never want to live with a woman. I know that is not the solution. I have a sixty percent good marriage. Today I get my strength from my work, my kids, and, above all, from myself—not from the necessity of having another woman. At the end of the day, there's the same pain."

She lists the qualities she has derived from her intimate friendships with women: "Tenderness. Sharing. Trust. Honesty. Support. Strong and clean emotions. Respect—above all respect. If you want those good things in your life in Saudi Arabia, you can only get them from a woman. You will seldom get them from a Saudi man, at least not from any Saudi man that I have met—especially not respect. There are very few Saudi men who treat their women as truly equal partners in life—not in their hearts."

Mashael believes that the problem lies in the overwrought, convention-obsessed atmosphere of the Kingdom itself, with its emphasis on appearances and "face."

"It's amazing," she says, "how my husband becomes a different man when we go on holiday and can escape from this country—even to Bahrain. We start to do things as a couple. We go shopping together. We play together in the swimming pool. The children become closer to us. The whole family benefits. I'm without my black [clothes], he's without his headdress. It's as if, by taking off our Saudi costumes, we've become ordinary human beings, not putting on an act, just natural and warm. He says he can feel my warmth.

"Then we bump into some friends from home, and he freezes. Once we were walking together in the street somewhere abroad, and we saw some Saudis coming from the other way. He just walked off in another direction, as if he was nothing to do with me."

The notion of "face" still holds the Saudi mentality in a rigid grip. "Is She a Disgrace?" asked Yasser Harib in a column of that title in *Al-Watan* in October 2008, pondering the common sight of a Saudi husband striding out alone in a shopping mall with his wife trailing yards behind with the children. "You might assume that these people have no connection with each other until they exit the mart and approach their car."

Harib noted how "the man will usually walk quickly when he sees a group of men sitting at a café in order not to tie him[self] to the woman walking behind him at a distance"—and how this shame extends into the language. A traditional Saudi husband will use "such euphemisms as 'my people' or 'my home' when talking about his wife, as if she were something obscure or disgraceful that he does not want other people to know about."

In 2008, it has to be said, it is possible to see young Saudi couples, presumably married, walking hand in hand in shopping malls—with the woman, usually, covered totally by a veil. But such public expressions of affection remain the exception, and traditionalists see nothing wrong with that. Social conservatism is the glue that is holding the Kingdom together, in their view, while more laid-back Arab societies have fallen apart.

"Look at our neighbors in the Middle East," says one traditional Saudi. "Look at the Lebanese. They are considered to be the sophisticates, the 'Europeans' of the area, so clever and free and easy, compared with us, the old-fashioned, conventional tribal stick-in-the-muds. They drink wine and hold hands. But look at the mess that the Lebanese have made of their government. They have great cooking and lousy politics—with militia carrying weapons in the streets. What's wrong with a bit of old-fashioned tribal toughness and deference to those in authority, saying your prayers and sticking to the rules?"

So is the convention-bound Saudi male destined never to become a normal member of the human race?

"I certainly do not blame Islam," says Mashael. "I wish that our Saudi men would study the life of the Prophet more closely—it's another example of how the religion of this country has been twisted by its tribal prejudices. We know that the Prophet was gentle with his women. He cherished his wives. He treated them with softness and respect. There is a hadith in which he tells men to take care of their women as if they were 'precious glass.' "

In the summer of 2008 the hottest show on Saudi television was a Turkish soap opera in which a husband took care of his wife in precisely that way. It cleared the normally crowded streets every evening. According to MBC, the Saudi-owned satellite channel, between three and four million viewers tuned in nightly to watch *Noor,* a 141-part series whose romantic and supportive hero, Muhannad, treated his wife Noor, a fashion designer and the title character, with respectful tenderness—as both a love object and an equal. The show became the rage of the season, with newspapers reporting divorces after men found pictures of Muhannad on their wives' cell phones. Several cartoonists slyly depicted husbands who missed the point by getting plastic surgery to try to *look* like the twenty-four-year-old Turk. Saudi women swooned over the blond and blue-eyed hero who was not afraid to show his soft side. Saudi men dismissed him as "gay."

Abdul Aziz Al-Asheikh, Bin Baz's successor as the Kingdom's grand mufti (and blind, like Bin Baz), was concerned with episodes in *Noor* that depicted dating and pregnancy outside marriage. He issued a fatwa condemning the show as "a declaration of war against Allah and his Messengers"—while the chairman of the Supreme Judiciary Council, Saleh Al-Laheedan, went further, denouncing the owners of Westernizing TV channels as being "as guilty as those who watch them. . . . It is legitimate," he said, "to kill those who call for corruption if their evil cannot be stopped by other penalties."

The chief justice was well aware that the principal owners of MBC were the Al-Ibrahim family, brothers-in-law to the late King Fahd, and he would only issue a halfhearted apology, pointing out defiantly that he had forty years' experience of shariah law, and was the oldest Islamic scholar in the country. The religious establishment was finally hitting back at the Al-Saud for its trickery over the introduction of the TV satellite dishes.

Meanwhile, the Turkish embassy announced that the number of Saudi travelers to Turkey that summer had increased to over one hundred thousand—from about forty thousand the year before.

"Basically," says Mashael, "Saudi men behave the way they do because their mothers indulged them as kids. We all know that Arab women put the man-child on a pedestal, which swells his head and encourages him to lord it over his sisters and other women. So if wives want husbands to change one day, the answer is quite simple—the solution lies in our own hands. The mothers of Arabia have got to stop spoiling their sons. They must treat them as true equals with their daughters."

CHAPTER 30

Illegitimate Occupation

The first time that George W., son of Bush, met face-to-face with Abdullah, son of Saud, they got on better than either of them had expected. It was April 2002, and few Americans could imagine why their president should extend any welcome to the leader of the country that had just given them 9/11, let alone greet him respectfully in a suit and tie—the first and only time Bush cleaned up so formally at his ranch in Crawford, Texas. The tie had been his mother's idea.

"This is royalty, George," said Barbara Bush. "You've got to dress properly."

After a communal lunch that lasted an hour, the two men retired to talk alone, with just their translators. It was four hours before they emerged. Abdullah had insisted that the president look at a ten-minute videotape he had brought along showing extracts of Arab news reports from Palestine. This is what his people saw every night on TV, he explained—these images were coming right into their homes. Tears came to his eyes as he appealed to Bush: "You've got to fix this."

Bush came out of the meeting slightly shocked, but also impressed by Abdullah's candor.

"This is a man I can trust," he said to his aides. "He's telling it to me like it is. All the others say one thing to me when they come over here, then go home and say something else when they get back to their country."

They went on a drive around the ranch together—the two leaders alone again, with just their interpreters.

"I think it helped that they were both very religious," recalls one of Abdullah's aides. "They were two men of faith, even though their faiths were very different."

• • •

All through the traumas of 9/11, Abdullah had remained preoccupied with Palestine. It was the reason why he had refused to meet Bush the previous summer, pushing the president to the brink of a new initiative, when 9/11 had intervened. Now, in 2002, the crown prince felt even more pressure. The intifada was in crisis. Yasser Arafat was a virtual prisoner in Ramallah, where the Israeli Army was surrounding his compound. *Al-Jazeera* burned with reports of West Bank violence, and Saudis were following the drama avidly on their satellite channels. Abdullah had been denounced on both Islamist and liberal websites for going to the United States at such a moment, and his Information Ministry had had to scrape the barrel in his defense. The crown prince, a spokesman announced, had loaded the hold of his Boeing with several thousand translations of the Koran that he would be distributing to educate Americans about Islam.

Abdullah had made careful preparations for the meeting. In the post-9/11 majlises that he had summoned in Riyadh for the businessmen, academics, members of the Shura, and for the ulema, his correspondence with Bush and Condoleezza Rice had been read out for all to hear. His staff had noted the feedback from the different crowds. During a February 2002 interview the crown prince startled the author and *New York Times* columnist Thomas Friedman by opening a drawer in his desk to produce a fully worked-out peace proposal that offered Arab recognition of Israel and normalization of relations in exchange for an Israeli return to its pre-1967 borders. A few weeks later Abdullah went to Beirut to push his peace plan through the twenty-two-member Arab League summit—the most developed and comprehensive Arab olive branch ever.

"We had carried out private polling inside Israel," recalls one of the crown prince's aides. "We hired a local company and never told them it was for Saudi Arabia. We found that 70 percent of Israelis thought that the Abdullah peace plan was a fair deal. Unfortunately 70 percent of them also supported Ariel Sharon—but I suppose that showed we'd gotten some authentic sampling."

The crown prince had had his staff prepare a scrapbook of news photographs to go with the heartrending video footage he took to Crawford. His aides had stayed up late the previous night in Houston sorting through a pile of news agency images and making photocopies at the local Kinko's.

"I'm not asking this for myself or the Kingdom," said Abdullah. "I'm asking for the sake of the Palestinians."

The pictures seemed to have a stronger impact on the crown prince than on his audience.

"It's the blood issue," he told Bush, returning to the theme that had made him emotional the previous summer. "You seem to care more about the lives of Israelis than of Arabs."

Bush demurred, but Abdullah would not be brushed off.

"You said you were willing to do something," he asked. "But what? I didn't want to come here, but you kept asking. Now you are giving me nothing. I can't go home empty-handed."

And with that the crown prince gathered his robes about him and rose to his feet. The meeting was over, he declared—there was no point in staying. He and the rest of his party would be going home at once. Bush sat on his screened porch with Condoleezza Rice, nonplussed.

"Are they playing games?" he asked.

Elsewhere on the ranch, Bandar bin Sultan and Colin Powell, usually the best of friends (and occasional racquetball partners) got into a shouting match.

"What the hell did you do?" the U.S. secretary of state demanded roughly of the Saudi ambassador. "How did you let it get to this?"

Their voices grew so loud that Bush himself appeared to investigate.

Powell suspected the ultimatum was a ploy that the Saudis had planned in advance, but Abdullah's staff denied it. Whatever their plain-speaking boss did came from his heart, they said—and the king's anger got results. Bush agreed to go public with a new U.S. approach on Palestine, essentially as he had worded it in private in the days before 9/11.

"My vision," the president declared, speaking in the White House Rose Garden on June 24, 2002, flanked by his defense secretary, Donald Rumsfeld, and his secretary of state, Colin Powell, "is of two states, living side by side in peace and security."

No American president had ever committed so explicitly or firmly to the creation of a Palestinian state, which flatly contradicted the vision of both hard-line Jews and the Christian Zionists. Bush hedged his promise with a multitude of caveats to comfort the Israelis; he consistently refused to deal with Yasser Arafat, and he proved over the years to be considerably less resolute in acting to secure his pledge than he had sounded in the Rose Garden. Still, the words had been uttered. The creation of a Palestinian state was now, for the first time, a declared objective of American policy, and Abdullah bin Abdul Aziz could take much of the credit for it.

. . .

The triumph—and the harmony—were short-lived. Several observers of the Crawford meeting noted how the king and the president appeared to be talking "past each other," for while the Saudi was focusing on the current emergency in Palestine, the American's vision was clearly set in another direction. Sixteen months earlier, as the new Bush administration was entering office, its defense secretary, Donald Rumsfeld, had proposed a startling new template for U.S. policy in the Middle East. "Imagine what the region would look like," he told a meeting of the National Security Council, "without Saddam and with a regime that's aligned with U.S. interests. It would change everything in the region and beyond."

A few weeks later, Bush speechwriter David Frum presented an even more explicit version of this Iraq-centered strategy to the *New York Times Magazine:* "An American-led overthrow of Saddam Hussein, and the replacement of the radical Baathist dictatorship with a new government more closely aligned with the United States, would put America more wholly in charge of the region than any power since the Ottomans, or maybe even the Romans."

September 11, 2001, offered the chance to put this grandiose vision into practice. America clearly needed to lash out at somebody sinister and Arab. Donald Rumsfeld frankly testified to the official 9/11 Commission that immediately after the attacks, on the afternoon of September 11, "his instinct was to hit Saddam Hussein," and the next day President Bush ordered Richard A. Clarke, his counterterrorism czar, to explore possible Iraqi links. Within hours the principal consequence of the Saudi-manned assault on Manhattan and Washington had been to open up the American path to war in Iraq.

Saudi reaction to this knee-jerk response was a mixture of suspicion and disbelief. As Sunni Muslims they knew instinctively what intelligence reports later confirmed, that 9/11 and Iraq were not connected—a pious Salafi like Bin Laden would never have serious dealings with a secularizing regime like Saddam's. U.S. attempts to prove a Saddam–Al-Qaeda conspiracy seemed laughable. At the same time, many Saudis fell victim to their own conspiracy theories. The fact that the U.S. was exploiting 9/11 as a pretext to direct its military power in the direction of Iraq confirmed their suspicion of Zionist involvement in the September 2001 attacks: Saudi reasoning ran that America's wish to be "wholly in charge" of the Middle East could only be to provide extra protection for its client state Israel.

Abdullah instructed his personal spokesman, Bandar's young, Westernized aide, Adel Al-Jubeir, to go out and make clear his opposition to a U.S. invasion of Iraq.

"There is no country in the world that supports it," declared Al-Jubeir in August 2002. "There is no legal basis for it. There is no international sanction for it. There is no coalition for it."

Al-Jubeir did the rounds of U.S. TV newscasts systematically rebutting a speech Vice President Cheney had recently made that called for invasion. So far as the Saudis were concerned, the same reasoning applied in 2002 as ten years earlier, when there were calls for the victorious Gulf War allies to march on Baghdad: better the devil you know . . . Saddam might be a villain, but he was a Sunni villain whose power kept the Shia—and the ayatollahs of Iran—at bay. Bringing down the Iraqi dictator risked making Tehran, not America, the new Rome in the Middle East.

The Saudis were also opposed to the neoconservative principle that America could intervene as it wished to reshape the area. In July that year Laurent Murawiec, a French analyst with the RAND Corporation, had given a twenty-four-slide presentation to the prestigious Defense Policy Board, an arm of the Pentagon, suggesting that the United States should consider "taking [the] Saudi out of Arabia" by forcibly seizing control of the oil fields, giving the Hijaz back to the Hashemites, and delegating control of the holy cities to a multinational committee of moderate, non-Wahhabi Muslims: the House of Saud should be sent home to Riyadh.

"Saudi Arabia supports our enemies and attacks our allies," argued Murawiec, a protégé of Richard Perle's, the neocon advocate of war with Iraq who chaired the Policy Board. "The Saudis are active at every level of the terror chain, from planners to financiers, from cadre to foot soldier, from ideologist to cheerleader." They were "the kernel of evil, the prime mover, the most dangerous opponent" in the Middle East.

The Pentagon rushed out a disavowal. "Neither the presentations nor the Defense Policy Board members' comments reflect the official views of the Department of Defense," said a spokeswoman in a written statement. "Saudi Arabia is a long-standing friend and ally of the United States. The Saudis cooperate fully in the global war on terrorism and have the Department's and the Administration's deep appreciation."

But it was not difficult to find voices in Washington who welcomed the airing of Murawiec's aggressive views, which he would later set out in a book, *Princes of Darkness,* praised by Perle as "brilliant" and "powerful."

"People used to rationalize Saudi behavior," said a Bush administration official to the *Washington Post*. "You don't hear that anymore. There's no doubt that people are recognizing reality and recognizing that Saudi Arabia is a problem."

The unnamed official set out the grand neoconservative strategy, with a menacing sting in its tail for the Kingdom: "The road to the entire Middle East goes through Baghdad. Once you have a democratic regime in Iraq, like the ones we helped establish in Germany and Japan after World War II, there are a lot of possibilities."

"I think this view defies reality," hit back Adel Al-Jubeir, quoted on Abdullah's behalf in the same newspaper report. "The two countries have been friends and allies for over sixty years. Their relationship has seen the coming and breaking of many storms in the region, and if anything it goes from strength to strength."

It was believed in the Washington press pool that many of these anti-Saudi sentiments were being promoted by the office of the pugnacious Dick Cheney—with the vice president also suggesting that, despite their public protestations, the Saudis were secretly in favor of an attack that would oust Saddam. Al-Jubeir let it be known that the crown prince had personally contradicted this suggestion face-to-face with Cheney when the two men had met earlier that year.

"No," Abdullah had said. "The answer is no. I said 'no' in Saudi Arabia. I say 'no' now, and I will say 'no' tomorrow."

The trouble was that Cheney had solid grounds for his suspicions, since the allegation that most of the leaders of the Arab world—including Abdullah—secretly wanted the United States to bring Saddam crashing down came from no other source than Abdullah's own ambassador, Prince Bandar bin Sultan.

• • •

It seemed to be a case of the flamboyant Bandar "flying solo." According to many, the Saudi ambassador had a long-standing personal grudge against Saddam Hussein. In the summer of 1990, only hours before Iraq's troops started rolling, the dictator had tricked Bandar into conveying solid personal assurances to both Margaret Thatcher and President George H. W. Bush that there would be no Iraqi invasion of Kuwait. Since then, Bandar believed, Saddam had also put out a contract to have him assassinated. The Saudi prince had strengthened his already substantial security squad.

A professional colleague of the prince's dismisses this idea as "utter nonsense."

"Prince Bandar" he says, "does not take things personally. And it is quite untrue to suggest that he would ever depart from officially determined Saudi policy."

But that was not how many observers saw the prince operating in Washington in the autumn of 2002. While Crown Prince Abdullah was doing his best from Riyadh to oppose and prevent a U.S. attack on Iraq, his nephew and ambassador seemed to be doing quite the opposite—effectively serving, as David Ottaway of the *Washington Post* put it, as "a de facto member of the U.S. neoconservatives' 'war party.'" In a replay of the previous Gulf conflict of 1990–91, Dick Cheney and Donald Rumsfeld were once again Bandar's best chums—indeed, on January 11, 2003, according to the investigative journalist Bob Woodward, the two men briefed Bandar on Bush's decision to go to war before they told Secretary Powell. Reinvigorated by the coming conflict, the Saudi envoy bustled to and fro between Riyadh and Washington. When finally questioned at home, he presented his rationale without apology—the United States was going to attack Iraq whatever anyone said, so why not make the best of it?

Abdullah's conclusion from the same grim reality was that Saudi interests were now best served by visibly distancing the Kingdom from Bush's America. The crown prince regarded the prospect of a U.S. presence in Iraq as bad for Iraq, bad for America, and bad for Saudi Arabia—an "illegitimate occupation," as he would subsequently put it publicly in a speech to the Arab League. Abdullah was appalled that Bush and his advisers did not even pretend to listen to the firsthand experience offered by those who knew the region. In Abdullah's own case, he could offer the perspective of his mother's tribe, the Shammar, to whose powerful chiefs he remained close and whose writ ran deep into the deserts of Iraq. Two of the crown prince's wives were (and are) Shammar.

"History teaches us the American track record in adventures like this," says a veteran Saudi diplomat. "They dive in without thinking, then they cut and run, leaving the mess to others."

But there were existing commitments to consider. Since the mid-1990s the U.S. Air Force had built up the Prince Sultan Air Base at Al-Kharj, south of Riyadh, to become the linchpin of its Middle East air command. Enforcement of the no-fly zone over Iraq had been coordinated from here, as had the 2001 attacks on Afghanistan. In 2003 the U.S. military was counting on Al-Kharj as the command center for its attack on Iraq.

Abdullah did a deal through his chameleon ambassador. The United States could go on using Al-Kharj and some other bases for the duration of the war, it was agreed, on a basis of strict military secrecy—after which the Americans must pack up their belongings and be gone. The U.S. campaign of "shock and awe" that overwhelmed Iraq in a few short weeks after March 20, 2003, relied heavily on Al-Kharj and also on the northern Saudi airports of Ar'Ar and Tabuk—U.S. Special Forces teams took off from these two bases near the Iraqi border for their undercover operations inside Baghdad and other cities.

But once the invasion was completed, American transporters flew in to start dismantling and shuttling U.S. Air Force assets eastward piece by piece, to the French-built Al-Udeid Air Base, in the Gulf state of Qatar. By the end of September 2003 there was not a single U.S. soldier, tank, or plane left on the soil of Saudi Arabia, apart from a few long-term military trainers. Abdullah had finally distanced the Kingdom from Bush's America as he had long wished—and, in the process, one of the principal demands that Osama Bin Laden had made in attacking the twin towers two years earlier had also been met. Saudi Arabia had helped brew the poison that was 9/11. Now Iraq would have to drink it.

CHAPTER 31

End of the Affair

Prince Bandar bin Sultan liked to compare the long-standing U.S.-Saudi relationship to a Catholic marriage. There might be rows and dalliances, he would say with a twinkle—he had known his share of both—but the marriage would go on forever. Then in the spring of 2004 his nominal boss, Prince Saud Al-Faisal, the long-serving and normally somber foreign minister, out-twinkled his cousin with a new definition.

"It's not a Catholic marriage," Prince Saud told David Ottaway of the *Washington Post*. "It's a *Muslim* marriage." The Muslim husband is allowed up to four wives, providing that he treats them all with fairness—so that would be Saudi Arabia's new course in the difficult days that followed 9/11. The Kingdom was not seeking a divorce from America, just looking for some extra partners.

The first of these was China, a country with whom the Kingdom had not even maintained diplomatic relations when Bandar went to Beijing shopping for CSS-2 missiles in 1985. A few years later the first Communist Chinese ambassador arrived in Riyadh—part of the international alliance amassed against Saddam in 1990–91—and the relationship grew closer through the 1990s as Saudi Arabia increased its oil exports to Japan, South Korea, and other countries in Asia. By the early 2000s the Kingdom had become China's principal supplier of crude oil. It was a coincidence that Ali Al-Naimi, the Saudi oil minister, happened to be in Shanghai in September 2001, just eight days after the Al-Qaeda attack on America, but what he chose to say there was not. Saudi Arabia, he declared, wished to build a "strategic relationship and partnership" with China "at all levels."

In 1998 Abdullah had made China one of his earliest destinations after he assumed more power as crown prince, and when he became king he pointedly made Beijing, not Washington, the object of his very first foreign visit. The king landed in January 2006 with a mixed delegation of Saudi men *and* women—another first—and promptly got down to business, laying plans for a massive $3.5 billion refinery to process high sulfur Saudi crude and discussing the provision of Saudi oil for a new Chinese hundred-million-barrel strategic reserve.

A few weeks later, China's president, Hu Jintao, returned the visit. Hu was on his way back from Washington, where the White House greeter had addressed him using the wrong title, welcoming him in Chinese as President of Nationalist China (Taiwan), and where he had also suffered the indignity of being heckled at his press conference. In Riyadh there were no protocol mishaps—and certainly no risk of hecklers. There was, furthermore, a curiously genuine warmth as two inscrutable and proudly non-Western cultures took their mutual measure. Both were on the rise. Both were seeking to modernize. Both were authoritarian and secretive—and both had had to endure patronizing lectures on that account from the know-it-all West. Speaking to the Majlis Al-Shura, Hu pointed out how China's relationship with Arabia went back a lot further than that of the United States. Two thousand years earlier, even before the time of the Prophet, the ancient Silk Road had linked China with the Middle East.

"Regarding history as a mirror," said the president, quoting an old Chinese proverb, "we can understand what will be rising and what will be falling."

This oblique reference to the world's shifting balance of power was echoed in the rest of Hu's speech. Rather than invading one another, he declared, nations should pursue dialogue, opposing "the use of force, or threatening each other with force at random." Sovereign states had the right to choose their own social and political systems, and each should respect the choice of the other. Without once uttering the word *America,* Hu laid out a worldview refreshingly different from that of George Bush, who had recently expressed his ambition to end what he described as his country's "addiction" to oil imports, especially from the Arab Middle East. China had no hang-ups: it was unashamedly eager for Saudi oil.

Oil for security had always been the basis for the U.S.-Saudi "special relationship." Now this was echoed in the new Sino-Saudi marriage—with the possibility of a sinister twist. Official reports described the signing of a "contract on defense systems," which analysts presumed to refer to the Kingdom's stock of fifty to sixty aging Chinese CSS-2 missiles purchased two decades earlier by Bandar and Khaled bin Sultan. These medium-range weapons had been designed to deliver nuclear warheads, and the years since 1985 had seen Saudi Arabia's closest Muslim ally, Pakistan, become a nuclear power—operating secretly, it was widely presumed, with China, since Pakistan and China were both worried about India's long-standing nuclear capability. Saudi Arabia, for its part, was worried about Iran and its development of nuclear technology. So it seemed obvious that the three nations should find ways of collaborating, preferably in some arm's-length fashion.

When the nuclear suggestion was put to Saud Al-Faisal he mustered all his authority as the world's longest-serving foreign minister to reject the suggestion that the Kingdom had any access to the bomb.

"We think it is stupidity incarnate because these weapons will not give security," he said in March 2004. There was "absolutely no truth" to reports that Saudi Arabia was pursuing the nuclear option.

But the Kingdom deliberately deceived the world and its closest ally to acquire and install China's missiles—and defense, after all, is the gravest matter of life and death. It would be foolish not to keep the country's stock of CSS-2 East Wind missiles in updated working order, and it would not be difficult for Pakistan to hold a matching stock of nuclear warheads on behalf of its wealthy Muslim ally, thus providing the Kingdom—and indeed Pakistan and China—with some element of deniability. The state of Israel continues to deny that it is a nuclear power. So why should the Saudis tell the truth?

• • •

Wife number three was also recruited from the very top of America's list of foes. The Soviet Union had been the first country in the world to recognize Abdul Aziz's conquest of the peninsula in 1926 and was the only foreign government that could claim the distinction of having given oil to Saudi Arabia: in the days of the Great Depression a Russian tanker delivered to Jeddah some £30,000 worth of petrol for which the poverty-stricken Saudis never managed to scramble up the cash. Through the Cold War the godless Soviets became one of the ritual devils that Saudi foreign policy statements loved to stone, and relations did not thaw greatly with the collapse of Communism. The two countries had been energy competitors for years, vying alternately for the position of the world's largest oil producer. The Saudis resented the way Russia declined to join or cooperate with OPEC, but happily enjoyed the enhanced oil prices produced by OPEC's production restraints.

Then America invaded Iraq, and suddenly Moscow became the object of another of Prince Abdullah's pioneering foreign visits. The competitors discovered that they were really collaborators, controlling between them no less than 26 percent of the world's known oil reserves and 31 percent of the gas. Since his accession to power in the late 1990s, Abdullah had been pursuing an ambitious pet project, his Oil and Gas Initiative, intended to encourage foreign investment in the development of new Saudi energy resources, including petrochemical and desalinization plants. Negotiations had not gone well with the largely American-led consortiums, particularly after 9/11, and had been broken off in the weeks following the U.S. invasion of Iraq, which, in the eyes of many Arabs, had been about nothing so much as the forcible laying of American hands on Arab oil. In January 2004 it was announced that Lukoil, a private Russian energy enterprise, along with some Chinese and European oil companies (Sinopec, Eni, Repsol YPF, Royal Dutch Shell, and TotalFinaElf) would now fill the space left by Exxon Mobil, Phillips, Marathon, Conoco, and Occidental.

Within months, Luksar, the joint venture formed by Saudi Aramco and Lukoil (with a $2 billion Russian investment) had gone to work, starting its first prospecting by the time Vladimir Putin arrived in Riyadh early in 2007. The Russian president set the tone for his visit with a speech delivered at the annual Munich Conference on Security Policy on his journey down from Moscow. Russia had had enough, he said, of the "unipolar world" created by America's "almost uncontained hyper-use of force . . . airily participating in military operations" to impose its policies on other nations. "Who," he asked, "is happy about this?"

Two days later Abdullah welcomed the Russian president to Riyadh, hailing him as "a statesman, a man of peace, a man of justice." As befitted a man of peace, Putin offered Saudi Arabia a shopping list of Russian military technology—150 T-90 battle tanks, 100 attack and transport helicopters, 20 mobile air-defense systems, and a large number of armored personnel carriers, along with a proposal to help with the development of nuclear technology. To round off the warm and successful visit—Russia, it was noted, had always supported the cause of the Palestinians—Abdullah presented Putin with the Kingdom's highest honor, the King Abdul Aziz Medal. At that date this medal had been presented to only two other foreign leaders, China's President Hu and Jacques Chirac of France, who had led the United Nations campaign to halt Bush's Iraqi invasion. It was difficult to think of a more satisfyingly anti-American trio.*

• • •

Catholic or Muslim, the old U.S.-Saudi special relationship had clearly become history, and a typically Saudi mix-up confirmed it. In July 2005 Prince Bandar bin Sultan resigned as Saudi ambassador to Washington, exhausted and disillusioned by what had become an impossible challenge. After inviting hundreds of friends and colleagues to a farewell party, he abruptly canceled it and vanished, as unpredictable in departure as he had been in his long tenure—to be replaced by his cousin and brother-in-law, Prince Turki Al-Faisal, the former intelligence chief who had been serving as ambassador to London since the departure of Ghazi Algosaibi. It was Turki who, more than a quarter of a century earlier, had first suggested that Bandar, then a young fighter pilot recently married to his sister Haifa, might do well in Washington as an advocate for Saudi causes.

When Turki arrived in the stand-alone, castlelike Saudi embassy beside the Watergate complex that September there was already a strategy in place for mending the broken relationship between the Kingdom and America—a "strategic dialogue" of U.S.-Saudi working groups to address the multitude of practical dislocations that had followed 9/11. These ranged from counterterrorism and business breakdowns to the strangling of U.S. visa procedures by the new Department of Homeland Security. Insensitive security restrictions had virtually extinguished the flow of Saudi students to U.S. universities and had also made entry into America an offensive and humiliating process for even the most respectable of Saudis. Six different working groups would be staffed by upper-level Saudi and U.S. officials who would meet face-to-face twice a year, alternately in Washington and Riyadh, and would maintain contact between meetings, hoping to build up the routine working relationships that had been neglected in Bandar's years of "room at the top" diplomacy.

"Now we would know who to call," explained a Saudi diplomat who was much involved in this reconstruction process.

*Subsequently Abdullah presented the medal to George W. Bush and to King Juan Carlos of Spain.

On the public front, Turki accepted every invitation to appear on U.S. radio and TV shows, from Fox to NPR, calmly answering the most aggressive questions, including many about his own personal role in events—he was the Saudi official, after all, who had tried and failed first to contain, then to recapture Osama Bin Laden. Alongside this painstaking media campaign, for which he also recruited the onetime Salafi and campaigning journalist Jamal Khashoggi, the prince embarked on a grueling schedule of visits to grassroots America, accepting invitations to speak at universities and on the country's rubber-chicken circuit of Rotary clubs and Kiwanis lodges, an unglamorous public diplomacy effort intended slowly to convert the views of the average American—"Joe Six-Pack," as Bandar liked to call him.

The trouble was that Bandar could not keep his fingers out of the pie. The flamboyant prince seemed to be only happy while being indispensable. Back in Riyadh, Bandar had taken charge of a recently-revealed but long-planned National Security Council on the U.S. model whose function, it soon turned out, was to keep the ex-ambassador at the center of events, giving him important reasons to jet to London, Beijing, and Moscow, still carrying messages for the king—and still traveling, quite frequently, on high-level missions to Washington.

For more than a quarter of a century, Turki's full brother Saud Al-Faisal, the foreign minister, had accepted Bandar's wholesale trampling on his personal bailliwick, but Turki was not so tolerant. He had been given charge of Saudi policy in Washington, only to discover his brother-in-law flying in regularly to cozy up to his old pals in the Bush administration.

It was not a matter of Turki's personal embarrassment—which he denied on the record, and, indeed, off the record. He had no problem, he said, with Bandar or anyone else carrying personal messages for the king. He well understood how the Saudi system worked, and he had himself carried royal messages in his days as intelligence chief. But it was embarrassing for lesser Saudi officials when they went to see a senior U.S. official to be asked whether they were "with Bandar or with Turki?" There were serious matters of foreign policy at stake. As the Bush administration increased its drumbeat of aggression toward Iran in the autumn of 2006, Turki was arguing for calm, hoping against hope that war might be avoided.

"For the United States not to talk to Iran," he said, "is a mistake."

In this Turki was voicing the official policy set by his brother Saud, who, the previous year, had called for the United States to engage in talks with Iran rather than indulging in threats. The Saudi foreign minister pointed out that if the Bush administration was now alarmed by the increasing regional influence of Iran they had only themselves to blame for "handing over Iraq on a golden platter."

Bandar bin Sultan, however, was saying something much more to the taste of his friends inside the White House, and in particular of Dick Cheney, whose confrontational instincts Bandar shared. The prince had supported the neocon attack on Iraq, and now he encouraged the United States to get tough with Iran—a message that the administration greatly preferred to being publicly lectured by the Al-Faisal brothers. George W. Bush knew what he wanted to hear, and if it came straight from Riyadh on a plane via an old friend who had just come from the king, it surely carried more weight than the disapproving comments of a locally based ambassador whom he did not know so well.

This all came at the same time as a financial crisis in the embassy that spoke to the endemic Saudi confusion between public and private, along with the Kingdom's deficiencies in administrative skills. For many years the large Saudi delegation in Washington had been running over budget, and Abdullah had ordered a cutback, in line with his attempts to impose financial discipline throughout government affairs. Bandar had blithely ignored the cutback—or had, rather, accepted the cutback, then made up the difference by deploying the lavish funds that poured monthly into his local Riggs Bank account from the Al-Yamamah project. The prince's multimillion-dollar support for his country's foreign service in Washington was one of the reasons he felt so confident in dismissing the accusations of corruption against him.

Turki Al-Faisal, however, had no Al-Yamamah slush fund. He did his best when he arrived in Washington to introduce economies—it was not difficult to conduct business in a less lordly style than his predecessor—but there were many commitments that he could not cut quickly. Qorvis Communications, the embassy's principal public relations adviser, and other suppliers were owed large sums of money that had mounted up over the months. Turki's appeals to Riyadh for help fell on deaf ears. Following budget overruns in both the intelligence service and the London embassy during the times of Turki's tenure, Abdullah had a poor opinion of his nephew's financial acumen. More important, he declined to back Turki in his turf war with Bandar.

The king held no special brief for his bumptious national security adviser. He would, on a later occasion, show no hesitation in slapping Bandar down when he felt that the prince had stepped out of line. But now Abdullah effectively took Bandar's side, refusing to extend Turki, his designated and incredibly hardworking official representative, any sort of helping hand. Perhaps the king agreed with Bandar that the United States should exert some pressure on Iran. Perhaps he was quite happy that mixed messages should be delivered to America. Perhaps—and this is the most likely explanation—Abdullah simply chose not to make a decision between the two cousins and felt that Turki should "get over it."

The son of King Faisal did not see it that way. The Al-Faisal (sons of Faisal) conduct themselves as aristocrats inside an already aristocratic clan. The news of Turki's resignation became public in December 2006, not much more than a year after he had started the job. Graceful to the end, the retiring ambassador declined to go into details. He insisted that he was leaving for personal, not political reasons, and with the full agreement of the king. But what was certain was that in just eighteen months, two senior and very talented princes—among the most able in the family—had given up on the unpalatable job of trying to represent Saudi Arabia in America.

• • •

If 9/11 took the special out of the U.S.-Saudi "special relationship," the U.S. invasion of Iraq killed it stone dead—for the time being, at least. Oil for security had always been the basis of the pact, but Iraq produced the very opposite of that. From being a guarantor of safety, George W. Bush's United States turned out to be a provider of chaos and jeopardy.

Oilwise, in 2002 Saudi Arabia ceased granting the discounted shipping rates with which it had for decades favored the successor companies of Socal, Texaco, Esso, and Mobil, the four U.S. oil majors that had made up the original, prenationalization components of Aramco. U.S. companies now had to pay the same price as everyone else, and the Kingdom rapidly ceased to be the United States' foremost oil provider. By 2006, that honor went to Canada, at 2.3 million barrels per day, followed by Mexico at 1.7 million. At 1.4 million barrels per day, Saudi Arabia competed for the honor of third place with that other good friend of the United States, Venezuela.

Oil was the main item on the agenda when Bush and Abdullah met at Crawford, Texas, for a second time, on April 25, 2005. Scarcely noticed in the months following 9/11, the price of oil had started to creep upward. The invasion and chaos in Iraq had intensified that trend, so that, at $55 a barrel, a gallon of gas was costing $2.42 in the United States, well on its way to double the $1.41 level when the two men had met three years earlier.

This second encounter became notorious for the picture of the two leaders walking hand in hand as Bush shepherded Abdullah through his garden to the ranch building where they were to meet—the weird intimacy of the gesture being so obviously at odds with the two men's clash of interests that it seemed to sum up Bush's cluelessness. Bush wanted Saudi Arabia to use its pumping power to flood the world market and bring down the price per barrel, but Adel Al-Jubeir, Abdullah's spokesman, pointed out the fallacy in that. The Kingdom could send a million or more extra barrels to America tomorrow, he said, but America did not have the refineries to process it. Saudi Arabia had been investing in new production, but the West—and America, in particular, had not been building refineries to match.

So the other half of the equation did not work either. America could not guarantee security and the Saudis could no longer guarantee cheap oil. It seemed scarcely surprising when, ignoring the media furor over the Al-Yamamah deal, the Kingdom turned back to Britain in 2007 to provide its new generation of high-tech fighter combat aircraft, a long-term contract worth some $40 billion, thus locking out U.S. manufacturers for the foreseeable future. "You go Uruguay" had come about with a vengeance—though the special relationship had an ally at its heart that might not have been expected.

"Why can't I send more of my sons to study in America?" asked King Abdullah when he welcomed Michael Chertoff, the U.S. secretary of homeland security, to his farm at Janadriya in the spring of 2008. By "sons" the king was referring to the thousands of young Saudis who had been denied visas to study in the United States in the aftermath of 9/11.

The American security czar shifted uncomfortably and was just starting to explain how his government had certain concerns about the dangers posed by young Saudi males, when the king cut him short.

"Thank you very much, Mr. Secretary," he said. "But think about this.

Do you imagine that America can possibly be more concerned about the radicalizing of my sons that *I* might be?"

Chertoff was one of a miniflood of American visitors that spring, including President Bush, who flew on to the Kingdom after attending celebrations in Jerusalem to mark Israel's sixty years of existence since 1948. In Riyadh there was another celebration—the seventy-fifth anniversary of U.S.-Saudi diplomatic relations, which had started with the signing of the oil contract in 1933. It was called the Oryx summit, because two of Arabia's native antelopes were being sent to the National Zoo in Washington.

Abdullah took some delight in the comparative longevity of the two anniversaries, cupping his palms open in front of him, as if weighing the relative poundage of sixty or seventy-five years of friendship in the scales. He balanced his hands in the air for some time, moving them up and down—sixty, seventy-five—then grinned knowingly at the American delegation. The U.S.-Saudi split that Osama Bin Laden had hoped to accomplish had clearly not come to pass—and then, a few months later, came the presidential election of November 4, 2008, and the triumph of the new African-American U.S. leader with the oddly similar name.

Barack Hussein Obama's transition team got a call from Saudi Arabia within hours of the candidate's victory. Abdullah was due in New York just three days later for a special United Nations session of the Inter-Faith Religious Dialogue, which the king had initiated earlier that year in Madrid. His Majesty wanted to call and congratulate the new president-elect.

"Don't call us, we'll call you," came the firm but courteous reply. It was a matter of protocol. If the king was arriving as a guest on U.S. soil, it meant that Obama should make the call to welcome *him*—and this way, the president-elect could prepare his agenda and have his interpreter beside him as he spoke.

The call came through within minutes of Abdullah's landing at Kennedy airport on November 7. The king and his staff were in their limousines heading toward Manhattan.

"I have heard much, Your Majesty, about your preference for frank and plain speaking," said Obama, who had clearly been studying his briefing notes. "That is the style that I appreciate and I look forward to the chance to talk together."

The president-elect wished the Saudi king well with his interfaith gathering, and also with his participation in the G-20 gathering in Washington (Saudi Arabia ranks about seventeenth in the list of the world's twenty most powerful economies, just behind Turkey and comfortably ahead of any other Arab country). The call went on for around seven minutes, and it finished with Abdullah expressing the wish that the two leaders might meet and talk face-to-face before too long—*"Inshallah"* ("If it be God's will").

"Inshallah," echoed Obama, making use of the pious Islamic expression with which he was obviously familiar.

Later the king recounted some details of the conversation to a group of Saudis who had assembled to welcome him to Manhattan.

"I clearly heard him say 'Inshallah,'" mused Abdullah to the little gathering.

"God willing," he added wryly, "we shall make a Muslim of him yet."

CHAPTER 32

Condition of the People

King Abdullah loves the French game of pétanque, also known as boules. He acquired the taste in the sandy boulevards of Lebanon, and he plays it for hours. He roundly defeated Prince Charles when Charles visited the Kingdom in February 2004—but in the rules of *pétanque à l'Abdullah,* the king always wins.

The game is played in the desert, where the players take their ease on cushions ranged around the walls of a tall, plushly carpeted, open-sided tent. Outside on the sand is laid a small square of green baize marked with black arrows, and the target ball is thrown out thirty feet or so into the desert.

One by one the players rise from their cushions to take their place on the green baize and toss their single boule, which has their name attached to it with tape. As in the normal game of boules, the aim is to finish up closest to the target, and it is permitted—in fact, it is rather encouraged—to knock your rivals out of the way.

When every other player has thrown, the king steps forward, and this is where the normal game changes. For Abdullah has a deadly aim, he always throws last—and on at least one occasion he has been known to have *two* boules to throw. So that is why the king tends to win Saudi Arabia's royal pétanque championship, and having won, he takes a little purse of gold and hands it graciously to the runner-up—since in this royal version of a plebeian game, the runner-up is, in a way, the winner.

• • •

Abdullah used to spend a lot of time camping in the desert with his falcons. Now he favors the comforts of his farm north of Riyadh, where he keeps his Arabian horses in neat white courtyards of hacienda-style stables. The huge picture window of his sitting room is arranged to give him a view of the animals as they graze around a lake. He likes to sit watching them on Thursday mornings, the beginning of the Saudi weekend. It is the one morning he gets some time to relax—though his staff are only happy when they see him emerge to take some exercise in his brightly colored, thick-soled athletic shoes. A daily walk and a daily swim help keep the Angel of Death at a distance.

As in the declining days of Fahd, there is a whole power structure around the king that is hugely concerned to keep their patron alive—though in Abdullah's case they are joined by most of the Saudi population.

"He is our Muawiyah," says Hala Al-Houti, thirty-four, a Jeddah business executive, one of the new generation of Saudi working women. "We can only hope he never loses hold of the thread."

The early caliph Muawiyah, who had been a scribe to the Prophet, once said that he would not draw his sword where a whip would suffice, nor use a whip where his tongue was enough—and that if he should ever find himself connected to his people by just a single strand of hair, he would never allow it to snap. As the people pulled, so he would give way with them; only when they relaxed the thread would he try to pull them gently in the direction that he thought it best to go. Governance Muawiyah-style was a delicate matter of mutual respect, and it is a mark of the Saudi school system that while it signally fails to teach its children how to think for themselves, it does instill snippets of classical learning like this.

The modern Muawiyah keeps in touch with his people from his book-lined study in Riyadh. Above his desk hang some richly embroidered black-and-gold Koranic inscriptions, of which his favorite comes from the "Thunder" sura: "God will never change the condition of a people until they change it for themselves." This is the basis for Abdullah's belief in bringing changes to Saudi society.

There is also an entire wall full of television screens—one huge flat screen, surrounded by twenty or more satellite monitors, all displaying the channels that the Saudi population are watching at that moment. Each monitor has a number, and if something catches the royal eye, Abdullah presses that number on the control pad beside him. Instantly its sound becomes live and the image switches to the main screen. Sitting alertly in front of his video bank, this eighty-six-year-old Arab could be navigating the starship *Enterprise*. He puffs on an occasional Merit cigarette as he samples what his people think.

To back up the king's personal sampling, full-time teams of researchers watch all the TV channels systematically and write daily digests that are read out to Abdullah every night. Parallel teams monitor the published press and also the radio, particularly the grievances on the call-in shows, while a fourth, rather more geeky group, scans the ferocious and often hostile fundamentalist bloggers and websites. Together they make up a quartet of polling outfits to rival that of any U.S. presidential candidate. Early in 2008, for example, the teams warned Abdullah of the grassroots anger engendered by widespread inflation. Dr. Mohammed Al-Qunaybit, an eloquent Shura member and newspaper columnist, appeared on television to express his vivid disappointment with virtually every area of the king's domestic policies.

"The king's advisers," said Dr. Al-Qunaybit, "are creating a cloud of confusion around him."

Dr. Al-Qunaybit was only saying what most people were thinking, and his case was strengthened when Hashim Yamani, the commerce minister, was questioned about the rising cost of rice. Once an exotic foreign delicacy, rice (and particularly basmati rice) has become, with prosperity, the staple of every Saudi meal, but the minister dismissed the question with the insouciance of Marie Antoinette.

"There are nineteen types of rice," he responded. "And it is not compulsory for people to eat the most expensive."

The Saudi system may not be democratic, but it usually seeks to be responsive. Abdullah acted quickly to increase food subsidies and raise government salaries, then brusquely sacked the minister of commerce. But he also let it be known that the people's tribune, the eloquent and critical Dr. Al-Qunaybit, should moderate his acerbic tone for a spell. In Saudi Arabia it is the king, and the king alone, who throws the last ball.

. . .

One day late in 2006, Mahdi Al-Mushaikhis, an engineering student in the Eastern Province, came to his uncle Fouad in a troubled state. Some of the young man's relatives had been receiving strange phone calls about his fiancée. The couple had been together only a few months. They had signed the *milka,* the formal plighting of the troth that permitted private time together and sexual relations, and until that moment Mahdi had felt very happy with his future wife. But the phone calls suggested she had been with other men. If that was the case, Mahdi did not wish to proceed to full marriage.

Fouad Al-Mushaikhis is a man to whom many in his family would turn for advice. A calm and sagely grizzled graphic designer in his middle forties, he is an activist among the Shia community in Qateef, in the Eastern Province, displaying all the self-composure of a man who went into exile with his fellow campaigners at the age of fifteen and had to parent himself through some very hard years. His right temple is scarred with a bullet mark, his personal souvenir of the 1979 intifada. Having returned to the Kingdom with his fellow exiles at the end of 1993, Fouad now mentors young Shia in the Qateef region, teaching them computer design at weekends and giving them personal advice.

"You must not be hasty. You must sit down and talk to her," he instructed his nephew, who was nearing the end of his studies at the University of Petroleum and Minerals in Dhahran. But when Fouad met with the couple, he saw that the girl had been traumatized in some way. She was terrified to speak.

"Will you give me my rights?" she blurted out aggressively after Fouad had asked his nephew to leave the two of them alone.

"What I can promise," he replied, "is that I will not pass on anything you say unless you are willing."

And so, for the first time, the "Qateef girl" spilled out the sensational story that would provoke headlines around the world in the closing months of 2007—and would provide a metaphor for all that was wrong, and a few things that were right, inside King Abdullah's Saudi Arabia. Before getting engaged to Mahdi, the girl confessed, she had been persuaded to hand over a picture of herself to a girlfriend who had passed it on to a male relative, a good-looking boy a year or so younger than them named Hassan, who would sometimes drive the two girls to the mall.

"Can I see her picture?" is a matchmaking ploy very common among young Saudis, so restricted in their opportunities to meet and date. Pakistani- and Indian-run picture studios do a roaring trade in Saudi souks—providing, in this case, a kitschy photograph that, as Fouad remembers it, showed the Qateef girl standing against a baby blue backdrop. The picture had been taken two years earlier. Her head was covered, and she was dressed demurely in a black skirt and orange top, posing beside a small plastic tree that had been copiously laden with every imagineable variety of plastic fruit.

The Qateef girl had never been alone with Hassan, she told Fouad, nor had she ever lifted her veil to show the boy her face. But after her family arranged her contract of marriage to Mahdi, she had started to worry about the photograph being in Hassan's possession. Affection had flowered between the newly betrothed couple, and the girl had also discovered that Mahdi was fiercely possessive. She characterized her fiancé-husband as *hemish,* an Egyptian colloquialism that male Saudis sometimes apply to being fully "in charge" of their women. Not wanting to risk losing the man she now loved, she contacted her girlfriend to ask if she could get the picture back.

The girlfriend reported a complication. Hassan wanted to meet his picture pal one last time. He would hand over the picture, he promised, at City Plaza, a mini-mall a couple of hundred yards from her family home, but only if he could meet her privately. So being keen to get the whole thing over, the Qateef girl set off from home, walking the distance to the mall by the time agreed, around 9 P.M. that night.

She was not at all pleased with Hassan for compelling her to go through this, and as she turned left off her street and started walking along the main road she grew still more annoyed when a car slowed down to crawl alongside her, its three male occupants leaning across to make suggestive comments. As she hurried into the mall, she upbraided Hassan for tipping off the men, whom she presumed to be his cronies. But he swore he knew nothing—and he was as horrified as she was when they escaped together through the mall's rear door, to find the men in their vehicle waiting there for them. As the couple drove away, they were followed by their pursuers, who, the moment that they were off the main street, overtook them and forced them off the road. A foolish escapade was turning into a scarcely believable true-life nightmare. At knifepoint, two of the gangsters forced their captives out of their vehicle and onto the floor in the back of their own car, where one sat in the middle with a foot planted firmly on each of them.

"Come on over!" they could hear him boasting on the phone to his friends. "We've got a boy and a girl for tonight!"

Fouad Al-Mushaikhis could not believe what he was hearing. But it got worse. His nephew's wife described how, arriving at a rough farm, the

Qateef girl's abaya was pulled off and she was dragged out of the car into a primitive majlis-style room. There were cushions around the walls, with a rough and dirty woven palm mat in the middle of the floor. Four more men had arrived, their headdresses swathed around their faces like balaclavas so she could not see their features. They told her to take off her clothes and to get ready for some "fun." When she refused to strip, they beat her with palm fronds and ripped off the thin shift she was wearing beneath her abaya. She pleaded with them, telling them that she was married and from a good family. She called out to God, but they just laughed at her. Then they pushed her down onto the thin palm mat and raped her one by one. As they waited their turn, the men made videos on their mobile phones, leering and cheering from their cushions around the room.

"If you talk," they threatened, "we will spread these movies all around."

The girl's ordeal went on for hours—till 2 A.M. she later reckoned—and while it was going on, four of the attackers tied up Hassan, then raped and videotaped him as well.

Fouad was in tears. He could not believe what he was hearing. The girl took forty minutes to get through her story. The final video-blackmailing detail convinced Fouad that the attackers were an organized gang who routinely kidnapped victims and had carried out these rape orgies before. They had worked out every detail, even copying the contact numbers from their victims' cell phones before they let them go. They understood Saudi society. Such is the importance of "face" in this family-based culture that it is not unknown for families to seek out their daughters' violators and pay them for their silence. The men who raped the Qateef girl had every reason to believe that the Shia community of Qateef would connive in their crime.

. . .

Fouad, who surely represents modernity in this drama, pondered for a week what to do. He was distraught. He found it difficult to do any work, and he spent a lot of time out walking, leaving his home so that his own family should not see his distress. He met with the girl again to try to get the details straight, then called another meeting with the couple.

"There is a really big problem that we have to face," he told his nephew. "When you hear what has happened, you will be shocked, and you are going to have to be strong. You have got to act as a man and stand by your wife—even though your family, when they hear what has happened, will insist that you have got to divorce."

Mahdi listened—then did as his uncle said. He stood by his woman. His sense of hemish made him determined to take his revenge on her violators, and the young man's aggression showed Fouad the way ahead. He could hardly have pursued the cause of the Qateef girl without the support of her future husband. Fouad had determined to play Sherlock Holmes.

"Do you remember anything about the men?" he asked.

The problem with bringing the rapists to justice was a total lack of solid evidence. When the girl had finally got home after the attack, sobbing and semicomatose, her family had assumed she was suffering from a problem she had long had with anemia. They rushed her to hospital, where she did not mention being raped. So she was not examined internally and no DNA samples were taken—not that any such procedure would have been guaranteed. Saudi hospitals have no standardized protocol for processing rape allegations, and in some emergency rooms it remains routine for doctors—male or female—to refuse to hear or acknowledge what the assaulted patient is trying to say.

Fouad knew that the local police would be worse. Even when presented with evidence, they would presume provocation on the part of the woman: her rendezvous with Hassan would sink her cause fatally. So what could the Qateef girl say to prove her innocence?

"I remember," she told Fouad, "that some of the men had a very strong smell. They smelt of something like fish."

Sherlock Holmes had his clue. Fouad contacted Hassan, whose intransigence had started the trouble. The boy could make some amends, Fouad told him, by accompanying him to the bustling Qateef fish market, the main fish market of the Saudi east coast, where he would have to walk slowly past the various stalls. It was Fouad's plan to follow at a distance and see if anyone reacted to Hassan's presence.

Fouad and Hassan went twice to the fish market, and on the second visit the plan worked. As the boy walked down the central aisle of the long and narrow fish shed, awash with pungent water and glittering fish scales, Fouad saw two stallholders nudging each other with alarm. They vanished together behind their high freezer cabinet, and did not reemerge until Hassan had safely passed.

Now Fouad needed confirmation from the other victim.

"They won't be able to see you," he reassured her, "through your veil."

The Qateef girl went to the stall as directed, and haggled over some fish. It was good fish, she later told Fouad, but she refused to hand over a single riyal to the animals who had abused her. She was terrified and had nearly fainted on the spot. Yes, she confirmed—the two men who had hidden behind their freezer were indeed the men who abducted her.

Fouad now had two suspects, and in the days that followed he gathered names and phone numbers and license plate details. He wrote everything down on a sheet of A4 paper, highlighting the main points, in the form of a letter from Mahdi asking for justice. "My wife has been raped," it stated bluntly. But Fouad did not take it to the police. He went instead to the majlis of the royal governor of the Eastern Province, Prince Mohammed bin Fahd.

Here is the next point to ponder in this ancient and modern morality tale. Mohammed, the eldest son of the late King Fahad, has presided over two decades of spectacular growth in Saudi Arabia's oil province, and his multifarious family businesses, run by his brother and his sons, have profited from it spectacularly. This linkage between public position and private profit would raise ethical questions in other parts of the world, but in Saudi Arabia it is the way things get done. Mohammed bin Fahd has many critics in the Kingdom's largest and most prosperous province, which he governs—but it was thanks to him that the rapists were brought to justice.

"I could tell from the prince's face," remembers Fouad. "He was totally shocked by some of the details. I had highlighted them in bold on the piece of paper that I gave to him. His color changed. 'Why haven't you gone to the Qateef police?' he asked. 'I'm more afraid of them,' I told him, 'than I am of those criminals.'"

A few days later Fouad was sitting at a table in the Dammam Corniche waterfront park talking to two Mabahith colonels, and as he watched the detectives gently interrogating his nephew's wife, he could not help admiring the way they went about their work. The colonels had been chosen by the prince's office to supervise the case, and over the days that followed they selected an investigative team that quickly got results. After making their own inquiries, the detectives arrested the two fish sellers, who promptly surrendered the names of their accomplices. Several of them confessed. As events took a positive turn, Mahdi and his wife decided that they would move in together, taking up residence in Mahdi's mother's house, not far from Qateef's Shia burial ground, and just across the street from Fouad's home. Adversity had helped them become fully man and wife.

...

Fouad assumed that justice would now take its course, but he had not reckoned on the Saudi court system, based on the shariah, God's eternal and unchanging law, derived from the Koran and the Hadith (Islamic traditions). Since law is a branch of religion, it follows that all Saudi judges are religious sheikhs, most of them of a conservative and distinctly Wahhabi inclination, very concerned to encourage their own view of virtue and to discourage vice, particularly when that vice might involve bidaa, innovations, of a Western nature. This meant, in the case of the Qateef girl, that the three judges started their deliberations by focusing on the premarital relationship that had drawn the young woman to the City Plaza that fateful night. This was the single undisputed offense before the court. The rapists had withdrawn their confessions and were now pleading innocence, while the girl's signed "confession" to the police remained on the record.

"The shariah is quite clear," declared Sheikh Abdul Muhsin Al-Ubaiqan, himself a former judge and now a member of the Majlis Al-Shura. "If she had confessed to adultery, she would have been sentenced to stoning. As it was, she confessed without reservation to an improper premarital closeness."

In the circumstances, the three Qateef judges, all devout Sunnis, considered that they were being lenient in sentencing this sinful young Shia woman—and the man with whom she had been in the car—to just ninety lashes each and two months in prison. As for the other defendants, the accusation of multiple rape was the allegation of one admitted sinner against a group of men who were all protesting their innocence—and who, if they turned out not to be innocent, could plausibly claim enticement by a woman whose looseness was now a matter of record. Kidnapping seemed proven, but who could tell exactly what had happened after that? It was her word against theirs. Considering the paucity of incriminating evidence, the judges could not possibly invoke the standard shariah death penalty for rape. Sentences ranging from ten months to five years, they considered, were more than harsh enough.

As the verdict was read out in court, the rapists sneered openly at their victim. She had been summoned to appear and stand alongside them not as their accuser, but as a fellow sexual offender. Fouad had secured Saudi justice for his nephew's wife, but it was not the justice for which he had hoped.

. . .

To most Western readers, Fouad Al-Mushaikhis will seem a hero in this tale. But that is not how he appeared to many people in Qateef. As soon as news of the arrests began circulating, people had started to take sides—and not Fouad's side, for the most part.

"Every evening when I got home from work," he remembers, "there would be a group of friends and neighbors hovering around."

Fouad would invite them in for tea, and after the preliminaries and normal courtesies had been negotiated, most of the visitors proffered the same piece of advice—"Just drop it. Don't stir things up."

His family begged him to abandon his mission, while his wife's family threatened to take her away and impose a divorce. One of Fouad's beloved uncles refused—and still refuses—to shake Fouad's hand, his attitude reflecting that of a local sheikh, the firebrand Nimr Al-Nimr ("Tiger of the Tigers"), who publicly denounced anyone who would have a hand in surrendering Shia boys into the ungodly clutches of the Sunni legal system. Some of the rapists were related to Fouad's own family, and their wives came to him pleading that he should drop the case.

"My husband has no sin in this," said one in tears. "I give him no blame. He was just invited by a sinful woman."

When the court issued its verdict, the sentences seemed very fair to the many segments of Qateef society who saw Fouad as a troublemaker. But for that very reason Fouad refused to give up.

"I told people, 'The more you push me, the more I shall expand the circle.' "

His nephew Mahdi agreed. The boy was determined to protect his wife from being lashed. Uncle and nephew decided to appeal the court's verdict, turning for reinforcement to the wider Saudi media and to Abdul Rahman Al-Lahem, a controversial young Riyadh lawyer specializing in human rights. Two of King Abdullah's cherished "agencies of civil society" were about to be tested as building blocks of modernity and reform.

"To start with," says Fouad, "I had avoided publicity. I could see that it would upset the judges. But then I got a local journalist friend to write a general sort of article about rape victims and society's response. He didn't mention any names, yet we got more than seven hundred responses, and a lot of them brought up the case. It was clear that people knew about it even though nothing had then been published—and most of them were against the criminals. They wanted the death penalty. So that encouraged me. I decided to widen the thing still further."

In the short term, widening the case seemed to make things worse. In November 2007, three judges of the General Court of Qateef agreed that the original sentences had not been severe enough—on anyone. They increased the sentences on the rapists to terms ranging from two to nine years. But they more than doubled the punishment of their victims, the Qateef girl and Hassan, to two hundred lashes and six months in jail. The judges also confiscated the professional license of her lawyer, Abdul Rahman Al-Lahem, on the grounds that he had tarnished the court's reputation by talking to the press about the case. In a rare public statement, a court official explained that the woman's sentence had been increased because of "her attempt to aggravate and influence the judiciary through the media."

The case of the Qateef girl went international overnight. The U.S. State Department gave its views. So did Hillary Clinton in her presidential primary campaign, and a regiment of columnists in every language. The Qateef judges' attempt to squash one young woman for publicizing her plight had exactly the reverse effect. In Saudi Arabia it became the issue everyone discussed. The idea that the victim was to blame and that she had somehow "invited" rape seemed to sum up the Kingdom's perverse and topsy-turvy code of traditional values. Observers noted how King Abdullah had announced ambitious plans in October to reform the Kingdom's entire legal system, reducing the power of individual clerics. Now it was November, and the clerics had struck back.

"If I had been a judge in Qateef that day," declared Ibrahim bin Salih Al-Khudairi, a judge on the Riyadh Appeals Court, "I would have sentenced all of them to death. The woman and her male companion were lucky not to get the death penalty."

Listening to this sort of assertion in a TV discussion that had turned to debating the subject of the Qateef girl's "honor," Mahdi Al-Mushaikhis decided to put in a call.

"Since all of you are presuming to gossip and pass judgment on my wife's 'honor,'" he said, "I would like to point out that none of you know her. I do. Listen. I am her husband. I am going to tell you the truth."

. . .

The firestorm of publicity got results. In less than a month Abdul Rahman Al-Lahem was given back his license to practice law, and a few weeks later King Abdullah announced pardons for the Qateef girl and Hassan.

"I never had any doubt," says the controversial Al-Lahem—now a liberal, once a Salafi fanatic—"that in the end King Abdullah would put right everything that was wrong with this case."

In his letter announcing the pardons, the king also set up an inquiry into what he called "the dark tunnel of iniquity" surrounding the rapists, their connections to the local police, and the faulty response of the judicial system—an inquiry that has still to report. Police investigations made it clear that the rapists, aged between twenty-six and forty-two, had long-established links with local drug and alcohol dealing. To both liberals and conservatives they represented the unacceptable face of modernization. Off-the-record, people close to the king disclose that Abdullah's personal verdict was uncompromising: The men should all be beheaded.

. . .

So what does it tell us, this slip-sliding Saudi drama of old and new? At the end of a book, people expect some prognosis for the future, and on the subject of Saudi Arabia, the think tanks and foreign-affairs societies can offer statistics and analyses aplenty. I prefer to offer, and have chosen to end with, the messy human story of the Qateef girl, since it defined Saudi Arabia to the world for a moment, and still provides, in my view, the best route into the muddle of tradition and progress that makes up the Kingdom today.

Take your pick as to the story's defining turn. You might select the exhilarating moment when Mahdi, a twenty-six-year-old student of petroleum engineering, picked up the phone to call MBC, the popular satellite broadcasting channel, to speak boldly to millions and to defend the honor of his wife. Here, in Saudi terms, was something very new.

You might select something very old—the interventions by the local prince-governor, Mohammed bin Fahd, and then by his uncle the king, who used their absolute powers to circumvent the established mechanisms of police and the law to secure the outcome that we in the West would certainly define as justice. In other chapters we have seen this arbitrary power deployed to ward off harm to Mansour Al-Nogaidan, the restlessly reflective Salafi, and to protect Mohammed Al-Harbi, the progressive chemistry teacher from Buraydah. So is autocracy the answer to the conundrum? Do we believe that benevolent despotism could or should offer Saudi Arabia the long-term way ahead?

Or you might reflect on the fact that, as this book goes to press, Mahdi is living separately from his Qateef girl, who packed her bags several months after the royal pardon and went back to live with her mother. Mahdi told her she had to leave. All his closest family—brothers and sisters, mother, cousins, and aunts—feel that his world-famous wife has brought unacceptable shame on their clan. The only dissent comes from his liberal and Westernized Uncle Fouad, who is still ostracized by many in the town. Everyone else in the family wants Mahdi to break off his marriage, and as of this writing, the young student, just graduating and starting adult life as a petroleum engineer, is under incredible pressure to act as his family requests. He has done his bit for her, after all—a great deal more than most other Saudi men would have dared. In the family-created, family-dominated Kingdom of Saudi Arabia, the story of the Qateef girl does not have a Western happy ending. By the Saudi rules of the game, it has got to end in divorce.

Epilogue

Shortly before this book was due to go to press, I was traveling by car toward Jeddah's *balad,* the picturesque ancient "downtown" that was forsaken in the oil boom and the rush to the suburbs. Three decades of tumultuous Saudi development have unrolled since I first laid eyes on the old quarter's crumbling array of carved wooden mansions, and I was just reflecting on the conflicting, push-and-pull progression of the Kingdom's life in those years—when I hit the traffic jam. Excited men, largely Pakistanis and Asians, were halting their cars and leaping out toward the sidewalk, abandoning their vehicles, in some cases, where they stood in the street, in order to dash toward an awning in the parking lot of a mosque beside the palm-fringed lagoon. There I could make out security vehicles gathered around a tall white ambulance, where policemen in khaki uniforms kept the all-male crowd at bay. The sun blazed down from almost immediately overhead. My watch said eleven o'clock—the hour when Saudi executions are held.

It was over by the time my car had drawn level with the scene. Saudi executioners pride themselves on performing their duties swiftly and efficiently, with a single wheeling blow from a razor-sharp sword. I could see the headless body still kneeling, bizarrely upright beneath the awning, while the suddenly subdued spectators turned back toward their abandoned cars. Vivid stripes of red blood ran down the brightly laundered white cotton robe in which the condemned man had met his end.

My driver sized up the victim's white costume in a glance.

"Afghan," he said—and drove on.

• • •

Public execution is the dark side of life inside the Kingdom, the medieval spectacle that is both pilloried and fondly gloated over by the Western media. In fact, very few Saudi men (and still fewer Saudi women) have ever witnessed an execution. Public beheadings today are disciplinary displays intended to make a point to the ever-swelling community of migrant workers—some ten million, legal and illegal, in a population of twenty-eight million—and the grim deterrent seems effective. By day or by night, you can walk the streets of any Saudi town without fear of muggers. People leave their cars unlocked. Gun crime against or between locals is virtually nonexistent, and if you raise the issue of capital punishment with Saudis, many will ask why their rate of executions, some seventy-three per year since 1985, according to Amnesty International, makes them so much more barbaric than the United States, where the rate has been forty-two per year over an equivalent period (China, of course, dwarfs both countries in this gruesome respect). With regard to voyeurism, they will point out that every U.S. execution chamber features its own viewing gallery, and that in June 2001 the U.S. government painstakingly assembled no fewer than three hundred people to witness in person, and on closed circuit television, the execution of the Oklahoma City bomber Timothy McVeigh.

They are on less solid ground when it comes to defending their country on questions of torture and detention without trial. Until quite recently the calculated infliction of pain was a tool routinely deployed by the Saudi secret police—in 2002 a group of largely British expatriates, some of them involved in the illegal alcohol trade, were shamefully tortured by the Mabahith when they were falsely accused of bombings that were actually the work of Al-Qaeda. King Abdullah has tried to put a stop to that. His human rights commissions are charged with pursuing all complaints of prisoner abuse—according to recently released detainees the first question in their nightly interrogations has often been "Have you been tortured or threatened today?" This reflects the influence of Prince Mohammed bin Nayef, whose "soft policing" techniques have been praised by foreign security experts. But the fact remains that the Saudi government claims the right to detain its citizens without charge for six months. As this book goes to press in the spring of 2009, there are at least eleven political prisoners, a group of Jeddah liberals and their associates, who have been detained without trial for nearly two years.

When Fouad Al-Farhan drew attention to the plight of these men in his popular Arabic blog, he was arrested himself—on December 10, 2007, International Human Rights Day.

"I came out of a coffee shop," he recalls, "to be surrounded by this group of guys in tracksuits and running shoes—no uniforms in sight. It was all very polite and even respectful in a weird way. No one would have known I was being arrested, unless I chose to make a scene or try to escape—in which case they were dressed to catch me very quickly. They looked like they were a running club who had come to invite me to the gym. They took me home to say good-bye to my wife and family while they rooted round in my books and my PC to get a profile of my politics."

When Al-Farhan told his captors the significance of the date, they thought it was a huge joke.

"Well, come and enjoy the anniversary with us!" said one of them. "We'll bake you a cake in prison!"

The food in the recently completed Mabahith jail north of Jeddah turned out, in fact, to be remarkably good—in line with the rest of the facilities. Al-Farhan was assigned his own air-conditioned cell, about ten by eleven feet, containing his own WC and shower. Prison rumor credited the creature comforts to pressure exerted by Amnesty International and Human Rights Watch in their post-9/11 visits to Saudi Arabia.

"Everything came from America," recalls Al-Farhan. "The handle on the WC was stamped CALIFORNIA. It did not happen with me, but I have heard of political prisoners in Riyadh who would pick up the phone when they received visitors and would order a huge plate of rice and *kharoof* (sheep) to be delivered to their room."

In the middle of this almost surreal material comfort, Al-Farhan discovered there was nothing that he could control for himself.

"I was totally helpless," he recalls. "Like a baby or an invalid. If I wanted the AC up or down, or even the lights on or off, I had to ask on the intercom for the guards to do it for me. I was at their mercy. When I did not cooperate with the questioners once, they just left me in my cell for thirty-two days. I have to say that no one hurt me or threatened me, and that I got my three meals a day. But they played with my mind. I went crazy with fear and self-doubt. I now know that a human being cannot live by himself for very long—I certainly could not. When they did finally call me for questioning again, I was actually grateful."

Fouad's interrogators were concerned that he had a friend—a "mole"—

inside their organization. In the prewritten letter that he had arranged to have posted on his blog if detained, he gave the false impression that he had had advance, inside knowledge of his arrest, and this worried the Mabahith very much.

"Here I am trying to hunt down Al-Qaeda," said Prince Mohammed bin Nayef in the course of one long conversation with the troublesome blogger, "and now I have to search out security leaks among my own men."

Prince Mohammed insists that Al-Farhan was not detained to limit his freedom of expression, but for security reasons. The blogger had been speaking out on behalf of a group of reformers whom the ministry accused of raising funds for anti-American insurgents in Iraq, and, once arrested, his blog was kept going by the exiled Tunisian activist Sami bin Garbiah, who is the scourge of the Tunisian government. Fouad says that these were only pretexts for government unhappiness with his writing, and points to the focus his captors placed on one of his most popular—and notorious—blogs, a list of the ten Saudis that he most disliked and least wished to meet.*

"That is not the Saudi way," his interrogators chided. "Be polite. You should be respectful to others in the community. You were creating discord"—using *fitna,* the shariah law term that denotes disagreement or "division among the people."

Fitna provides the legal justification for the Saudi system of detention without trial. Under shariah law the ruler is responsible for preserving harmony in the community, so if "those that govern" determine that you pose a threat to the security of society or to public order, they are required to detain you for the sake of the community as a whole. It is a divine duty. One American ambassador who was negotiating with Prince Nayef in the 1990s about the detention of a U.S. citizen recalls the normally impassive interior minister throwing his arms into the air to proclaim, "I can do nothing except as God commands!"

*The ten "most hated" included Hashim Yamani, the commerce minister who had told Saudis they were not compelled to eat expensive rice; Saleh Al-Laheedan, the chief justice, who would later call for the death sentence on the owners of satellite TV channels; and Prince Waleed bin Talal, the successful royal businessman whose plans for a kilometer-high skyscraper—potentially the world's tallest building—had pushed up real estate prices in the north Jeddah area, making it impossible for Fouad to buy the house he had wanted there. (In February 2009 Al-Laheedan was dismissed by King Abdullah in the reform reshuffle that saw Norah Al-Faiz appointed Deputy Minister of Education.)

The ambassador's interpreter must have shortened or conflated several things that the prince probably said. The interior minister would have pointed out that the prisoner had been either detained or sentenced according to the law, that the law in Saudi Arabia is the law of God, and that the prince was an instrument of the law. But it comes down to the same thing. If, as a country, you adopt the Koran as your constitution, then all your wars must be holy wars, those who die for their country are all holy martyrs—and the secret police are doing the work of God. Habeus corpus is not a shariah concept.

"They kept telling me they were respecting my rights," recalls Fouad Al-Farhan. "They came to my wife and gave her thirty thousand riyals (about $8,000) to help with her living expenses, and when I came out they gave me forty thousand ($11,500) to compensate me for my loss of business, though I lost ten times that. To get out I had to sign a statement promising to be a good Saudi citizen and not to write online criticizing the Saudi government. They make everyone sign something like that, so if you 'misbehave' again, they can wave it at you, saying that you've let them down. All through my time there they kept reminding me that I had not been physically or mentally abused, and that is true. But what does that mean? The world stopped for me for 137 days. I was not allowed to read any books or newspapers. Months after my release I discovered that Benazir Bhutto had been assassinated. I could never go out once and see the sun. Isn't that mental—and physical—abuse?"

The much-imprisoned reformer Mohammed Saeed Tayeb, who is also campaigning on behalf of his fellow constitutionalists in prison, puts it another way.

"We have never used violence. We have never taken up weapons. The only thing we did was to have a different opinion, and for that we got put in prison."

Saeed Tayeb's prison tally to date is five spells behind bars adding up to more than seven years, and at the age of seventy, he was still banned from leaving the country.

"When we, the constitutional reformers, come out of jail, the government does not give us rewards as they give to those violent terrorists. We are not given a job, or a car, or a new wife—we do not even get the dialogue and discussions that those extremists are granted. The last time I saw Prince Mohammed bin Nayef I said to him, 'I want to be in *their* basket!' He smiled at me. 'No, no, no,' he said. 'That is not your thobe.' He was very friendly. 'I am quite sure things will be all right,' he said. 'Try to be patient. Things will be happening, inshallah.'"

Prince Nayef's son has promised that the Saudi system of travel bans is in the course of revision by the Ministry of the Interior. In the future, he says, bans will only be issued for security reasons that have been certified by a judge—in the middle of March 2009 he phoned Mohammed Saeed Tayeb to tell him that his ban had been lifted: Mohammed was now free to travel.

"Where are you planning to go?" asked a friend of the ancient agitator.

"Anywhere in the world," replied Saeed Tayeb, "so long as there are no reformers there."

FINDING THE RIGHT PATH

A pilgrim was delayed on his journey to Mecca, and when he finally caught up with his companions, he discovered that they had already made their first visit to the Grand Mosque to pray. He found them back at their hotel taking tea together around an open-air table at the edge of the souk.

"It's easy to get there," they said, pointing to the jumble of alleys and shops that made up Mecca's souk in the old days. "Set off in that direction. Turn left at the incense seller, and you're sure to reach the Mosque."

The pilgrim had had a stressful journey. He was eager to pray. He felt he needed to commune with his God. So he set off at once into the colorful maze of little shops, and when he found the incense seller he turned left. But he had only gone a short way down that passageway when he found another incense seller—and another one after that, who was located beside yet another junction. Each time, the pilgrim stopped to ponder the correct route to his destination. Which one should he choose? What if he chose the wrong path, got lost, and missed the cherished spot at which he aimed?

After carefully navigating the twists and turns of the marketplace, the traveler was delighted to find himself at an entrance to the Grand Mosque, where he entered and said his prayers. Returning joyfully to take tea with his friends, he told them of his navigational problems and of his eventual good fortune—to be gently informed that *any* route he might have chosen would have landed him at the huge Mosque. Choose your own incense seller. There are many paths that we can take to reach our God.

. . .

It is early September 2008, and the pilgrims are flying in to Jeddah. Every seat on the plane is occupied, the women wearing black robes and headdresses, the men swathed in white pilgrim towels.

"I am responding to Your call, oh Allah, I am responding to Your call. I am obedient to Your orders. You have no partner . . . "

The men are chanting with their heads bowed—some of them in unison, some of them bent over into their own, intense, privately mouthed prayers. The public-address system crackles: The plane is still thirty thousand feet above the ground, but now, reports the captain, we are about to enter the area of holiness that surrounds Mecca. This is the pilgrims' last chance to wash and to change into their towels. The chanting gets louder; the excitement is mounting—Ramadan is due to start tomorrow.

Most people have heard of the hajj, the annual pilgrimage to Mecca that every Muslim man or woman must try to make at least once in their lives. Less well known is the migration inspired by Ramadan, the holy month of fasting, when the devout travel to spend the whole of that month in Mecca. Every hotel, apartment block, and boarding house in the city is booked, and the Grand Mosque overflows with visitors. Up in Medina the story is the same. A prayer said during Ramadan is worth double the prayer said at any other time, and a prayer said in either of the two holy cities is worth double that. So in terms of storing up credits for heaven, this is bumper bargain time—multiple mileage-point upgrades.

In one sense, Ramadan is all about subduing your appetites. Saudis cherish the tale of the battle of Badr, fought in Ramadan two years after Mohammed's migration to Medina, when a small force of fasting Muslims defeated a much larger army of Meccans who had been fully fed.

"When you can control your hunger, you can control your human desires," says the student Ahmed Sabri. "And when you control yourself, you are strong."

Yet in another sense, Saudi Ramadan is like Carnival—ultimately a riot. The vast majority of the population fasts conscientiously from dawn to dusk, as required, and that is not an easy accomplishment, even if many choose to spend long stretches of the daylight hours asleep. Once the sun has gone down, however . . .

It is day for night. The Saudis celebrate their God, who has given them the strength to fast—no food, no sex, and, most difficult of all, no liquid of any kind for more than twelve hours, not even a sip of water. They celebrate their religion with its complicated array of demands and rewards that, as they know in their hearts, no other religion can rival. But, most important, they celebrate the company of their friends and family. As the moon runs its course, they feast and chat, play games, laugh, joke, and pray, with the prayers getting longer and louder and ever more poetic as the month progresses. It is the "glory time." There are Ramadan gifts, and gaudy Ramadan lights and decorations. The children run around getting far too excited. There is special Ramadan food. Shops overstock. People overeat. Ramadan is the Saudis' monthlong, after-dark Christmas.

The king, the court, and all the government ministers move to Jeddah for the month, doing business for abbreviated hours in the day, then shuttling up and down the highway to Mecca at night. Batches of prisoners get released—those who have not been convicted of drug offenses or crimes of violence. There are no executions. It is the season of "Ramadan breath," since the rules do not permit you—or, more relevantly, others—to suck on a breath freshener to perfume the fumes from an empty stomach. It is also the season of the office party, when filing clerks and sales directors nervously nibble dates together over *iftar,* the sunset breaking of the fast. Without alcohol, the atmosphere of the Saudi office party is emphatically different from that of its ribald Western equivalent: it starts with everyone, from managing director to office boy, forming lines, kneeling down together, and saying their prayers. In Ramadan 2008 the governor of the Mecca region, Prince Khaled Al-Faisal, announced that, for the first time, it would be permissible for female workers to break the fast at such gatherings in the company of their male colleagues.

• • •

Ramadan is the season when the Saudi TV channels stage special editions of their top-rated shows, the most popular of which is *Tash Ma Tash*—literally "Splash, No Splash," or "You either get it or you don't"—an irreverent, satirical mixture of *Little Britain* and *Saturday Night Live.* For Ramadan in 2007 the series opened with its two comic heroes planning to open a new *dish* (satellite) television channel. They hired themselves a couple of busty blondes to present round-the-clock news—and the channel failed. They tried a "love advice" channel, then a music channel, and finally a psychic channel offering help against black magic, dressing the blondes in ever more alluring costumes (while also attempting to seduce the girls themselves). Nothing worked, until they had a brainwave—"Go Islamic." They hid the girls completely behind veils and put on long, Osama-style beards to present a gloomy program called *Repentance*. The advertisers came flocking in.

King Abdullah is said to be *Tash Ma Tash*'s greatest fan—and they need that level of support. From its first broadcast in 1993 the program has provoked the fury of the strictly religious community, earning fatwas as if they were Emmys. In 2000 the permanent committee of the grand ulema itself pronounced condemnation—with its creators, Nasser Al-Qasabi and Abdullah Al-Sadhan, receiving death threats from the terrorist groups whom they frequently lampooned. *Tash Ma Tash* has ridiculed Saudi tribes and tribal customs, bureaucratic delays and corruption, religious extremists, the religious police, greedy investors, wasta (influence and pulling strings), unfaithful Saudi husbands, arrogant Saudis abroad, ignorant Saudi teachers, the ban on women driving and the subjugation of women. One episode imagined a household where the women ruled the roost and the men were kept on their knees doing the housework all day. Fans of the show reckon it has become even more scathing since Ramadan 2006, when it moved from the official government channel to satellite TV in Dubai, and, in 2008, renamed itself *Kullena Eyal Garyah* ("We Are All Village People"). Yet in all its sixteen years on the air, *Tash Ma Tash* has never once made fun of a greedy prince or a pompous government minister.

"Our leaders make mistakes," says Nasser Al-Qasabi, "and we enjoy laughing at the results of those mistakes. But we don't make fun of the leaders personally. That is not the Saudi way."

That is not likely to change anytime soon—but once upon a time it was not the custom for Saudis to sit down in front of the television and laugh at themselves.

. . .

If you switch on the TV just before iftar, the breaking of the fast, you can catch a special Ramadan version of Khaled Bahaziq's popular counseling program, *Yalla Saadah*—"Let's Go for Happiness." The onetime mujahid has adapted his marriage guidance work for television, trying to spread his message about the need for men to behave more gently and sweetly toward their wives.

"Since the men won't come to my therapy sessions," he says, "I am taking the message to them. I hope that just a few of them will listen—though

I fear that it will only be just a few. Women will be driving cars in this country, I believe, long before their men start to change—and it will be from that sort of practical change, inshallah, that some sort of mental change may follow."

Waiting for that long-delayed and deeply symbolic innovation—which, according to ongoing popular rumor, King Abdullah is perennially preparing to make—the pioneer women drivers of the 1990 demonstration gather every year on November 6, the anniversary of their great adventure, to share their memories and look to the future.

"We discuss," says Fawzia Al-Bakr, "what we can do to empower the younger women. Since 9/11 women have the right to work in the private sector, but like any other activity outside the home, they can do it only with the written permission of their mahram [male guardian]."

The problem of the male guardian was one of the issues discussed at the Third National Dialogue, held in Medina in June 2004, which Dr. Al-Bakr attended as a member of the organizing committee. The former political prisoner was invited to help set the agenda and suggest the names of participants. As at the Second Dialogue, the previous year, male and female delegates were kept in separate conference rooms, with women making their contributions to the men's gathering via closed-circuit television.

"We had separate accommodation," she recalls, "and even our own elevator—WOMEN ONLY."

But the segregation fostered unexpected harmony.

"Most of the women delegates were very religious and very conservative," recalls Dr. Al-Bakr. "I was one of the few liberals, and to start with, the atmosphere was definitely prickly. Neither side trusted the other—there was so much hostility. But as we lived together and ate together, we came to see the human side. They were very honorable women, with very fine intellects. I developed great respect for them, and I think they felt the same for me. We became a sort of sisterhood. By the end of the day we were all talking away together, sharing our problems and ideas about our children and our work."

The June 2004 gathering came up with three specific recommendations: that women should be able to work and study without the permission of a mahram; that female-only courts should be established with female judges to adjudicate on women's issues; and that a high-quality national public-transportation system be established for the benefit of all women, and particularly for poorer women and girls who could not afford drivers.

King Abdullah received Dr. Al-Bakr and all the women delegates afterward to thank them publicly for their work and to promise that their proposals would be considered in depth. Four and a half years later, in the spring of A.D. 2009 (A.H. 1430), there is no sign that a single one of the women's recommendations has been seriously studied, let alone acted upon.

. . .

Husayn Shobokshi, the dreamer who wrote of his lawyer daughter driving him home from the airport, is writing his column again and has his talk show back—in a better time slot, with a still larger audience. He is setting up a new twenty-four-hour news and comment TV channel in Jeddah. He has also become a Sufi.

. . .

After months of reconstructive surgery and rehabilitation, Frank Gardner has resumed his work as the BBC's security correspondent, in a wheelchair most of the time. In October 2005 he went to Buckingham Palace to receive the Order of the British Empire from the Queen—standing up and shuffling thirty yards across the ballroom to meet her on crutches.

"How very gallant of you to come like this," said Her Majesty.

. . .

"T-1," Abdul Aziz Al-Tuwayjri, passed away in 2007, aged over ninety, having had the satisfaction of seeing many of his projects come to fruition and to be succeeded as principal royal adviser by his son Khaled. Less gregarious than his father but equally hardworking, Khaled is responsible, among other things, for the running of the new Allegiance Commission, which will choose the next king or crown prince. Once known as "T-4" because of his relatively lowly position in the heirarchy of the Tuwayjri family, Khaled has been promoted. Today he is known as T-1 among the foreigners who seek to make sense of the confusing array of names who cluster around the king.

. . .

The outspoken and reforming Prince Khaled Al-Faisal has been promoted by King Abdullah. He is now governor of Mecca and the Jeddah area, where, in October 2007, he allowed the reinstatement of Ramadan celebrations in the streets. The street vendors and sweets makers could sing their songs—watched for the first time in thirty years by mixed crowds of men and women not segregated into separate sections. Should the nineteen grandsons in the royal family's new council of electors prove brave enough to select one of their own generation for the succession—a very long shot—Khaled is the grandson on whom you might put your money to become crown prince.

His half brother Turki, the former head of Saudi intelligence and short-lived ambassador to Washington, is now directing his family's learned research institute in Riyadh—the Kingdom's leading center for independent scholarly study—and is doing some research of his own into what happened in the Muslim year 1000 (1591–92 in the Christian calendar). He is hoping that the topic might make a book. As the book you're reading goes to press, the prince is a visiting professor of government at Georgetown University in Washington, D.C., a Wahhabi "between quotation marks," as he puts it, lecturing at a school that was founded and is still staffed to some degree by Jesuits.

His brother-in-law Bandar bin Sultan is still national security adviser to his uncle the king, but has not featured in the headlines recently. In October 2007, during a series of state visits to European capitals, King Abdullah settled down to watch the first of a multipart TV series on his life and reign, to discover the voluble Bandar dominating the screen and claiming personal credit for a number of royal policy initiatives—including, crucially, the 2001–2 confrontation that led George W. Bush to endorse the creation of a separate Palestinian state. His Majesty was dismayed. Accounts differ as to what happened next, but the TV series was not seen again—and nor was Prince Bandar when the Saudi party arrived in Rome. His staff explained that the prince had had to leave for a long-delayed shoulder operation in Geneva. As to Bandar's new foreign policy role as national security adviser, one of his aides explained that the prince considers his new responsibilities to be "low profile" and not a matter for discussion in books or newspapers.

• • •

Osama Bin Laden has also been keeping a low profile—hiding somewhere, it is presumed, in the tribal areas of Pakistan, whence reports occasionally emanate of his death. These are examined very seriously by the lawyers of the Bin Laden family, since they are administering his assets and share of the family fortune, confiscated at the time that his brothers renounced him in 1994. When Osama dies, this sum—some seventy million riyals ($20 million) according to a family friend—will be distributed according to Islamic law among his surviving wives and children.

• • •

Mansour Al-Nogaidan resides in Ajman, in the United Arab Emirates, with his wife, who is a doctor, and their two small children. He returns to Buraydah from time to time, but he can no longer find a Saudi newspaper that will publish his work. He has paid a high price for his plain speaking. He is a columnist for the Bahraini paper *Al-Waqt* ("Time"), where he expounds his great hope for the appearance of an Islamic Luther who will reform Islam as Martin Luther reformed Europe's medieval church.

"Muslims are too rigid," he wrote in the summer of 2007, "in our adherence to old, literal interpretations of the Koran. It's time for many verses—especially those having to do with relations between Islam and other religions—to be reinterpreted in favor of a more modern Islam. It's time to accept that God loves the faithful of all religions. It's time for Muslims to question our leaders and their strict teachings, to reach our own understanding of the Prophet's words and to call for a bold renewal of our faith as a faith of goodwill, of peace, and of light. . . . This is the belief I've arrived at after a long and painful spiritual journey."

• • •

There is still no sports or organized physical activity for girls in Saudi state schools. Saudi Arabia did not send a female team to the Beijing Olympics for reasons of "decency"—athletic costume in almost every Olympic contest except shooting is considered too revealing. Women's sports clubs are criticized by traditionalists as "leading to the spread of decadence"—though three of the conservative sheikhs who argued for the ban, Abdul-Rahman Al-Barrak, Abdullah Al-Jibreen, and Abdul Aziz Al-Rajhi, have recently suggested a way by which it would be possible for a woman to take exercise in an Islamic fashion. "A woman can practice sports at home," they said, "and there are many ways to do that: she can, for example, race her husband in a deserted area, like the Prophet Mohammed—peace be upon Him—who raced with his wife Aisha twice."

• • •

The Mabahith continue their work as the social control system, the Ministry of the Interior's own private monitoring service on dissent and the national mood. It released Fouad Al-Farhan from jail after 137 days, but, at the time of this writing, seven of the dissidents on whose behalf he protested remain behind bars. By Western standards this is deplorable. By Saudi standards it is an improvement on Fawzia Al-Bakr's 1980s experience of disappearance without a trace. Today the Mabahith operate according to defined protocols—the spouses and families of those detained, for example, must be notified within twenty-four hours—and their work is the subject of increased public comment.

Even more scrutinized are the activities of the religious police. In late 2008 a number of religious policemen were awaiting trial on charges that ranged from harassment to the unlawful killing of a suspect taken into custody—though no one reckoned that the religious courts would treat them with the harshness that secular folk felt they deserved. At the heart of the Saudi state lies the bargain between the religious and the royals, and though the misalignments in that delicate balance have inspired the problems of the past thirty years—inside the Kingdom and beyond—that fundamental deal is also the reason why the royal family has weathered the storm. Looking ahead and wondering what might assist the cohesion of this complicated society as it rattles into the twenty-first century, it would seem unwise to abandon the grounding of religion.

• • •

Among the Shia in the east the steps to reform continue, albeit at pigeon-step pace. Tawfiq Al-Seif is working with Jaffar Shayeb and Sheikh Hassan Al-Saffar for Saudi Arabia to adopt more flexible interpretations of the Koran—what Muslims call *tafsir*.

"There is a verse in the Koran that says that in order to be strong in war against your enemies you have to prepare 'swords and horses,'" says Tawfiq. "Well, if you take that literally nowadays and go into battle with swords and horses you will find yourself hopelessly *weak* against your enemies. So here is a case where everyone would agree that you have to reinterpret what the Prophet said. Literalism can only represent the outside of things, and in the last thirty years it has taken us badly off the path. We must search for the value that lies *inside* the words. What the pious Muslim—Sunni or Shia—should be asking himself today is not what the Prophet did then, but what he *would* do now if he were confronted by the realities of modern life."

. . .

Ahmad Al-Tuwayjri, one of the framers of the 1992 Memorandum of Advice, believes it is very possible for Wahhabism to reform itself and lead the way in new directions.

"In the beginning," he says, "Wahhabism was an extremely progressive, reformation movement that shook up a world of superstition and blind imitation. Mohammed Ibn Abdul Wahhab tried to correct the fundamentals in a way that was dynamic and modern for its time. It is only in the twentieth century that the dawah wahhabiya [Wahhabi mission] became identified with those who pull backward and refuse to change."

The man who spent forty days in prison after he presented the Memorandum of Advice in 1992 now has a successful law practice in the Saudi courts and is working with activists from other countries to create a World Forum for Peace.

"People talk as if there are only two ways for us in the Kingdom," says Al-Tuwayjri, "to imitate the West slavishly or to preserve everything and resist any change. But there is a third way, the way of *ijtihad*—to find out and follow the truth. If our Muslim scholars do not lead the way and have the courage to change, they will be left behind and Islam will pay a heavy price. Our current king, Abdullah, is a good man. We know that he is reform-minded. But as of 2008, I have to say that the political institutions are evolving too slowly."

. . .

Abdullah bin Abdul Aziz thinks the same—at eighty-six, he is an old man in a hurry. For more than thirty years his most cherished ambition has been the creation of an internationally prestigious college that will bear his name, the King Abdullah University for Science and Technology (KAUST), a graduate-only, Arabian equivalent of the Massachusetts Institute of Technology. The world's leading scientists and scholars will gather and mingle freely on its campus, dreams the king—men and women, East and West, all united in their pursuit of learning.

The inspiration for Abdullah's romantic ambition is the Bayt Al-Hekma, the House of Knowledge, which flourished in Baghdad between the ninth and thirteenth centuries as the center of study in the Muslim world—in the entire Western world, in fact. It was the Bayt Al-Hekma that kept civilization alive as Europe endured the travails of the Dark Ages. Mathematics, astronomy, medicine, chemistry, geography, zoology, and philosophy all survived and thrived in these centuries thanks to the Arab House of Knowledge: from its Kitab Al-Jabr (Book of Equations) came the study of what we call algebra. The ideas of Galen, Pythagoras, Plato, Aristotle, Euclid, and Hippocrates were researched, preserved, and embellished by the Bayt Al-Hekma, so it was Muslim scholars who passed on the raw material that inspired Europe's intellectual rebirth at the end of the Middle Ages. Without the Arab House of Knowledge there could have been no Thomas Aquinas, no Bacon or Galileo.

This is the early Islam to which modern Muslims should look back and aspire, thinks King Abdullah—to an age that was characterized by tolerance and the pursuit of knowledge. The scholars of the Bayt Al-Hekma followed inquiry wherever it led, opening their minds to new ideas. To understand the miracle of God's universe is to understand God's handiwork, they believed, and following in the tradition of that big idea, KAUST aims higher than the processing of international graduate students. The university represents the king's considered response to the joyless and totalitarian aspects of Salafism—the starting point, he hopes, of a trickle-down change of educational attitudes that will eventually illuminate every madrasa in the land.

In the spring of 2007, Abdullah offered the state oil company, Aramco, almost any sum they needed to pick up his project and make it happen. KAUST already has a $10 billion endowment to match that of MIT, and is heading for $25 billion, according to the *Financial Times,* which would place its wealth in the world second only to that of Harvard. In the king's view Aramco has always been the most efficiently managed Saudi enterprise in or out of government, light-years ahead of the tradition-bound Ministry of Higher Education. Abdullah had originally intended that the campus be located on the cool, green plateau of Taif, above Mecca, but was persuaded to shift it to the site of the proposed new economic city that bears his name on the Red Sea coast. His one proviso was that he wanted to see the students and professors at work on the campus in two years' time—September 2009.

A few months later the king decided he would like to inspect the progress of his university, so he called up the royal bus, his preferred manner of transport. It is a nightmare for his security detail. A bus makes a very large target. But the king enjoys the laughter and camaraderie of bus travel. There are jokes and songs when you travel on King Abdullah's bus, and, high above the road, you also get a very good view.

The bus rattled up the coastal highway from the royal palace in Jeddah, drawing to a halt outside the new King Abdullah Economic City a hundred miles away.

"Where's the university?" asked the king, getting down from the bus.

When he discovered that this was a preliminary, courtesy stop at his new economic city, he got straight back on the bus, leaving a bewildered reception committee in the dust. He had come to see where his students would study, and when he reached the correct site, to discover nothing much more than palm trees and sand, he was not pleased. He pretended to show an interest in the plans and projections hurriedly unrolled for him, but his family could see that he was both angry and depressed.

It was not a jolly bus ride back down the coast to Jeddah, and when the bus stopped, the king went straight out to the beach to say his sunset prayer—seated, since Abdullah has some difficulty kneeling these days. Muslims who suffer from disability are permitted to pray seated—or, indeed, to pray lying in bed if they are completely incapacitated.

It was a poignant sight, the king dressed in white, sitting in his chair quite alone on the beach, praying earnestly toward Mecca. He was holding his hands up, cupped before his face, imploring his God. His family said they had never seen him look sadder—so much to do, so little time in which to do it.

That evening, the king stayed longer at his prayers.

TIME LINE

1744 Founding of the first Saudi state, in Dariyah, Nejd, Central Arabia
1803 Saudi armies conquer Mecca
1818 Turkish cannons flatten Dariyah
1824 Beginning of the second Saudi state
1891 Second Saudi state falls to the Rasheed family of Hail
1902 Abdul Aziz (aged around twenty-five) captures Riyadh to become sultan of Nejd
1913 Abdul Aziz annexes Qateef and Al-Hasa in the east
1921 Abdul Aziz conquers Hail, seat of the Rasheeds
1926 Abdul Aziz enters Jeddah to become king of the Hijaz and sultan of Nejd
1929 Battle of Sibillah. Abdul Aziz defeats rebel Ikhwan
1932 Proclamation of the Kingdom of Saudi Arabia
1933 Oil prospecting begins in the Eastern Province
1938 First significant oil "strike" at well number seven, Dhahran
1945 Abdul Aziz meets U.S. President Roosevelt on the Great Bitter Lake, Egypt
1953 Death of King Abdul Aziz. Accession of King Saud bin Abdul Aziz
1964 Faisal bin Abdul Aziz replaces his brother Saud as king
1965 The creation of Medina's Salafi Group, Al-Jamaa Al-Salafiya Al-Muhtasiba
1973 King Faisal announces a boycott on oil sales to the United States
1975 Faisal assassinated. Khaled bin Abdul Aziz becomes king
1979 Iranian Revolution. Shah deposed
Juhayman seizes Mecca's Grand Mosque
Intifada uprising by Shia protesters in the Eastern Province
The Soviet Union invades Afghanistan
1980 Saddam Hussein invades Iran, starting the Iran-Iraq War of 1980–88
1982 Death of King Khaled. Fahd bin Abdul Aziz becomes king
1983 Bandar bin Sultan appointed ambassador to Washington
1984 Mohammed bin Fahd becomes governor of the Eastern Province
1985 Sultan bin Salman orbits earth in NASA *Discovery* flight
1986 Oil Minister Ahmad Zaki Yamani dismissed
1987 402 pilgrims die following Iranian political demonstration in Mecca
1988 Osama Bin Laden and "Arab Afghans" active in Afghanistan
1989 Last Soviet soldiers leave Afghanistan
1990 Saddam Hussein invades Kuwait
Women's driving demonstration in Riyadh
1991 Gulf War. Iraqi forces ousted from Kuwait. Battle of Al-Khafji
1992 Following reform petitions, King Fahd establishes the Majlis Al-Shura
1993 Osama Bin Laden active in Sudan
1994 Bin Laden stripped of Saudi citizenship
1995 National Guard Center bombed in Riyadh
King Fahd suffers stroke. Crown Prince Abdullah assumes more power
1996 Al-Khobar Towers building bombed in Eastern Province

1998 Al-Qaeda bombs U.S. embassies in Nairobi and Dar es Salaam, East Africa
Taliban refuse to surrender Osama Bin Laden to Saudi Arabia
2000 Al-Qaeda bombs USS *Cole* in Aden
2001 Al-Qaeda 9/11 attacks on World Trade Center and Pentagon
2002 Fire in Mecca girls' school kills fifteen
Abdullah Peace Plan offers Arab recognition to Israel
2003 Al-Qaeda attacks in Riyadh. BBC cameraman Simon Cumbers killed
Crown Prince Abdullah initiates first National Dialogue
2004 Third National Dialogue addresses women's issues
2005 Death of King Fahd. Accession of Abdullah bin Abdul Aziz
Bandar bin Sultan resigns as Saudi ambassador in Washington
King Abdullah sets up domestic Human Rights Commissions
2006 King Abdullah visits Beijing
2007 Founding session of Allegiance Council to decide future succession
"Qateef girl" rape case
2008 King Abdullah initiates interfaith dialogue in Madrid, then New York
Oil price falls from $147 per barrel in July to $40 in December
2009 King Abdullah removes conservative religious figures from his government
Norah Al-Faiz named deputy minister of education
Prince Nayef bin Abdul Aziz named second deputy premier

GLOSSARY OF NAMES AND ARABIC TERMS

All characters are listed here by their first names. When searching for a word, please ignore *Al-*, the definite article. Rendering Arabic words and phrases into their precise English phonetic equivalents, complete with accents, gaps, and symbols, is an exercise of great complexity—and not a little snobbery in a book for the general reader. The results are also confusing, since *Q'run, badawin,* or *Ramzan* do not correspond to the spellings most people recognize.

Unless you are a devotee of a particular system, you can, in fact, spell Arabic words just the way they sound to you—*Abdullah, Abdallah, Abd'Allah.* T. E. Lawrence certainly did so in *Seven Pillars of Wisdom,* even changing spellings as he went along, writing *Jeddah* or *Jiddah* as the mood took him, and declining his publisher's attempts to impose uniformity. He was, in fact, quite restrained, since modern transliterations of that city's name have included *Jaddah, Jedda, Jidda, Judda, Juddah, Djiddah, Djuddah, Djouddah, Gedda, Djettah,* and *Dscheddah,* to name only some—and all are acceptable.

The general rule I have adopted in this book, as in *The Kingdom,* is that Arabic words and names are rendered here whenever possible in the spellings that Western readers will most easily recognize—Koran, bedouin, Ramadan. The transliterations do not take account of the difference between Arabic's "sun" and "moon" letters, so the definite article is invariably spelled *Al-,* whether or not it elides. *Bin* and *ibn,* meaning "son of," are used interchangeably.

abaya—black, full-length outer gown worn in public by Saudi women—and, today, by most expatriate women.

Abdul Aziz bin Abdul Rahman Al-Saud (1876–1953)—creator of modern Saudi Arabia, often known as "Ibn Saud" (Son of Saud). Father of the brothers and half brothers who have ruled the Kingdom since his death (see the family tree, page xxiv).

Abdul Aziz Al-Muqrin—leader of Al-Qaeda inside Saudi Arabia during the 2003 attacks.

Abdul Aziz Al-Tuwayjri—known as "T-1." Died June 2007. Historian and principal adviser to Abdullah bin Abdul Aziz as crown prince.

Abdul Aziz Bin Baz (1912–1999)—mufti (chief religious sheikh) and principal religious adviser to Saudi kings. Blind from a young age. Notorious for reputedly asserting that the earth is flat.

Abdullah Azzam—Palestinian scholar and jihadi who mentored Osama Bin Laden in Afghanistan.

Abdullah bin Abdul Aziz (b. 1923)—crown prince of Saudi Arabia 1982–2005, and king since August 2005. Head of the National Guard since 1962.

Abdul Rahman Al-Lahem—human-rights lawyer. Imprisoned 2005–6. Defender of the "Qateef girl."

abu—"father of," as in "Abu Abdullah," the father of Abdullah.

agal—double black rope ring, worn on top of the traditional cotton headdress, the *shomagh,* by Saudi men and other Arabs of the Gulf states.

Ahmad Al-Tuwayjri—lawyer and petitioner for constitutional rights.
Ahmed Badeeb—assistant to Turki Al-Faisal in the Istikhbarat (foreign intelligence).
Ahmad Zaki Yamani—long-serving Saudi oil minister (1962–86)
Aisha Al-Mana—women's rights campaigner. Helped organize the women's driving demonstration in Riyadh in October 1990.
Al-hamdu lillah!—"Thanks be to God!" An all-purpose exclamation that extends from greeting safe delivery in childbirth to "(May God) bless you!" following a sneeze.
Ali Al-Marzouq—Shia-rights activist who went into exile. Now returned.
Allahu Akbar!—"God is the greatest!"
anno hegirae—year of the Hijrah (the migration by the Prophet Mohammed to Medina, the starting point of the Islamic calendar). Hijrah years are made up of twelve lunar months, about 354 days. See *Hijrah* below.
Al-Asheikh—family name borne by the descendants of Mohammed Ibn Abdul Wahhab, literally "the family of the sheikh."
Ashura—"the tenth" of Muharram, the first month of the Muslim year, an annual period of mourning among the Shia to commemorate the slaying of Husayn bin Ali, the grandson of the Prophet, by Sunni forces in Karbala, Iraq, in A.H. 61 (A.D. 680).
Asir—southern Saudi province on the border with Yemen. Home to Ismaili Shia, Sufis, gunrunners from Yemen—and four of the 9/11 hijackers.
Assalaamu alaykum—"Peace be upon you!" A greeting often shortened to *"Salaam!"*

balad—"downtown." Used in Jeddah to describe the old quarter of narrow alleys and coral-rock homes remaining from the walled city of pre–oil boom days.
bedu—or bedouin, from the Arabic *badawi*—desert-dwelling Arab nomads.
Bandar bin Sultan—Saudi ambassador to the United States 1983–2005. Now secretary-general of the Saudi National Security Council.
bin or ibn—"son of."
bint—"daughter of."
bidah—innovation (plural *bidaa*).
Buraydah—a town in Qaseem that prides itself on its religious purity.

Caliph—literally "successor," from *kalifah,* the title bestowed on leaders of the Muslim community in the years after the Prophet's death.

dawah wahhabiya—Wahhabi mission

Eid Al-Adha—one of the two Muslim holidays, the day of sacrifice, marking the end of the annual pilgrimage.
Eid Al-Fitr—the other Muslim holiday, the breaking of the fast at the end of Ramadan.

Fahd bin Abdul Aziz (1922–2005)—crown prince 1975–1982. King of Saudi Arabia 1982–2005. Eldest of the brothers known as the Sudayri Seven.
Faisal bin Abdul Aziz (1904–1975)—king of Saudi Arabia 1964–1975. Assassinated by his nephew Faisal bin Musaed, who was declared insane and beheaded in Riyadh.
Fajr—The predawn Islamic prayer.
al-faseqoon (subject), *al-faseqeen* (object)—"those who are immoral."
fatwa—a judgment issued by an Islamic scholar.
Fawzia Al-Bakr—an academic and women's rights campaigner. Imprisoned in 1982.
fitna—strong disagreement leading to conflict.

Fouad Al-Farhan—Jeddah blogger jailed in December 2007 for 137 days.
Fouad Al-Mushaikhis—uncle of Mahdi, the husband of the Qateef girl.
Frank Gardner—BBC journalist shot in Riyadh, June 2004.

Hadith—sayings and acts of the Prophet that have been collected and serve as a guide to Islamic belief and practice alongside the direct revelation of the Koran.
Al-Haier prison—Interior Ministry prison in the south of Riyadh.
Hail—town in northern Arabia that was formerly the headquarters of the Al-Saud's rivals the Al-Rasheed family.
hajj—the pilgrimage, one of the five "pillars" of Islam. All Muslims are required to make their *hajj* to the holy city of Mecca at least once in their lives, if they can afford it.
Al-Hamra (the Red One)—upscale residential neighborhoods in Riyadh, Jeddah, and other Arab cities, named after the red Alhambra citadel of Moorish Grenada in Spain.
Al-Haraka Al-Wataniya—the National Movement, a group of Saudi liberals who were campaigning for reforms in the late 1970s and early '80s.
Haramain—the two holy places, the grand mosques of Mecca and Medina.
haram (pronounced with a short "a")—a holy place.
haram (pronounced with an extended "a")—forbidden.
Al-Hasa (Al-Ahsa)—historical name of the Eastern Province home to most of the Shia in Saudi Arabia and to the world's largest palm tree oasis. Beneath Al-Hasa lies the world's largest oil field, Ghawar, from which has come for more than five decades over half of Saudi Arabia's oil production, some 8 to 9 million barrels per day in 2008–9.
Hassan Al-Banna—Egyptian founder of the Muslim Brotherhood, assassinated in 1949.
Hassan Al-Saffar—Shia spiritual leader in exile 1980–93, now back in Qateef.
Al-Hayah—the Commission (for the Promotion of Virtue and the Prevention of Vice), known to Westerners as the religious police.
Al-Hijaz—the western region of Arabia along the Red Sea coast, containing the cities of Mecca, Medina, Taif, and Jeddah; an independent kingdom ruled by the Hashemite family until its conquest by Abdul Aziz in 1926.
Hijrah—the migration. The turning point in the birth of Islam when the Prophet Mohammed left Mecca in A.D. 622 and migrated to the community that would become known as Medina, starting point of the Islamic calendar. See *anno hegirae.*
hilal—new moon, crescent moon.
hisbah—to promote good and discourage evil.
husayniya—Shia meeting room (named for Husayn bin Ali, the martyr of Karbala).

ibn or *bin*—"son of."
Ibn Nimr—"Son of the Tiger," a Wahhabi preacher in Riyadh in the 1930s.
iftar—breaking of the fast at sunset, during Ramadan.
ijtihad—independent judgment, meaning literally to struggle with oneself using reason, logic, and deep thought. In law *ijtihad* is a method of legal reasoning that does not rely on the traditional schools of jurisprudence.
Ikhwan—Brethren or Brotherhood, the name given to the settled bedouin who fought alongside Abdul Aziz from around 1912 until 1926 in his conquest of Arabia.
Al-Ikhwan Al-Muslimoon—Muslim Brotherhood, the austere and sometimes violent Islamic opposition movement active in many Arab countries, particularly in Egypt, where the Brotherhood was founded in 1928 by Hassan Al-Banna.
imam—the righteous religious leader of a community. A religious teacher who calls for prayers and leads his congregation.

inshallah—"God willing."
intifada—uprising.
Al-Islahiyoon (subject), *Al-Islahiyeen* (object)—"the Reformists."
isterham—a plea for mercy.
istikhara—the Muslim prayer for guidance, a brief recitation which can be repeated as many times as needed.
Istikhbarat—Saudi foreign intelligence, or GID, the General Intelligence Department.

Jaffar Al-Shayeb—Shia activist formerly in exile, now returned to Saudi Arabia. Elected a municipal councillor in Qateef in 2005.
Al-Jamaa Al-Salafiya Al-Muhtasiba—The Salafi Group That Commands Right and Forbids Wrong, spiritual inspiration of Juhayman Al-Otaybi.
Al-Jazeera—Island (of the Arabs), the poetic name given to the Arabian Peninsula, which is surrounded by the Red Sea to the west, the Arabian Sea to the south, the Persian (or Arabian) Gulf to the east, and the Syrian desert to the north. The name *Al-Jazeera* has been adopted in current times by a daily newspaper in Riyadh, by an airline in Kuwait, and by the TV news station based in Qatar.
jihad—holy war. From which comes *jihadi,* holy warrior.
Juhayman Al-Otaybi—leader of the religious zealots who captured the Grand Mosque in November 1979. Executed January 1980.

Kaaba—the cubelike building in the center of the courtyard of the Grand Mosque in Mecca, traditionally covered in gold-embroidered black cloth. Believed by Muslims to date back to the time of Abraham, the Kaaba is the most sacred site in Islam. At the time of the Prophet, the Kaaba was home to more than three hundred idols, which Mohammed removed and destroyed.
kabsa—the Saudi national dish of lamb and rice.
kafir (singular), *kuffar* (plural)—"infidel," from the noun *kufr,* "blasphemy."
Kandahar—second largest city in Afghanistan.
Khadem Al-Haramain Al-Shareefain—Servant or Custodian of the Two Holy Mosques, the title borne by Saudi kings since 1985.
Al-Khafji—a town on the Saudi-Kuwaiti border, briefly captured by Iraq in 1991.
Khaled Al-Faisal—poet and painter. Former governor of Asir Province. Today governor of Mecca. Son of King Faisal and elder half brother to Saud and Turki Al-Faisal.
Khaled Bahaziq—marriage counselor. Former jihadi and steel salesman.
Khaled bin Abdul Aziz (1912–82)—fourth modern Saudi monarch (1975–1982) in succession to his father Abdul Aziz and his half brothers Saud and Faisal.
Khaled bin Sultan—son of Sultan bin Abdul Aziz. Saudi Joint Forces commander during the Gulf War 1990–91. Now assistant minister, and effectively acting minister, to his father the crown prince, and minister of defense and aviation.
Khaled Al-Hubayshi—a jihadi who was imprisoned in Guatánamo Bay.
khalawi—prayer and meditation rooms beneath the Grand Mosque in Mecca.
khawajah—colloquial term for Christian Westerner formerly applied to the landed gentry of Egypt and the Sudan.
khawarij—"those who come out and depart," splinter movements from mainstream Islam over the centuries, sometime violent.
Al-Khidr—"the Green One," a legendary Islamic figure sometimes confused with the Mahdi.
Khitab Al-Matalib—"Letter of Demands," a reform petition circulated by activists in 1992.

Al-Khobar—a city in the Eastern Province of Saudi Arabia, adjacent to Dammam.
Khorassan—Afghan-based empire of the Prophet's time.
Koran (Qur'an)—Islam's central text, the divine revelation to the Prophet Mohammed.

Mabahith—secret police, a department of the Ministry of the Interior. Literally "investigations," "investigators," or "the detectives."
Madinah—officially decreed Saudi spelling of "Medina" in English.
madrasa—a religious school.
Mahdi—a prophesied Islamic redeemer described in some Islamic traditions, but not mentioned in the Koran.
Mahdi—fiancé of the Qateef girl.
mahram—a male guardian.
Majlis—"the place of sitting." The main reception hall in a Saudi home—usually two: one for men and one for women.
Majlis Al-Shura—Consultative Council of 150 "learned and experienced" male citizens appointed by the king.
Makkah—official Saudi spelling of "Mecca" in English—said to have been first decreed to set the name of the holy city apart from the British chain of Mecca dance halls.
Maktab Al-Khadamat—Office of Services, a relief and recruitment network financed by Osama Bin Laden to support his 1980s Afghan campaign against the Russians.
Mansour Al-Nogaidan—writer. Former Salafi preacher and video-store bomber.
"Mashael"—pseudonym for the former lesbian featured in chapter 29.
milka—the plighting of the troth that allows Muslim couples to have private time for sexual relations if their families agree. More serious than a Western engagement, slightly less than full marriage.
Mohammed Abdullah Al-Qahtani—the "Mahdi," proclaimed by his brother-in-law Juhayman Al-Otaybi. Killed in the siege of the Great Mosque, November 1979.
Dr. Mohammed Al-Qunaybit—Shura member and newspaper columnist.
Mohammed Ibn Abdul Wahhab—eighteenth-century scholar, born in Nejd around 1703, whose puritannical teachings were championed by the House of Saud and form the basis of the austere interpretation of Islam known in the West as Wahhabism. His descendants, who bear the name Al-Asheikh, literally "Family of the Sheikh," occupy many of the prominent religious positions in modern Saudi Arabia.
Mohammed Bin Laden—Yemeni-born builder-by-appointment to successive Saudi kings and remodeler of the Grand Mosque in Mecca. Founder of the Bin Laden construction company. Father to Osama Bin Laden and some fifty other children.
Mohammed bin Fahd—businessman son of King Fahd. Governor of the Eastern Province since 1984.
Mohammed bin Nayef—assistant to his father, the minister of the interior, and himself director of the ministry's Terrorist Redemption Program.
Mohammed Saeed Tayeb—Jeddah lawyer and constitutional reformer.
mufti—an Islamic scholar who is an interpreter of shariah law. The "grand mufti" is the supreme religious figure in Saudi Arabia.
mujahid (plural subject *mujahidoon,* plural object *mujahideen*)—holy warrior; a Muslim serving in a military force led by an imam to defend Muslim communities.
Mullah Omar—Afghan Taliban leader.
murshid—spiritual mentor.
Al-Muslimoon—"The Muslims," the name of a magazine whose title can be rendered into English as *Muslim World.*

mutawwa—a volunteer, or enforcer of virtue. The Saudi name for members of the religious police, "those who promote virtue and prevent vice."

Mudhakkarat Al-Nasiha—"Memorandum of Advice," a 1992 reform petition.

muwahiddoon (subject), *muwahiddeen* (object)—monotheists, the name favored by Wahhabis for their interpretation of Islam, sometimes rendered into English as "Unitarian."

National Guard—tribally based domestic defense force under the command of Abdullah bin Abdul Aziz since 1962. Also known as the "White Army."

Nayef bin Abdul Aziz (b. 1934)—minister of the interior from 1975 to the present. Named second deputy premier in March 2009 and hence a possible future king.

Nejd—"Highland"; the central plateau of the Arabian Peninsula, regional power base of the House of Saud.

niqab—a veil that covers the face.

Osama Bin Laden (b. 1958)—founder of Al-Qaeda, inspirer of 9/11. Son of construction magnate Mohammed Bin Laden.

Pashtu—Language of the forty million or so Pashtun people of southern Afghanistan and northwestern Pakistan.

Peshawar—town in northern Pakistan, close to the border with Afghanistan.

qadi—Islamic judge.

Al-Qaeda—Osama Bin Laden's terrorist organization, founded in the late 1980s. *Qaeda* means "foundation" or "basis"—"the rule" even—and can also refer to a military base or database.

Qaseem—the area of Nejd to the north of Riyadh, containing the towns of Unayzah and Buraydah, often described as the heartland of Wahhabism.

"Qateef girl'—Rape victim sentenced to ninety lashes by an Islamic court in Qateef in October 2006. Pardoned in December 2007 by King Abdullah.

qibla—the direction of Mecca: a Muslim should face this way during prayer.

rafada—"rejectionists," a term used by Sunni Muslims to characterize Shia rejection of the early line of succession in Islamic leadership.

Ramadan—the Islamic holy month of fasting (the ninth Islamic month of the year).

Saddam Hussein—president of Iraq 1979–2003.

Safa-Marwah corridor—once a separate site, this 490-yard-long gallery has now been incorporated into the Grand Mosque in Mecca. Pilgrims move to and fro along the corridor, replicating the Koranic story of how Abraham's wife Hagar ran desperately between the hills of Safa and Marwah looking for water for her son Ishmael.

Safar Al-Hawali—a Sahwah sheikh who called for Islamic revival in the 1990s and was imprisoned. Now released.

Sahwah—"Awakening," the name embracing the various Islamic revival movements originating in the 1980s and 1990s.

sakina—"serenity," a state of spiritual calm.

Salafi—a Muslim seeking to live in the style of a *salaf,* one of the seventh-century Companions of the Prophet Mohammed.

Salman Al-Awdah—Sahwah sheikh who was imprisoned following his outspoken calls for Islamic revival in the 1990s. Today the host of a popular TV show.

Salman bin Abdul Aziz (b. 1936)—governor of Riyadh since 1962.

Al-Saud—the House of Saud. Eighteenth-century rulers of Dariyah in central Nejd who enlisted the austere teachings of the preacher Mohammed Ibn Abdul Wahhab to create a succession of three Saudi states, the latest of which became the Kingdom of Saudi Arabia in 1932. There is a definitive list of members of the royal family at the royal court and also in the branch of the Riyadh Bank that pays their monthly stipends, but this is treated as a state secret, concealed from most members of the family. Those Al-Saud who are willing to discuss the matter—and most are—set their number today at around seven thousand princes and princesses.

Saud Al-Faisal—foreign minister since 1975. Son of King Faisal's reforming wife Queen Iffat and full brother of Turki Al-Faisal.

Saud bin Abdul Aziz (1902–69)—second modern Saudi monarch (1953–64), forced to relinquish the throne in favor of his half brother Faisal.

Sayyid Qutub—Egyptian author of *Milestones,* one of the guiding works of the Muslim Brotherhood. Executed by the Nasser regime in 1966.

shaheed—"martyr" who sacrifices their life for God and goes straight to heaven.

Shareef—successor of the Prophet, the title employed by the Hashemite family when they were kings of Al-Hijaz.

shariah—meaning "way" or "path to the water source." Islamic law.

shaytan—devil or Satan.

Shia—Muslims who assign special importance to Ali, the cousin and son-in-law of the Prophet. *Shiat Ali* means the party of Ali. The Shia, or Shiites, make up the majority of Muslims in Iran, Iraq, and in certain areas in the Eastern Province of Saudi Arabia, Bahrain, Lebanon, Morocco, Pakistan, and Yemen.

shirk—polytheism.

shomagh—commonly a red and white checkered cloth headdress, worn beneath the double black rope rings of the agal. An all-white cloth *ghutra* is a more formal indoor headdress.

Al-Shumaysi—a pious neighborhood of Riyadh. Home to Abdul Aziz Bin Baz.

Sibillah—the battle, north of Riyadh, in which Abdul Aziz defeated the rebel members of the Ikhwan in March 1929.

souk—market.

Sudayri Seven—the seven sons of Abdul Aziz by Hissa Al-Sudayri, making up the most significant power bloc in the Saudi royal family: Fahd, Sultan, Abdul Rahman, Turki, Nayef, Salman, and Ahmad bin Abdul Aziz (see family tree, page xxiv).

Sultan bin Salman—born 1956, the son of the governor of Riyadh. The first Arab and first Muslim to fly in space, orbiting the earth in June 1985. Today secretary general of the Saudi Commission for Tourism and Antiquities.

sunna—words, actions, and example of the Prophet.

Sunni—the largest denomination of Islam: those who follow the *sunna* of the Prophet.

Al-Suwaydi—the Riyadh neighborhood where Frank Gardner was shot.

taahud—"pledge" or "promise."

tafsir—commentary on the Koran.

tahliah—"to sweeten," the name given to principal shopping streets in Jeddah and Riyadh that are near the local desalination plants or terminals.

takfeer—religious condemnation.

Talal bin Abdul Aziz—maverick prince who served as communications minister and finance minister, before going into exile 1961–64 with a group of his brothers, the "Free Princes." Later a special envoy to UNESCO.

talib, plural *taliban*—pupil, student. These Afghan-Persian words derive from the Arabic word *talib ilm,* someone who wishes to be educated.

tal omrak—an abbreviation of *tal allah omrak,* "May God lengthen your life," a greeting of respect to elders, often used to royalty.

taqiya—discretion or cautionary dissimulation, a tradition by which Shia Muslims may conceal their faith if under threat or persecution.

Tawfiq Al-Seif—Shia spokesman who helped negotiate the return from exile in 1993.

Turki Al-Faisal—son of King Faisal. Head of Saudi foreign intelligence 1977–2000, later Saudi ambassador to Britain and to the United States.

thobe—the long, white, shoulder-to-ankle cotton garment worn by most Saudi males. Also spelled *thawb.*

ulema—"those who possess knowledge'—plural of *alim,* a learned man. The supreme council of Islamic scholars entitled to make definitive interpretations of the Koran, hadiths, and shariah.

umm—mother, or "mother of," as in "Umm Abdullah," the mother of Abdullah.

umma—the Islamic community.

umrah—the minor or lesser pilgrimage that a Muslim can undertake at any time.

Unayzah—a pious and traditional town in Qaseem.

Wahhabism—Western name given to the austere interpretation of the Islamic faith enunciated by Mohammed Ibn Abdul Wahhab in eighteenth-century Nejd, championed by the House of Saud and prevailing today in Saudi Arabia.

wali al-amr, plural *awaliyn al-amr*—responsible person, from a father to a mayor, governor, tribal chief or king. The authorized leader of a community or family.

Wallah! ("By God!") and *Wallahi!* ("By my God!")—common exclamations.

wasta—string-pulling and influence.

White Army—nickname of the National Guard, derived from its original white thobe uniform.

Al-Yamamah—"The Dove," an historic name for part of the plateau of Nejd, and the name given to the lucrative and controversial 1985 contract whereby Britain supplied Tornado fighters and other military equipment to Saudi Arabia for more than twenty years.

Yasser Arafat—Palestinian leader. Nobel Peace Laureate 1994.

Yasser Al-Zahrani—Saudi jihadi said to have committed suicide in Guantánamo Bay.

Yathrib—original name of oases later known as *Al-Medina*, "The City" of the Prophet.

Zaynab—sister of Husayn, daughter of Ali, and hence the granddaughter of the Prophet, through Ali's marriage to Mohammed's daughter Fatima.

Zulfiqar—the legendary sword of the Islamic leader Ali.

NOTES

Preface: Welcome to the Kingdom

xviii **portable darkrooms:** The glass negatives of Captain William Shakespear, the earliest of these photographer-explorers, are in the archives of the Royal Geographical Society in London.

xxi **Persian Gulf:** In recent years many Arabs have claimed the Persian Gulf as "Arab," and one side of it certainly is. But this book will continue to use the Gulf's longstanding historical title.

xxii **its Internet translation:** http://www.rasid.com/artc.php?id=20576.

Chapter 1: Angry Face

3 **nearly five times:** In the course of 1973, the year of the oil boycott, the price of oil went from $2.10 a barrel to $10.40. *New York Times*, August 13, 1990.

4 **money in their pockets:** Dr. Horst Ertl, interview with author, Jeddah, August 1, 2006.

4 **"lost in your own town":** Prince Amr Mohammed Al-Faisal, interview with author, Jeddah, July 11, 2006.

4 **scent of moisture:** Zahra S. Al-Moabi, "Souq Al-Nada," in Akers and Bagader, pp. 11–15.

4 **"iron and cement":** Prince Faisal bin Abdullah, interview with author, Riyadh, February 25, 2006.

5 **attributed to the Prophet:** "In *bidah* lies Hell-fire." Hadith source Tirmidhi. http://islamknowledge.faithweb.com/danger_of_bidah.htm.

5 **"in some modern hotel":** Khaled Bahaziq, interview with author, Jeddah, December 9, 2006.

6 **"blankets pulled over us":** Nasser Al-Huzaymi, interview with author, Riyadh, September 20, 2006.

6 **What God revealed to Mohammed:** This simplified account is based on Karen Armstrong's works on Mohammed and Islam, and also on Reza Aslan's *No God but God*.

6 **"Recite!":** Koran, 96:1, sura 96, verse 1.

8 **"single lightbulb acceptable":** Nasser Al-Huzaymi, interview with author, Riyadh, September 21, 2006.

8 **"the flesh of fowls":** Koran, sura 56, verse 21.

9 **Medina's Salafi Group:** This account of the Salafi Group is based on a series of interviews with Nasser Al-Huzaymi in Riyadh, 2006–7, and on articles written by him in *Ar-Riyadh* newspaper, May 19 and 26, 2003, June 10, 2003, and September 6, 2004. The subject was well covered by Yaroslav Trofimov in his book *The Siege of Mecca*, on which I have also drawn. The definitive article in English is by

Thomas Hegghammer and Stéphane Lacroix, "Rejectionist Islamism in Saudi Arabia: The Story of Juhayman Al-Utaybi Revisited," *International Journal of Middle East Studies* 39 (2007), pp. 97–116. I am grateful to Thomas Hegghammer for his help on this and several other aspects of recent Islamist history.

9 **"Hanging a picture on a wall":** *Fatawa Islamiya* (Riyadh, Dar es Salaam, 2002), vol 8, p. 112. Cited in Trofimov, p. 28.

9 **from around the age of eight:** Some accounts say that Bin Baz became blind in his late teens or even twenties. A senior prince who spent time with him recalls the sheikh saying that he became blind before he was ten.

9 **surrendering Muslim land:** Guido Steinberg, "The Wahhabi Ulama and the Saudi State: 1745 to the Present," in Aarts and Nonneman, p. 25. Steinberg's account is based on Saudi records of Bin Baz's time in Al-Kharj, and also on U.S. State Department documents.

10 **mixing with local women:** Dr. Abdullah H. Masry, letter to author, September 22, 2008.

10 **The First "Wahhabi":** This simplified history of the Wahhabi mission is based on the accounts of the Nejdi historians Ibn Bishr (d. 1871/2) and Ibn Ghannam (d. 1811), as translated and collated by George Rentz, *The Birth of the Islamic Reform Movement in Saudi Arabia.*

11 **"rule lands and men":** Quoted in Rentz, p. 50.

11 **"ancient disciples":** Dr. Ali Saad Al-Mosa, interview with author, Abha, June 5, 2006.

12 **"antigovernment drift":** Ibid.

12 **"coins, not banknotes":** Nasser Al-Huzaymi, Riyadh, interview with author, November 19, 2006.

13 **not true salafis:** Nasser Al-Huzaymi, interview with author, Riyadh, November 22, 2006.

13 **police informers:** Hegghammer and Lacroix, pp. 102, 103.

Chapter 2: The Brothers

15 **flabby cooks:** John S. Habib, *Ibn Saud's Warriors of Islam,* p. 140.

15 **"camel bags without handles":** Almana, p. 103.

16 **cold-blooded:** Mohammed Almana, who was present at the battle, makes clear that Abdul Aziz gave orders for his machine-gunners to hold back and conceal themselves until they could fire with most lethal effect. Almana, pp. 103 ff.

16 **"no further useful purpose":** Harry St. John Philby, *Saudi Arabia,* p. 313. Harry Philby was the khawajah who took the first photo King Khaled could remember (see p. xix), and father of Kim Philby, the famous double agent.

16 **"Never give up":** Trofimov, p. 18.

16 **fathered a son:** It was thought for many years that Juhayman's grandfather Sayf fought with the Ikhwan at Sibillah, but Nasser Al-Huzaymi, speaking in November 2006, was adamant it was Juhayman's father, Mohammed.

17 **car auctions of Jeddah:** Nasser Al-Huzaymi, interview with author, Riyadh, February 11, 2007.

17 **"most of the money":** Nasser Al-Huzaymi, interview with author, Riyadh, September 20, 2006.

17 **"all released":** Nasser Al-Huzaymi, interview with author, Riyadh, September 21, 2006.
17 **"at the front":** Nasser Al-Huzaymi, interview with author, Riyadh, November 19, 2006.
17 **Thirty of the Brothers:** Nasser Al-Huzaymi, interview with author, Riyadh, November 22, 2006.
17 **friendly dentist:** Hegghammer and Lacroix, p. 104.
18 **"The Letters of Juhayman":** See Hegghammer and Lacroix, pp. 104, 105, for a meticulous analysis of Juhayman's letters, once thought to be only seven, and how they were published.
18 **"evil and corruption":** Hegghammer and Lacroix, p. 105.
18 **"recited his thoughts":** Nasser Al-Huzaymi, interview with author, Riyadh, February 11, 2007.
18 **"a bit kooky to me":** Nabil Al-Khuwaiter, interview with author, Dhahran, January 17, 2008, and e-mail to the author, September 27, 2008.
19 **"pious people in power":** Ibid.
19 **"When kings enter a village":** Koran, sura 19, verse 27.
20 **the identity of the Mahdi:** Nasser Al-Huzaymi, interview with author, Riyadh, September 20, 11, 2006.
20 **reports of the angels:** Nasser Al-Huzaymi, interview with author, Riyadh, February 2007.
21 **slipped away:** Nasser Al-Huzaymi, interview with author, Riyadh, November 22, 2006.
21 **"The fact that we dream":** Nasser Al-Huzaymi, "The Dreams—from Happiness to Ego." *Al-Riyadh*, September 6, 2004.
23 **"the Green One":** Dr. Ali Saad Al-Mosa, interview with author, Abha, June 5, 2006.

Chapter 3: Siege

24 **King Khaled with horror:** *Kingdom* interview, off-the-record, 1980.
24 **in the 1960s:** Reluctant to take his elder brother's place for some time, Khaled eventually bowed to family pressure and became crown prince in 1965.
25 **"important issues in Tunis":** Prince Turki Al-Faisal, interview with author, Riyadh, February 11, 2008.
25 **driving a new Lamborghini:** Information from the prince's co-driver.
25 **bullet shattered the glass:** Trofimov, p. 86.
26 **by nine that morning:** Ibid., p. 79, based on an interview with an officer in the force.
26 **escape from the Mosque:** Ibid., p. 74, based on the interviews subsequently given by Ibn Subayl.
27 **an emergency fatwa:** *Arab News*, November 26, 1979.
27 **a bullet had pierced his fuselage:** Mahdi Zawawi, interview with author, Jeddah, April 12, 2007.
28 **"snipers up in the minarets":** Khaled Al-Maeena, interview with author, Jeddah, July 10, 2006.
28 **in range of the minarets:** Girls' interview, Jeddah, August 1, 2006.

28 **"You'll get us all killed!":** Matooq Jannah, interview with author, Jeddah, December 9, 2006.
28 **sensed a business opportunity:** Hussein Ali Shobokshi, interview with author, Jeddah, January 22, 2007.
29 **Loss of life did not matter:** Trofimov, p. 132.
29 **had been swallowed up:** Abdul Aziz Qudheibi, "Al Riyadh Yaqaddem Qissat al-Qital fil Masjid al-Haram," *Al-Riyadh*, December 12, 1979.
30 **the coming of the Mahdi:** Trofimov, p. 134.
30 **"save the Holy House of God":** Ibid., p. 120.
30 **"Do not fight with them":** Koran sura 2, verse 191.
31 **"had been a pupil":** Turki Al-Faisal, interview with author, Riyadh, February 11, 2008.
31 **"people intervened for their release":** Interview with *Al-Safir,* Lebanon, translated by the official Saudi press agency (SPA) and published in *Arab News,* Jeddah, January 14, 1980.
31 **"fighting inside the Sacred Mosque":** Fatwa text as translated by the Saudi Press Agency, *Arab News*, November 26, 1979.
31 **"You have to surrender":** Trofimov, p. 152.
32 **proof of his mortality:** Ibid., p. 160.
33 **"If my son is the Mahdi":** Ibid., p. 166.
33 **aura of the evil:** Ibid., p. 162.
33 **death in sufficient concentrations:** Ibid., p. 192.
34 **helpless in their luxurious hotel:** The degree of help by the French has been the subject of much speculation and exaggeration. Yaroslav Trofimov deals with it well in chapters 21 and 23 of his comprehensive book, *The Siege of Mecca*.
34 **"had the advantage":** Turki Al-Faisal, Riyadh, interview with author, February 11, 2008.
34 **oddly subdued reply:** Trofimov, p. 213.
34 **rebel's head:** Interview with confidant of King Fahd, Riyadh, November 17, 2008.
35 **"that's Islamic?":** Turki Al-Faisal, interview with author, Paris, September 2, 2006.
35 **"tribal way":** This account is from one of the witnesses on the balcony.

Chapter 4: No Sunni, No Shia

37 **loosened the purse strings:** Dr. Majid Al-Moneef, interview with author, Riyadh, November 18, 2008.
37 **"on camels' milk":** Prince Turki Al-Faisal related this story most recently in his address to the U.S.-Arab Policy Conference in Washington, DC, October 31, 2008.
38 **"Yanbu and Jubail":** Author interview with an associate of Fahd's as crown prince, November 30, 2008.
38 **ten elephants:** Off-the-record interview, London.
39 **anniversary of Ashura:** Ali Al-Marzouq, interview with author, Qateef, January 27, 2007.
39 **Arabic for "tenth":** From *Ashara*, the figure ten in Arabic.
39 **five hundred thousand or so Shia Muslims:** The precise size of the Shia population, and other issues, is well discussed in Toby Craig Jones, "Rebellion on the Saudi

Periphery: Modernity. Marginalization, and the Shia Uprising of 1979," *International Journal of Middle East Studies* vol 38 (2006), p. 216.

40 **"my brothers":** Ali and Issa Al-Marzouq, interview with author, Al-Khobar, January 27, 2007.

41 **"Ali as his master":** Nasr, pp. 37, 38.

42 **"his Zulfiqar!":** Ibid., p. 37.

42 **"no authority except God":** Aslan, p. 135.

43 **barricade of death:** Ibid., pp. 172, 173.

43 **sentence of death:** Sheikh Ahmed bin Hajar al-Tami, *Sheikh Mohammed ibn Abdul Wahhab, His Fundamental Belief and Reformist Call and the Ulama, Praise Be Upon Him* (Riyadh, 1999), p. 79, cited in Ibrahim, p. 23.

43 **destroyed the tomb of Husayn:** Ibn Bishr, *The Landmark of Glorification in the History of Nejd* (Riyadh, 1982), vol. 1, pp. 121–22, cited in Ibrahim, p. 23.

43 **Sunni foreman:** Ben Dyal, interview with author, January 22, 2008.

43 **cow straddling:** The cartoonist, Ali Al-Kharji, went to prison for his pains. Ahmed Al-Ajaji, interview with author, November 14, 2008.

44 **got the point:** Ibrahim, p. 98.

44 **"criminal Al-Saud":** Quoted in Toby Craig Jones, "Rebellion on the Saudi Periphery: Modernity, Marginalization, and the Shia Uprising of 1979," *International Journal of Middle East Studies* 38 (2006), p. 218.

45 **"so much blood":** Ali and Issa Al-Marzouq, interview with author, Al-Khobar, January 27, 2007.

45 **"remained empty":** Jon P. Parssinen, interview with author, Al-Khobar, January 15, 2008.

45 **killed in the riots:** Ibrahim, p. 120.

45 **burned:** Toby Craig Jones, "Rebellion on the Saudi Periphery."

45 **ransacked:** Clive Morgan, e-mail to author, November 2, 2008.

45 **"Vietnam War":** Ibid.

45 **ayatollahs' take:** Bronson, p. 147.

45 **"not want you!":** Toby Craig Jones, "Rebellion on the Saudi Periphery."

Chapter 5: Vox populi, Vox Dei

46 **"national opinion survey":** Quoted in the introduction to Al-Nadwah, *When Sense Is Dying* (Riyadh, 1980).

46 **talking about the Shah:** Adnan Khashoggi, interview with author, Riyadh, March 2007.

47 **power of religion:** Ironically, Saudi Arabia had contributed to Iran's economic woes by increasing oil production in 1977, thus sabotaging an oil price increase on which the Shah had been depending. Andrew Scott Cooper, "Showdown at Doha: The Secret Oil Deal That Helped Sink the Shah of Iran," *Middle East Journal* 62, no. 4 (Autumn 2008), p. 567.

47 **"God's punishment to us":** Interview with a member of the royal family who prefers not to be named.

48 **Council of Ministers:** Reported to the author by a minister of the time, Jeddah, November 30, 2008.

48 **"must move gradually":** Interview with *Al-Safir*, Beirut, January 9, 1980, cited in Middle East Economic Survey (MEES), vol. 23, no. 14, January 21, 1980.

48 **a committee to reexamine:** MEES, vol. 23, no. 23 (March 24, 1980).
48 **"no coming back":** Reported to the author by a close associate of the committee member, who is now deceased.
49 **"four cinemas in Jeddah":** "The first was behind the house of Zainal at the Al-Nahda Hotel in Balad. There was the Abu Safiya Cinema in Hindawiya, another opened by Fouad Jamjoom and Khalil Baghdadi in Ammariya and the Al-Attas Hotel Cinema in Obhur." *Arab News*, October 25, 2007 (Shawwal 14, 1428). "The Importance of Preserving Tolerance in Jeddah," by Mahmoud Abdul Ghani Sabbagh.
49 **"reading the news":** Samar Fatany, interview with author, Jeddah, March 5, 2006.
49 **combative Ikhwan:** For details of the Njedi and Wahhabi assimilation of Jeddah, see William Ochsenwald's chapter, "The Annexation of the Hijaz," in Ayoob and Kosebalaban, *Religion and Politics in Saudi Arabia: Wahhabism and the State*, pp. 75 ff.
49 **"poor dears":** Sami Nawar, interview with author, Jeddah, February 16, 2006.
49 **"No more Valentine's":** Dr. Enam Abdul Wahhab Ghazzi, interview with author, Jeddah, October 31, 2006.
50 **"going to hell":** Mahdi Al-Asfour, interview with author, Qateef, February 20, 2006.
50 **judged inappropriate:** E-mail from Jon S. Parssinen, April 20, 2008.
50 **"copies after class":** Jon P. Parssinen, interview with author, Al-Khobar, January 15, 2008.
50 **vanished very early:** Hassan Al-Husseini, interview with author, Al-Khobar, January 15, 2008.
50 **Koran by heart:** Mohammed Al-Rasheed, interview with author, Riyadh, September 20, 2006.
51 **"'fanatics with eyes'":** Off-the-record interview with author, Jeddah, April 3, 2007.
51 **"misleaders of men":** Ibid.
51 **in the fire:** Ben Dyal, interview with author, Jeddah, September 14, 2007.
52 **"go to the mosque":** Abdullah Masry, interview with author, London, July 22, 2007.
53 **singing songs:** Mahmoud Abdul Ghani Sabbagh, *Arab News*, October 25, 2007 (Shawwal 14, 1428).
53 **"my wife was my wife":** Khaled Al-Maeena, interview with author, Jeddah, March 5, 2006.

Chapter 6: Salafi Soccer

54 **degenerate Western culture:** Hala Al-Houti, interview with author, Jeddah, April 4, 2006.
55 **"straight path":** Koran, sura 1 verse 6.
55 **"thirsty lips":** *Amrika allati Raaytu* ("America That I Saw") quoted on http://gemsofislamism.tripod.com/milestones_Qutub.html#footnote_16.
56 **"Westoxification":** Reza Aslan credits this word, *Gharbzadegi,* to the Iranian social critic Jalal Al-e-Ahmad: Aslan, p. 238.
56 **"behavior like animals":** Qutub, p. 119.
56 **"Islam . . . is the answer":** Ibid., p. 32.
56 **"Islamic way of life":** Ibid., pp. 21, 62, 71.

56 **perfect Islamic state:** Jamal Khashoggi, interview with author, Jeddah, April 10, 2008.

56 **challenge the establishment:** I am grateful to Abdullah Al-Muallimi for his analysis of these points.

57 **"mosque was full":** Jamal Khashoggi, interview with author, Jeddah, September 7, 2008.

57 **football enthusiast:** Khaled Batarfi, interview with author, Jeddah, September 23, 2006.

58 **trachoma:** Information from one of the grandsons of Abdul Aziz.

58 **lost his eye:** Information from one of the sons of Mohammed Bin Laden.

59 **director of public works:** In the 1940s, departments like Public Works and Agriculture that later became ministries operated as departments of the Ministry of Finance.

59 **"Then behead them":** This remark has been quoted in several versions by several sources. See, for example, Trofimov, p. 162.

59 **"seize the holiest place":** Khaled Batarfi, interview with author, Jeddah, September 23, 2006

59 **no evidence:** Jamal Khashoggi, interview with author, Jeddah, September 7, 2008.

60 **Bin Laden construction company:** From the SBG (Saudi Binladin Group) website, before its removal from the Internet after September 11, 2001. Bergen, *The Osama Bin Laden I Know*, pp. 152, 153.

60 **separateness:** Osama did have half sisters through his mother's second marriage.

61 **"liberated in that home!":** Interview with a member of the Al-Thagr School group who prefers not to be named, Jeddah, November 15, 2006.

Chapter 7: Jihad in Afghanistan

62 **"in cash":** Ahmed Badeeb, interview with author, Jeddah, July 26, 2006.

63 **"freedom fighters":** Prince Turki Al-Faisal, interview with author, Washington, DC, May 10, 2006.

63 **sum was in the millions:** U.S. Bureau of Engraving and Printing: 490 notes weigh 1 lb. www.bep.treas.gov.

64 **crisp $100 bills:** Coll, *Ghost Wars*, p. 72.

64 **support the mujahideen:** Khaled Batarfi, interview with author, Jeddah, September 23, 2006.

64 **some historians:** See, for example, Thomas Hegghammer's *Jihad in Saudi Arabia*.

64 **protest could be permitted:** Alexei Vassiliev, *The History of Saudi Arabia,* p. 296.

65 **"brave men in the mountains":** Recollection to the author by a government minister, Jeddah, November 30, 2008.

65 **Koran printing plant:** Ottaway, pp. x, xi.

65 **handed a check:** MEES, vol. 23, no. 32 (May 26, 1980).

66 **the Safari Club:** Prince Turki Al-Faisal, interview with author, Paris, September 1, 2006.

66 **"Soviet atheism":** Prince Turki Al-Faisal, interview with author, Riyadh, April 10, 2007.

67 **"any means necessary":** State of the Union address, January 23, 1980.

67 **undercover guerrilla campaign:** Bronson, p. 149.

67 **$3 billion each:** Rachel Bronson, "Understanding U.S.-Saudi Relations," in Aarts and Nonneman, p. 383.

Chapter 8: Special Relationship

68 **annual flow of pilgrims:** Monroe, p. 173.
68 **entertain the chiefs:** Public Records Office, Kew, ibid.: E1119/266/25, Biscoe to SSC, February 5, 1932, para. 8.
68 **oil in Arabia:** Philby, p. 78.
69 **1933:** This tale is dated to 1933 by Madawi Rasheed in her *History of Saudi Arabia*, p. 91, and she has confirmed this date in e-mails with the author. Other Saudi historians maintain that the incident occurred as many as twenty years earlier, when Abdul Aziz was entertaining the British officer Captain Shakespear in Nejd. One grandson of the king says that Abdul Aziz actually lifted the preacher bodily off the podium, and that the British official whose presence offended the sheikh was Sir Percy Cox, who negotiated the first pension paid by the British government to Ibn Saud. It is possible that similar incidents occurred more than once.
69 **"fire will seize you":** Koran, sura 11, verse 113.
69 **"To you be your way":** Ibid., sura 109, verses 1–6.
69 **three hundred thousand mainland patients:** Thomas Lippman, "The Pioneers," *Aramco World* 55, no. 3 (May–June 2004).
70 **king's aging father:** Ibid.
70 **"you are very far away!":** Hart, p. 38.
70 **"after the money":** Al-Mana, p. 223.
70 **on board the USS *Murphy*:** This account of Abdul Aziz's journey to Suez and his meeting with Roosevelt is based on William Eddy's monograph *F.D.R. Meets Ibn Saud*.
71 **"Arabs wage war":** Ibid., p. 34.
71 **"favor":** Encyclopedia Britannica Online, retrieved July 3, 2007, "Balfour Declaration."
71 **"no move hostile":** Eddy, p. 34.
72 **America's largest:** Vitalis, p. 9.
72 **"trust the United States":** Rachel Bronson, "Understanding U.S.-Saudi Relations," in Aarts and Nonneman, p. 392.
72 **caught him visiting:** Vitalis, p. 233.
73 **Louisiana:** Simpson, p. 57.
74 **"all the votes":** Ibid., p. 58.
74 **"factual inaccuracies":** E-mail of October 1, 2008, to author from Peter J. Johnson in David Rockefeller's office.
74 **switched funds:** "As for the movement of $200 million in and out of Chase in 1978, the bank had two principal vehicles for work with Saudi Arabia, the Saudi Industrial Development Fund, which began operations in 1975, and the Saudi Investment Banking Corporation, which opened its doors in 1977. Both had been undertaken at the request of SAMA and involved Chase in direct economic development efforts in Saudi Arabia. SAMA's principal correspondent bank in the United States was Citibank, which held huge deposits. Why SAMA would have moved money from Chase to Morgan and not Citibank is unclear, as is the fact that the Saudis even had

$200 million on deposit for whatever reason at Chase to begin with." E-mail of October 1, 2008, to author from Peter J. Johnson in David Rockefeller's office.

74 **met with Bandar:** E-mail of June 10, 2008, to author from Peter J. Johnson in David Rockefeller's office.

75 **result of a brief encounter:** Close female family sources say that Bandar's mother was a servingwoman in the household of one of Sultan's sisters.

75 **"mother was a concubine":** Simpson, p. 13.

75 **"a different color":** Ibid., p. 13.

75 **getting the last pick:** Ibid., p. 15.

75 **faking his date of birth:** Ibid., p. 15.

76 **"son of the slave":** Interview with one of Bandar's circle of friends in his youth, January 2007. To this day there are those who detect dismissiveness in the attitude of his father, Prince Sultan, toward Bandar, by comparison with his more respectful stance toward his other sons.

76 **call from the crown prince:** Walter Cutler, interview with author, Washington, DC, April 30, 2007.

76 **personal request:** Author interview with a Saudi diplomat present at the breakfast meeting.

76 **$1 million a month:** Bronson, p. 184.

76 **secretly channeled:** Ibid., p. 184.

77 **more material assistance:** For details of covert Saudi and U.S. funding of anti-Communist operations in the Reagan years, see chapter 9 of Bronson, pp. 168–90.

Chapter 9: Dawn Visitors

78 **"Women used to hide":** These paragraphs are based on interviews with Dr. Fawzia Al-Bakr, in person and on the telephone, in Riyadh on February 27, April 4, and July 30, 2006.

79 **black-market whisky:** Author's recollection, Jeddah, 1980 and 1981.

80 **freethinkers and atheists:** Interview with a former member of the National Movement.

81 **"sparing their family":** Conversation with Mabahith officer.

82 **"connection cut out":** Peter Theroux, telephone interview, November 8, 2007.

83 **"Syria is an Arab sister":** Ibid.

83 **number of the room:** Theroux, p. 107.

84 **an official letter:** Maha Fitaihi, interview with author, Jeddah, March 7, 2006.

Chapter 10: Stars in the Heavens

86 **divine requirements:** "King Fahd Makes First Policy Statement—July 24, 1982," translation in *Middle East Economic Survey* 25, no. 2 (August 2, 1982).

86 **corrupt pleasures:** Ibid.

86 **"without even leaving his house":** Author interview, off-the-record.

87 **"respect to show":** Ibid.

87 **"gone to heaven":** Ibid.

87 **gift . . . from John Latsis:** information from a business associate of Latsis, April 2009.

87 **was the longest:** Built by the Helsingor Vaerft shipyard in Denmark and fitted out in Southampton by the British designer David Hicks, the *Prince Abdul Aziz* was the largest motor yacht built in the twentieth century (www.superyachttimes.com).

87 **hedonistic economy:** On news of the Saudis' arrival, the supermarkets filled their cold cabinets with legs of lamb, while fleets of car transporters set off from Germany laden with luxury limousines. Jim Mackie, "Marbella's Favorite Son—King Fahd of Saudi Arabia," *Andalucia Travel Guide*, November 22, 2007.

87 **Saudi monarch's honor:** Giles Tremlett, "Marbella Feels the Loss of the Saudi King: Three Days of Mourning for Royal Who Spent Millions in Town," *The Guardian*, August 6, 2005.

87 **only one trip:** This information comes from Al-Fahd family members. The author has been unable to confirm it in Marbella, where people recall the Saudi king visiting more than once in the ten-year spell following his strokes in the late 1990s.

87 **man-made island:** information from a business associate of John Latsis, April 2009.

87 **"Going into Orbit":** "On the Possibility of Going into Orbit," Shaaban 1389. I am grateful to Dr. Sheikh Mohammed Al-Shuwayl for providing me with a copy of this fatwa, and to Hala Al-Houti for translating it for me.

88 **"men may reach the moon":** Ibid., p. 3.

88 **"sufficient proof":** Ibid., p. 1.

88 **"seemed to be flat":** Memory of someone who read Bin Baz's writings.

89 **"rules about traveling":** Sultan bin Salman, interview with author, Riyadh, June 2, 2007.

89 **"Ramadan finished in two days":** Ibid.

89 **"Keep your eyes open":** Ibid.

90 **"'stars in the heavens'":** Koran, sura 15 "Al-Hijer," verse 16.

90 **"not be the last time":** Sultan bin Salman, interview with author, Riyadh, June 2, 2007.

90 **felt beneath his feet:** These paragraphs are based on Bin Baz's fatwa of Shaaban 1389 and on conversations with his son Ahmed Bin Baz; with Dr. Sheikh Mohammed Al-Shuwayl, the sheikh's close friend and assistant; with Prince Turki Al-Faisal; with Prince Sultan bin Salman; with Dr. Abdullah Al-Muallimi; with Dr. Ghazi Algosaibi; and with Fouad Al-Ibrahim—whose differing perspectives I have sought to reconcile in this narrative.

90 **world glut of energy:** "Oceans of Oil," *Texas Monthly*, October 1984.

91 **decline steadily:** Niblock and Malik, pp. 55, 56.

91 **he would complain:** Off-the-record interview, Nicosia, October 19, 2006.

91 **"*ustaz*—Mister Yamani":** Explanation to the author by an adviser to the royal court, Jeddah, November 29, 2008.

91 **after long discussions:** Recollection of a member of Fahd's immediate family.

92 **"I don't know how":** Recollection of a relative of the ministerial colleague.

92 **Turn up the volume:** recollection of a family member, June 2009.

92 **"low oil prices":** Dr. Ibrahim Al-Muhanna, interview with author, Riyadh, December 5, 2006.

92 **Saudi oil production would fall:** Niblock and Malik, pp. 55, 56.

93 **"pay the salaries":** Off-the-record recollection to the author, November 30, 2008.

94 **beside Sigourney Weaver:** Elizabeth Kastor and Donnie Radcliffe, "Fahd's Night: Fanfare Fit for a King," *Washington Post*, February 12, 1985. "After Caballe sang,

the Reagans escorted Fahd and his son to the door. Then the band struck up 'Shall We Dance?' The Reagans did."

94 **"to my brother Faisal":** Recalled by a royal adviser.

95 **"the propagation of Islam":** Ottaway, p. 185.

95 **$27 billion:** Ibid.

95 **"closest to my heart":** The recollection of one of Fahd's ministers who later discussed the title with him.

96 **"clean the place properly":** Recalled to the author by two U.S. diplomats of the time. The cartoon was one of a series depicting "Captain Nejd," a Saudi version of Superman, who came flying into crisis situations to apply Wahhabi solutions to the problem.

Chapter 11: Into Exile

97 **soapbox orator:** Sir David Gore Booth, interview with author, January 16, 2003.

98 **"modern infrastructure":** Clive Morgan, e-mail to author, December 8, 2008.

98 **"people try to test you":** Mohammed bin Fahd, interview with author, Damman, January 30, 2007.

98 **"embraced each other":** Ibid.

99 **prisoners were released:** Ibrahim, p. 136.

99 **"seek peace":** Ali Al-Marzouq, interview with author, Al-Awjam, October 11, 2007.

100 **"freedom that Islam can give":** Ibid.

100 **Iranian money:** Author interview with Saudi security official, London, December 8, 2008.

101 **"should have confessed":** Ali Al-Marzouq, interview with author, Al-Awjam, October 11, 2007.

101 **princely "oppressors":** Scott Cooper and Brock Taylor, "Power and Regionalism: Explaining Regional Cooperation in the Persian Gulf," in Finn Laursen, ed., *Comparative Regional Integration* (Aldershot: Ashgate Publishing, 2003), p. 115.

101 **promote their cause in Mecca:** Theroux, p. 145.

102 **plastic explosives:** Walter Cutler, interview with author, Washington, DC, April 30, 2007.

102 **"a new life":** Ali Al-Marzouq, interview with author, Al-Khobar, January 27, 2007.

102 **violating Islamic tradition:** John Kifner, "Mecca Pilgrims Say Iranians Concealed Weapons," *New York Times*, August 8, 1987. Dr. Martin Kramer's long and thorough investigation of the 1987 Mecca tragedy concluded: "The available evidence indicates that a group of undisciplined Iranian pilgrims, acting under the influence of at least one provocative statement by a leading Iranian official, wished to enter the Great Mosque as demonstrators. Saudi security authorities, who had been alerted to this possibility but lacked self-confidence in the face of provocation, employed deadly force to thwart the Iranian crowd." Martin Kramer, *Arab Awakening and Islamic Revival* (New Brunswick, NJ: Transaction, 1996), pp. 166–87.

103 **"remain independent":** Hassan Al-Saffar, interview with author, Qateef, June 7, 2007.

103 **"their games":** Jaffar Shayeb, interview with author, Qateef, January 30, 2007.

103 **"They do not rule":** Hassan Al-Saffar, interview with author, Qateef, June 7, 2007.

103 **"one chicken per month":** Ali Al-Marzouq, interview with author, Al-Khobar, January 27 2007.

Chapter 12: The Dove and the East Wind

105 **Saudi Air Force:** Ottaway, p. 55.
105 **shot the intruder down:** Sultan and Seale, p. 144.
106 **Palestinian friends:** Bronson, p. 165.
106 **"hell of a man":** Author interview with an associate of Prince Bandar's, Jeddah, November 26, 2008.
106 **tens of billions:** On August 22, 2006, the London *Sunday Times* quoted Mike Turner, CEO of BAe Systems, as saying that BAe and its predecessor had earned £43 billion in twenty years from the contracts and that it could earn £40 billion more.
106 **in its history:** Ottaway, p. 67.
107 **U.S. defense industry:** Simpson, p. 133.
107 **£170,000 Rolls-Royce:** "BAe Probed on £60m Saudi Slush Fund," by David Leppard and Robert Winnett, *Sunday Times*, July 25, 2004.
107 **Lee Strasberg Institute:** "Prince Turki, the RAF Wing Commander, a Secret £60m BAe slush fund . . . and Me," by Ian Gallagher, *Mail on Sunday*, April 7, 2007.
107 **registered to the Saudi Air Force:** Information from a Saudi government official, November 26, 2008.
107 **price tag:** "BAe bought £75m Airbus for Saudi Prince," by David Leigh and Rob Evans, *The Guardian*, June 15, 2007.
108 **Bandar's unapologetic reply:** Video interview, June 7, 2007, *Guardian* website, "The BAe Files."
108 **total £1 billion:** "MoD accused over role in Bandar's £1bn," by David Leigh and Rob Evans, *The Guardian*, June 12, 2007.
108 **"a utopian arrangement":** Simpson, pp. 148–149.
108 **untraceable cash:** Ibid., p. 150.
108 **Saudi $10 million:** Ibid., pp. 100–101.
109 **"audited . . . every penny":** Off-the-record interview, Jeddah, November 26, 2008.
109 **attack capacity:** Simpson, p. 143.
110 **War of the Cities:** Bronson, p. 164.
110 **"the Lance":** Bandar bin Sultan, interview with CBS *Nightwatch,* cited in Simpson, p. 152.
110 **no recollection:** E-mail of May 31, 2008, from Susan Schendel in the office of Secretary Shultz.
111 **"give them to Iraq":** Simpson, p. 152.
111 **launchers and trainers:** Ibid., p. 165.
111 **negotiate in whispers:** Sultan and Seale, p. 140.
111 **"timings of the satellite":** Khaled bin Sultan, interview with author, Riyadh, March 6, 2007.
111 **"they are alive":** Ibid.
112 **middle of 1989:** Sultan and Seale, p. 150.
112 **men in beards:** Ibid.
112 **camping in the desert:** Off-the-record interview, Riyadh, November 2008.
112 **"Nuclear weapons":** Simpson, p. 159. Richard Murphy has given no response to an

e-mailed request, received and acknowledged by his office, to confirm, deny, or correct this quotation and version of events.

112 **cut off all links:** E-mail of May 31, 2008, from Susan Schendel in the office of Secretary Shultz.

112 **Israelis' targeting package:** Simpson, p. 162; see also Bronson. Richard Armitage has given no response to an e-mailed request, received and acknowledged by his office, to confirm, deny, or correct this quotation and version of events.

112 **"Israelis don't bomb":** Ibid. According to Simpson, Bandar's approved biographer, Powell described this encounter in a personal interview with Simpson. However, Secretary Powell has given no response to an e-mailed request received and acknowledged by Powell's office, to confirm, deny, or correct Simpson's version of events.

113 **back in Washington:** Saudi sources claim that Horan was put on a plane to the Sudan that very night. But this is denied by at least one U.S. diplomat who has recalled attending the ambassador's rapidly summoned farewell party a few days later.

Chapter 13: Vacationing Jihadi

114 **"discounts on air tickets":** Khaled Bahaziq, interview with author, Jeddah, January 9, 2006.

114 **actually come to fight:** Prince Turki Al-Faisal, whose Istikhbarat had orders to stay aloof from the volunteers, reckons that, starting in 1981–82, there were at the most "a couple of thousand" Arab-Afghans fighting in Afghanistan. He recalls the local mujahideen telling him that they did not want men from Saudi Arabia—they were more in need of medicine, weapons, and supplies. Conversation with the author, Paris, December 15, 2008.

115 **"'This has got preservative'":** Khaled Bahaziq, interview with author, Jeddah, January 9, 2006.

115 **"helping jihad":** Khaled Bahaziq, interview with author, Jeddah, December 9, 2006.

116 **"taking a grenade":** Ibid.

117 **"I had sinned":** Azzam, *The Lofty Mountain,* p. 113.

117 **a military base:** Bergen, *The Osama Bin Laden I Know*, p. 49.

118 **"think tactically":** Jamal Khashoggi, interview with author, Riyadh, March 28, 2008.

118 **"Reliance upon God":** *Arab News*, May 4, 1988.

118 **"God's will":** *The Lofty Mountain,* p. 113.

118 **"you love death":** "Robert Fisk on Osama Bin Laden at 50," interview with Amy Goodman, March 5, 2007, www.democracynow.org.

118 **survey of exit stamps:** Author interview with Saudi government adviser, December 8, 2008. This is significantly greater than the estimate of only a few hundred Arab-Afghans by Peter L. Bergen in *The Osama Bin Laden I Know,* p. 49.

118 **175,000 to 250,000 native Afghans:** Urban, p. 244.

119 **died martyrs:** Ali Al-Johani, interview with author, Riyadh, November 24, 2006.

119 **an oversize beehive:** The author visited this mosque in January 2007.

120 **bunking off school:** Mansour Al-Nogaidan, interview with author, Ajman, November 9, 2007.

120 **"The beheading platform":** Mansour Al-Nogaidan, interview with author, Ajman, November 9, 2007.
120 **"tales of hellfire":** Abdullah Thabit, interview with author, Jeddah, July 2006.
122 **arrested by the Mabahith:** Mansour Al-Nogaidan, e-mail to author, September 22, 2008.
123 **another target:** Khaled Batarfi, interview with author, Jeddah, September 23, 2006.

Chapter 14: Desert Storm

127 **"armored cars and tanks":** Ahmed Badeeb, interview with author, Jeddah, July 26, 2006.
127 **landing special troops:** Ambassador Chas Freeman Jr., U.S. Diplomatic Oral Histories, Library of Congress, Washington, D.C.
127 **"Escape at once!":** Ahmed Badeeb, interview with author, Jeddah, July 26, 2006.
128 **the BBC's monitors:** BBC, Summary of World Broadcasts, August 2, 1990.
128 **"leave the border":** Mohammed bin Fahd, interview with author, Damman, January 30 2007.
128 **to Dammam:** E-mail from Hassan Al-Jasser, Governor's Office, Damman, December 1, 2008.
128 **Palestine Liberation Organization:** Bowen, p. 124. This figure has been confirmed by a Saudi familiar with the figures.
128 **largest financial supporter:** Saudi government analyst, Geneva, December 11, 2008.
129 **"Helping the Palestinians":** Princess Latifa bint Musaed, interview with author, Riyadh, September 17, 2006.
129 **"a British colonial fiction":** Ottaway, p. 91.
129 **"call me *shareef*":** Sultan and Seale, p. 210.
129 **weather map:** Ahmed Badeeb, interview with author, Jeddah, July 26, 2006.
129 **"We'll be back":** Interview with Dr. Ali Saad Al-Mosa, Abha, June 5, 2006.
129 **distanced themselves:** Sultan and Seale, pp. 183–184.
129 **leaked recording:** Rime Allaf, "Success Measured by Attendance," *Bitterlemons* 6 edition 12, (March 20, 2008).
130 **"the consensus":** Off-the-record interview, Jeddah, June 1, 2006.
130 **unanimous No:** Nawaf Obaid, "The Power of Saudi Arabia's Islamic Leaders," *Middle East Quarterly* (September 1999), http://www.meforum.org/article/482.
131 **wisdom that he delivered:** Sheikh Abdul Aziz Ibn Baz Religious Teaching Center, Al-Shumaysi, Riyadh, visit of March 12, 2008.
131 **"supports all measures":** Saudi Press Agency, pp. 40–42.
132 **"his permission":** Norman Schwarzkopf interview, Tampa, FL, May 11, 2006.
132 **"listen to my briefing":** Ibid.
132 **U.S. photographs:** Ibid.
133 **"trespassed on Saudi":** Ibid.
133 **"tanks were facing south":** Ibid.
133 **"no permanent bases":** Ibid.
133 **"hotel rooms in London":** Ambassador Chas Freeman Jr., Diplomatic Oral Histories Project, Library of Congress, Washington, D.C.
134 **driving their cars:** ABC News, London, February 19, 2007.

134 **she recalls:** Dr. Aisha Al-Mana, interview with author, Al-Khobar, January 27, 2007.
134 ***Arabia Unified:*** See Suggested Reading.
135 **"piece of the cake":** Dr. Aisha Al-Mana, interview with author, Al-Khobar, January 27, 2007.
135 **"ban just melts away":** Ibid.
137 **woken from his afternoon nap:** Family information.
138 **"angry lump of indignation":** Interview with Reem Jarbou, Jeddah, July 12, 2006.
138 **without his consent:** Dr. Fawzia Bakr, interview with author, Riyadh, February 27, 2006.
139 **"control your women":** Dr. Fawzia Bakr and Dr. Fahd Al-Yehya, interview with author, Riyadh, February 27, 2006.
140 **"un-Saudi to demonstrate":** Interview with Bassim Alim, Jeddah, July 11, 2006.
140 **"falling on the nation":** Raja and Shadia Aalim, interview with author, Jeddah, June 8, 2006.
140 **"Communist whores":** Fandy, p. 49.
140 **spat on their teachers:** Ambassador Chas Freeman Jr., U.S. Diplomatic Oral Histories Project, Library of Congress, Washingont, D.C.
140 **"'You are our daughters'":** Princess Latifa bint Musaed, interview with author, Riyadh, September 17, 2006.

Chapter 15: Battle for Al-Khafji

141 **Al-Khafji stood deserted:** These paragraphs on the battle of Al-Khafji are based on a three-day visit to the town in June 2007 and with interviews with soldiers who took part in the battle, including Major General Suleiman Al-Khalifa. I am grateful to Douglas Baldwin for coordinating the trip and to Jan Baldwin for her photographs documenting the town and landscape of the battle. I am also grateful to Prince Khaled bin Sultan for an interview on March 6, 2007, in which he discussed Al-Khafji and the Gulf War.
141 **town was undefendable:** Sultan and Seale, p. 362.
141 **thirty-eight days and nights:** Ibid., p. 344.
142 **eighteen thousand hospital beds:** Ibid., p. 362.
142 **Saddam's crack units:** Schwarzkopf and Petre, p. 495.
142 **"I am lucky":** Sultan and Seale, p. 377.
142 **an Iraqi attack:** Morris, p. 10.
142 **"I need the Tornados":** Sultan and Seale, p. 374.
143 **surrounded by Iraqi troops:** *Storm on the Horizon*, by David J. Morris, recounts the story of Al-Khafji from the point of view of the deep-reconnaissance Marines who were trapped in the town.
143 **"get the Marines out":** Sultan and Seale, p. 374.
143 **"difficult to bear":** Ibid.
143 **"a real war":** Suleiman Al-Khalifa, interview with author, Al-Khafji, June 6, 2007.
144 **"keen on looting":** Ibid.
144 **more than four hundred prisoners:** Sultan and Seale, p. 387.
144 **the prince's jeep:** Ibid., p. 388.

145 **military refugees:** Ibid., p. 389.
145 **finest armored units:** Schwarzkopf and Petre, p. 496.
145 **martyrs:** Morris, caption facing p. 153.
145 **the only pitched battle:** Khaled bin Sultan, interview with author, Riyadh, March 6, 2007.
145 **"war aims":** Chas Freeman, interview with author, Washington, DC, May 7, 2007.
145 **the question "shocking":** Ibid.
146 **"restraining a smile":** Ibid.
146 **remained in his palace:** Ambassador Chas Freeman Jr., Oral Histories Project, Library of Congress, Washington, D.C., p. 293.
146 **"get out fast":** Sultan and Seale, pp. 421 and 426.
146 **"dinosaur in the tarpit":** Schwarzkopf and Petre, p. 579.
146 **"bitterly hostile land":** *Middle East Report*, May–June 1992. Cited August 18, 2007, on the Gulf 2000 Project website: Marsha B. Cohen, Florida International University.
147 **replied without hesitation:** http://www.youtube.com/watch?v=YENbElb5-xY&NR=1.
147 **"additional dead Americans":** Ibid.

Chapter 16: Awakening

148 **"He rang me":** Jamal Khashoggi, interview with author, Riyadh, March 28, 2008.
148 **"jihad needed fighting":** Ibid.
148 **the Salafi cause:** Bergen, *The Osama Bin Laden I Know*, pp. 108–109.
149 **"one last shot":** Turki Al-Faisal, interview with author, Riyadh, April 10, 2007.
149 **"greatly concerned about security":** Ahmad bin Abdul Aziz, interview with author, Riyadh, February 5, 2009.
149 **"eldest brother, Bakr":** Bakr Bin Laden today says he has no particular memory of this encounter, and is happy to accept the recollection of Prince Ahmad as definitive. Meeting with author, Jeddah, February 5, 2009.
150 **"black" with anger:** Burke, p. 136.
150 **"the infidels *inside*":** Ibid., p. 139.
151 **to destroy Islam:** Guido Sternberg, "The Wahhabi Ulama and the Saudi State: 1745 to the Present," in Aarts and Nonneman, p. 31.
151 **"remove injustice":** http://ibnbaz.org/mat/8345.
151 **"some infidel states":** Ibid.
152 **"banner of Islam":** Fandy, p. 95.
152 **his real target:** Ibid., p. 97.
152 **"'working in a shoe store'":** David Rundell, interview with author, Riyadh, March 6, 2007.
152 **wearing gold:** David Rundell, e-mails to author, October 30, 2008.
153 **"supporting the women":** Mansour Al-Nogaidan, interview with author, Ajman, November 9, 2007.
154 **"tight little group":** Off-the-record interview, Dubai, November 9, 2007.
154 **Royal Victorian Chain:** Buckingham Palace Press Office, February 9, 2009.
155 **"don't discuss this subject":** Bergen, *The Osama Bin Laden I Know*, pp. 59, 60.

155 **"jihad in Yemen":** Jamal Khashoggi, interview with author, Riyadh, March 28, 2008.
155 **"stop making speeches":** Ibid.
155 **"stopped talking himself":** Mohammed Saeed Tayeb, interview with author, November 27, 2008.
156 **sources differ:** I have followed Peter Bergen's book *The Osama Bin Laden I Know* as my principal guide to the chronology of these dates in Afghanistan and the Sudan. I am also grateful for the personal insights of Thomas Hegghammer.

Chapter 17: Stopping the Sins

157 **new jihadi friends:** Mansour Al-Nogaidan, interview with author, Ajman, November 9, 2007.
160 **reform in a petition:** Stéphane Lacroix, "Islamo-Liberal Politics in Saudi Arabia," in Aarts and Nonneman, p. 41.
160 **elitist and Westernized:** Off-the-record interview, April 1, 2006.
160 **restoration of Islamic values:** For a chronological list of major reform petitions since the 1990s, see Abdul Aziz Sager, "Political Opposition in Saudi Arabia," in Aarts and Nonneman, table 6, p. 268.
161 **"kept the radio":** Dr. Ahmad Al-Tuwayjri, interview with author, Riyadh, April 1, 2006.
162 **"intervened with the king":** Ibid.
162 **"to be patriotic":** Ibid.
162 **"received the Memorandum":** Ibid.
164 **"advice for the sake of God":** Teitelbaum, p. 40.
164 **"better class of jail":** Dr. Ahmad Al-Tuwayjri, interview with author, Riyadh, April 1, 2006.
165 **early websites:** Andrew Hammond, telephone conversation with author, November 22, 2008.
165 **destructive influence of oil:** http://www.iiwds.com/said_aburish/index.htm.
165 **an official decree:** In 1994 Decree 128 banned the private ownership of TV satellite dishes. Mai Yamani, "Saudi Arabia's Media Mask," in Madawi Al-Rasheed, ed., *Kingdom Without Borders*, p. 330.
166 **TV business:** See Al-Rasheed, ed., *Kingdom Without Borders,* (Madawi Al-Rasheed, ed.) for the proceeedings of a conference held at King's College, London, in September 2007 to examine the spread of Saudi media.
166 **"control or influence":** A member of Fahd's private phone call circle, March 2007, Jeddah.
166 **telephone think tank:** Ibid.

Chapter 18: In from the Cold

167 **the Saudi Shias:** Hassan Al-Saffar, interview with author, Qateef, June 7, 2007.
167 **being recounted:** Ibid.
167 **"rights and worship":** Ibid.
167 **"reformed Saudi Arabia":** Tawfiq Al-Seif, interview with author, Tarut Island, June 8, 2007.
168 **"Saudi arrests and scandals":** Ibrahim, pp. 149–52.

168 **"our human rights":** Sadiq Al-Jabran, interview with author, Al-Hasa, January 27, 2007.
168 **"Saudis demonstrating":** Faiza Ambah, interview with author, Jeddah, February 7, 2007.
169 **"nightmare for them":** Off-the-record interview, Al-Khobar, June 2007.
169 **"defending the country":** Ibrahim, p. 157.
170 **"As for 'sorry'":** Off-the-record interview, London, October 2007.
170 **"admit mistakes":** Tawfiq Al-Seif, interview with author, Tarut Island, June 8, 2007.
170 **"Islamist state with Sunni rule":** Off the record interview.
171 **"bring about change":** Tawfiq Al-Seif, interview with author, Tarut Island, June 8, 2007.
171 **"yes to them all":** Sadiq Al-Jabran, interview with author, Al-Hasa, January 27, 2007.
171 **telegram to Saudi embassies:** Ibrahim, p. 190.
172 **"They let us in":** Sadiq Al-Jabran, interview with author, Al-Hasa, January 27, 2007.
172 **"Shia are equal citizens":** Ibid.
173 **"*Playboy* magazine":** Author interview with a source familiar with the discussion.
173 **Iranian aid:** Information from a security adviser to the Saudi government, December 8, 2008.

Chapter 19: Change of Heart

174 **found himself at liberty:** Mansour Al-Nogaidan, interview with author, Ajman, November 10, 2007.
174 **"King Fahd is kafir":** Ibid.
175 **"kick out the angels":** Ibid.
175 **"take what I want":** Ibid.
176 **using the British media:** See Al-Rasheed, *A History of Saudi Arabia*, pp. 177–184.
176 **a huge bomb:** National Commission on Terrorist Attacks, p. 60.
176 **"change things with bombs":** Mansour Al-Nogaidan, interview with author, Ajman, November 10, 2007.
176 **eliminate the House of Saud:** Wright, p. 246.
176 **372 wounded:** Ibid.
176 **ideas had influenced them:** Fandy, p. 3.
176 **Iranian involvement:** See http://www.fbi.gov/pressrel/pressrel01/khobar.htm for details of the 29-page indictment dated June 21, 2001.
177 **farms by the Blue Nile:** Bergen, *Holy War Inc.*, p. 80.
177 **Luxembourg and Switzerland:** Author interview with a Saudi diplomat familiar with the information discovered by the U.S. government.
177 **philanthropic Saudi sheikh:** "Robert Fisk on Osama Bin Laden at 50," interview with Amy Goodman, March 5, 2007, www.democracynow.org.
177 **"waiting for this road":** Robert Fisk, *The Great War for Civilization*, p. 5.
177 **not all of them successful:** Tim Niblock, e-mail to author, November 9, 2008.
178 **government's number one critic:** Bin Laden family member, interview with author, Jeddah, September 2007.
178 **"condemnation of all acts":** Bergen, *The Osama Bin Laden I Know*, p. 152.

178 **supervised trust for his children:** Information from a senior Bin Laden family member.

178 **turn homeward:** Bergen, *The Osama Bin Laden I Know*, p. 151.

178 **"Osama's changed":** Jamal Khashoggi, interview with author, Riyadh, March 28, 2008.

178 **nostalgically enjoying *kabsa*:** Wright, p. 200.

179 **"forget about the flight":** Jamal Khashoggi, interview with author, Riyadh, March 28, 2008.

Chapter 20: Enter the Crown Prince

180 **words in a rush:** Off-the-record interview, Jeddah, March 7, 2003.

180 **cell without light:** Off-the-record interviews with several associates of the king, including a former National Guard officer, who say that Abdullah recounted this story to them personally. Family members concur with the tale.

180 **"right out of the desert":** Walter Cutler, interview with author, Washington, DC, April 30, 2007.

181 **huge communal supper:** Ibid.

181 **weeping and crying out:** Ali Al-Johani, interview with author, November 15, 2008.

181 **tap the offending head:** Brigadier General Nick Cocking, interview with author, London, November 4, 2008.

181 **"groveling on the floor":** Ibid.

181 **honest and reform-minded:** Fandy, pp. 133, 187.

181 **"If Abdullah becomes king":** Wright, p. 199.

182 **"rights of the citizen":** DeGaury, p. 104.

183 **sniffed at extreme ideas:** Family source.

183 **"constitution inspired by God":** DeGaury, p. 106.

184 **"not his business":** Brigadier General Nick Cocking, interview with author, London, March 5, 2008.

184 **"be the very best":** Abdul Rahman Abuhaimid, interview with author, Riyadh, January 25, 2007.

185 **"My father, of course":** Brigadier General Nick Cocking, interview with author, London, March 5, 2008.

185 **speech therapy lessons:** James E. Akins, interview with author, Virginia, May 10, 2007, confirmed by members of the royal circle.

185 **"totally fluent":** Brigadier General Nick Cocking, interview with author, London, March 5, 2008.

185 **land grants:** Information from a Jeddah businessman, October 2008.

185 **"lives like a prince":** Off-the-record interview, Jeddah, May 13, 2008.

186 **"close the doors and windows":** Abdul Rahman Abuhaimid, interview with author, Riyadh, November 18, 2008.

186 **deny the truth:** Turki bin Abdullah, interview with author, Paris, September 2005.

186 **sat down with his sons:** Abdullah is known as "Abu Miteb" ("Father of Miteb") after his firstborn son, who died in infancy. His next son was named Khaled. The present Miteb was born after the death of his elder brother.

186 **"in the business cabin":** Off-the-record interview, March 26, 2008.

186 **special flying privileges:** These remain for sons and daughters of Abdul Aziz and for all provincial governors. Abdullah has cut free royal travel by 80 percent, accord-

ing to an informed source inside Saudia. The fleet of planes dedicated to royal travel has been reduced from fourteen to five. Princes may use these planes for private travel, but must pay at market rates.

187 **"difficult for Abdullah":** Off-the-record interview, Jeddah, June 6, 2006.

187 **wheeled in:** The recollection of one of his ministers, March 4, 2007.

187 **"sort of pathetic":** Off-the-record interview, January 29, 2007.

187 **"strengthen the ties":** Off-the-record interview, September 19, 2006.

187 **"don't change the curtains":** Adviser to King Abdullah.

188 **"leader of the opposition":** This remark by the late Abdul Aziz Al-Tuwayjri was reported to the author by one of his close associates.

188 **"minister without portfolio":** Weston, p. 375.

188 **beloved elder brother:** Recollection by a European ambassador to Riyadh.

188 **"to bring him his shoes":** Recollection to the author, Jeddah, November 30, 2008.

188 **sink to nine dollars:** Niblock and Malik, table 4.1, p. 100.

189 **"different way of life":** BBC News Room, January 19, 1999.

189 **stringent austerity budget:** Ibid.

189 **"could not provide":** Dr. Ahmad Gabbani, interview with author, Jeddah, July 11, 2006.

189 **"money in the past":** Businessman, interview with author, Jeddah, February 12, 2006.

189 **"not enough lines":** Ali Al-Johani, interview with author, Riyadh, November 24, 2006.

189 **"Just six?":** Ali Al-Johani, interview with author, Riyadh, November 24, 2006.

190 **"sneaking an extra photocopy":** Ibid.

191 **"impossible to privatize":** Ali Al-Johani, telephone conversation, May 13, 2008.

191 **"outdated information":** Ibid.

191 **"*wanted* my job":** Ibid.

191 **not work with Al-Johani:** Interview with a member of the board who submitted his resignation, December 2006.

191 **been liberated:** When Ali Al-Johani took over the PTT in 1995, there were 1.8 million landlines, with 360,000 mobile numbers. Privatization was completed early in 1998, and ten years later there are 4 million landlines in the Kingdom with more than 20 million mobile numbers on two competing cellular networks and a third network just getting started.

192 **"as a pretext":** Author interview with economic adviser to King Abdullah, November 18, 2008.

Chapter 21: The Students

193 **"orders to shell Kabul":** Ahmed Badeeb, interview with author, Jeddah, July 26, 2006.

194 **"alternative to fighting":** Ahmed Badeeb, interview with author, May 11, 2008.

194 **"joint U.S.-Saudi project":** Off-the-record interview, Jeddah, November 26, 2008.

194 **"allocated $300 million":** Ahmed Badeeb, interview with author, May 11, 2008.

195 **"an incentive":** Turki Al-Faisal, interview with author, Jeddah, September 9, 2008.

195 **"working with Allah":** Rashid, p. 22.

195 **Taliban:** In Arabic the plural of *talib* is *tullab.*

195 **shot them dead:** Coll, *Ghost Wars*, p. 283.
195 **"time of the Prophet":** Rashid, p. 43.
196 **willingly paid:** Ibid., pp. 22 and 29.
196 **"These are my boys":** Turki Al-Faisal, interview with author, Jeddah, September 9, 2008.
196 **"a country boy":** Ibid.
197 **"lost an eye":** Ahmed Badeeb, interview with author, May 11, 2008.
197 **cut out his right eye:** Coll, *Ghost Wars*, p. 288.
197 **"laws of God on earth":** Ibid.
197 **restoring some order:** Ahmed Badeeb, interview with author, May 11, 2008.
197 **"I will do":** Coll, *Ghost Wars*, p. 295.
198 **"hundreds of new pickups":** Rashid, p. 45.
198 **"may have been Saudis":** Turki Al-Faisal, interview with author, Jeddah, September 9, 2008.
199 **"Saudi aid":** Ahmed Rashid, e-mail to author, September 24, 2008.
199 **Chevrolets:** According to an American diplomat who has studied the battle of Sibillah, a number of the Saudi vehicles were Chevrolets.
200 **"cursed by the Islamic sharia":** "A Sample of Taliban Decrees," Appendix 1 in Rashid, *Taliban,* p. 217.
200 **fundamentalist vigilantes:** Nawaf Obaid, "Improving U.S. Intelligence Analysis on the Saudi Arabian Decision Making Process," Harvard University, 1998.
200 **"training and salaries":** Ahmed Rashid, e-mail to author, September 24, 2008.
201 **led between the goalposts:** Rashid, *Taliban,* pp. 1–4.
201 **his protection:** Bergen, *The Osama Bin Laden I Know*, p. 164.
201 **singled out Bin Laden:** Coll, *Ghost Wars*, p. 342.
202 **"young, misguided kid":** Ottaway, p. 157.
202 **"offered him sanctuary":** Turki Al-Faisal, interview with author, Jeddah, September 9, 2008.
202 **"keeping his mouth shut":** Coll, *Ghost Wars*, p. 342, quoting an interview Prince Turki gave to *Nightline*, December 10, 2001.
202 **the lone Saudi exile:** Bergen, *The Osama Bin Laden I Know*, pp. 160ff.
203 **"only killing and neck-smiting":** Burke, p. 163, and Wright, p. 234.

Chapter 22: Infinite Reach

204 **"It was genocide":** Khaled Al-Hubayshi, interview with author, Jeddah, April 19, 2008.
205 **detainee's Basic Course:** Summary of Evidence for Combatant Status Review Tribunal—Al-Hubayshi, Khaled Sulayman Jaydh, September 24, 2004, no. 000156, unclassified.
205 **"explosives instructor":** Khaled Al-Hubayshi, interview with author, Jeddah, May 12, 2008.
206 **"come to die":** Khaled Al-Hubayshi, interview with author, Jeddah, April 19, 2008.
206 **"the U.S. visa automatically":** Off-the-record interview.
206 **"for the elite":** Khaled Al-Hubayshi, interview with author, Jeddah, April 19, 2008.
207 **"kill you for a hundred dollars":** Ibid.

207 **"to scare people":** Khaled Al-Hubayshi, interview with author, Jeddah, May 12, 2008.
207 **"videos in our lessons":** Ibid.
207 **eight thousand non-Afghans:** This number included charity workers, according to a Saudi defense analyst. The Saudi Ministry of the Interior estimated more.
207 **"Jihad Against Jews and Crusaders":** Bergen, *The Osama Bin Laden I Know*, p. 195.
208 **"they are all targets":** National Commission on Terrorist Attacks, p. 47.
208 **"like locusts":** Bergen, *The Osama Bin Laden I Know*, p. 195.
208 **"humiliating its people":** Ibid.
208 **followers with missiles:** Coll, *Ghost Wars*, p. 397.
208 **U.S. consulate in Jeddah:** Thomas Hegghammer, "Islamist Violence and Regime Stability in Saudi Arabia," *International Affairs* 84, no. 4 (July 2008), p. 708.
208 **"fieldwork at home":** Turki Al-Faisal, interview with author, Jeddah, September 9, 2008.
209 **"give us Bin Laden":** Wright, p. 268.
209 **the talibs' Gulf sponsors:** Ahmed Rashid, e-mail to author, September 24, 2008.
209 **ghastly reprisals:** Rashid, p. 72.
210 **baked alive:** Ibid., pp. 73–74.
210 **suicide bombers:** Figures from Steve Coll, *Ghost Wars,* and Lawrence Wright, *The Looming Tower.*
210 **wired into the dashboard:** Wright, p. 272.
210 **extramarital affair:** Off-the-record interviews with Saudi and U.S. diplomats who were present at the meeting.
210 **"not swayed by the breeze":** Off-the-record interview with a diplomat present at the meeting.
211 **"I am alive!":** Wright, p. 285.
211 **"martyr on CNN":** Interview with Mustapha Mutabaqani, Jeddah, July 15, 2006.
212 **"gave us your word":** Coll, *Ghost Wars*, p. 414.
212 **tea with his fellow spymaster:** Turki Al-Faisal, interview with author, Jeddah, September 9, 2008.
212 **"a translator's mistake":** Wright, pp. 288–289.
212 **"courageous, valiant Muslim":** Coll, *Ghost Wars*, p. 414.
213 **the Tomahawk missiles:** Rashid, *Taliban,* p. 134.
213 **"back on his word":** Turki Al-Faisal, interview with author, Jeddah, September 9, 2008.
213 **reverence for God:** Craig Whitlock, "In Hunt for Bin Laden, a New Approach," *Washington Post*, September 10, 2008.
213 **"an occupied country":** Wright, p. 289.
213 **directly to Omar:** Turki Al-Faisal, interview with author, Jeddah, September 9, 2008.
213 **"harm to the Afghan people":** Wright, p. 289.

Chapter 23: New Century

214 **ignoring each other:** Ottaway, p. 115.
214 **diplomatic corps:** Ibid., p. 127.
215 **"hit Abdullah up":** Freeh, *My FBI*, p. 25, cited in Ottaway, p. 121.

215 **about $10 million:** John Solomon and Jeffrey H. Birnbaum, "Clinton Library Got Funds from Abroad," *Washington Post*, December 15, 2007.

215 **"no such request":** Wyche Fowler, interview with author, October 30, 2008.

215 **"special relationship":** Ottaway, p. 126.

216 **bouts of . . . depression:** Information from a member of the Saudi embassy in Washington in the 1990s.

216 **"the invisible dean":** David Ottaway documents this difficult period well in "Midlife Crisis," chapter 8 of his book *The King's Messenger*. Prince Bandar's office acknowledges that the prince gave numerous interviews and briefings to Ottaway over the years, but say that the prince did not collaborate with the book. They also state that he would not willingly miss the celebration of Saudi National Day.

216 **"more pro-Saudi than us":** Ottaway, p. 143.

216 **"too good to be true":** Ibid.

217 **"success of Zionism":** Eddy, p. 37.

217 **three times that:** Ancestry information beyond "Mother Tongue" was not collected in those days. I am grateful to Yasmeen Shaheen-McConnell of the Arab-American Institute for providing these figures.

217 **6.4 million U.S. Jews:** There are numerous estimates that set the Jewish population of the US in the range of 5–7 million. This figure is from the *American Jewish Yearbook* population survey of 2006.

217 **"to stand against Israel":** Shindler, Colin, "Likud and the Christian Dispensationalists," *Israel Studies*, Vol. 5, no. 1, Spring 2000, pp. 153–182.

217 **Israeli attempts to assassinate:** Ottaway, p. 148.

218 **"Turning Friends into Enemies":** Ibid.

218 **"found him a writer":** Author interview with a senior official familiar with the exchange, November 30, 2008. Confirmed by a second Saudi official who processed the U.S. official protest.

218 **"the ultimate insult":** Interview with a senior Saudi official, Jeddah, October 31, 2006.

219 **"Palestinian children":** Robert G. Kaiser and David Ottaway, "Saudi Leader's Anger Revealed Shaky Ties," *Washington Post*, February 10, 2002.

219 **"a terrorist act":** Ibid.

219 **"he can do a better job":** Remarks by the president, 10.44 CDT, August 24, 2001, www.whitehouse.gov/news.

219 **disingenuous simplification:** Interview with a senior Saudi official, Riyadh, April 3, 2006.

220 **particular buttons:** This description of how Bandar would develop and amplify his instructions from Riyadh comes from a Saudi official who has worked with him for many years.

220 **"our own interests":** Interview with a senior Saudi official, Jeddah, October 31, 2006.

220 **Powell to Bandar:** Reported by a high-level Saudi official familiar with the exchange, December 2008.

220 **"We scared ourselves":** Robert G. Kaiser and David Ottaway, "Saudi Leader's Anger Revealed Shaky Ties," *Washington Post*, February 10, 2002.

221 **"last chance":** Confirmed by a high-level Saudi official, Jeddah, November 2008.

222 **"kisses and licks":** Off-the-record interview, Riyadh, November 24, 2006.

222 **"taking the day off":** Confirmed by a high-level Saudi official, Jeddah, November 2008.

Chapter 24: Fifteen Flying Saudis

225 **"hit the twin towers":** Prince Khaled Al-Faisal, interview with author, Jeddah, September 25, 2007.

226 **"come after us":** Khaled Al-Hubayshi, interview with author, Jeddah, May 12, 2008.

226 **"end up with wackos":** Fouad Al-Farhan, interview with author, Jeddah, December 2, 2007.

227 **an outpoken columnist:** Al-Nogaidan was told to stop for a time, but after September 11 he took up his pen again. He wrote two full-page articles in *Al-Watan* condemning Bin Laden—the first in a Saudi newspaper by someone who had once been in the Islamist camp.

227 **"defied human thinking":** Mansour Al-Nogaidan, interview with author, Ajman, November 10, 2007.

227 **"Us versus Them":** Cited in Unger, p. 197.

228 **"a huge, dangerous enemy":** "Try the Gores, You Won't Get a War," Nathan Gardels interview with Gore Vidal, *Saudi Gazette,* December 13, 2006, p. 13.

228 **God brought it:** Ahmed Al-Ajaji, interview with author, Riyadh, February 9, 2008.

228 **"refuse to believe":** Interview with Khaled Al-Maeena, July 10, 2006.

229 **"disempowering ourselves":** Interview with Somaya Jabarti, Jeddah, July 12 and 14, 2006.

229 **"daring people":** Prince Amr Al-Faisal, interview with author, Jeddah, July 11, 2006, and e-mail to author, November 24, 2008.

229 **"The jihad has started":** Mohammed Al-Harbi, interview with author, Riyadh, February 13, 2007.

230 **"were helpless":** Ibid.

231 **"invalid as its king":** Robert Jordan, interview with author, Washington, DC, May 1, 2007.

231 **flattery that was required:** Ahmad Sabri, interview with author, Jeddah, September 16, 2007.

231 **"congressmen wearing Jewish yarmulkes":** Prince Sultan made this remark to *Al-Sharq Al-Awsat* ("Middle East," Saudi daily published in London) following a ceremony at the Saudi Public Institution for Military Industries. *Al-Sharq Al-Awsat,* June 23, 2002.

231 **"protagonists of such attacks":** Prince Nayef interview, reported by Alaa Shahine, Associated Press, December 5, 2002, cited in Bronson, p. 236.

232 **"conflicting advice":** Robert Jordan, interview with author, Washington, DC, May 1, 2007.

234 **sued the bureau:** Legal action confirmed by U.S. diplomat to author, November 2008.

235 **approval of the Sheikh:** Rentz, p. 116.

235 **"totally wrong!":** Prince Turki Al-Faisal, interview with author, Riyadh, March 3, 2007.

235 **"those who govern":** Abdullah Muallimi, interview with author, Jeddah, September 25, 2006.

Chapter 25: Fire

237 **directorate practice:** Some informed Saudi accounts of the tragedy maintain that the fatalities stemmed simply from the school gates being kept locked.

237 **guardians of their morality:** *Arab News*, March 14, 2002, cited on BBC News website, March 15, 2002.

238 **"hands to beat us":** Ibid.

238 **"Directorate of Girls' Education":** Qenan Al-Ghamdi, interview with author, Jeddah, September 12, 2006.

238 **"get revenge":** Said Al-Surehi, interview with author, Jeddah, October 31, 2006.

239 **Norah Al-Fayez:** *Arab News*, February 15, 2009.

239 **dangerous "atheist":** Mohammed Al-Rasheed, interview with author, Riyadh, September 20, 2006.

240 **"no ethics":** Ibid.

240 **"girls educated":** Abdullah Obaid, interview with author, Riyadh, February 26, 2006.

240 **University of Oklahoma:** Mohammed Al-Rasheed had studied in Indiana to gain his Ph.D.

240 **Al-Aghar:** Prince Faisal bin Abdullah's think tank took its title from its first meeting in the Riyadh equestrian club of that name. It has produced a number of cultural and economic reports in addition to its work on the knowledge-based society. Author conversation with Fahd Abu-Alnasr, February 17, 2009.

241 **poisonous text messages:** Mansour Al-Nogaidan, interview with author, Ajman, November 10, 2007.

241 **"seventy-five lashes":** Mansour Al-Nogaidan, e-mail to author, September 22, 2008.

242 **"humiliating punishment":** http://www.nytimes.com/2003/11/28/opinion/28MANS.html.

242 **"price of reforms":** Ibid.

Chapter 26: Al-Qaeda in the Arabian Peninsula

244 **"come to kill you!":** Gardner, p. 271.

244 **death toll that night:** *New York Times*, May 14, 2003. Also Saudi Press Agency, June 7, 2003.

245 **battle to the Al-Saud:** Thomas Hegghammer, "Islamist Violence and Regime Stability in Saudi Arabia," *International Affairs* 84, no, 4 (July 2008), p. 709.

245 **Riyadh black market:** Douglas Baldwin, interview with author, Riyadh, March 5, 2007.

245 **by memorizing the Koran:** The concept of halving a prisoner's sentence if he memorized the Koran was introduced in 1979 by General Yahya Al-Muallimi, director general of Saudi prisons, who felt that religious education was a good way to reform convicted criminals.

245 **bloodthirsty exploits:** Frank Gardner, interview with author, London, March 3, 2008.

246 **authorized the location:** Frank Gardner, e-mail to author, November 10, 2008.
246 **drew out a gun:** These paragraphs are based on an interview with Frank Gardner in London on March 3, 2008, and on the account in his book *Blood and Sand*.
246 **bullet in his leg:** Gardner, p. 26.
246 **"pure hatred and fanaticism":** Ibid., p. 27.
246 **feeling the bullets:** Ibid., p. 28.
247 **killed or captured:** Saudi embassy, Washington, D.C., Press Release of April 11, 2005. www.saudiembassy.net.
247 **not sufficiently trained:** Gardner, pp. 269, 270.
248 **"Bin Laden's 'own goal'":** David Rundell, interview with author, March 6, 2007.
249 **"people of the caves":** Mohammed Al-Harbi, interview with author, Riyadh, February 13, 2007.
250 **dream of a better place:** Hussein Shobokshi, "The Dream," *Okaz*, May 30, 2003.
251 **no less than 40 percent:** *Arab News*, December 11, 2007.
252 **could only be a Sufi:** The Maliki family of Mecca have a large following in the Hijaz and throughout the Muslim world, especially in Indonesia, where millions of people follow their teachings and practice Sufism in their tradition.
252 **"Know your limits":** "Shobokshi Article Provokes Vibrant Debate," *Arab News*, July 16, 2003.

Chapter 27: Prodigal Sons

253 **"simply vanished":** Khaled Al-Hubayshi, interview with author, Jeddah, April 19, 2008.
254 **"over the horizon to die":** Khaled Al-Hubayshi, interview with author, Jeddah, May 12, 2008.
254 **"They shackled us":** Ibid.
254 **"'Cuba?'" I said:** Khaled Al-Hubayshi, interview with author, April 19, 2008.
254 **137 Saudis detained:** "List of Individuals Detained by the Department of Defense at Guantánamo Bay, Cuba, from January 2002 through May 15, 2006," http://www.defenselink.mil/news/May2006/d20060515%20List.pdf.
257 **"a virus in the brain":** Mohammed bin Nayef, interview with author, Riyadh, March 7, 2007.
257 **"transform each detainee":** Ibid.
257 **"a sort of Saudi Guantánamo":** Mohammed bin Nayef, interview with author, Riyadh, February 3, 2009.
258 **went to Yemen:** "Saudi Suspects Seeking to Revive Al-Qaeda," *Khaleej Times*, February 8, 2009.
258 **eighty-five radical young Saudis:** "Eighty-five on Wanted List of Militants," *Saudi Gazette*, February 3, 2009.
258 **"Whoever wins society":** Mohammed bin Nayef, interview with author, Riyadh, February 3, 2009.
259 **the phone call:** Talal Al-Zahrani, interview with author, Taif, July 27, 2006.
259 **"duty to God":** Talal Al-Zahrani, interview with author, Jeddah, July 16, 2006.
259 **captured alongside Yasser:** "Abu Fawwaz," interview with author, Jeddah, January 22, 2007.
260 **misled his interrogators:** Summary of Evidence for Combatant Status Review Tribunal—Al-Zahrani, Yasser, September 24, 2004, no. 000149, unclassified.

260 **"committed suicide":** See Wikipedia, "Guantánamo Suicide Attempts" for a comprehensive survey of the press coverage of the suicides. Also "U.S. Group Sues Pentagon over 2 Guantánamo Suicides—Claims Filed on Behalf of Relatives," Associated Press in *International Herald Tribune*, June 11, 2008; Carol J. Williams, "Covering Gitmo," *Los Angeles Times*, June 18, 2006; Michael Melia, "Saudi Arabian Guantánamo Detainee Dies in Apparent Suicide," *San Diego Union Tribune*, May 31, 2007.

260 **"entrance to hell":** "Abu Fawwaz," interview with author, Jeddah, January 22, 2007.

261 **larynx had been removed:** Final Autopsy Report on Al Zahrani, Yasir T., 02 August 2006, Armed Forces Institute of Pathology, Naval Hospital, Guantánamo Bay, Cuba. This report describes the larynx as "lined by intact white mucosa."

262 **"three thousand lies":** Talal Al-Zahrani, telephone conversation with Hala Al-Houti, November 26, 2008.

262 **"a coordinated suicide pact":** Andy Worthington, "Guantánamo Suicide Report: Truth or Travesty?" Web report on Antiwar.com, the Huffington Post, CounterPunch, Znet, and AlterNet.

262 **"my son's handwriting":** Talal Al-Zahrani, telephone conversation with Hala Al-Houti, November 26, 2008.

262 **like a corpse:** Hala Al-Houti, interview with author, Taif, July 27, 2006.

Chapter 28: King Abdullah

264 **"The Angel of Death":** Off the record, August 2006.

265 **new private jet:** Information from a senior pilot with Saudia, April 2, 2008. Confirmed by a senior member of the royal family.

265 **required to pay:** Saudi journalist, Jeddah, July 2006.

265 **"same schedule":** Off-the-record interview, December 2008.

266 **chlorinated water vapor:** From a member of Abdullah's inner circle.

266 **poolside ponderings:** From one of Abdullah's advisers

266 **intellectual dimension:** Dr. Majid Al-Moneef, interview with author, November 18, 2008.

266 **Al-Jabri . . . Arkoun:** Ibid.

267 **"Eid Al Adha . . . Eid Al Fitr":** http://www.2eids.com/introduction_to_eid.php.

268 **"nonroyal Saudis":** Defeated candidate, interview with author, Al-Khobar, April 2007.

268 **Saudi voting craze:** Abdullah interview with *Le Monde,* reprinted in Saudi-U.S. Relations Information Service (SUSRIS), www.saudi-us-relations.org., April 14, 2005, p. 2.

269 **"Allegiance Council":** Abdullah personally worked out the role and mechanisms of the council, according to a senior member of the royal family.

269 **nomination for crown prince:** "Saudi Arabia Issues Rules for Succession Council," Reuters, October 9, 2007.

269 **"We should do it now":** Information provided to the author by a senior member of the royal family.

270 **news of the council's creation:** Information from a local journalist who covered the story.

270 **television viewers:** Mohammed Saeed Tayeb interview with author, Jeddah, November 27, 2008.

270 **Allegiance Council met:** P. K. Abdul Ghafour, "Mishaal Named Allegiance Commission Chairman," *Arab News*, December 11, 2007.

270 **late father's vote:** Description from a member of the Allegiance Commission.

271 **"the principle of tolerance":** Remarks by King Abdullah bin Abdul Aziz at the United Nations "Culture of Peace" Conference, New York, November 12, 2008.

271 **"respect the opinions":** *Arab News*, June 23, 2003.

271 **"institutions of civil society":** Abdullah interview with *Le Monde,* reprinted in SUSRIS, April 14, 2005, p. 2.

272 **rocketed in three years:** Weston, p. 483.

272 **improvement was tangible:** See Country Tables in World Bank, *Doing Business 2009* (London: Palgrave Macmillan, 2008).

273 **eighteen million natives:** The CIA's *World Factbook* is one of several sources that estimates the Saudi population at around 28 million in July 2008, with 5.5 million legal nonnationals.

273 **13 percent of GDP:** Henny Sender, "What the U.S. Can Learn from Saudi Arabia," *Financial Times*, February 6, 2009.

273 **$513 billion:** Saudi Arabian Monetary Authority figures in "GCC Sovereign Funds: Reversal of Fortune," by Brad Setser and Rachel Ziemba, Working Paper, Center for Geoeconomic Studies, Council on Foreign Relations, January 2009, p. 2.

Chapter 29: Girls of Saudi

275 **"do not exist":** Suzanne Al-Mashhadi, "I am Black and You are White," *Al-Hayat,* February 22, 2007.

275 **"good at being ready to die":** Khaled Bahaziq, interview with author, Jeddah, December 9, 2006.

277 **"Unconditional love":** Ibid.

277 **"crazy about him":** "Mashael," telephone interview, January 29, 2008, and meeting, February 11, 2008.

278 **Saudi female campuses:** Numerous Saudi women.

281 **"Is She a Disgrace?":** *Arab News*, October 10, 2008.

281 **"euphemisms":** *Ibid.*

282 **"cherished his wives":** Hadith 170, book 73, narrated by Anas bin Malik: "The Prophet came to some of his wives among whom there was Umm Sulaim, and said, 'May Allah be merciful to you, O Anjasha! Drive the camels slowly, as they are carrying glass vessels!' "

282 **pictures of Muhannad:** Faiza Saleh Ambah, "A Subversive Soap Roils Saudi Arabia," *Washington Post*, August 3, 2008.

282 **condemning the show:** http://www.ammaro.com/2008/07/divorces-tv-shows-fatwas.htm.

282 **"call for corruption":** http://news.bbc.co.uk/go/pr/fr/-/1/hi/world/middle_east/7613575.stm.

282 **oldest Islamic scholar:** "Al-Laheedan Raps Distortion of Remarks," *Arab News*, September 13, 2008.

Chapter 30: Illegitimate Occupation

284 **"This is royalty":** From a member of the Crawford Ranch gathering.
284 **appealed to Bush:** Ibid.
284 **"a man I can trust":** Ibid.
285 **"two men of faith":** Ibid.
285 **several thousand translations:** *Arab News*, April 22, 2002.
285 **peace proposal:** Thomas L. Friedman, "An Intriguing Signal from the Saudi Crown Prince," *New York Times*, February 17, 2002.
285 **"some authentic sampling":** Adviser to Abdullah, interview with author, Riyadh, February 2007.
285 **scrapbook of news photographs:** Glenn Kessler and Karen DeYoung, "Saudis Publicly Get Tough With U.S.," *Washington Post*, March 30, 2007.
286 **Kinko's:** Recollection of a Saudi official who helped collate the photo album.
286 **"empty-handed":** And previous sentences. Recollection of an official present at the meeting.
286 **"playing games?":** Robert Jordan, Interview with the author, Washington, DC, May 1, 2007.
286 **voices grew so loud:** DeYoung, p. 386.
286 **"in peace and security":** http://www.whitehouse.gov/news/releases/2002/06/20020624-3.html.
287 **talking "past each other":** Ottaway, p. 237.
287 **"aligned with U.S. interests":** Michael Schwartz, "When Success Is Failure in Iraq," September 10, 2008, http://www.atimes.com/atimes/Middle_East/JI10Ak01.html.
287 **"An American-led overthrow":** Ibid.
287 **"hit Saddam Hussein":** National Commission on Terrorist Attacks, *("9/11 Report")*, p. 335.
287 **possible Iraqi links:** Clarke cited in National Commission on Terrorist Attacks *("9/11 Report")*, p. 334.
288 **"no legal basis for it":** Bill Sammon, "Saudis Want Inspections, Not Iraq Attack," *Washington Times*, August 28, 2002.
288 **sent back to Riyadh:** Thomas E. Ricks, "Briefing Depicts Saudis as Enemies," *Washington Post*, August 6, 2002. For details of the twenty-four slides, see Jack Shafer, "The PowerPoint That Rocked the Pentagon," *Slate*, August 7, 2002, http://www.slate.com/id/2069119/.
289 **"the kernel of evil":** Ibid.
289 **"Saudis cooperate fully":** Thomas E. Ricks, "Briefing Depicts Saudis as Enemies," *Washington Post*, August 6, 2002.
289 **aggressive views:** Murawiec, book jacket quotations.
289 **neoconservative strategy:** Thomas E. Ricks, "Briefing Depicts Saudis as Enemies," *Washington Post*, August 6, 2002.
289 **"allies for over sixty years":** Ibid.
289 **"The answer is no":** Dana Milbank and Glenn Kessler, "Bush Moves to Ease Tensions with Saudis," *Washington Post*, August 28, 2002.
290 **Saddam crashing down:** Ottaway, p. 214. See also Elsa Walsh, "The Prince," *New Yorker*, March 24, 2003.
290 **have him assassinated:** Ottaway, p. 214.

290 **"utter nonsense . . . Saudi policy":** Information from a long-standing professional colleague of Prince Bandar's, Jeddah, November 26, 2008.

290 **"a de facto member":** Ottaway, p. 214.

290 **briefed Bandar:** Woodward, pp. 264–266.

291 **Two . . . wives . . . Shammar:** Information from a member of the royal court, December 2008.

291 **"cut and run":** Personal opinion of a senior Saudi diplomat involved in the U.S.-Saudi communications in these years.

291 **air base at al-Kharj:** Thomas E. Ricks, "American Way of War in Saudi Desert," *Washington Post*, January 7, 2003.

291 **undercover operations:** Rowan Scarborough, "U.S. to Pull Forces from Saudi Arabia," *Washington Times*, April 30, 2003.

Chapter 31: End of the Affair

292 **"a *Muslim* marriage":** Ottaway, p. 226.

292 **other countries in Asia:** Between 1991 and 2001 Saudi oil sales were running at approximately 2 million barrels per day (mbd) to Japan and South Korea, 2 mbd to other Asian countries including China, 2 mbd to Europe, 2 mbd to the U.S., and 1 mbd on domestic consumption. Information from an oil consultant based in Bahrain.

292 **China's principal supplier:** Between 2002 and 2008 China increased its oil consumption to about 8 mbd, of which 50 percent was imported. Saudi Arabia provided about a quarter of those imports (1 mbd).

292 **"strategic relationship":** Ali Al-Naimi, "The Asian Outlook and Saudi Arabia's Oil Policy," World Petroleum Congress, Shanghai, China, September 29, 2001.

293 **$3.5 billion refinery:** *Arab News*, January 23, 2006.

293 **"history as a mirror":** Ibid., April 24, 2006.

294 **Chinese CSS-2 missiles:** Simon Henderson, "Chinese–Saudi Cooperation: Oil but also Missiles," Washington Institute, Policy Watch #1095, April 21, 2006.

294 **the nuclear option:** Ottaway, pp. 228–29.

294 **poverty-stricken Saudis:** For the early history of Saudi-Soviet relations, see Lacey, pp. 240, 241.

295 **vying alternatively:** the two countries continue to compete in the 8-9 mbd range. Information from an oil consultant based in Bahrain.

295 **26 percent . . . 31 percent:** *World Almanac and Book of Facts* (New York: World Almanac Books, 2007), p. 113.

295 **In January 2004:** The deal was signed in November 2003 for a 40-year concession covering 81,000 square miles. *Arab News*, January 27, 2004.

295 **the "unipolar world":** Vladimir Putin, speech at the 43rd Munich Conference on Security Policy, February 10, 2007.

295 **nuclear technology:** According to one royal adviser, this Russian "shopping list" has since been discarded because of Abdullah's suspicions of Saudi kickbacks in the deal.

296 **reconstruction process:** Diplomatic official, interview with author, Riyadh, November 2006.

297 **carried royal messages:** Prince Turki Al-Faisal, conversation with author, Paris, December 15, 2008.

297 **embarrassing for lesser Saudi officials:** Ottaway, p. 259.

297 **arguing for calm:** "Transcript of Prince Turki Al-Faisal Remarks," October 4, 2006, Royal Embassy of Saudi Arabia, http://www.suadiembassy.net/2006News/Statements/SpeechDetail.asp?cIndex=644.

298 **influence of Iran:** Saud Al-Faisal, "The Fight Against Extremism and the Search for Peace," Council on Foreign Relations, September 23, 2005.

298 **large sums of money:** Robin Wright, "Royal Intrigue, Unpaid Bills Preceded Saudi Ambassador's Exit," *Washington Post*, December 23, 2006. A Saudi official involved in the contract denies the sum of $10 million mentioned in the *Washington Post*—setting the figure closer to a tenth of that.

299 **honor of third place:** Ottaway, p. 249.

300 **double the $1.41 level:** Ibid., p. 247.

300 **refineries to match:** States News Service, April 25, 2005.

301 **"the radicalizing of my sons":** Recollection by an official present at the meeting at the king's Janadriyya farm. Adel Al-Jubeir, who translated for the king in his meetings with Michael Cherthoff during this visit, says he has no recollection of this conversation taking place.

301 **"relative poundages":** Recollection by an official present at the meeting, Riyadh, November 19, 2008.

302 **"make a Muslim of him yet":** This story circulated soon after Abdullah's arrival in the U.S. in November 2008. Adel Al-Jubeir, the Saudi ambassador who was with the king for much of the time, agrees that Abdullah received a private call from Obama soon after his arrival in November 2009, but says that the king did not make the comment attributed to him.

Chapter 32: Condition of the People

303 **open-sided tent:** Named a *fillabee* after Harry St. John Philby (1885–1960), the English explorer, bird-watcher, and colonial servant turned adviser to King Abdul Aziz, who was said to have brought the first of these tall, straight-sided marquees from India. Philby converted to Islam, taking the name Abdullah, and wrote several books about Arabia. Apart from the fillabee, he is remembered in ornithology for Philby's partridge (*Alectoris philbyi*)—and in non-Saudi history for being the father of Kim Philby, the British spy turned Soviet double agent.

303 **into the desert:** In France this small wooden ball is known as the *cochonnet,* or piglet.

303 **king tends to win:** Related by a foreign player of Saudi boules. Several Saudi sources have denied that the king plays with an extra boule, but people in Prince Charles's party in 2004 have a clear memory of the home advantage.

303 **comforts of his farm:** These details were described to the author by a confidant of the king's.

304 **"He is our Muawiyah":** Hala Al-Houti, interview with author, Jeddah, February 1, 2009.

304 **pull them gently:** Algosaibi, *Yes, (Saudi) Minister!,* p. 17.

304 **classical learning:** Ibid.

304 **the "Thunder" sura:** Koran, sura 13, verse 11.

304 **the royal eye:** Adviser to King Abdullah, interview with author, Riyadh, November 20, 2006.

305 **"cloud of confusion":** http://www.youtube.com/watch?v=8Kt40FP_N1k.

305 **"nineteen types of rice":** *Al-Jazirah* (newspaper), August 17, 2007.

306 **been with other men:** This account of the rape of the Qateef girl is based on an interview with Fouad Ali Al-Mushaikhis in Al-Awjam, January 16, 2008, and on follow-up conversations in Dhahran and Qateef, November 24, 2008; on visits to some of the sites of the incident with Al-Mushaikhis and with Ali Al-Marzouq; on interviews with Abdul-Rahman Al-Lahem in Riyadh, February 9, 2008, and March 10, 2008, and on interviews with Ebtihal Mubarak, Suzan Zawawi, and other journalists who covered the case.

307 **a small plastic tree:** Fouad Al-Mushaikhis, interview with author, Dhahran, November 24, 2008.

307 **"a boy and a girl":** Fouad Al-Mushaikhis, interview with author, Al-Awjam, January 16, 2008.

308 **importance of "face":** Interview with clinical psychologist, Riyadh, March 2008.

309 **processing rape allegations:** Survey by Safaa Al-Ahmad, 2007.

310 **"'more afraid of them'":** Fouad Al-Mushaikhis, interview with author, Dhahran, November 24, 2008.

311 **"improper premarital closeness":** Sheikh Abdul Muhsin Al-Abaiqan, interview with author, Riyadh, March 11, 2008.

312 **"hovering around":** Fouad Al-Mushaikhis, interview with author, Dhahran, November 24, 2008.

313 **"invited by a sinful woman":** Ibid.

313 **tarnished the court's reputation:** "Saudi Arabia: Rape Victim Punished for Speaking Out," *Human Rights Watch*, New York, November 17, 2007. http://hrw.org/english/docs/2007/07/18/saudia16399.htm.

313 **"the death penalty":** Interview in *Okaz*, November 27, 2007, reported in "Saudi Rape Case Spurs Calls for Reform," by Rasheed Abou-AlSamh, *New York Times*, December 1, 2007.

314 **"my wife's 'honor'":** Ebtihal Mubarak, interview with author, Jeddah, February 24, 2008.

314 **pardons for the Qateef girl:** Abdul Rahman Al-Lahem, interview with author, Riyadh, March 10, 2008.

314 **"the dark tunnel of iniquity":** Abdul Rahman Al-Lahem, interview with author, Riyadh, February 9, 2008.

315 **had to leave:** Fouad Al-Mushaikhis, interview with author, Dhahran, November 24, 2008.

Epilogue

317 **some ten million:** Galal Fakkar, "Many Land Lucrative Jobs Dodging the Rules," *Arab News*, November 13, 2008.

317 **seventy-three per year:** Robert F. Worth, "Saudi Arabia: Executions Rose in 2008," *New York Times*, October 15, 2008.

317 **forty-two per year:** "Facts About the Death Penalty," http://www.deathpenaltyinfo.org/FactSheet.pdf, Death Penalty Information Center, April 1, 2008.

317 **three hundred people:** "Ashcroft Announces Closed-Circuit Telecast of McVeigh Execution," CourtTV (2001-04-12).

317 **shamefully tortured:** Hollingsworth and Mitchell.

317 **"Have you been tortured":** Off-the-record interviews.

317 **"soft policing":** See, for example, Christopher Boucek, *Saudi Arabia's "Soft" Counterterrorism Strategy: Prevention, Rehabilitation, and Aftercare* (Carnegie Endowment for International Peace, Middle East Program, no. 97, September 2008).

318 **were a running club:** Fouad Al-Farhan, interview with author, Jeddah, November 12, 2008.

318 **"a cake in prison":** Ibid.

318 **rice and sheep:** Fouad Al-Farhan, interview with author, Jeddah, February 5, 2009.

319 **"hunt down al-Qaeda":** Fouad Al-Farhan, interview with author, November 12, 2008.

319 **security reasons:** Prince Mohammed bin Nayef, interview with author, Riyadh, February 3, 2009.

319 **"as God commands":** Off-the-record interview, Washington, October 2008.

320 **"Isn't that mental—and physical—abuse?":** Fouad Al-Farhan, interview with author, November 12, 2008.

320 **"a different opinion":** Mohammed Saeed Tayeb, interview with author, November 27, 2008.

321 **"'not your thobe'":** Ibid.

321 **in the course of revision:** Prince Mohammed bin Nayef, interview with author, Riyadh, February 3, 2009.

321 **middle of March 2009:** Mohammed Saeed Tayeb, telephone conversation, March 15, 2009.

321 **"no reformers there":** Fouad Al-Farhan, March 16, 2009.

322 **"control your hunger":** Ahmad Sabri, interview with author, Jeddah, September 20, 2007.

324 **earning fatwas:** Pascal Ménoret, "Saudi TV's Dangerous Hit," *Le Monde Diplomatique*, September 16, 2004.

324 **receiving death threats:** Mahmoud Ahmad, "Tash Ma Tash Actors Receive Death Threats," *Arab News*, October 27, 2004.

324 **"don't make fun":** Nasser Al-Gasabi, interview with author, Dubai, November 8, 2007.

325 **"mental change may follow":** Khaled Bahaziq, interview with author, Jeddah, September 12, 2007.

325 **"permission of their mahram":** Dr. Fawzia Al-Bakr, telephone conversation, June 8, 2008.

325 **"a sort of sisterhood":** Ibid.

325 **The June 2004 gathering:** Weston, p. 435.

327 **"a Wahhabi between quotation marks":** Turki Al-Faisal, U.S.-Arab Policy Conference, Washington, DC, October 31, 2008.

327 **dominating the screen:** This description comes from several who saw this single episode of the canceled TV series.

327 **shoulder operation:** Statement to the author by a representative of Prince Bandar, Jeddah, November 26, 2008.

327 **"low profile":** Explanation to the author by a member of Prince Bandar's staff.

327 **tribal areas of Pakistan:** Nico Hines, "CIA Says Osama Bin Laden Cut Off from al-Qaeda," *Timesonline*, November 14, 2008.

327 **some seventy million riyals:** Statement to the author by an adviser to the Bin Laden family, Jeddah, November 29, 2008.

328 **surviving wives and children:** Bin Laden family member, interview with author, Jeddah, September 2007.

328 **"a more modern Islam":** http://www.washingtonpost.com/wpdyn/content/article/2007/07/20/AR2007072001188.html.

328 **"sports at home":** http://www.islamlight.net cited in Faiza Ambah, "A Drive Toward the Goal of Greater Freedom," *Washington Post*, April 15, 2008.

329 **"realities of modern life":** Tawfiq Al-Seif, interview with author, Tarut Island, June 8, 2007.

330 **"evolving too slowly":** Dr. Ahmad Al-Tuwayjri, interview with author, Riyadh, April 1, 2006.

330 **more than thirty years:** Interview with a confidant of King Abdullah, Jeddah, November 30, 2008. Abdullah had to wait until he became king—and until the price of oil rose—to afford his dream.

330 **House of Knowledge:** I am grateful to Ambassador Chas Freeman for this insight into the Bayt Al-Hekma and its role in King Abdullah's vision for KAUST.

331 **$10 billion endowment:** *New York Times*, March 6, 2008.

331 **second only to that of Harvard:** *Financial Times*, May 19, 2008.

332 **palm trees and sand:** This account was related to the author by someone who traveled on the bus.

332 **stayed longer at his prayers:** recounted by a member of the family who was with the king that evening.

SUGGESTED READING

Aarts, Paul, and Gerd Nonneman, eds. *Saudi Arabia in the Balance: Political Economy, Society, Foreign Affairs*. London: Hurst, 2005.

Aburish, Said K. *The Rise, Corruption, and Coming Fall of the House of Saud*. London: Bloomsbury, 1995.

Akers, Deborah S., and Abubaker Bagader, trans. and eds. *Whispers from the Heart: Tales from Saudi Arabia*. Beirut: ICCS, 2002.

Al-Amri, Hasan Zuhair, ed. *Post September 11: The Arab Perspective*. Riyadh: Ibn Baz Foundation, 2003.

Algar, Hamid. *Wahhabism: A Critical Essay*. Oneonta, New York: Islamic Publications International, 2002.

Algosaibi, Ghazi. *Yes, (Saudi) Minister! A Life in Administration*. London: London Center for Arab Studies, 1999.

———. *The Gulf Crisis: An Attempt to Understand*. London: Kegan Paul International, 1991.

Alireza, Marianne. *At the Drop of a Veil*. Boston: Houghton Mifflin, 1971.

Almana, Mohammed. *Arabia Unified: A Portrait of Ibn Saud*. London: Hutchinson Benham, 1980.

Alsanea, Rajaa. *Girls of Riyadh*. London: Fig Tree–Penguin, 2007.

Al-Suud, Faisal ibn Mishal. *Islamic Political Development in the Kingdom of Saudi Arabia*. Washington, DC: National Association of Muslim American Women, 2002.

Armstrong, Karen. *Muhammad: A Biography of the Prophet*. London: Phoenix, 2001.

Aslan, Reza. *No God but God: The Origins, Evolution and Future of Islam*. London: Arrow, 2005.

Ayoob, Mohammed, and Hasan Kosebalaban, eds. *Religion and Politics in Saudi Arabia: Wahhabism and the State*. London: Lynne Rienner, 2009.

Azzam, Abdullah. *The Lofty Mountain*. London: Azzam Publications, 2003.

Baer, Robert. *Sleeping with the Devil: How Washington Sold Our Soul for Saudi Crude*. New York: Crown, 2003.

Bergen, Peter L. *Holy War Inc.: Inside the Secret World of Osama Bin Laden*. New York: Free Press, 2001.

———. *The Osama Bin Laden I Know: An Oral History of the Making of a Global Terrorist*. New York: Free Press, 2006.

Boucek, Christopher. *Saudi Arabia's "Soft" Counterterrorism Strategy: Prevention, Rehabilitation, and Aftercare*. Washington, DC: Carnegie Endowment for International Peace, Middle East Program, no. 97, September 2008.

Bowen, Wayne H. *The History of Saudi Arabia*. Westport, CT: Greenwood Press, 2008.

Bradley, John R. *Saudi Arabia Exposed: Inside a Kingdom in Crisis*. New York: Palgrave Macmillan, 2005.

Bronson, Rachel. *Thicker Than Oil: America's Uneasy Partnership with Saudi Arabia*. New York: Oxford University Press, 2006.

Burke, Jason. *Al-Qaeda: The True Story of Radical Islam*. London, New York: Penguin, 2004.
Cave Brown, Anthony. *Oil, God, and Gold: The Story of Aramco and the Saudi Kings*. New York: Houghton Mifflin, 1999.
Coll, Steve. *Ghost Wars: The Secret History of the CIA, Afghanistan, and Bin Laden, from the Soviet Invasion to September 10, 2001*. London: Penguin Press, 2004.
———. *The Bin Ladens: An Arabian Family in the American Century*. New York: Penguin Press, 2008.
Commins, David. *The Wahhabi Mission and Saudi Arabia*. London: I. B. Tauris, 2006.
Cook, Michael. *Forbidding Wrong in Islam: An Introduction*. Cambridge: Cambridge University Press, 2003.
Cordesman, Anthony H., and Nawaf Obaid. *National Security in Saudi Arabia*. Westport CT: Praeger Security International, 2005.
Dawood, N. J., trans. *The Koran*. London, New York: Penguin Books, 1974.
DeGaury, Gerald. *Faisal, King of Arabia*. London: Arthur Barker, 1966.
Delong-Bas, Natana J. *Wahhabi Islam: From Revival and Reform to Global Jihad*. New York: Oxford University Press, 2004.
DeYoung, Karen. *Soldier: The Life of Colin Powell*. New York: Vintage, 2007.
Eddy, William. *FDR Meets Ibn Saud*. New York: American Friends of the Middle East, 1954.
Esposito, John L., and Dalia Mogahed. *Who Speaks for Islam? What a Billion Muslims Really Think*. New York: Gallup Press, 2007.
Fandy, Mamoun. *Saudi Arabia and the Politics of Dissent*. London: Palgrave MacMillan, 1999.
Fisk, Robert. *The Great War for Civilization: The Conquest of the Middle East*. London: Harper Perennial, 2006.
Fourmont-Dainville, Guillaume. *Géopolitique de l'Arabe Saaudite: La Guerre Intérieure*. Paris: Ellipsis 2005.
Gardner, Frank. *Blood and Sand*. London: Bantam, 2006.
Habib, John S. *Ibn Saud's Warriors of Islam*. Leiden: Brill, 1978.
Hart, Parker T. *Saudi Arabia and the United States: Birth of a Security Partnership*. Bloomington, IN: Indiana University Press, 1998.
Heck, Gene W. *Islam, Inc.* Riyadh: King Faisal Center for Research and Islamic Studies, 2004.
Heck, Gene W., and Eng. Omar Bahlaiwa. *Saudi Arabia: An Evolving Modern Economy*. Riyadh: Saudi Council of Chamber of Commerce and Industry, 2006.
Hegghammer, Thomas. *Jihad in Saudi Arabia: Violence and Pan-Islamism Since 1979*. Cambridge: Cambridge University Press, 2010.
Hertog, Steffen. *Princes, Brokers, Bureaucrats: the Politics of the Saudi State*. Ithaca: Cornel University Press, 2010.
Hollingsworth, Mark, and Sandy Mitchell. *Saudi Babylon: Torture, Corruption and Cover-up Inside the House of Saud*. London: Mainstream, 2005
Ibrahim, Fouad. *The Shi'is of Saudi Arabia*. London: Saqi, 2006.
Jones, Toby Craig. "Rebellion on the Saudi Periphery." *International Journal of Middle East Studies,* vol. 38 (2006).
Kepel, Gilles. *Jihad: The Trail of Political Islam*. London. I. B. Tauris, 2002.
———. *The Roots of Radical Islam*. London: Saqi, 2005
Kepel, Gilles, and Jean-Pierre Milelli, editors, translated by Pascale Ghazaleh. *Al Qaeda In Its Own Words*. Cambridge, MA: Belknap Press, 2008.

Khan, Riz. *Alwaleed: Businessman, Billionaire, Prince*. New York: William Morrow, 2005.
Lacey, Robert. *The Kingdom: Arabia & the House of Saud*. London: Hutchinson, 1981.
Levine, Mark. *Heavy Metal Islam: Rock, Resistance, and the Struggle for the Soul of Islam*. New York: Three Rivers, 2008.
Lippman, Thomas W. *Inside the Mirage*. Cambridge, MA: Westview Press, 2004.
Long, David E. *The Kingdom of Saudi Arabia*. Gainesville: University Press of Florida, 1997.
Menoret, Pascal. *The Saudi Enigma: A History*. London: Zed Books, 2005.
Monroe, Elizabeth. *Philby of Arabia*. London: Faber, 1974.
Morris, David J. *Storm on the Horizon: Khafji—The Battle That Changed the Course of the Gulf War*. New York: Ballantine, 2005.
Munif, Abdelrahman. *Cities of Salt*. Translated by Peter Theroux. London: Cape, 1988.
Murawiec, Laurent. *Princes of Darkness: The Saudi Assault on the West*. Translated by George Holoch. Lanham, MD: Rowman & Littlefield Publishers, Inc., 2005.
Nasr, Vali. *The Shia Revival: How Conflicts Within Islam Will Shape the Future*. New York: Norton, 2006.
National Commission on Terrorist Attacks upon the United States. *The 9/11 Commission Report: Final Report of the National Commission on Terrorist Attacks upon the United States*. New York: W. W. Norton, 2004.
Nawwab, Nimah Ismail. *Poems: The Unfurling*. Vista, CA: Selwa Press, 2004.
Niblock, Tim. *Saudi Arabia: Power, Legitimacy, and Survival*. London: Routledge, 2006.
———, and Monica Malik. *The Political Economy of Saudi Arabia*. London: Routledge, 2007.
Obaid, Nawaf. *The Oil Kingdom at 100: Petroleum Policymaking in Saudi Arabia*. Washington, DC: Washington Institute for Near East Policy, 2000.
Ottaway, David B. *The King's Messenger*. New York: Walker, 2008.
Philby, Harry St. John. *Saudi Arabia*. Beirut: Librairie du Liban, 1955.
———. *Arabian Oil Ventures*. Washington, DC: Middle East Institute, 1964.
Qutub, Sayyid. *Milestones*. Indianapolis: American Trust Publications, 1990.
Al-Rasheed, Madawi. *A History of Saudi Arabia*. Cambridge: Cambridge University Press, 2002.
———. *Contesting the Saudi State: Islamic Voices from a New Generation*. Cambridge: Cambridge University Press, 2007.
———, ed. *Kingdom Without Borders: Saudi Political, Religious and Media Frontiers*. London: Hurst, 2008.
Rashid, Ahmed. *Taliban: The Story of the Afghan Warlords: Including a New Foreword Following the Terrorist Attacks of September 11, 2001*. New Haven, CT: Nota Bene, 2001.
Rentz, George S. *The Birth of the Islamic Reform Movement in Saudi Arabia*. London: Arabian Publishing, 2004.
Rivlin, Paul. *Arab Economics in the Twenty-first Century*. Cambridge: Cambridge University Press, 2009.
Ross, Dennis, and David Makovsky. *Myths, Illusions, and Peace: Finding a New Direction in the Middle East*. New York: Viking, 2009.
Robinson, Jeffrey. *Yamani: The Inside Story*. New York: Atlantic Monthly Press, 1988.
Saudi Press Agency. *The Echoes of the Saudi Position During the Events of the Arab Gulf, 1411 H*. Riyadh: Ministry of Information, 1991.
Schwarzkopf, Norman, and Peter Petre. *It Doesn't Take a Hero: The Autobiography*. New York: Bantam Books, 1992.

Simpson, William. *The Prince: The Secret Story of the World's Most Intriguing Royal, Prince Bandar bin Sultan*. New York: Regan, 2006.
Sultan, Khaled bin (Al-Saud), and Patrick Seale. *Desert Warrior: A Personal View of the Gulf War by the Joint Forces Commander.* London: HarperCollins, 1995.
Teitelbaum, Joshua. *Holier Than Thou: Saudi Arabia's Islamic Opposition*. Washington, DC: Washington Institute for Near East Policy, 2000.
Theroux, Peter. *Sandstorms: Days and Nights in Arabia*. New York: Norton, 1990.
Trofimov, Yaroslav. *The Siege of Mecca: The Forgotten Uprising.* New York: Doubleday, 2007.
Unger, Craig. *House of Bush, House of Saud: The Secret Relationship Between the World's Two Most Powerful Dynasties*. London: Gibson Square, 2006.
Urban, Mark. *War in Afghanistan*. London: Macmillan, 1988.
Vassiliev, Alexei. *The History of Saudi Arabia.* London: Saqi, 1998.
Vitalis, Robert. *America's Kingdom: Mythmaking on the Saudi Oil Frontier.* Stanford, CA: Stanford University Press, 2007.
Weston, Mark. *Prophets and Princes: Saudi Arabia from Mohammed to the Present*. Hoboken, NJ: John Wiley, 2008.
Woodward, Bob. *Plan of Attack*. London: Simon & Schuster, 2004.
Wright, Lawrence. *The Looming Tower: Al-Qaeda and the Road to 9/11*. London: Allen Lane, 2006.
Yamani, Mai. *Changed Identities: The Challenge of a New Generation in Saudi Arabia*. London: Royal Institute of International Affairs, 2000.
———. *Feminism and Islam: Legal and Literary Perspectives*. New York: New York University Press, 1996.

ACKNOWLEDGMENTS

Far are the shades of Arabia,
Where the Princes ride at noon
'Mid the verduous vales and thickets
Under the ghost of the moon . . .
They haunt me—her lutes and her forests;
No beauty on earth I see
But shadowed with that dream recalls
Her loveliness to me;
Still cold eyes look coldly upon me,
Cold voices whisper and say—
"He is crazed with the spell of far Arabia,
They have stolen his wits away."

—Walter de la Mare

I write this after an evening driving around the laid-back northern town of Ar'Ar on the Saudi border with Iraq, where I have been greeted with a mountain of rice and sheep and the warm Saudi welcome to which, over the years, I have grown accustomed. We are talking now of more than thirty years, and my debt to those who have helped me in that time is immeasurable—starting in 1978, when my beautiful and intrepid wife, Sandi, gamely agreed to pack up our home in London and brave the hazards of life in oil-boom Jeddah. The friends I made back then are friends to this day, chief among them being Khalid Ahmed Youssuf Zainal Alireza and his wife, Ghada Abduljawad, the staunchest of allies and battlers on behalf of an inquisitive *khawajah* whose curiosity has not always brought them popularity.

Looking through the acknowledgments to *The Kingdom,* published in 1981, I see that I thanked no less than 380 people, with Sandi at the head of the list. She and I have since separated, but my admiration and thanks to her remain boundless. This sequel has run up a comparable debt of gratitude to the family, friends, colleagues, and total strangers an author exploits ruthlessly as he seeks out secrets, contacts, perspective, correction, encouragement, reliable facts—along with the occasional cup of tea, of which there is no shortage in the Kingdom. The following have helped me in one or more of those varied departments, starting with those who agreed to be interviewed on the record.

Raja and Shadia Aalim; Dr. Abdul Khalik Abdul Haq; Kamal Ali Abdel Qader; Abdullah Abu Al-Samh; Rasheed Abou Al-Samh; Abdul Rahman Abuhaimid; Muna Abu Sulayman; Dr. Hamoud Abutalib; Ali Al-Ahmed; Ahmad Al-Ajaji; Yussuf Al-Ajaji; Madeha Al-Ajroush; Ahmad Ali Al-Qaisi; Dr. Abdul Muhsin Al-Akkass; Amb. James Akins; Bassim A. Alim; Sheikh Ahmad Yussuf Zainal Alireza; Hamida Alireza; Tareq Alireza; Al-Johara Al-Angary; Dr. Sami Angawi; Dr. Issa Al-Ansari; Mahdi Al-Asfour; Colonel Adel Al-Sheikh; Asya Al-Asheikh; Dr. Abdullah Al-Askar; Husayn Al-Sayed Ali Al-Awwami; Sheikh Salman Al-Awdah; Abdullah Al-Ayyaf; Ahmad Badeeb; Dr. Lamia Al-Baeshen; Dr. Abu Bakr Bagadr; Dr. Khalid Bahaziq; Douglas Baldwin and Judy Baldwin; Dr. Fawzia Al-Bakr; Alan Barton; Dr. Fawzia Ba Shattah; Dr. Khaled Batarfi; Shaid Al-Bayat; Saud Al-Behari; Ahmad Bin Baz; Abdullah Bin Laden; Sam Blatteis; Brad Bourland; Marian Bukhari; Ibrahim Al-Bulayhid; Dan P. Cagle; Brigadier Nick Cocking; Sir Sherard Cooper-Coles; Dr. Paul Thomas Cox; Amb. Walter Cutler and Didi Cutler; Amr Dabbagh; Yusuf Al-Dainy; Turki Al-Dakheel; Ali Domaini; Nancy Dutton; Nicholas Egon; Dr. Horst Ertl; Sheikh Abdullah Faddaq; Abdul Aziz H. Fahad; Ahmad Al-Abbadi; Dr. Matrook Al-Faleh; Farida Farsi; Dr. Hatoon Al-Fassi; Samar Fattany; Sheikh Hadi Mattar Al-Fayfi; Maha Fitaihi; Dr. Walid Fitaihi; Amb. Wyche Fowler; Amb. Chas W. Freeman, Jr.; Dr. Ahmad Gabbani; Frank Gardner OBE; Sheikh Abdullah Al-Garni; Gus Gennrich; Tatian C. Gfoeller; Hayat Al-Ghamdi; Qenan Al-Ghamdi; Khalid Al-Ghannami; Dr. Enaam Ghazi; Richard Goffin; Dr. Ghazi Algosaibi; Armond Habiby; Dr. Ali Al-Haji; Turki Al-Hamad; Mohammed Salama Al-Harbi; Bandar Al-Hasan; Dr. Sulayman Al-Hatlan; Hassan Hatrash; Dr. Gene W. Heck; Dr. Thomas Hegghammer; Dr. Steffen Hertog; Abbas Hidawi; Al-Anoud Al-Houti; Khaled Al-Hubayshi; Sheikh Saleh Al-Humaid; Saleh Al-Humaidan; Lubna Hussain; Hassan Al-Husseini; Dr. Sadad Al-Husseini; Wajeeha Al-Huwaider; Fouad

Ibrahim; Sheikh Khalid Al-Ibrahim; Nisreen Al-Idrisi; Soheir Al-Idrisi; Professor Ekmeleddin Ihsanoglu; Dr. Samira I. Islam; Majdi Islami; Somayya A. Jabarti; Mustafa Jalali; Matouq H. Jannah; Shireen Jawa; Mohammed Al-Jazary; Mohammed Jazzar; Salman Al-Jishi; Dr. Yahya M. Ibn Junaid and the staff of the King Faisal Center for Research and Islamic Studies in Riyadh; Dr. Ali Al-Johani; Amb. Robert Jordan; Adel Al-Jubeir; Dr. Sadeeq Al-Jubran; Abdullah Saleh Jum'ah; Major Omar Al-Kahtani; Eng. Tariq Al-Kasabi; Sean Keeling; Hasna Al-Keneyeer; Dr. Khalil Al-Khalil; Seema Khan; Adnan Khashoggi; Jamal Khashoggi; Ghassan Al-khunaizi; Najeeb Al-khunaizi; Dr. Hind Al-Khutailah; Nabil Al-Khuwaiter; John S. Kincannon; Usamah Al-Kurdi; Zuhair Kutbi; Abdul-Rahman Al-Lahem; Dr. Haifa Jamal Al-Lail; Sheikh Hattim Lutfallah; Eyad Madani; Dr. Ghazzi Madani; Khaled Al-Maeena; Mohammed Mahfoodh; Abdullah Al-Majdouie; Hassan Farhan Al-Malki; Dr. Sadiq A. Malki; Dr. Aisha Al-Mana; Dr. Hamed Al-Mana; Haifa Al-Mansour; Ali Al-Marzouq; Isa Al-Marzouq; Suzanne Al-Mashhadi; Dr. Abdullah H. Masri; Samar Al-Migrin; Fouad Al-Moushaikhis; Dr. Ali Saad Al-Mosa; Dr. Abdul Elah Al-Moayyad; Dr. Hamza Al-Mozainy; Abdullah Al-Muallimi; Faisal Al-Muammar and the King Abdul Aziz Center for National Dialogue; Ebtihal Mubarak; Ibrahim Muftar; Ibrahim Al-Mugaiteeb; Dr. Ibrahim A. Al-Muhanna; Dr. Majid Al-Munif; Dr. Wafa Al-Munif; Mustapha I. Mutabaqani; Hassan Al-Nakhali; Sheikh Nimr Al-Nimr; Mansour Al-Nogaidan; Dr. Zakir Naik; Dr. Saleh Al-Namlah; Sheikh Abdullah Naseef; Professor Tim Niblock; Fouad Nihad; Dr. Abdullah S. Obaid; Ahmad Al-Omran (www.saudijeans.org); Abdul Wahhab Al-Oraid; Dr. Yousef Al-Othaimeen; Sir William Patey; Dr. Abdullah A. Al-Rabeah; Lawrence M. Randolph; Turki Faisal Al-Rasheed; Dr. Madawi Rasheed; Dr. Mohammed Rasheed; Owain Raw-Rees; Dr. Hamid Al-Rifaei; Cecile F. Roushdie; David H. Rundell; Ahmad Mustafa Sabri; Sheikh Hassan Al-Saffar; Dr. Abdul Aziz O. Sager; Dr. Abdul Rahman Al-Said; Dr. Tawfiq Al-Saif; Adnan K. Salah; Sami Salman; General Norman Schwarzkopf; Dr. Fahd A. Al-Semmari and the King Abdul Aziz Foundation for Research and Archives; Ian Seymour and the staff of MEES, the *Middle East Economic Survey;* Dr. Jameel Shami; Jafar M. Al-Shayeb; Husain Shobokshi; Dr. Mohammed S. Al-Showayer; Ahmad Al-Shogairy; Dr. Kamal Shukri; Dr. Naila Al-Sowayel; Jawaher Al-Sudairi; Turki K. Al-Sudairi; Mohammed Al-Suhaimi; Dr. Said Al-Surehi; Dr. Faleh Al-Sulaiman; Lama Suleyman; Dr. Fahd Al-Sultan; Zahir Tahlawi; Dr. Abass Tashkandi Leila Tayba; Mohammed Sayed Tayyib; Abdullah Thabit; Peter Theroux; Nada Al-Tobaishi; Dr. Abdullah Turki; Khalid Ali Al-Turki and Sally Al-Turki; General Mansour Al-Turki; Abdul-Aziz Al-Tuwayjri; Dr. Ahmad Al-Tuwayjri; Sheikh Abdul Muhsin Al-Ubaiqan; Graham Wisner; Dr. Adnan A. Al-Yafi; Dr. Mohammed Abdo Yamani; Faisal Yamani; Hani Yamani; Dr. Mai Yamani; Ali Al-Yami; Manea bin Saleh Al-Yami; Hassan Yassin; Sabbah Yassin; Sheikh Sahal Yassin; Fawwaz Al-Zahrani; Colonel Talal Al-Zahrani; Dr. Abdul Rahman Al-Zamil; Mahdi Zawawi; Dr. Mohammed Al-Zulfa.

I am grateful to the following members of the royal family for their help: Abdul Aziz bin Nawaf bin Abdul Aziz; Abdul Aziz bin Salman bin Abdul Aziz; Abdullah bin Faisal bin Turki; Ahmad bin Abdul Aziz; Amr Al-Faisal; Bandar bin Abdullah bin Abdul Rahman; Bandar bin Khaled Al-Faisal; Princess Fahda bint Saud bin Abdul Aziz; Faisal bin Abdul Aziz bin Faisal; Faisal bin Abdullah bin Mohammed; Faisal bin Bandar bin Abdul Aziz; Dr. Faisal bin Mishaal bin Saud bin Abdul Aziz; Dr. Faisal bin Salman bin Abdul Aziz; Khaled Al-Faisal; Khaled bin Bandar bin Sultan bin Abdul Aziz; Khaled bin Faisal bin Turki; Khaled bin Sultan bin Abdul Aziz; Princess Latifa bint Musaid bin Abdul Aziz; Princess Loulua Al-Faisal; Princess Maha bint Mishari bin Abdul Muhsin; Mansour bin Miteb bin Abdul Aziz; Princess Mishael bint Faisal; Mishaal bin Mohammed bin Saud bin Abdul Aziz; Mohammed bin Khaled bin Abdullah Al-Faisal; Mohammed bin Mansour bin Miteb bin Abdul Aziz; Mohammed bin Nawaf bin Abdul Aziz; Mugrin bin Abdul Aziz; Mohammed bin Nayef bin Abdul Aziz; Nawaf bin Nasr bin Abdul Aziz; Nayef bin Ahmad bin Abdul Aziz; Princess Sara bint Talal bin Abdul Aziz; Dr. Seif Al-Islam bin Saud bin Abdul Aziz; Sultan bin Fahd bin Abdullah; Sultan bin Salamn bin Abdul Aziz; Talal bin Abdul Aziz; Turki Al-Faisal; Dr. Turki bin Mohammed Saud Al-Kabeer; Dr. Turki bin Saud bin Mohammed; Turki bin Talal bin Abdul Aziz.

I should also like to thank: Dr. Abdul Rahman Abdul Waheed; Dr. Hassan Abedin; Fahd Abu Al-Nasr; Safa Al-Ahmad; Bandar Mohammed Al-Aiban; Neal Allan; Maja Ahmad Al-Anaizy; Reza Aslan; Alan Barton; Shajahan Chandrathil; Sir James Craig; Sir David Gore-Booth; Dr. Christopher Boucek; Yvonne Butcher; Jim Chapman; Dr. Jeevan S. Deol;

Samia Al-Edrisi; Ishtiyaq Eftekhar; Ahmed Eitezaz; Matt Elliott; Jacqui Powell, and Kirsty MacArthur at Coutts; Zaki Farsi; Professor F. Gregory Gause III; Camilla Goslett; Mohammed Hanif; Roger Hardy; Roger Harrison; Dr. Waleed Hassanen; Mounir Hassanieh; Aldine Honey; Saud Al-Houti; Hamdan Al-Hunaiti; Christopher H. Johnson; Albert Beckford Jones; Colonel Brian Lees; Thomas Lippman; Leslie McLoughlin; Yasmin Malik; Reehab Massoud; Reema Memon; Ben Montanez; Ann Morris; William D. Morrison; Sir Alan Munro; Dr. Joshua Muravchik; Caryle Murphy; Khadija Nehfawy; Professor Tim Niblock; Dr. Farhan Nizami; David B. Ottaway; K. P. Pillai; Sultan Ghalib Al-Quaiti and his wife Sultana; Raid S. Qusti; Lawrence P. Randolph; Hugh Renfrew; Dr. Eugene Rogan; Shaheeda Sabir; Abdulbaset Al-Sahafi; Dr. Abdul Aziz bin Salamah; Dr. Sami Salman; Najat Al-Shafie; Mansour Al-Shalhoub; Professor Avi Shlaim; Gary Sick and the refreshingly disputacious members of his Gulf 2000 web forum; Qazi Suhail; Kevin Sullivan; Kirsty Sutherland; Dr. Abdullah Al-Thayer; Jan and Anna Thesleff; Jim Thomas; Ismail Tutla; Siraj Wahab; Dr. Ayman Samir Wahba; Val Weir; David Wells and John Whitbeck; Sir John and Maureen, Lady Wilton; Suzan Zawawi; and Rustom Zere.

I arrived in Jeddah in February 2006 to find Lawrence Wright winding up the research on his classic, *The Looming Tower.* With true collegiality he shared with me his finest contacts, including the finest of them all, Faiza Saleh Ambah. Life beside the Red Sea would not have been the same without her—nor without Friday lunches in the acerbic and genial company of Ben Dyal, a "virtual" Saudi whom I have known for thirty-one years, since we first met in the Polyglot Language School in London. With his knowledge and love of Jane Austen, Ben is an eighteenth century person living in the twenty-first century—like a good number of folk in this country.

On the east coast, I have benefited immeasurably from the support and wisdom of my friends Nabil Al-Khuwaiter and Hassan Al-Husseini, the latter of whom has generously assumed the burden of checking the Arabic aspects of the manuscript. In Riyadh, Lubna Hussein has kept me laughing and given me more plugs that I deserve on her television show, *Bridges.*

My greatest debt of all in the Kingdom has been to Ms. Hala Al-Houti, the executive assistant of Khaled Alireza, whom Khaled generously seconded to translate, organize, and shepherd me through my three years of research. Hala has been a joyful and ever resourceful companion—living proof, like many a determined young woman I have met here, that the Saudi future resides with the sex that wears black. The "whites" are discovering, day by day, that they cannot match the dynamism of women like Hala.

Back home, my mentor has been my calm and shrewd young literary agent, Jonathan Pegg, who has brought me home to harbor with two superb publishing teams and editors in Kevin Doughten of Viking Penguin, New York, and Caroline Gascoigne of Hutchinson—the house that published *The Kingdom,* as chance would have it, and who are now part of the Random House group in London. My additional thanks to Carla Bolte, Emily Votruba, Veronica Windholz, and Wendy Wolf at Viking. I am grateful to my former colleagues from the *Sunday Times Magazine* Suzanne Hodgart and Ian Denning for their work on the research and design of the pictures sections, and to Mateen Munshi and L. Ramnarayan Iyer at *Arab News* in Jeddah, who heeded the generous call of their editor Khalid Al-Maeena to unlock their picture archive. My thanks to Camilla Panufnik for her Photoshop expertise.

My friend Kieran Baker of Political Bytes Productions has enlivened my recent months by bringing the talented Heidi Ewing and Rachel Grady of LOKI Productions to the Kingdom to shoot two documentary films that have grown out of my work here. Thank you to Kieran and to his wife, Nancy, for their hospitality in Washington, D.C.—and to David Sherwood and James Brooker of Flamble for keeping my e-mails and Apples buzzing. My thanks to Mr. and Mrs. Ian Seymour for their hospitality in Cyprus while I was researching the archives of the Middle East Economic Survey—and thank you to MEES for access to their invaluable records.

Cut off from home, whatever "home" has come to mean, it has been consoling to buy up the latest special offer of Mobily minutes and to talk long-distance with my supportive friends Lili Agee; Nafeesa Chinoy; Joe Feinberg; Prentis Hancock; Neil Letson; Daniel St. George; Bob and Patricia Shaheen—and to Jane Rayne, my most inspiring and supportive friend of all. "Home" for me, I have come to realize in the last three years, is the joy of being with Jane.

My children, Sasha and Scarlett, provide me with home whenever I can get to stay with them in Oregon and California, while Bruno looks after what used to be my home in Pimlico. My thanks to Thomas and Stephane Walde for being the most accommodating tenants for which a landlord could hope.

Before I had a publisher for this book, I had my old friend and editor Bill Phillips, who encouraged me and corrected me as I stumbled through early drafts of the text and who showed me, as ever, how to locate the story in the *meaning* of what I was discovering. He and his wife, Gladys, had been warm and gracious hosts on my annual visits to Massachusetts. In England Diana Melly made cheering and insightful comments on the manuscript, while Claus von Bülow and Christophe Gollut have been cheering and insightful in general. My thanks too to Gregorio Kohon.

Hana Moazzeni did calm and crucial work in organizing the source notes and reference section of the book when I was rushing to finish the manuscript, and, as always at such junctures, my old friend and colleague Jacqueline Williams came to the rescue with countless details from her mind-boggling research bank of electronic, documentary, and personal contacts. For *The Kingdom,* Jackie and I went to the desert together. For this book, we found gems in Marbella.

My most unexpected and welcome support came from my brother, Graham. Our mother, Vida Lacey, fell ill last year, and it was Graham who cared for her unstintingly, with the help of his companion, Gabriella Merry. My brother made it possible for me to keep working on my book. More important, he made the final months of our mother's life a relaxed and warm experience in her own home, surrounded by those she loved. Thanks to Graham, I was there when she died.

Robert Lacey
Ar'Ar, Saudi Arabia,
March 2009

INDEX

Page numbers in *italics* refer to illustrations and maps; and *n.* indicates a footnote. Non-personal names beginning with Al-, the Arabic definite article, are listed here in the A's under Al-. Surnames beginning with Al- are listed under the starting letter of the name: e.g., Banna, Al-. For members of the House of Saud, see the dedicated index of names and topics beginning on page 401. *Indexes by Cohen Carruth, Inc.*

General Index

House of Saud Index

PHOTOGRAPHIC SOURCES

Picture research by Suzanne Hodgart

Insert 1

The Saudi army on the march in 1911 photographed by Captain William Shakespear (© Royal Geographical Society)

Abdul Aziz and his family in 1918 photographed by Harry St. John Philby (Middle East Centre Archive, St Anthony's College, Oxford GB 165-0229, Philby Collection PA 10/1202)

Oil well number 15, Dhahran, 1939 (Aramco)

Abdul Aziz meets FDR, 1945 (Naval History and Heritage Command, Washington, D.C.)

An Aramco typing lesson in the late 1940s (Aramco)

Ahmad Zaki Yamani, Saudi oil minister, 1962–1986 (Getty Images)

TIME Cartoon. OPEC plucks U.S. feathers (Don Wright © 1979 Palm Beach Post. Image supplied by the British Cartoon Archive, University of Kent)

King Faisal with hawk, 1967 (Jean-Claude Sauer/Paris Match, Camera Press, London)

Kings Faisal, Khaled, Fahd, and Abdullah dance the *ardha (Arab News)*

Juhayman Al-Otaybi, December 1979 (AFP/Getty Images)

Juhayman's followers under arrest (AFP/Getty Images)

Sheikh Abdul Aziz Bin Baz *(Arab News)*

Sheikh Hassan Al-Saffar, Shia leader *(Arab News)*

Ali Al-Marzouq, Eid Al-Ghadeer, November 1979 (Ali Al-Marzouq Private Collection)

Insert 2

Prince Fahd at Kidbrooke Comprehensive School, November 1954 (© Topfoto)

King Fahd arrives in Nice, April 1987 (SIPA/Rex Features)

King Fahd with Saddam Hussein (AFP/PHOTO/HO)

King Fahd's yacht, the *Prince Abdul Aziz* (Chris Wood/Rex Features)

Ronald Reagan greets King Fahd in Mexico, October 1981 (AFP/Getty Images)

King Fahd's palace in Marbella (SIPA Press/Rex Features)

Prince Turki Al-Faisal with hawk *(Arab News)*

Prince Bandar bin Sultan as a fighter pilot (© Ron McGaffin)

AWACS (Airborne Warning and Control System) aircraft (Getty Images)

Prince Sultan bin Salman in space, July 1985 (© UPPA/Topfoto)

Prince Salman bin Abdul Aziz *(Arab News)*

Prince Nayef bin Abdul Aziz *(Arab News)*

Prince Sultan bin Abdul Aziz (Popperfoto/Getty Images)

Osama bin Laden in Afghanistan, 1988 (SIPA Press/Rex Features)

King Fahd and General Norman Schwarzkopf, January 6, 1991 (SIPA Press/Rex Features)

Saudi troops in Al-Khafji, January 30, 1991 (Durand-Hudson-Langevin-Orban/Sygma/Corbis)

Insert 3

Bandar bin Sultan with George H. W. Bush, 1989 (AP/Topfoto)

Bandar bin Sultan with George W. Bush, 2001 (Rex Features)

Al-Watan ("The Nation") reports 9/11 (Courtesy of *Al-Watan*)

Khalid Al-Hubayshi in Afghanistan (Khalid Al-Hubayshi, Private Collection)

Khalid Al-Hubayshi today (Khalid Al-Hubayshi, Private Collection)

Mansour Al-Nogaidan in 1995 (Mansour Al-Nogaidan, Private Collection)

Mansour Al-Nogaidan with his family, November 2008 (Mansour Al-Nogaidan, Private Collection)

Fifteen flying Saudis, the hijackers of 9/11 (AP/PA Photos)

Yasser Al-Zahrani's letter to his father of December, 2002 (Talal Al-Zahrani, Private Collection)

Yasser Al-Zahrani in Guantánamo (Talal Al-Zahrani, Private Collection)

Frank Gardner shot in Riyadh, June 2004 (Internet screen grab—no credit)

Frank Gardner, October 2005, Buckingham Palace (Fiona Hanson/PA Archive/PA Photos)

Mohammed bin Nayef Extremist Rehabilitation Center, Riyadh (Hassan Ammar/AFP/Getty Images)

Abdullah bin Abdul Aziz in National Guard uniform *(Arab News)*

Fire in Mecca Girls' School, March 2002 *(Arab News)*

Abdullah bin Abdul Aziz visits a poor man's shack *(Arab News)*

King Abdullah at the G20 conference in New York, November 2008 (Getty Images)

King Abdullah at the April, 2008 National Dialogue convened in Abha to discuss women's issues (http://www.sha6e.com/up/sha6e/images/sha6e-fdd72b93b5.jpg)